D0768859

E-Boat Alert

E-Boat Alert

Defending the Normandy Invasion Fleet

James Foster Tent

Naval Institute Press

Annapolis, Maryland

Library of Congress Cataloging-in-Publication Data
Tent, James Foster, 1944–
    E-Boat alert : defending the Normandy invasion fleet / James
Foster Tent.
        p.   cm.
    Includes bibliographical references and index.
    ISBN 1-55750-805-4 (acid-free paper)
    1. World War, 1939–1945–Campaigns–France–Normandy.
2. World War, 1939–1945–Naval operations, German. 3. Torpedo-boats–
Germany. 4. Normandy (France)–History, Military.   I. Title.
D756.5.N6T46   1996
940.54′5943–dc20   95-43711

∞ Printed in the United States of America on acid-free paper
03 02 01 00 99 98 97 96   9 8 7 6 5 4 3 2
First printing

In Loving Memory of Robert L. Janowitz, 1944–1968

If given a choice, Bob would probably have preferred that his name appear in a work devoted to his life-long heroes, the New York Yankees. However, he would also be pleased with this study of a subject that fascinated us both since childhood: the men and women who answered the call to arms in World War II. Like so many of them, Bob volunteered for duty, but in another war, deliberately placing himself in harm's way even though he was by nature a gentle man. Like so many of the heroes of our childhood, he refused to abandon friends in danger, and, like them, he paid with his life. We miss you every day, Bob.

Contents

Illustrations

Big Joe McCarthy's 617 Squadron crew

Navigator Tom Bennett and Pilot Gerry Fawke in front of their Mosquito marker aircraft

Pilot Nick Knilans as a USAAF lieutenant

The German Navy's experimental fast boat "Bodo"

Prewar E-boats with the Lürssen Yard's fast planing hull and "effect" rudders

Front view of a prize E-boat

Rear view, showing the main rudder and the two side rudders

Rear view, showing the flat hull in the stern

Two S-26 class boats at den Hoofden, the Netherlands

Two 1944 boats with rounded skullcap bridges

Late-war E-boat with the armored skullcap bridge that became standard in 1944

S-111 after her capture by British coastal forces

Late-war E-boat arriving in Felixstowe to surrender, 13 May 1945

E-boat crossing the Channel for internment, accompanied by coastal forces MTBs

LST 507 with an LCT piggy-backed aboard

LSTs carrying heavy combat equipment

LST 283 enters the Channel for exercises

Two LSTs carrying barrage balloons

LST 289 under tow after the E-boat attack in Lyme Bay

LST 289 in Dartmouth harbor

Casualties of the Lyme Bay disaster being offloaded

Typical scene on Britain's South Coast on the eve of the Normandy Invasion

Rear Adm. Alan G. Kirk, USN, on the bridge of the USS *Augusta*

View of Omaha Beach from a Mulberry

American Mulberry wrecked by the gale of 19–22 June 1944

U.S. soldiers taking German prisoners at fortresses around Cherbourg, 26 June 1944

Tables

Acknowledgments

Two seemingly unconnected events in World War II—the April 1944 sinking of two Allied ships off the English coast and an Allied bombing raid on a French town the following June—provided the incentive for this study. The perpetrators of the first action, the so-called Slapton Sands incident, were German torpedo boats. Six weeks later, Britain's RAF Bomber Command launched a special raid on German targets in the Bay of the Seine. Research in six archives on two continents plus interviews with veterans and eyewitnesses from four nations proved that the first incident set in motion the second—and revealed a little-known episode connected to the Normandy Invasion.

Preparation of this study required help from many wonderful colleagues and friends. I thank the staff of the Bundesarchiv-Militärarchiv as well as Maj. Rüdiger Overmans from the Militärgeschichtliches Forschungsamt. Hans-Georg Ruppel of the Stadtarchiv Offenbach alerted me to several sources, as did Douglas Peifer in Durham, North Carolina. Hans-Werner and Ingrid Koeppel in Bonn kindly put me in contact with former naval personnel, as did Ralph C. Greene of Chicago. Heinz and Angelika Ferstl aided my research in Hamburg. Sönke Neitzel supplied two documents on German naval installations. The Le Havre Archives offered unique materials, and director Sylvie Barot deserves special thanks for introducing me to eyewitnesses. Chicago attorney Marvin Green, formerly of the U.S. Navy's 358th Harbor Craft Company in Le Havre, volunteered an excellent historical report. The Marine Offizier Vereinigung in Bonn, including Fregattenkapitän a.D. Peter Borstel, provided useful secondary sources about the former Kriegsmarine. Britain's Public Record Office (PRO) contained invaluable documents. I am forever indebted to one of its staff members who overrode the computer and hand-delivered an invaluable document. Martin Middlebrook and Chris Everitt advised me on PRO sources. Michael R. D. Foot explained the intricacies of special intelligence. The U.S. Air Force Historical Research Agency in Montgomery, Alabama, and the nearby Air University Library provided useful materials. The National Archives produced one-of-a-kind documents. I thank archivists Will Mahoney, Tim Mulligan, Ed Reece, Harry Riley, Amy Schmidt, and John Taylor for their help, as well as Kathy Lloyd at the Washington Navy Yard.

Eyewitness accounts aided this study. RAF 617 Squadron veterans Tom Bennett, Nick Knilans, and Big Joe McCarthy offered insider information. I am deeply indebted to 617 Squadron historian Robert M. Owen also. E-boat commanders Günther Rabe, Bernd Rebensburg, Ullrich Roeder, Hans Schirren, and Felix Zymalkowski added first-hand information, as did engineer Wilhelm Gördes and radioman Ernst Benda. Stephen Z. Ross provided materials from the Nick Knilans Collection.

Birmingham, Alabama, residents also helped this investigation. Gen. James Brown, Maj. James Fitts, and Staff Sgt. Taylor Robinson of the 117th Photo Reconnaissance Wing of the Alabama Air National Guard provided rare aerial photographs. RAF Flt. Lt. (Ret.) Ian Sturrock, instructed me about photoreconnaissance. Owen Sheppard and William C. Walker, LST veterans and fellow Birminghamians, shed light on the Slapton Sands tragedy and put me in touch with Eugene E. Eckstam in Wisconsin and William F. Gould in New York. Birmingham attorney Edward M. Friend, a VII Corps veteran, briefed me about ground operations at Normandy. UAB presidents S. Richardson Hill, Charles A. McCallum, and J. Claude Bennett generously supported this project. UAB History Department Chairman James Penick helped, too, as did Debbie Givens, Hank Inman, Albert McCarn, Mike McConnell, André Millard, John Morgan, Frank Patton, and Lonnie Shoultz. David B. Wyman provided original illustrations. Margaret Wyman Tent demonstrated unflagging editing skills, as did Anne R. Gibbons. Help me though they all did, any errors in this work are my responsibility alone.

E-Boat Alert

Prologue

The Antagonists

In the early hours of 28 April 1944, two flotillas of fast German torpedo boats attacked a convoy of LSTs on Lyme Bay off Britain's South Coast, sinking two, savaging a third, and killing 749 U.S. soldiers and sailors. This fact is well known.

Six weeks later at Le Havre on the Bay of the Seine, an armada of RAF Bomber Command Lancasters, fitted with special bombs, caught up with those selfsame fast boats, sinking two flotillas, killing or maiming their most experienced commanders, and wrecking Germany's last remaining naval threat in the Normandy battle zone. This fact is not well known. Because of one strategic bombing raid, the Allies' critical buildup of forces continued after the invasion, and no LST ever succumbed to torpedo boat attack again.

In recent years the public has become aware of the deaths of hundreds of U.S. servicemen on a moonlit night in late April 1944, only five weeks before D-day. They were the first American victims of German torpedo boat (or E-boat) attacks, and in the aftermath of the disaster, fears arose that others in the invasion fleet would soon fall victim to similar attacks. The casualties on Lyme Bay were a special force, mostly combat engineers, on their way to a practice amphibious landing at Slapton Sands in Devon. Those sands bore a striking resemblance to another shore, the Normandy coast in German-occupied France. The timing of the tragedy could scarcely have been worse, occurring as it did so close to Operation Neptune/Overlord, the Allied invasion of Europe. As public awareness of it has grown, the maritime disaster that unfolded that night around Convoy T-4's LSTs has come to symbolize other wartime calamities marked by enormous loss of life. Many such incidents have been swallowed up in the historical record, lost in the whirl of events, and repressed in the memories of survivors plagued by a sense of guilt that they survived when others did not. Over and above the human dimension, the sinkings had ominous implications for the Allied invaders. They demonstrated the extreme vulnerability of landing craft to Germany's swift coastal forces.

Although the German naval success in Lyme Bay gave the appearance of being a fluke, highest Allied counsel viewed it with foreboding. It set in motion a series of complex and interrelated reactions that reveal much about how the Allies and their Axis foes organized for and conducted operations in World War II. Tardily, the Allies discovered they had underestimated a dangerous opponent on the Narrow Sea. German naval leadership was agreeably surprised by the E-boats' success and hoped to achieve many more. It was the Allies, however, who drew the right conclusions and made the right responses. The disaster that befell Convoy T-4 spurred the leaders at SHAEF, General Eisenhower's invasion headquarters, to mobilize their resources for a sea and air war against a hitherto unheralded opponent: the Schnellbootwaffe (E-boat Force). Belatedly the Allied commanders realized that this force was composed of some of the world's highest-performance, fast fighting boats of World War II. They could ignore it only at their own peril.

The Allies have been criticized by some in recent years for artlessly pummeling their Axis foes into submission, that is, for using brute force. Yet when called upon to defend the Normandy Invasion Fleet, those same Allies displayed a measure of subtlety. They employed new, hard-won skills to outwit a cunning enemy and husbanded their newly created special forces to land a strategically placed blow with excellent timing. Superior handling of intelligence, particularly the employment of special intelligence such as the Ultra Secret, eliminated much guesswork. Skilled photoreconnaissance provided the raw material for expert photointerpretation. Painstaking operations analysis and imaginative use of prisoner of war information allowed them to know their enemy better. In combination, all these newly displayed skills enabled the Allies to integrate the elements of war and arrive at an effective counteraction. Within a week following the invasion, the last pieces of a puzzle slid into place and gave the defenders of the Allied invasion fleet the opportunity to determine where and when they could close with their elusive naval foe. In doing so, they demonstrated that they had institutionalized lessons learned early in the war by brilliant innovators in the use of intelligence, such as Professor R. V. Jones.

Functioning for all practical purposes as a one-man committee in 1939–40 to draw together disparate strands of intelligence to identify dangers and find solutions at a time of Britain's military weakness, physicist Jones succeeded in countering secret German weapons such as its highly accurate navigational beams and later its V-weapons, such as the V-1 Flying Bomb. His feat became a model for others. On the eve of the invasion, other organizations such as the Admiralty's highly secret Operational Intelligence Centre in London were beginning to duplicate Professor Jones's achievements on a sustained institutional basis.

Additionally, various Allied combat forces had been honing their skills and perfecting new weapons. Britain's RAF Bomber Command was able to use the new precision tactical capability of its famed 617 Dambuster Squadron as well as the awesome destructive power of its increasingly accurate main force squadrons to achieve results no one had foreseen even a few months earlier. With little fanfare, Bomber Command had crossed a significant threshold by D-day. It had achieved the capability to aid Allied ground forces on an operational and tactical level despite claims of being strictly a strategic air force. The airmen were significantly aided by brilliant scientific and engineering advances such as scientist Barnes Wallis's earthquake bombs, which could mete out telling blows against seemingly impregnable targets such as the German Navy's massive concrete naval pens.

The victory over the E-boats was not achieved exclusively in actions on water or in the air. Allied ground operations in the D-day invasion provided unforeseen dividends for those who had to fight on the Channel. American land forces, highly trained airborne troops as well as untested infantry divisions, had long intended to wrest early control of a French harbor to ease the logistical needs of their Second Front. By isolating Cherbourg, they also happened to choose the naval base most favored by the E-boat Force because of its proximity to Britain's western ports on the Channel. After 6 June 1944 Cherbourg assumed even greater strategic significance as the western German linchpin for attacks on the invasion fleet. The Allies' unexpectedly rapid advance up the Cotentin Peninsula to that strategic port degraded the German naval response far sooner than is generally realized and brought to a sudden end their ability to disperse their forces around the Channel harbors.

The sum total of these Allied initiatives, seemingly unrelated, climaxed in a strategic bombing attack at the right place, at the right time, and with precisely the right destructive weapons. That raid, when it came, was not the area bombing generally associated with Bomber Command. Using advanced technology, the raiding force executed a rapier thrust instead and in one night eliminated the naval threat posed by Germany's E-boat Force. In performing that feat, the Allied air forces measurably decreased the threat the Normandy Invasion Fleet's workhorse LSTs faced from Germany's "greyhounds of the sea." It also assured a successful buildup phase for Operation Neptune/Overlord in the weeks that followed. The raid achieved something else rare in modern warfare: a decisive victory. Privately, the Germans admitted that the raid fundamentally altered their naval dispositions in the invasion area.

By eliminating the last maritime threat to the Allied forces entering Normandy, the Allies won a high-stakes game. They guaranteed the safety of their six-thousand-ship invasion fleet, especially its landing vessels, which were indispensable for off-loading men and arms onto beaches when no intact port was available and when storms had rendered the artificial harbors useless. Time was a critical factor here. The rapid buildup of Allied ground forces over open beaches proceeded at a pace the amazed Germans could not match. It was no fluke that D-day was followed seven weeks later by the crucial breakthrough at St. Lo on 25 July 1944. This in turn was followed days later by the all-important breakout into the Second Front. That war-winning move doomed Hitler's Wehrmacht in the West.

Another factor that makes the 14 June raid worthy of attention is the human element involved. It was a feat of arms accomplished by young citizen-soldiers, almost all of whom had been pursuing civilian vocations only a few years or even months previously. They did it with the help of scientists equally unacquainted with war and weapons development until forced by circumstances to develop such expertise at a pace that is hard to comprehend in times of peace.

In focusing on a hitherto underrated naval threat, namely a few dozen E-boats, I hope to add a historical corrective to our understanding of World War II. In one sense this study covers the Normandy Invasion effort from the perspective of those who had to protect our forces from a vulnerable flank: the sea. Within the context of Operation Neptune, the Allied forces responsible for defending the Normandy Invasion Fleet had to find a way to quickly counter a threat that planed nightly across the Channel

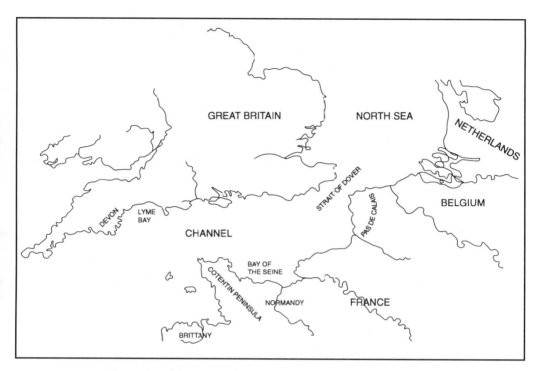

Map 1. Channel and lower North Sea

waters, seemingly oblivious to the disparity of numbers. Outwardly, a contest pitting a few dozen wooden-hulled boats against a fleet of six thousand ships seemed grossly one-sided. Yet it was the unorthodox nature of the threat that challenged the planners of Operation Neptune. In the aftermath of the sinkings in late April 1944, the vulnerability of landing ships and their complements to torpedo attack became obvious and led to urgent discussions. The debate was not without rancor, and it caused friction between the responsible U.S. and British naval leaders. In the end, however, those discussions bore fruit: an unorthodox solution to an unorthodox threat. It was not Allied naval forces that administered the decisive blow against Germany's coastal forces. The endgame came with a clash between two unlikely adversaries: the naval base strongholds from which E-boats operated, and Britain's strategic air force whose leadership had looked askance at "panacea" targets until the E-boat threat presented itself.

The raid on Le Havre was an unusual operation in the long air war because of the unique targets in its port and the tactics used to engage those targets. So secret were the special bombs and the special intelligence used in the raid that at the moment he signaled congratulations to his crews, Air Chief Marshal Sir Arthur Harris also labeled his communication to them top secret and forbade further mention of the raid to the public. When wartime restrictions ended a year later, the attack on Le Havre had become but a dim memory for most, one of many actions that the participants-turned-civilians were happy to forget.

Although this book concentrates on an obscure episode of World War II, it points to issues directly affecting national defense policies today. The naval and air threats used by both sides in 1944 may seem old. But they were developed by the combatants to counter threats that are with us still. In the aftermath of the Persian Gulf War of 1991, the U.S. Navy realized that it was ill equipped to counter expendable, high-speed vessels as well as mines in the narrow seas of a hostile gulf. After years of internal debate, it has issued contracts for two classes of coastal vessel. One is the PB Mk. V (Patrol Boat Mark Five), a forty- to fifty-knot vessel about 70 feet in length, and carrying the 1990s equivalent of 1940s torpedoes: compact seaborne missiles. Sailors aboard British MTBs, American PTs, or other compact patrol boats of two generations ago would understand perfectly the value of such a craft. The U.S. Navy's other coastal vessel is the PC 1 (Patrol Craft One). With a waterline length of 170 feet and utilizing light construction and powerful diesels, it is a first-class coastal vessel that can make thirty-five knots or more and is capable of standing farther offshore. The PC 1's ancestor is the powerful 1944 E-boat that once posed a threat to the Allies when they too had to approach a hostile shore. Both classes of vessel address a need by the United States and other maritime powers to reinvigorate their "brown water" navies, as coastal forces are called today.

The Gulf War provided another instructive lesson about weaponry that seemingly had become obsolete. In February 1991, as the land phase of the Gulf War was reaching its climax, the Allies were perplexed. How could the Iraqi military continue to exercise command and control of its forces despite complete Allied air supremacy? The use of special intelligence, which drew upon information from many sources, revealed disquieting answers. Saddam Hussein had constructed two extraordinary command centers a hundred feet underground and encased in steel and concrete containment walls twenty feet thick. Existing Allied weaponry was useless. Military necessity compelled American scientists and engineers to produce the GBU 28, a 1990s successor to Barnes Wallis's Tallboy, the bomb that played a central role at Le Havre. Much about this smart, deep-penetration, ultra-high-explosive bomb is still classified, but one fact is clear: the

GBU 28 bore through the Iraqi warlord's hundred feet of earth and his twenty feet of hardened concrete with ease. Within hours of its impact, Hussein and his military sued for peace and ended the war.

The problems the Allies of 1991 faced, although not on the same scale as those of the generation fighting in 1944, were similar. Technological and organizational responses in 1991 parallel the actions traced in this book, when an earlier generation effectively countered the efforts of a skilled and resourceful foe.

Chapter **1**

The Lyme Bay Disaster

Petty Officer 3d Class Bill Gould, USN, was aboard LST 507, crossing Lyme Bay just off Britain's South Coast. With two other LSTs they had sailed out of the English port of Brixham in Devon on the afternoon of 27 April 1944, falling in behind five more landing ships that had put out that morning from Plymouth. Soldiers and sailors alike had had a busy day as the eight ships in Convoy T-4 joined a practice landing called Exercise Tiger. They were transporting a battalion of combat-ready engineers from the U.S. 4th Infantry Division to a featureless shore called Slapton Sands.

Midnight had come and gone, and many of the soldiers had bunked down as best they could. A few remained topside, too keyed up to sleep. They were joined by some restless sailors, although most off-duty crewmen were trying to sleep. Gould, serving as a small-boat coxswain on LST 507, was responsible for a thirty-six-foot LCVP (landing craft, vehicle and personnel), which he would launch from the LST in a few hours. Gould had gone below to the first deck and was in one of the troop compartments in the company of soldiers who would soon be boarding his landing craft. They were barely under way, making little more than three knots; the sound of the LST's twin diesels was muted. The weather had calmed too. Almost complete quiet reigned on the dark coastal waters. Suddenly Gould and several of his shipmates froze. "It was around 1:30 in the morning [0130 hours]," he recalled, "when some of us heard a sound we had never heard before. It was a kind of growling, grinding noise that scraped along the bottom of the hull and then stopped. Nobody knew what it was."[1] Gould and the others waited, wondering if they would hear it again. Quiet returned. After a short pause, they shrugged and went back to work. Men aboard other LSTs in the convoy, some of whom were playing poker on the tank deck, reported hearing the same scraping sounds. They, too, assumed it was just flotsam that their ships had nudged aside.

To anyone looking from a distance, the LSTs must have presented a strange sight, lumbering across the dark waters of Lyme Bay, twelve miles south of Portland and thirty miles east of Slapton Sands. All eight American LSTs, including LST 507 as "tail end Charlie," continued to glide along at three and a half knots. Convoy T-4 was the last convoy in the two-day practice landing called Exercise Tiger, and there was good reason why they were out on the waters of the English Channel. They were practicing for the invasion of Europe, only five weeks away. Exercise Tiger was the next to last in a series of practice landings intended to give green troops practical experience in attacking from the sea. The convoy moved slowly in order to reach the practice zone at the correct time.

The LSTs were new. The vehicles packed row upon row on their decks were new. So too were the citizen-sailors who crewed the LSTs. Most were recently arrived in Europe. All desperately needed seasoning to prepare them for the assault on what they called the Far Shore: Occupied France, less than a hundred miles away to the south and east.

LSTs were part of a new concept of war. They were awkward looking, flat-bottomed ships of five thousand tons registry, intended to carry men and heavy equipment, such as tanks and mobile guns, and float them onto a hostile beach. They were a kind of roll-on, roll-off ferry that needed no dock at the other end. Like ferries, they were open-ended to allow rapid embarking and debarking. Unlike ferries, they were combat-loaded, meaning they could off-load first the equipment that was urgently needed in battle. Although their builders did not say so, the LSTs were also expendable. Rapidly constructed on a mass production basis, they were designed to carry out one of the most dangerous assignments of World War II: amphibious assault on a defended coast. Because they were intended to enter a hostile environment, there was no point in installing in them more than the bare essentials. But the builders did lavish two special features on the

LST. First, they gave the landing ship a strong, reinforced-steel lower deck to hold forty-ton tanks, as well as a sturdy upper deck on which to crowd additional combat vehicles. Few ships could accommodate such a load. Second, they built onto the bow huge clam-shell doors that could disgorge large vehicles quickly, including Petty Officer Gould's LCVP and others like it. Other than those two features, the LSTs were designed with economy in mind—and just enough performance to do the dangerous job of placing men and equipment on firm soil. Exhibiting a vein of dark humor, navy regulars dubbed the LST "Large Slow Target" or simply "T."

The LSTs were indeed slow; their twin twelve-cylinder diesels propelled them at a maximum speed of twelve knots if the seas were calm—which they usually were not on the turbulent Channel. Lacking a keel, their ability to maneuver might be described as glacial. They were lightly armed, depending on more orthodox ships like destroyers to protect them. They had almost no bulkheads or watertight compartments to protect them against flooding. Like a child's toy boat, the hold of an LST was one large cavity. Once breached there was little to stop the flow of water, and like a toy boat this landing ship would then go in only one direction: down. This unorthodox structure, a British design, was built primarily in U.S. shipyards in unlikely places like Seneca, Illinois, and Evansville and Jeffersonville, Indiana. These so-called cornfield shipyards of World War II could turn out generic steel products without worrying much about traditional shipbuilding designs or methods.[2]

At the time of Convoy T-4's sailing, the LSTs were among the most urgently needed ships in the world. The highest Allied counsels fretted about them constantly from mid-1943 through most of 1944, hoping to scrape up a few more for the invasion of Europe. "The destinies of two great empires seem to be tied up in some goddamned things called LSTs," Prime Minister Churchill was heard to growl one day.[3] Given enough LSTs the Allies would be less dependent on port facilities, and there was no guarantee that their expeditionary force would capture a port quickly or intact at Normandy. In fact, so central were the LSTs to the Normandy enterprise that SHAEF (Supreme Headquarters, Allied Expeditionary Force) postponed D-day one month, from May to June 1944, simply to obtain that extra month's production of the precious landing ships.[4] The Allied fleet scheduled to assemble for D-day numbered over 6,000 ships of which 236 were LSTs. Although less than 4 percent of that fleet, they were indispensable for the rapid buildup of forces once the lodgment was secure.

Now, here were eight of them floating a dozen miles out in Lyme Bay heading toward Slapton Sands, still thirty miles distant. Proximity to the friendly shore lent some comfort to these final participants in Exercise Tiger. Several convoys had already touched down on the first day as part of Task Force U, a predominantly U.S. task force under the command of Rear Adm. Don P. Moon, USN. Moon's ships were responsible for lifting Maj. Gen. J. Lawton Collins's VII Corps onto French soil at one specific beach. Senior commanders from SHAEF had been watching their troops perform. Lt. Gen. Omar Bradley was there, as well as Major General Collins. There had been confusion, and H-hour had been postponed by an hour, causing a monumental failure of coordination among the combined arms in the exercise. Everyone hoped the final landings, scheduled for 0730 on 28 April, would go more smoothly. Exercise Tiger preceded Exercise Fabius, the last of several large practice assaults that would culminate sometime in early June in the real thing—the assault on the Far Shore at Normandy.

Plans had called for the presence of two Royal Navy escorts to shepherd the newcomers of Convoy T-4 to the practice beach. Leading the column was HMS *Azalea,* a fifteen-knot antisubmarine corvette with a four-inch forward gun. For most of the war its main weapons had consisted of depth charges and a mortarlike "hedgehog" with which it could lob an oval-shaped pattern of charges ahead of the ship while still maintaining sonar contact with the submerged German U-boat. Its captain, Lt. Comdr. George C. Geddes, RNVR, and his crew had gained much experience in protecting convoys from U-boat attacks on the Atlantic reaches. They were relative newcomers to Britain's coastal waters.

The second vessel ordered to escort duties, HMS *Scimitar,* was larger, an old U.S.-built four-stack destroyer of World War I vintage, traded to the British in 1940 as part of President Roosevelt's destroyers-for-bases deal. The aged *Scimitar* had begun to develop defects after twenty-six years of service and had undergone repairs in January 1944. Perhaps for that reason she was no longer plying the high seas and had been assigned as one of the Royal Navy's S-class destroyers to guard the flank of amphibious practice convoys such as Convoy T-4. Two escorts were barely adequate for an LST column in dangerous waters, as the British well knew, and events soon conspired to remove the *Scimitar* from the convoy's defense. But the Royal Navy was stretched to the limit, trying to scratch up any and all escorts for the drastically increased shipping in home waters prior to the invasion. The officer in overall charge of Force U for this phase of Exercise Tiger, Rear Adm. Don Moon, estimated that by the night of 27–28 April he had accumulated 221 ships and boats under his jurisdiction in Lyme Bay, including 21 LSTs.[5] The notion of two "real" warships as escorts

for Convoy T-4 added to the crews' sense of security as they glided westward in a bay crowded with Allied ships.

Convoy T-4 headed farther out into Lyme Bay, moving line astern
through the night. They moved slowly in order to approximate the time
they would spend at sea in the real crossing to Europe. They were pacing
themselves for a dawn arrival off Slapton Sands. There they would provide
a finale for Exercise Tiger with a realistic practice assault using fully armed
combat equipment including tanks. The beach looked like another one on
the French Coast out toward the neck of the Normandy region on the Cotentin Peninsula. That look-alike landing zone now had a secret Allied designation: Utah Beach. Admiral Moon's naval task force would soon be
landing on it.

The crews and assault troops shivered in the chilly air on Lyme Bay on
that brisk morning of 28 April. The water temperature was forty-two degrees Fahrenheit. It was dark on the water at first, but the moon rose
steadily so that by 0200 visibility had improved somewhat.

Commanding the convoy as flag commodore on the bridge of the first
landing ship, LST 515, Comdr. Bernard Skahill, USN, glanced around his
convoy but could see little in the blacked out conditions. He and the crews
of the other seven LSTs had received their sailing orders the previous
morning with the usual information about course and speed, makeup for
the convoy, times of arrival, radio frequencies for emergency communication, and much more. Wireless communications were highly restricted.
Everyone knew that they were to maintain radio silence except in the
most desperate circumstances. Unnecessary communication would violate
security and help the enemy locate shipping. The Allies knew that Germany's B-Dienst, its expert deciphering service, monitored all frequencies
from listening posts at Dunkirk and the Isle of Jersey, looking for signs of
unusual radio traffic. In addition, the convoy was out on the contested
Channel, scene of sinkings in earlier years by German U-boats, aircraft,
and the fast torpedo boats known as E-boats. The briefing staff for Exercise
Tiger had warned Convoy T-4 as it had warned other convoys to take the
usual security precautions. True, the practice exercises had experienced
no trouble in any of the preparations in 1944, but prudence dictated that
the landing force take into account the possibility of enemy attack.

What few of the Americans knew on that dark night was that several of
their assumptions about safety precautions were wrong or illusory. The
first in a series of calamities involved escorts. The flank escort, HMS *Scimitar,* was not on station either to port or starboard. *Scimitar* had been
rammed in Plymouth Harbor the previous morning by an American LCT, a

fifteen-hundred-ton vessel that was a smaller version of the LST. Despite the captain's request to proceed, Plymouth's port commander had ordered her to return to harbor for repairs. A mix-up in the shore command prevented her replacement from sailing with Convoy T-4, a fact that became known only after the ships were at sea and committed to the exercise. For the newly arrived Americans, the absence of *Scimitar* was not unduly disturbing. "Our attitude was what the hell, live today, die tomorrow; full speed ahead," recalled Eugene E. Eckstam, a medical officer aboard LST 507. "But we were nervous inside," he admitted.[6]

Another critical but as yet unrecognized problem was that Convoy T-4's sailing orders contained a vital flaw, either a typographical error in the radio frequencies or an omission that failed to acknowledge a shift in frequencies at a certain time. With Exercise Tiger under way, the much larger Exercise Fabius about to begin, and the massive final orders for Operation Neptune/Overlord in the process of being distributed to all commands, mix-ups in communication procedures were an unfortunate probability. In this instance, the Americans could not have communicated with their British escorts or with any other Royal Navy ship or installation if they had tried. And because of the need for radio silence none had tried. The LSTs heading into contested waters were unaware of any problems, a custom-made recipe for disaster in a war zone.

HMS *Azalea,* equally unaware of any difficulties, steamed in front, convinced that nothing was amiss in the security arrangements for her vulnerable charges following astern at six-hundred–yard intervals over a span of several miles. Commander Geddes should have wondered why, after seeing *Scimitar* steam back into harbor past his convoy the previous morning, he had received no replacement escort. But apparently neither he nor Convoy Commander Skahill on LST 515 had considered the consequences of the *Scimitar's* absence.

Shortly after midnight, at 0007 hours on 28 April, *Azalea* received a terse radio message from the naval commander in chief at Plymouth, which warned of "ships on port wave," indicating an E-boat alert. Although Commander Geddes and his bridge staff began studying the new information, they did not change course or attempt to issue any warnings to the LSTs. Oblivious to approaching peril, Convoy T-4 continued to glide ahead at little more than walking speed, strung out across Lyme Bay.[7]

Shortly after 0130 hours crewmen on several of the ships saw green tracer far off the port side of the convoy to the south, followed by the sound of gunfire on the horizon. Lacking radio communication, they were unaware of a running fight developing between E-boats and British destroyers that had begun to track the fast coastal craft. Troops milled about talking about how realistic the organizers had made their practice amphibious assault exercise. Medical Officer Eckstam was in the wardroom of LST 507 near the stern when the commotion began. "I heard shots," he recalled, and commented to one of his shipmates that "they better watch out or someone will get hurt." It was at this time that PO Bill Gould and a few of his shipmates heard the strange grinding noises underneath their hull. Lt. (jg) James Murdock, USN, also saw the distant green tracer. At about the same moment he and the bridge personnel aboard LST 507 began tracking a pair of tiny blips on their radar, indicating two small craft approaching from the starboard, or northern, side of the convoy. Prudently, they sounded general quarters, and all over the ship navy and army personnel pulled on combat gear and went to their battle stations. A few minutes later those on the bridge could see the faint blur of two fast boats pulling abreast of them off the starboard side of the column. They scarcely had time to take in that fact when something crashed into LST 507, followed by a deafening explosion. At exactly 0203 hours an object hit the auxiliary engine room. Power failed immediately, and LST 507 was plunged into darkness. The ship had been torpedoed. In that instant Bill Gould knew what he and his fellow crew members had heard just minutes before: the first torpedo in an E-boat attack. Set to run too deep, it had grazed 507's hull without exploding.[8]

The attack took everyone by surprise. Medical Officer Eckstam, who had heard gunshots earlier, went on deck to investigate. "I decided to see what was going on," he recalled, "when BOOM, I was tossed up and landed on my knees on the steel deck." Luckily, he sustained no injuries.[9] However, the situation quickly worsened. With no propulsion, the ship lay dead in the water. Worse, fires had erupted in her auxiliary engine room and on the tank deck where army vehicles, tanks, trucks, mobile guns, jeeps, and landing vehicles called DUKWs were lashed together waiting to off-load at Slapton Sands. Before leaving port the exercise crews had topped off all the vehicles with gasoline, and most had full stores of ammunition aboard for the next morning's simulated landing. LST 507, like her sister landing ships, was carrying an extremely volatile cargo.

Medical Officer Eckstam, his curiosity quickly satisfied, was one of the first to go back below, anxious to see if anyone needed medical assistance. "As I opened the hatch to the tank deck," he recalled, "I was thrown back by the inferno." Fires had spread rapidly from vehicle to vehicle as gasoline flowed in rivulets along the decks. Soon the entire hold was ablaze. Crew and soldiers above decks could hear signs of distress below. "I heard the screams and cries for help," Eckstam continued, "but there was no way anyone could get out or go in." With a heavy heart he made a move that all sailors dread but that had to be done. "I followed navy regulations to preserve water-tight integrity," Eckstam stated, "and dogged the hatch."[10]

Soon the outer walls and decks on LST 507 began to glow cherry red. It was now 0230 hours, and the crew received orders to abandon ship. It hardly seemed possible that the torpedo had struck only twenty-seven minutes before. Survival now depended on the availability of emergency rescue equipment like lifeboats and rafts. Petty Officer Gould and fellow crew members had already set about unfastening and lowering LST 507's two undamaged small-boats in the bow, a difficult job amid the chaos and panic.

Inexperience among the crew and troops complicated matters. The ship had been in European waters only a month, and some of the crew, such as its small-boat specialists, had been aboard a bare two weeks. They had had precious little time to conduct emergency drills with the permanent crew and its young officers. Motor Machinist Mate 2d Class Owen Sheppard shouted a warning to a green navy lieutenant who had started to lower one of the two operable LCVPs on his own initiative. Sheppard was too late. The descending davits struck two safety pins, bending them, and delaying the launch. While panicky soldiers and sailors crowded around, Sheppard ordered the boat winched up again and, wielding a sledgehammer, he pounded the safety pins out. Down came the boat again, released by the same panicky lieutenant before Sheppard could free a final securing cable. The tough cable ripped through the small-boat, parted the engine throttle and steering gear, and impeded the launch yet again.[11]

From their vantage point forward, small-boat crewmen Sheppard and Gould became aware of a stark fact: there were too few boats and rafts available for the hundreds of survivors. Men began jumping individually or in groups into the icy water, convinced that the life belts around their waists would help them survive. Lacking proper instructions, they did not know they were supposed to secure the belts under their armpits before inflating them. Some of them, still encumbered with equipment, dove head-first into the water only to slip completely out of their belts into the deep. Other men already afloat were discovering that belts in the waist position tipped their heads and upper torsos into the icy water, accelerating the effects of hypothermia. The soldiers, especially, revealed that they had not had enough safety drills. Some men were still wearing their heavy steel helmets when they jumped overboard despite instructions to remove them. Falling a distance of twenty feet or more into the water, their heads snapped forward or backward upon impact, breaking many a soldier's neck. For the members of Convoy T-4 a maritime disaster had begun, and luck as much as anything would determine who lived and who did not.

Pharmacist's Mate 2d Class Bill Walker, a native of Alabama, was one of thirty-nine medical corpsmen aboard LST 507. He was asleep in his bunk when General Quarters sounded. He and the other corpsmen had just completed a training course on gas attacks, and in his groggy state Walker assumed they were having another drill. He grabbed his gas mask and proceeded topside only to discover that no drill was under way. Confused, Walker went below again but found the bosun and another sailor securing the water-tight hatches. Unable to reach his quarters, he had just returned to the ladder leading topside when the torpedo struck. Dazed by the shock of the explosion he clambered upward somehow, the last person to emerge from that compartment. By this time heavy smoke was issuing from amidships, and a fellow Alabamian, Medical Corpsman Bill Rogers, calmed Walker by agreeing to share his life jacket if they had to go into the water. Through the smoke the alert Rogers spied a lifeboat being prepared for launch and steered his buddy to it. Along with nearly eighty of the ship's company they crowded into the boat just as it lowered away. Unfortunately, the boat hung up on a fouled cable, and finally the coxswain ordered everyone off. Walker and his guardian angel, Rogers, began clambering back onto the deck again. Still without a life jacket, Walker hung behind for a moment, inadvertently separating himself from his friend. Unsure of what to do next, he began undressing to permit easier swimming, a decision that might easily have proved fatal given the frigid waters below. Just then one of his compartment mates, a soldier known by the nickname "Wrench," yelled to the coxswain that he could part the cable with his rifle. The first shot produced little effect, and many of the erstwhile occupants continued to move away. However, by the fourth shot "Wrench" parted the cable and amid shouts of relief the coxswain pulled the small-boat away from the ship. Scarcely able to make sense of his good fortune, Bill Walker finished dressing again and along with everyone else aboard the small craft began fishing less fortunate survivors out of the water. Bill Rogers was not one of them.[12]

A more typical experience was that of Medical Officer Eckstam who had not been fortunate enough to encounter a small-boat. "I climbed down a cargo net," he recalled, "and eased into the water." It was as icy as it looked, but Eckstam had no choice but to swim away from the stricken vessel toward a raft. Many others had the same idea, and since there were so few rafts, the men began to form concentric rings around them, each member in a ring holding onto one of the ship's company closer in. "At first I was on the sixth or seventh ring," Eckstam said. However, the numbing water quickly took its toll. "As the men lost consciousness," he remembered, "they drifted away. There was no way to hold so many. Finally, I got a hand around a rope on the raft. Then I blacked out."[13] The hardy Eckstam was lucky. Although he was unaware of it, at the very moment he lost consciousness, help had finally arrived.

Meanwhile crews and army personnel aboard the other landing ships had swiveled around to see what was happening at the rear of the convoy. Aboard LST 515 nearly three miles away at the head of the column, Commander Skahill was convinced that the stricken ship was not part of his convoy. Radio operators requested information but received no replies of any kind. The convoy continued in line, but by this time a wave of apprehension had begun to sweep from ship to ship.

At 0217 a landing vessel in the middle of the column, LST 531, exploded in flames when first one torpedo then another hit her. Onlookers from other ships watched the debris and rising column of flame. They also witnessed a gun firing red tracer to starboard passing incoming green tracer. The LST's deck gun was a heavy .50-caliber machine gun. Suddenly the gun swung vertical. Some speculated that a dead man's hand was still on the trigger. In reality the foundering ship had begun listing heavily to port, elevating the gun and making its fire useless. The green tracer continued crisscrossing the column, but no one could track it to its source. Experienced German armorers had taken good precautions. Tracer from the E-boats ignited only when well along its trajectory, so that the American gunners searched in vain for its source and for their German opposites.

Agony for LST 531 was brutal but short. It slid beneath the waves in less than ten minutes carrying all but 29 of its complement of 496 men down with it. No one below decks escaped. For a time only its bow hovered above water, a refuge for no one. On the contrary, by the remorseless logic of war it had become a hazard to navigation.

Following this second torpedoing, ships were zigzagging frantically, and deck crews had begun firing machine guns and cannon everywhere. One soldier in a half-track on the upper deck of LST 496 fired at a shadowy outline to starboard. Far from hitting the enemy, he poured rounds into LST 511, causing casualties with his "friendly fire." Up and down the line crews reported near misses from torpedoes that appeared to be coming from two different directions. Moving at flank speed by this time—eleven knots—the LSTs were desperately trying to fend off the E-boats, whose deep-throated diesels they could hear clearly now. Some, like LST 496 were lucky. Others were not. LST 289 had avoided two of the deadly missiles when suddenly a surface-running torpedo caught her from astern and detonated under the fantail. The explosion blew upward, destroying the ship's rudders and mangling the gun crew who had continued to fire their 40-mm cannon until the moment of detonation. Everyone expected LST 289 to founder like LST 507. Thirteen men died in that explosion, but miraculously, the crippled ship continued to float, its engines and hull spared from the worst of the surface torpedo blast. Later, the plucky crew lowered two LCVPs, and using them as improvised tugs, they towed their stricken ship to safety.

The sea seemed to churn with torpedoes for minutes on end, and there were numerous near misses as the ungainly ships turned this way and that. Sailors aboard the command ship, LST 515, reported seeing one torpedo miss them by a matter of a few inches. For those who survived, it seemed a miracle that more ships had not gone down. But the occupants of three LSTs experienced no miracles. For many of those on board the agony of slow death was just beginning as they abandoned ship, jumping or falling into the icy waters of the Channel. As they jumped, many must have wondered what had happened to their armed escort.

When the first torpedo hit LST 507, Lieutenant Commander Geddes aboard HMS *Azalea* immediately turned sharp about and zigzagged down the starboard side of the convoy, looking for the attackers. Because he had chosen to position himself far forward, one nautical mile in front of the lead ship, and because his corvette could only make fifteen knots, Geddes's counterattack was necessarily delayed by local conditions. It was still dark, but the frustrated captain dared not throw up illumination flares because he was not sure from which side of the convoy the enemy boats were attacking. If he fired off flares to port, and the E-boats were to starboard, he would only succeed in illuminating the LSTs, increasing their peril. Because he was tied to a different radio frequency than the one used by the Americans, he could not obtain reports from anyone on the LSTs. As commander of a subchaser, Geddes was more practiced in detecting U-boats; he gave every sign of being baffled by the E-boats and their tactics. When the attack came he was caught unaware, out of position, and seemingly oblivious to the midnight warning issued from Plymouth Command. His inexperience was also evident as he groped his way down the column, unable to locate his elusive enemy even once during the entire attack by nine E-boats. But Geddes was not alone in his confusion. Few aboard the ships of Convoy T-4 actually saw the E-boats that night. Many more heard their diesels or saw their speeding torpedoes.

At the head of the LST column, Commander Skahill aboard LST 515 also reacted hesitantly. For some minutes he continued to gaze from the bridge at the mounting confusion astern. The first explosion had taken place five miles south of his column, he claimed, and along with the ship's captain, Lt. John Doyle, USN, and his crew, he was baffled by it. They thought that the victim, if it was a victim, was not part of their convoy. In reality they had witnessed the opening attack on LST 507. When some fifteen minutes later LST 531 exploded in the middle of the column, there could no longer be any doubt as to the peril confronting Convoy T-4. Obeying long-standing instructions in case of enemy attack, Skahill radioed all LSTs to make for the nearest friendly shore, in this case Chesil Beach and Cove approximately fifteen miles to the north. This order effectively abandoned LSTs 507, 531, and 289 to their fate, the rationale being that ships attempting to rescue survivors would themselves become victims of further E-boat attacks.

Although the senior officer in charge of Convoy T-4, Skahill was not a strong or decisive personality. The skipper of his command ship, Lieutenant Doyle, was much more forceful, and he judged the situation differently, claiming that E-boat tactics were hit-and-run. By this time they had already hit hard, and now the attackers were undoubtedly on the run back to France. Doyle demanded that they turn about and help rescue the soldiers and sailors from the doomed ships. An argument broke out on the bridge that lasted for some time. Finally, in a curiously American twist, the LST captain broadcast their options over the ship's public address system to the ship's complement, and when they heard the choices, the men clamored support for Doyle's position and demanded a rescue attempt. Obeying the majority opinion, LST 515 turned about, lowered its LCVPs into the water, and became the first ship to engage in the belated rescue.

What they confronted in the cold waters of Lyme Bay two hours after the attack was a tragedy of daunting proportions. Hundreds of bodies and parts of bodies were floating in the Channel. Most of the men who had failed to adjust their life belts properly had paid with their lives, as had those who hit the water still wearing their steel helmets. The few life rafts and boats afloat still had concentric rings of men around them. By this time, however, most of them were dead or near death. Hauling in the few survivors was an arduous task for the rescuers; the victims were so weakened by hypothermia that they could no longer aid in their own rescue. Medical Officer Eckstam was one of the lucky ones. The usual figure given for loss of life that night is 749 servicemen. It may have been even more.[14]

The navy crewmen in the small-boats assisted as best they could in the belated rescue effort. After Petty Officer Gould from LST 507 had freed his boat and pulled away, he and Motor Machinist Mate Sheppard improvised a throttle for the hastily repaired engine. Coordinating rudder and engine, they set about picking survivors out of the water. They pulled a dozen men out of the water in the immediate vicinity of LST 507 before moving away from the foundering vessel. Although their LCVP had not been crowded when they launched it, within a short time the landing craft was so packed that the survivors could not raise their arms above their heads in the confined space. Sheppard recalled that the only reason the boat did not swamp under the load was because the Channel waters were extremely smooth that night. Two hours later, when the first British warship arrived, seventy-eight men off-loaded from the LCVP, which normally had a maximum capacity of thirty-six.[15]

When HMS *Saladin,* the relief escort for the rammed *Scimitar,* finally reached the site, its crew began picking up victims. Sections of the sea were literally covered with bodies. Sailors and soldiers watched in horrified fascination as bow waves parted the floating corpses. LST 507's bow was still protruding from the water two hours after the torpedo attack. HMS *Saladin* warned all survivors that it was about to open up on the hulk, which now posed a menace to navigation. She opened fire with her four-inch gun and finished off LST 507.

At about the same moment, a major security flap developed: Allied officials could not account for several officers who had been "bigoted," that is, they had been apprised of the Normandy Invasion plans. Eventually, search crews accounted for all bigoted personnel. The Germans had picked up no survivors, so no Allied military personnel had compromised details of the impending attack. Meanwhile nine gray E-boats filed back into Cherbourg harbor unscathed, having eluded all Allied air and naval forces on the Channel.

While the German crews were tying up safely in their giant concrete pens, Albert Nickson, a young survivor from LST 507, stood shakily on the deck of LST 515. He knew he was lucky to be alive. Fished out of the water by LCVP crewmen and somewhat revived, Nickson steadied himself at a rail and looked down at the bodies still floating in the sea. Finally, he turned to a superior officer, Ensign Fred Beattie, who had also survived the sinking of LST 507 and articulated what many of the freshly arrived Americans were starting to realize: the Germans were playing to win.[16]

Others shared his opinion. Writing from his office in London on the day following the sinkings, the Supreme Allied Commander, General Eisenhower, cabled to JCS Chief of Staff George C. Marshall about the Lyme Bay incident, lamenting the loss of life, and as commander in chief of the imminent invasion, indicating what the losses implied. "Apparently we lost a considerable number of men," Ike informed Marshall. "I got the news just as I was finishing a long hard day, and I must say it was not a restful thought to take home with me." As Supreme Commander, General Eisenhower had a less compassionate but nevertheless sound military reason for regret: "We are stretched to the limit in the LST category." As of 28 April 1944, the Allies no longer had any reserves of the indispensable LSTs in the European Theater of Operations.[17]

How could such mayhem have been committed against the mighty Allied forces in a friendly bay only a few miles from shore with scores of Allied war vessels and entire aircraft squadrons in the vicinity? How could a few wooden torpedo boats have inflicted such damage and then escaped unharmed? The Americans, as newcomers to the Channel area, might ask those questions. The British, who had been fighting the E-boat menace for at least four years, had no answers that seemed adequate in the aftermath of such a disaster. The episode was especially humiliating because little more than a year earlier, on the night of 26–27 February 1943, four E-boats from the Cherbourg-based 5th Flotilla had also entered Lyme Bay and in quick succession sunk the five-thousand-ton British freighter *Moldavia,* two trawlers, and the British-built LCT 381.[18] What were these E-boats anyway? Given the impending invasion of Europe, the Allies had to decide quickly what they could do to prevent a far greater tragedy once the LSTs and other Allied ships put to sea again, heading for the Far Shore where the German Navy's Schnellbootwaffe awaited them.

Chapter **2**

Enemy Torpedo Boats

Most of the major combatants of World War II produced coastal forces equipped with fast torpedo boats as part of their naval arsenals. Hardly a war-winning weapon by themselves, high-speed, torpedo-equipped craft such as the American PT boats, British MTBs, Italian MAS boats, and German E-boats were nevertheless an important component of naval warfare, and nowhere was this more important than in the English Channel and North Sea. Coastal forces were a relatively new branch of the world's navies, in large part because the technology that drove them was itself rather new. Fast torpedo boats were complicated, unforgiving vessels that challenged their crews and demanded careful balancing of hull design, power, weight, and weapons systems. Most navies had mixed results with them. In common with other recently developed branches such as air forces and mechanized ground units, they depended on major advances in science and technology to become feasible components in a nation's arsenal, and the various combatants arrived at different solutions to the technological puzzles they posed.

Of the warring nations that produced fast torpedo boats in the 1940s, Germany stood out by establishing a coastal force employing advanced technology and attracting some of the ablest young officers of the Kriegsmarine. From the moment the war started, it could project naval power considerable distances from Germany's shores. Along with the submarine, which the Germans developed into the ultimate naval menace of the war, their Schnellbootwaffe proved to be a valuable complement, carrying the naval war to Britain's shoreline and threatening for a time that island nation's life-sustaining coastal convoys. More threatening still, those same fast torpedo boats demonstrated convincingly that they could sink Allied LSTs, as they did at Lyme Bay in April 1944, possibly jeopardizing the impending Allied invasion of Europe. Of all the weapons remaining in the German arsenal that fateful spring, the one naval threat in the West capable of offensive operations against the Allies on the shallow Channel waters was Germany's E-boat Force. The Germans patiently developed the fast torpedo boat into a modern weapon of war, one that fought on despite growing Allied preponderance in naval and air power. It was a considerable accomplishment.

Origins

Had they foreseen its potential at the outset of World War II, the British Admiralty might not have dubbed the German fast torpedo boat simply "E-boat," meaning enemy torpedo boat. Perhaps the British naval authorities were unconsciously placing it in the same category as their new and untried MTB (motor torpedo boat), the standard small vessel for Britain's newly constituted Coastal Forces. The degree of respect afforded that infant organization can be easily deduced by the Royal Navy regulars' nickname for it: "Costly Farces." In any case, Germany's high-speed motor torpedo boats were first called E-boats and the name stuck.[1]

It may seem odd that of all the world's navies in World War II, the Germans would emerge with the most formidable fast torpedo boat. Yet there were historical reasons for this development. The German Navy, although in existence only since 1871, had been conceived as a small Continental navy, concentrating on defense of its restricted North Sea and Baltic coasts. Before unification, the various German states, including Prussia, had assigned a lower priority to blue-water navies and merchant marines than did Atlantic-oriented nations like Great Britain, France, the Netherlands, Spain, and Portugal. This remained the case for at least two decades following Bismarck's declaration of the German Empire in 1871. In an age when the Great Powers were having to choose between a Mahanian big-gun, blue-water navy, or commerce raiding with smaller vessels, Imperial Germany chose the latter. Almost immediately, technical advances began to make those seemingly clear-cut choices less obvious. Specifically, the monopoly on power that a ship's main cannon had enjoyed for four centuries was coming to an end.

Since the onset of the black powder revolution, the most successful navies had been composed of large ships bristling with guns. Ships' cannon had been the premier weapon, and as late as the 1850s they seemed destined to remain so. Wood and sail might give way to steel and steam, but heavy-caliber guns, albeit greatly modified, seemingly would reign on. The assumption was that a good big ship would always beat a good little ship—and a good many more besides. Then technology took an unexpected twist. In 1866 during a brief Austro-Italian conflict, Austrian naval officer Giovanni de Luppis jerry-built a small wire-guided charge, propelled by a kind of clockwork mechanism, that he hoped to deploy from the Adriatic shore. It contained an underwater charge that de Luppis intended to steer onto a ship's hull. Not mechanically adroit, he asked an expatriate English engineer living in Fiume, Robert Whitehead, for help with his coastal weapon, which he called a *Küstenbrander* because of the spar-torpedo projecting from its bow. His device proved unworkable but had a fortuitous consequence. The brilliant Whitehead, with considerable experience in building marine engines, became fascinated with the notion of developing a self-propelled torpedo as opposed to floating static charges or spar torpedoes of the type that today would be classified as mines. He called his invention a fish torpedo; contemporaries referred to it variously as an automobile or locomotive torpedo.

Whitehead fashioned a slender tubelike missile, with a charge in its nose, propelled by a miniature compressed-air motor, and designed for underwater launching. After two years of experimentation he achieved a breakthrough, a hydrostatic valve with which to prevent porpoising. It held the torpedo at a steady depth. For several years Whitehead experimented in Fiume. Then at trials in Britain in 1870, he demonstrated his torpedo's practicality with one that made six knots and traveled seven hundred yards, striking targets consistently and sinking a sizable hulk. The skeptical Royal Navy officers present became instant converts, and by 1872 Whitehead was producing torpedoes commercially for many of the world's navies. Eventually, he fitted a gyroscope to his invention, which in combination with advances made by various naval research establishments, transformed the torpedo into a reliable, destructive weapon. For example, experimenters discovered that a hemispheric head rather than a pointed one was the least resistant shape for an underwater missile, and it allowed space for a far larger and deadlier charge in the torpedo's head. Thus by the eve of World War I, Whitehead's invention had broken the monopoly of the ship's cannon at the same time that the world's navies were evolving all-big-gun dreadnoughts.[2]

Aware of the potent effects of underwater explosions on ships' hulls, German naval authorities immediately recognized Whitehead's torpedo concept as an effective coastal weapon. In 1873 they dispatched none other than Alfred von Tirpitz, one of the German Navy's rising young weapons experts, to visit Whitehead in Fiume, where he spent weeks in Whitehead's company. The German Navy became a steady customer. By 1879 they were producing their own torpedoes to launch from shore or from coastal vessels they proposed to build. Thus began a German Navy tradition in which the torpedo was to figure prominently, initially in torpedo-firing surface craft and later in submarines. By contrast, Great Britain forged ahead with the development of large-caliber cannon and revolutionary gunnery techniques and, while the Royal Navy did not ignore torpedoes, neither did it place the highest priority on them.[3]

Development of the light, high-speed surface craft to deliver the torpedo was hardly as steady as the weapon itself, even though the attractions of cheap and potentially deadly torpedo boats were obvious to smaller Continental navies. In the 1880s the French even went so far as to build a revolutionary school of thought, their updated commerce-raiding *Jeune École,* around the fast torpedo vessel as yet another means to end Britain's monopoly in naval strength. Soon architects from many nations, especially among the smaller navies, began contemplating new designs with which to utilize Whitehead's fish torpedo. What they all discovered was that an effective design for torpedo boats was extremely elusive. The ideal vessel had to be fast, light, maneuverable, steady, strong, seaworthy, and stealthy enough to get within range to launch its weapons against more powerful foes. Since most of those characteristics worked against one another, the search for a successful fast torpedo boat lasted for decades. In many respects the search continues today.[4]

Although the performance requirements for a successful torpedo boat demanded many technological advances, the central need was for a proper power plant mated to a proper hull. Britain's Alfred Yarrow had been experimenting with fast expendable steam launches for spar torpedoes in the early 1870s, and then steam launches as platforms for the fish torpedo after 1877. In 1897 on the occasion of Queen Victoria's diamond jubilee, Sir Charles Parsons captured public attention with *Turbinia,* a slender-hulled vessel powered by his new steam turbine and capable of thirty-four knots. However, those long, narrow "toothpick" hulls and temperamental steam turbines were more suited to the sporting world than to naval vessels.

They were simply too fragile for combat conditions. Extreme length made them hard to maneuver, and they heeled badly when turning. The concept of a planing hull in which hydrodynamic lift carried most of the vessel out of the water had been around since the 1870s, but it proved difficult to obtain proper hull design and sufficient power. A Frenchman, M. Campet, built the first genuine planing boat in 1905. By then better, lighter power plants were available.[5]

A proper engine for small, light craft had proved elusive in the age of steam. The German Navy had the advantage of starting slightly later with a more promising technology produced nearby. Gottfried Daimler and Wilhelm Maybach revolutionized the world of propulsion with the world's first practical internal combustion engine in 1882. First used in automobiles, the engines were propelling motor boats within a few years. Suddenly motor torpedo boats, specifically German coastal craft, appeared as a feasible threat to costly, slow battleships. Then German naval development took another turn, influenced by an aggressive new head of state.[6]

In 1888 Kaiser William II, a headstrong personality, ascended the throne of Imperial Germany. Aged twenty-nine, William looked with mixed feelings of admiration and envy on his Victorian relatives in England. He especially envied them their great navy. Of impetuous temperament, William adopted the pseudo-Clausewitzian theories of the U.S. naval theorist Alfred Thayer Mahan and became a convert to the grand fleet concept. To achieve Germany's "place in the sun," William needed a great navy of capital ships, and in order to do that he appointed a new naval adviser: Alfred von Tirpitz. Tirpitz, one-time visitor to Whitehead, had steadily improved his reputation by becoming the premier organizer of Germany's coastal torpedo vessels in the 1870s and 1880s. William's ascension coincided with technological breakthroughs that allowed the building of ever more powerful, heavily armed and armored surface ships, and Tirpitz decided that he needed a larger springboard for his ambitions in the age of German *Weltpolitik*. With the rise of William II and Tirpitz, Imperial Germany broke with its older defensive naval tradition, which had much in common with the French *Jeune École*. Together they set out to build Germany's own big-gun high seas fleet to rival Great Britain's grand fleet. This significant shift in priorities slowed German advances in fast torpedo boat design in the decade and a half before World War I.[7]

German naval authorities, however, did not totally ignore developments coming from Germany's talented new boat designers and builders. Starting with the era of internal combustion engines, German powerboat designers had been among the world's leading innovators. Otto Lürssen, a young naval architect and pioneer powerboat builder with a shipyard on the Weser River at Bremen/Vegesack, designed one of the world's earliest power craft in 1890. A subsequent advanced design, *Donnerwetter*, powered by a 40-horsepower engine, made thirty-eight knots of limited endurance and impressed the German Navy. It was characteristic of Lürssen's skills that in one of the early international speedboat races, held in Monaco in 1911, the winner was neither Britain's pioneering designer John I. Thornycroft nor Italy's famed SVAN Company team. Lürssen's entry, the *Lürssen-Daimler*, powered by two 102-horsepower engines and averaging twenty-eight knots, crossed the finish line first. Nevertheless, despite undoubted successes, the trend in that imperial era was clearly toward huge battleships. Consequently, Lürssen and his competitors found an on-again, off-again reaction from the German Navy with respect to their vessels during World War I.[8]

For example, the German Navy had shown some interest in remotely controlled high-speed craft before World War I, then dropped the idea at the outset of hostilities, only to seize it again in 1915 when the British blockade began to bite. After the British installed mine net barrages off Belgian ports, the Germans tried to blow them up with explosives-laden remotely controlled craft called FL *(Fernlenk)* boats. Lürssen's six-ton boats were forty feet long, made thirty knots, and trailed a thin electric cable behind them back to a directing station on shore. The experimenters steered others by radio, sometimes with a seaplane overhead to give directions. The FL designs had a range of about 30 miles, and although a clever idea, they and their explosive cargo were too small and too unpredictable to destroy the nets.[9]

In 1913 Lürssen also produced a manned thirty-one-foot powerboat, the *Boncourt*, a planing craft that could reach over thirty knots, but official interest lagged early in the war. In fact, not until 1917 was Lürssen able to sell his idea of a high-speed manned craft to the German Navy, and even then it was ordered as a dispatch boat. To it he had added as a defiant gesture a torpedo tube centered over the bow of his sleek racing vessel. Impressed by the sight of this unexpectedly armed high-performance powerboat, the naval authorities took a renewed interest in the torpedo-boat concept and immediately ordered a second vessel that was delivered in April 1917. Powered by two 240-hp gasoline engines, this *Sonderkommando-Gleitboot* (special operations planing boat) could also make a respectable thirty knots but was so short-ranged that it had to be carried on the deck of a mother ship to the vicinity of the target and then swung over the side with its muzzle-loaded eighteen-inch torpedo already installed.

Thus the crew had only one chance in an attack. Despite these severe limitations, this weird little craft succeeded in September 1917 in sinking a Russian minelayer in the eastern Baltic Sea, the only success German torpedo boats scored in the First World War.[10]

Encouraged, the German admiralty ordered more craft, known as LM *(Luftschiff Motoren)* boats because of their aeroengines, and several served off the Belgian Coast as World War I drew to an end. These vessels were powered by three gasoline engines—the Zeppelins they once powered had been withdrawn from service—but the development was hardly trouble free. The gasoline engines and their volatile fuel were hazardous and unreliable, and at least two boats blew up. When the Germans next built a torpedo boat, they vowed it would be powered by diesel engines. Lürssen quietly preserved the unused LM hulls at the end of the war, and the firm conducted extensive testing with them in the mid-1920s.[11]

The Germans' uneven experience with fast torpedo boats in World War I was typical. In fact, with the possible exception of Italy, no navy in the era of World War I successfully developed the real potential for this class of vessel because of its demanding and contradictory design requirements. John I. Thornycroft's coastal motor boat (CMB) used a stepped planing hull to achieve high speed with a relatively low-powered gasoline engine. The step design featured a sharp break in the bottom curve of the hull roughly amidships, with the stern portion stepped up higher than the forward hull area. When planing, the stern portion rose above the water, reducing drag. Stepped hulls were commonly used on flying boats or aircraft pontoons where minimum resistance was needed. Although fast, they had serious limitations. Such hulls were time-consuming and expensive to build, placed enormous strains on the step, and could support only light loads. The CMBs were short-ranged, lightly armed, and had limited seakeeping abilities. Experiments with hard-chine, hydroplaning hulls also exhibited seakeeping problems, and crews complained about their slamming effect in the rough North Sea. Britain virtually abandoned further development of fast torpedo boats after 1918.

The climate for defeated Germany was even less promising. The clauses of the Versailles Treaty were hostile to offensively designed German naval vessels, and what developments did take place occurred clandestinely. Nevertheless, the downsized naval staff as well as private individuals and groups began a protracted effort to find the formula for a successful fast fighting boat that hitherto had eluded everyone. By 1925 Otto Lürssen had assembled a team of able naval architects and engine builders at his yard in Vegesack and returned to civilian markets. They built quantities of round-bilge displacement-hulled pleasure craft for American sportsmen under the label "Express Motor Cruiser." Success in the commercial market encouraged further development of that hull design, which was suitable to the choppy North Sea waters. In 1926 the Lürssen Yard began building a larger luxury yacht, the *Oheka II,* for an American client with a taste for both speed and luxury. Showing its wartime ancestry, *Oheka II* was powered by three gasoline engines, 550-hp Maybachs. With a top speed of thirty-four knots, she was rumored to be the fastest private yacht in the world.

Impressed, Germany's naval staff requested a look at Lürssen's plans and then ordered a similar vessel, the main difference being the addition of two removable torpedo tubes forward. Working in secrecy, the builders presented the German Navy with its modified vessel in August 1930, fulfilling the requirement to fit removable tubes and to add light metal covers over the indented bow fairings. After all, Allied inspection teams gave little notice of their approach. Naval authorities issued the new coastal craft several boat number and letter identifications, implying antisubmarine work, but encouraged by the halt to Allied inspections, they finally designated it in March 1932 for its proper function: S-1, Germany's first true *Schnellboot.*[12]

Besides designing a superior fast torpedo boat, another telltale sign that the German Navy was still imbued with a stronger tradition of coastal defense than rivals like Great Britain was its willingness even in the interwar years to assign capable regular navy personnel to its coastal forces. Once Germany began to rebuild its light units in the 1920s and early 1930s, it allocated outstanding officers to draft proposals for future craft, to develop tactics, and to organize support facilities.

A somewhat shadowy figure, Kapitän zur See Walter Lohmann was an administrative officer in the German Navy who helped in armistice negotiations with the Royal Navy at the end of the war, transferred as Naval Transport Officer to the Reichswehr in the chaotic postarmistice period, and fed government funds to various North German shipyards and "sporting clubs" for the preservation and development of high-performance coastal craft and tactics. Restrictions in the Versailles Treaty placed severe limits on the postwar navy, and Lohmann perceived fast torpedo boats as an important class of vessel to develop. He probed the limits of those restrictions until press attention and an ensuing public outcry over his financial manipulations forced him to resign from the Reichsmarine in 1928.[13] However, his artful funding had left its impact on torpedo-boat development and other secret projects. In the summers of 1925 and 1926, reserve officers manned holdover LM boats from the war, plus a few postwar craft built with surplus wartime materials such as Lürssen's *Liesel,* to conduct a series of unarmed low-profile exercises against veteran light cruisers off Fehmarn. One reserve officer, Kapitänleutnant Eduard N. Rabe, commanded LM *Bodo* among others and in spare hours allowed his young son to join the crew. Nearly two decades later the youth became a familiar name to Allied naval authorities. By then he was Kapitänleutnant Günther Rabe, "The Raven," destined to become one of the most successful E-boat commanders of World War II.[14]

The brief exercises of the mid-1920s demonstrated that such boats were a potent weapon if used in groups of two or more at night in relatively calm seas. Low silhouettes and gray camouflage paint made them extraordinarily stealthy. The exercises confirmed the German Navy's preference for the round-bilge (or round bottom) displacement hull. They also reinforced its aversion to gasoline engines: there were several explosions and fires during the trials. Convinced that fast torpedo boats had a promising future, Lohmann continued to support these quasi-legal activities throughout the 1920s.[15]

The future fast torpedo boat needed a concept and role to justify it as a class of naval vessel. In 1920–21, Leutnant Friedrich Ruge, fated to be one of Germany's outstanding naval officers in the next war, prepared a carefully researched thesis about fast torpedo boats. He investigated the experiences of the British, Italian, and German navies in World War I and helped lay the framework for a future German coastal force. Ruge's optimistic predictions for the new boats were amply justified in the summer exercises Lohmann organized in the mid-1920s. Ruge helped to establish general standards for future torpedo boats of several class sizes.[16]

Besides a dozen 930-ton mini-destroyers of the closely related predator mammal and predator bird classes—they sported names like *Jaguar* and *Falke* (Falcon)—Weimar Germany was permitted a dozen coastal defense vessels not to exceed 200 tons each. Convinced of the potency of torpedoes as a navy's most lethal weapon, the Weimar naval leadership designed both classes to include torpedoes as well as gun armament. The dozen 930-ton vessels carried three 10.5-cm cannon, one forward and two aft, but they also carried a hefty second punch: six torpedoes in two banks of three tubes, the first set mounted between the two funnels and the second just aft of the rear funnel. Despite their original designation as destroyers, these ships—after upgrading their tubes to take the 53-cm standard torpedo—were reclassified by 1931 for what they had become: torpedo boats. They were fast for their day, making speeds up to thirty-three and thirty-five knots respectively for the two mini-destroyer classes, and they were capable of firing deadly salvoes from their twin banks of tubes. Although large for the concept, they were properly called *Torpedoboote* by the German naval authorities and in flotilla strength could loose a score or more of torpedoes on select targets, a feat the Allies would witness first-hand on the opening day of the invasion of Europe. After the Nazi seizure of power in 1933, Hitler ordered eighteen 850-ton Type 35 torpedo boats, which were fast—nearly forty knots—but whose high-pressure steam turbines were notoriously temperamental. Like the *Schnellboot,* they dispensed with individual ship's names. T-24 was typical of that later class of T-boat.[17]

What the German Navy could do with the smaller 200-ton vessels was less clear. Rather than attempting to build up to the maximum weight limit, Ruge concluded that only fast motor torpedo boats, weighing half that much and taking advantage of lessons learned from World War I and since, could produce a worthy class of vessel. They would be multi-engined—preferably diesels—fast attack, planing craft with multiple reloadable torpedo tubes.

Once Ruge's outlines were transformed some years later into tangible boats and crews, the German Navy placed in command of its E-boat flotillas highly respected regular officers such as Erich Bey, who labored assiduously to mature the tactics and explore the potential of the new boats. Bey, among others, trained a talented new generation of E-boat commanders, including the future flag officer for E-boats, Rudolf Petersen, and many other talented personalities: Heinz Birnbacher, Kurt Fimmen, Kurt Johannsen, Friedrich Kemnade, Bernd Klug, Werner Lützow, Karl Matzen, Götz von Mirbach, Karl Müller, Hermann Opdenhoff, Kurt Sturm, and Felix Zymalkowski, to name only a few. It was characteristic of the respect the German Navy accorded to its coastal forces that one of Grossadmiral Karl Dönitz's two sons, Klaus, elected to serve aboard E-boats. Frequent exercises after 1935 with E-boats in groups up to flotilla strength confirmed the findings of the first tentative maneuvers of the mid-1920s and produced a more mature doctrine for Germany's coastal forces before the outbreak of hostilities. No other navy could make that claim.[18]

The physical and mental requirements for successful E-boat commanders were commensurate with the first-class coastal vessels the German Navy had in mind. The commanders had to be young, in their early twenties. They had to be intelligent, with quick reactions and capable of making snap decisions in tense combat situations at night. Keen night vision, a rugged physique, and an unflappable nature were essential. They had to be attractive personalities and strong leaders who inspired their crews to do their best in spite of the harsh conditions on heavy seas in a small-boat. In this respect they shared many of the same traits as successful U-boat commanders or the Luftwaffe's outstanding squadron leaders. The best crews grew into tight-knit families under their youthful commanders, and they developed intense ties of loyalty to each other and to the Schnellbootwaffe as a whole. Not surprisingly, these qualities, as well as the excellence of their boats, made this coastal force one of Germany's most efficient fighting organizations in World War II.[19]

The Making of a Wonder Boat

Although a number of features about German E-boats set them apart from the torpedo boats of all other navies, one of the builders' most fundamental design decisions centered on the E-boat's hull. In order for a short naval vessel of less than one hundred feet to reach forty knots or more, it must eliminate drag by skimming over the water. This solution is simple and elegant. Most of the hull must rise up out of the water to escape the two main sources of resistance: friction from the thick fluid that is water and resistance from the pressure wave created by the boat's own motion as it parts the water. Tremendous power and light construction are imperative to make the boat get up and run, but power and lightness alone are not enough. A special hull is also required.[20]

The most obvious design for this purpose is a hard-chine hull with a V-shape in the bow, spreading out into a flat bottom at the stern. It is the classic hydroplaning hull type associated with most powerboats, including American PT boats and British MTBs. The hard-chine hull starts with a wide V-shape at the bow to part the water and to avoid the most severe effects of slamming into waves. As the hull flares out from the centerline, it suddenly makes a hard bend upward—hence the term "hard chine"—to form the sides of the boat. With enough power, the boat raises its bow, letting the flat-bottomed stern carry most of the weight, and at an inclined angle it rises because of hydrodynamic lift and skims over the water. The hard-chine design separates the wave created by the boat's motion from the sides of the vessel. This minimizes the so-called wetted surface of the boat, namely that portion of the hull over which the water flows. Water flowing up the sides of the hull or over onto the deck creates just as much resistance as water flowing under the hull. By forcing the water to part company with the hull at the sharp bend, the hard chine significantly reduces water friction. It has the added advantage of flinging the spray out and away from the hull, improving visibility for the crew. The hard chine also gives this type of vessel a very large "bone in its teeth," or bow wave, when it reaches planing speed. Using flatter surfaces, it is also less expensive to construct. Hard-chine hulls are especially attractive for sustained speeds above forty knots.[21]

Such a design, however, has drawbacks. It works best in relatively calm waters. Heavy waves cause a hard-chine planing hull to smack against successive crests, degrading its ability to function as a war vessel, and eventually causing hull damage. Therefore, a hard-chine hull implies that such craft should operate in relatively calm weather or on somewhat more protected seas such as the Mediterranean. Britain's designers like John I. Thornycroft, Hubert Scott-Paine, and Peter du Cane were compelled by economics to design short sixty- and seventy-foot craft on the eve of World War II. Inevitably, they settled upon hard-chine hulls as the only solution for bulk production of short, high-speed combat craft, and their designs heavily influenced the U.S. Navy.[22]

The German Naval High Command and the design team at the Lürssen Yard in Vegesack looked at the problem differently. For them, coastal defense meant operating especially in the North Sea and the Channel area where the waters are considerably rougher than on the inland seas. Even the Baltic and Mediterranean are not immune to heavy conditions. Stormy east winds can also produce short steep chop that would make life unpleasant for the E-boat crews. The alternative to a hard-chine hull was a round-bilge, keeled hull such as larger displacement vessels use. This round-bottomed hull design provides greater stability in heavy seas. The problem with it is that it is not normally associated with planing vessels possessing a waterline length exceeding one hundred feet. Nevertheless, round-bilge hulls can, if carefully designed and given enough power, compete well with hard-chine designs in speeds up to approximately the forty-knot range.[23]

The German designers were looking at a coastal vessel that would be at the upper size range for a fast torpedo boat. A longer hull offers undoubted advantages if speed is desired. The longer the waterline length of the hull, the faster it can go through the water. This is expressed in nautical engineering terms as a speed/length ratio. Most normal displacement hulls have a speed/length ratio of about one. For example, a 400-foot merchant ship with a displacement hull can make up to twenty knots. Its speed/length ratio is exactly one because its speed of twenty knots is in relation to the square root of its 400-foot length, which is twenty. The power requirements for such a ship to reach that speed are not exorbitant. That, incidentally, is why most sailing records are still held by the slender, long-hulled clipper ships of the nineteenth century. In short, long ships achieve high speeds more easily than short ones. Higher performance from shorter vessels must see the speed/length ratio rise to 3:1, 4:1, or even more. Thus hull design becomes critical in order to produce such a favorable ratio. A 70-foot Elco boat would have to have a higher speed/length ratio than a 115-foot E-boat if both are traveling at forty knots.

The Germans lessened the problem somewhat by settling on a long hull that nearly doubled the length of its Allied competitors, but high performance from so large a vessel demanded other characteristics. Finding a way to make it light and strong offered a considerable challenge. By painstaking and lengthy experimentation, the Lürssen designers came up with their solution, a modified round-bilge hull that gave greater seaworthiness but also allowed a full planing capability.

Seen from the front, it looked like a round-bilge displacement hull, but from midships to the stern the round-bottom form gave way to a virtually flat bottom with just the keel and propeller shafts protruding slightly below the rest of the flat surfaces under the transom. As planing began and the boat settled aft, the flat-bottomed stern supported the boat better, and it sank less deeply into the trough produced by the boat's motion. A vessel that wallowed by the stern was said to "squat," increasing its wetted surface and therefore the amount of drag. The older "toothpick" hulls, although fast, had squatted badly because of their narrow sterns. A new hull design was imperative for high-speed combat vessels.

Another refinement was the addition of a narrow knuckle or spray guard midway up the round-bilge hull in order to separate the bow wake from the hull, an effect achieved naturally by the hard-chine design. This knuckle, or rub rail, reduced the boat's wetted surface and lowered water friction. Like the hard-chine hull, it also allowed the crew greater visibility by reducing spray at high speeds.

At low speeds the round-bilge design with a genuine keel protruding deepest amidships acted like a displacement hull and could take a relatively heavy sea because its rounded form cushioned the craft from slamming against waves, and the keel improved directional stability. When power was applied to its three screws, the forward end of the hull rose as the vessel began to plane. It was at this stage that the designers added another remarkable feature to this unusual vessel.

When speed increased to about twenty-five knots, a crew member cranked the E-boat's two side, or outer, rudders mounted on either side of the main rudder so that they flared symmetrically outward at about thirty degrees. Although this produced considerable resistance at first, an unexpected phenomenon took place above twenty-five knots, when the water rushing past the flared rudders suddenly separated to create a *Druck-Kissen,* or air-filled hollow space, under the stern. What happened next was called the "Lürssen Effect," after designer-engineer Otto Lürssen. For that reason the rudders were also called "effect" rudders.

The cavity produced three highly desirable effects. First, it altered the pattern of water flow around the screws. Inevitably, some of the propeller thrust would be dissipated to the side. Once formed, the low-pressure cavity proceeded to draw most of that deflected thrust toward the center and stern, and the propellers cut more efficiently into the slightly dammed body of water directly in front of the hollow. Because the propellers were now biting more efficiently, they increased velocity anywhere from one to three knots despite the drag penalty induced by the flared side rudders. Even that could be diminished. Once the cavity had formed, the helmsman cranked the side rudders back toward the centerline from thirty degrees to only about seventeen degrees without losing the Lürssen Effect. Because three screws propelled the E-boat, and two of the three inevitably had to turn in the same direction, the thrust was asymmetrical. Therefore, one of the rudders had to have a slightly larger angle of incidence, up to twenty degrees, to compensate. Given minute variations in hull, rudders, and screws, each boat had to be trimmed separately based upon experimentation.

Almost as desirable as increased speed was the effect the cavity had on the vessel's wake. High-speed boats typically produce a "rooster tail" behind them, a dramatic effect that is visually impressive in peacetime racing. It is anything but desirable in a war vessel since the enemy can spot a raised wake from miles away—even at night. Unmodified, the E-boat produced a rooster tail nearly ninety feet in length until the Lürssen Effect kicked in. Then suddenly the archlike wake disappeared and the stern wave was considerably diminished. The energy wasted in raising the rooster tail was now directed more horizontally and added to the boat's efficiency. Wake reduction contributed to the boat's increased speed, besides helping create a much stealthier vessel.

Finally, the cavity raised the stern by two and a half feet and settled the bow. At planing speed the boat was nearly horizontal. Resistance at the waterline was reduced further because the pressure wave created by the boat's motion was flowing nearly off the bottom lip of the stern when the E-boat was in its planing mode. Trimming wedges added to the bottom of the stern enhanced this effect and directed the water flow downward. This, too, reduced drag, and the result was to fool the water's "resistance genies" into thinking that the vessel was twice as long as it actually was since the pressure wave parted company with the transom at the bottom of its sine curve.

As a result of these design features, remarkably little of the E-boat's hull remained in the water at high speeds, an advantage in the frequently mined waters between Britain and the Continent and a remarkable feat for a 115-foot vessel weighing more than a hundred tons.

The E-boat had the best of two worlds. It could, within limits, handle like a displacement ship when seas were rough and could run almost silently at six knots. Its light gray camouflage paint and low silhouette made the E-boat difficult for even the sharpest eyes to detect at night. In calmer sea conditions its planing hull could fly with the best of the enemy torpedo boats when speed was the key to survival. In fact, there were certain sea conditions in which the British Admiralty admitted (privately to be sure) that the E-boat could travel fully sixteen knots faster than its British or, by implication, American rivals.[24] This was especially true in a medium sea when hard-chine hulls could not ride waves, slamming from crest to crest instead. Such conditions were a frequent fact of life in the seas around Europe. The inherent advantages of a round-bilge hull in the waters of the North Sea and the Channel translated into a significant tactical advantage for E-boats over MTBs in the main theater of engagement. Thus, the thorough design work of many years at Lürssen Yard paid off. After meticulous and intensive experimentation, the Germans achieved a final, mature hull design by 1939. Despite further testing, they could scarcely improve upon it thereafter. Henceforward increased speed came only from more power applied to the same hull.

The heart of this nautical greyhound lay in its mighty diesel engines. Remembering their bitter experience with gasoline engines in World War I and after, the naval leadership settled on diesels from the start. Despite teething problems and the outright failure of two M.A.N. (Maschinen-Fabrik Augsburg Nürnberg) designs—a seven-cylinder engine and its successor, an eleven-cylinder one—the navy settled by about 1935 on two Daimler Benz diesels. The first, a sixteen-cylinder engine known as the MB 502, produced 1,320 hp. It was compact, light, and trouble free, a considerable accomplishment considering that no other nation overcame the obstacles of producing a lightweight high-powered diesel. The real breakthrough, however, was the twenty-cylinder Daimler Benz MB 501 diesel that was almost as light as the MB 502. It was strong, relatively vibration-free, and reliable. Rated at 1,500 hp at first, its Daimler design team upgraded the MB 501 to 2,000 hp on the eve of World War II, so that the standard three-engine E-boat had an impressive 6,000 horsepower. The E-boats were fitted with three screws, one to each diesel in order to avoid cavitation, a phenomenon where excess power made the high-speed screw part company with the water it was supposed to bite through, turning it into a kind of froth that greatly robbed efficiency. The designers considered adding a fourth diesel but decided that it would add more weight without significantly increasing horsepower. They abandoned the idea in favor of upgrading performance on the existing three diesels.[25]

Compact and lightweight though the three diesels were, they occupied considerable space within the streamlined hull, and the engine crew who serviced them had to work in cramped, uncomfortable conditions. Funker (Radioman) Ernst Benda felt lucky to be working topside on the armored bridge. "Those crew members who served below decks tending the diesels were trapped men," he observed. Prevailing opinion among the crew, Benda added, was that if an E-boat sustained combat damage and began sinking, the "black gang" would never get out in time. Conditions were, however, crowded for everyone. By 1944 each crew included three radiomen: one, preferably a bright, young, high school graduate like Benda, manning the Enigma machine; another for boat-to-boat communications; and the third working the FuMB, or passive radar equipment. Crew's quarters for two of those radiomen consisted of having them take turns sleeping on the boat's collapsible navigation table—when it was not in use.[26]

By 1943 increased armor and firepower demands made the S-100 series heavier. The Daimler-Benz engineers kept pace with increased power requirements by adding 25 percent supercharging to the new MB 511, bringing horsepower output up to 2,500 per unit or 7,500 hp overall. They retrofitted MB 511s to S-130 in October 1943, and she performed so beautifully in sea trials that all E-boats received them thereafter. A crude index of the raw power available to the E-boats is evident when one considers that the triple expansion engine installed in a 6,000-ton, 400-foot long Liberty Ship also produced 2,500 hp, and it could make 11 knots. In its last wartime variant, the more fully supercharged E-boat MB 518 diesel delivered an astonishing 3,000 horsepower, totaling 9,000 hp per boat, although it also displayed many teething problems that were still unresolved at war's end. For a 115-foot vessel weighing only 113 tons combat loaded, that horsepower translated into a heavily armed and judiciously armored vessel that could hurl itself over the water at 43.5 knots or more. Starting with a power plant that produced roughly 1,000 horsepower and modifying it to produce 3,000 horsepower was an impressive accomplishment akin to Britain's Rolls Royce teams that produced the better-known

Merlin aeroengine. Even by today's standards a coastal craft with gas turbines and computer designed hulls can perform only marginally better—assuming that the touchy gas turbines do not break down. The E-boat's dependable diesels were the envy of Britain's Coastal Forces, and it is no exaggeration to say that most MTB commanders would gladly have traded their boats for a late-war *Schnellboot.*

The diesels not only provided a great reserve of power but were also more fuel efficient, allowing the E-boat a range of 700 to 750 nautical miles. The later variants could cruise economically at thirty-four or thirty-five knots and could attain a fast extended cruise of thirty-eight knots. Because of the lower volatility of diesel fuel, fires and explosions from combat damage were much less likely to occur than in gasoline-powered craft with large tanks of hundred-octane aviation fuel aboard. Their one drawback was that they were loud, despite the installation of complex muffling and underwater exhaust systems. Consequently, a small 100-hp auxiliary engine was installed, which allowed nearly silent running up to six knots as this hunter approached its prey. When the diesels were engaged, noise ended any game of stealth. However, at a flank speed of forty-two knots the German E-boat of 1944 had no fear that anything on the water would overtake it. It was truly a greyhound of the Narrow Sea.

One of the primary secrets in the success of the E-boat design was its lightweight construction, a must in planing vessels. At 115 feet it was on the large side for a wooden warship of World War II. It made judicious use of light metal construction to reinforce the keel and the mahogany frames. This light metal was Al-Cu-Mg, an aluminum-copper-magnesium alloy remarkably strong for its day. The designers fitted steel foundation plates under the diesels to mate them to the multilayered oaken keel, which absorbed the vibrations of the three powerful engines. However, the bulk of the double hull was made from cleverly selected woods. On the inside of the mahogany ribs, or frames, that sprouted from the keel to give the hull its shape, the builders created a 23-mm thick inner hull (called a ceiling) of Oregon pine, Germany's best domestically produced white pine. Light and strong, this longitudinal pine planking, which might have dented or splintered if exposed to the outer surface, formed a relatively watertight inner hull of great strength and integrity.[27]

On the outside of the alloy-reinforced ribs, the builders overlaid an outer hull composed of two layers. This double-hull construction effectively transformed the ribs into I-beams, with the inner pine ceiling, or planking, and the double layer of outer planking forming the flanges of the I-beam and the reinforced ribs forming the web. This added tremendous strength to the entire vessel. The inner layer of this outer skin was composed of a thin 12-mm planking of white cedar. This choice wood of great tensile strength is extremely light, weighing only twenty-three pounds per cubic foot. But it is soft and dents easily. Over it the builders laid a sheet of treated muslin and then placed a 21-mm outer layer of mahogany. Mahogany is much heavier, weighing thirty-two pounds per cubic foot. It also has a hard, dense surface that is resistant to the pounding and scraping such boats must constantly endure on the water.

Months of prolonged weathering in unforgiving seas under combat conditions demonstrated that the light-construction hulls needed strengthening at certain points. Therefore, the builders added heavier-duty longitudinals forward to cope with stress, plus oaken planking around the engine area. They also added light alloy transverse bracing at strategic spots to stiffen the hull and prevent buckling in heavy seas. E-boats also had stout watertight bulkheads made of sheet steel below the waterline and Al-Cu-Mg alloy above it.[28]

The builders took pains to design the superstructure as lightly as combat conditions would allow. Crew quarters, decking, and superstructure were often made of light metal construction and generous use of plywood. However, combat experience in which returning crews constantly upgraded the builders' knowledge prompted the Germans to add armor in certain crucial places. Most remarkably for its time, the 1944 E-boat carried a rounded armored wheelhouse called a *Kalottenbrücke,* or skullcap bridge. It was streamlined and posed a very low silhouette while giving welcome protection to its commander and bridge personnel. Gun crews also enjoyed the shelter of armored shields at their battle stations. Many a crew returned unharmed from combat thanks to those strategically placed pieces of armored housing.

By contrast, crews on Britain's unarmored MTBs were virtually unprotected, and they paid the price. In August 1943 Coastal Forces' most brilliant young commander and innovator, Robert "Hich" Hichens, died instantly on the bridge of his MTB in the last seconds of a long-range duel when a German E-boat gunner found the range.[29]

The E-boat's many advanced features served to enhance its main function: to fire torpedoes. Its most effective role was to close with an enemy vessel and fire a direct shot with one or two of its G-7a torpedoes. These twenty-one-inch "eels," as they were called in German naval slang, were of the same size and power as those used by U-boats. Typically the E-boats carried two torpedoes in the tubes and could carry two more amidships for reloading. Reloading took approximately forty-five seconds. The E-boat was a combat vessel to reckon with in the confined coastal waters around Europe. Without the reserve torpedoes it could carry six half-ton sea mines, a lethal cargo that caused nearly as many losses to Allied shipping as did the torpedoes. The E-boat, however, could not launch its torpedoes while skimming along at forty-two knots. The kick of the surging, 3,300-pound torpedoes was not so destabilizing in itself. But the torpedo, which could make only forty-four knots on its own, might destabilize after hitting the water at such high speed and strike the E-boat instead of the intended target. Losses from their own torpedoes were not unknown. Therefore, standard practice was to reduce speed to ten knots at the moment of launch when the E-boat's hull was back in its displacement mode. Ten knots was the E-boat's *Schleichfahrt,* or stealth speed, and successful commanders like Günther Rabe quickly learned that a stealthy torpedo firing improved the odds: an unsuspecting target was better than an alerted one.[30]

Wartime experience brought added refinements. The earlier boats had been flush-deckers with rounded torpedo tubes facing over slightly indented channels cut into either side of the bow. Extended voyages showed that in heavy seas this arrangement shipped a great deal of water over the bow. Starting with S-26, the designers installed a larger, built-up forecastle that enclosed the tubes. The design change exaggerated the hull's torpedo track channels in the bow, giving the craft a highly distinctive look. Combat also showed that E-boats needed more firepower forward when Allied aircraft began making head-on attacks. Realizing that the enlarged bow could accommodate a larger weapon, the designers nestled a gun mount with a retractable 20-mm Oerlikon cannon between the torpedo tubes, making the E-boat a worthier opponent against frontal assault. To be sure, the gun mount was not ideal. It took time to raise or lower it. When lowered, the Oerlikon could aim high, but then the gunner could not depress it sufficiently to fire low or horizontally. Still, it added measurably to an E-boat's protective firepower from the bow position.[31]

One unintended result of the redesigned forecastle was that it altered the boat's profile from above. Instead of describing a graceful curve at the bow, the E-boat's tube channels suddenly scooped away the normal bow curve, interrupting it to form an almost straight line upon the boat's profile until the hollow space of the channel curved back up to meet the forecastle again. At that point the E-boat's profile resumed its normal hull curve. Seen from an aircraft, the S-26–style E-boat bow made it unique among all ships. Later, with the addition of the skullcap bridge, the E-boat presented a crescent-shaped lightened area to aerial observers as well.

They were quick to spot odd features such as halo effects from enemy targets. It remained to be seen how desirable such features were in a combat vessel whose builders prized low visibility.[32]

Although a stealthy craft designed to operate almost exclusively at night in search of enemy merchant shipping, the E-boat was, as the redesigned forward gun mount suggested, upgraded periodically with ever more powerful antiaircraft weaponry as Allied air and sea countermeasures increased. An E-boat's defensive armament varied, but by 1944 a typical boat was mounting one 40-mm (2-pounder) Bofors gun or a quick-firing 37-mm antiaircraft cannon on the stern. A twin 20-mm Oerlikon mount was installed amidships—a few E-boats even had a *Vierling*, or quadruple Oerlikon mount—and the single Oerlikon was on the bow, plus lighter, removable machine guns on the bridge. The E-boat packed a powerful defensive armament, and it seldom worked alone. Operating in flotillas of eight to ten boats, the E-boats posed a formidable threat to any Allied coastal vessels or aircraft that tried to take them on. Typically, they moved in line-astern formation to and from the battle area. Then, upon approaching known Allied convoy routes, they broke up into units of two boats each, line abreast and spaced about seventy-five feet from each other for the attack formation. Sometimes, depending on the number of boats available, they moved in a double column formation to the combat zone. In any case, knowing that firepower for each craft was limited, they tried always to avoid situations where just one E-boat faced the enemy in isolation.[33]

The alloy and wood construction with judiciously placed heavy metal reinforcing made the E-boat a remarkably light but rugged craft weighing 92.5 tons empty, although it certainly did not venture into contested waters at 92.5 tons. Fitted with four large torpedoes or two in combination with six sea mines, mounting heavy and light cannon with hundreds of medium-size shells and as many as six thousand 20-mm rounds, carrying a full load of diesel fuel, lubricants, drinking water, stores and provisions, personal equipment, electronic accessories, and a crew of twenty-six to thirty officers and men, a fully combat-loaded E-boat of 1944 weighed 113 tons. Even so, it was a planing vessel, and at 42.5 knots it was, by 1944, one of the world's fastest and one of the deadliest torpedo boats ever built. It was strong where it had to be, hardened where it had to be, and definitely as light as it had to be. Two crucial questions that could be answered only with the passage of time were whether the German war economy could produce sufficient numbers of this expensive vessel and whether German scientific and technological advances could keep pace with the Allies.

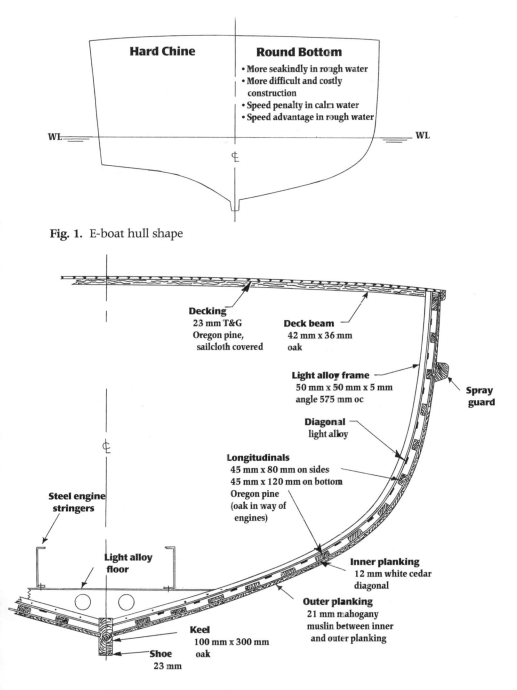

Fig. 1. E-boat hull shape

Within Fig. 1:

Hard Chine

Round Bottom
- More seakindly in rough water
- More difficult and costly construction
- Speed penalty in calm water
- Speed advantage in rough water

WL   WL

Within Fig. 2 labels:

Decking
23 mm T&G
Oregon pine,
sailcloth covered

Deck beam
42 mm x 36 mm
oak

Light alloy frame
50 mm x 50 mm x 5 mm
angle 575 mm oc

Spray guard

Diagonal
light alloy

Longitudinals
45 mm x 80 mm on sides
45 mm x 120 mm on bottom
Oregon pine
(oak in way of
engines)

Steel engine stringers

Light alloy floor

Inner planking
12 mm white cedar
diagonal

Outer planking
21 mm mahogany
muslin between inner
and outer planking

Keel
100 mm x 300 mm
oak

Shoe
23 mm

Fig. 2. Midships section, 1943 E-boat construction

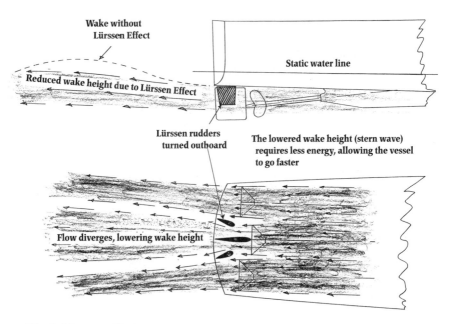

Wake without Lürssen Effect

Static water line

Reduced wake height due to Lürssen Effect

Lürssen rudders turned outboard

The lowered wake height (stern wave) requires less energy, allowing the vessel to go faster

Flow diverges, lowering wake height

Fig. 3. Lürssen effect

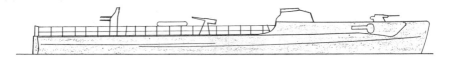

Fig. 4. 1944 E-boat silhouette

Chapter **3**

Wartime Operations to June 1944

Although it had been under development for a decade by 1939, and many design and technological advances had matured the E-boat, it was, nevertheless, a new class of vessel, and there was some confusion within the German naval leadership about how best to use it. They started the war with eighteen boats in two flotillas. The 1st Flotilla under Kapitänleutnant Kurt Sturm operated in the Baltic but played no appreciable role in the campaign in Poland, that unfortunate nation's tiny naval forces being disabled on the first day. The 2d Flotilla under Kapitänleutnant Rudolf Petersen moved from Wilhelmshaven to the strategically important island of Heligoland, essentially for picket duty against possible British or French attack. Harsh storms harassed all German naval units that autumn. Petersen's flotilla was fitted out with older E-boats powered by the M.A.N. diesels, whose poor performance justified earlier fears that those units were too long, top-heavy, and vibration-prone for service with a lightly built vessel. As a result, several of Petersen's E-boats experienced hull fractures in heavy seas. By contrast the Daimler engines in Sturm's 1st Flotilla performed beautifully, ample testimony to the accomplishments of the design team at Untertürkheim.

In April 1940 the E-boat Force joined in the Norwegian campaign, but their duties consisted primarily of placing small contingents of mountain troops in isolated areas, patrolling, and rounding up light surface units of the Norwegian Navy. While accomplishing those tasks successfully, the E-boat Force complained that their own naval leadership was using them in a role for which they were not intended. Their high-performance engines needed heavy maintenance after a few hundred hours of running time, and the boats experienced frequent propeller damage along the treacherous Scandinavian coast. Other, more durable naval craft with different performance characteristics could have performed such duties, leaving the E-boats free to make contributions more suited to their potential.

A hint of their deadliness came on 9 May 1940 when a British force of one cruiser and seven destroyers entered the Skaggerak to investigate sightings of minelayers and the whereabouts of the damaged torpedo vessel *Möwe*. With E-boats located in Stavanger and Wilhelmshaven as they moved south from the successful Norwegian campaign, the German naval leadership discovered that their untested coastal craft were in the best position to intercept the British forces. Led by Petersen, a group of four boats engaged for the first time in a night action against larger enemy warships. Constant training and night exercises during the 1930s paid off. Petersen led his boats in groups of two, and although it was a confused night action, S-31's commander, Werner Lützow, launched a standard two-torpedo spread, one of which struck destroyer HMS *Kelly*, skippered by Lord Louis Mountbatten, amidships. While maneuvering to avoid torpedoes from one two-boat element, the *Kelly* had run straight into those launched by a second two-boat element. The German E-boat commanders were gratified. Practice exercises designed to catch targets in a cross fire had paid off. Also typical was the fact that one E-boat, S-33, accidentally rammed a destroyer in the high-speed nocturnal maneuvering and was seriously damaged. Collisions became a common occurrence in those confused night actions. Somehow the *Kelly* limped under tow back to port, an epic ninety-one-hour struggle, and the Germans could be excused for assuming they had sunk her. S-33 was laid up for repairs for four months. The E-boat Force had shown that it could inflict damage to much heavier forces in night actions. Whether it was the best application for Germany's light coastal forces was another matter. Prewar studies indicated that their prey of choice were merchant ships, especially those plying coastal waters.[1]

The pace of operations in the West quickened as the Germans' western offensive rolled on. With the E-boats operating out of Germany's North Sea base at Borkum, and later, with the fall of the Netherlands, out of Den

Helder, they played a useful if atypical role in the war's next dramatic episode—the Allied evacuation of Dunkirk—by devoting much of their attention to war vessels. During those crucial days of intense naval action, several British and French destroyers, as well as a dozen merchant vessels, fell victim to the fast little boats. All too often, the sinkings were accompanied by heavy loss of life as the sealift carried thousands upon thousands of soldiers off the Continent. French Ships (FS) *Jaguar, Siroco,* and *Cyclone,* fell victim to E-boat attacks as did HMS *Wakeful* and *Abukir.* Those actions of late May and early June 1940 established the North Sea and Channel areas as the main arena of conflict involving the Schnellbootwaffe. It became the prime testing ground for coastal forces in World War II, and that contest would continue for virtually the rest of the war.[2]

With the fall of France, the German Navy was quick to make use of the newly available Dutch, Belgian, and French Atlantic ports, which, along with the captured airfields, allowed the German armed forces to project unprecedented strength into the Atlantic reaches. Their navy established bases to serve all surface units, specifically E-boats, at Rotterdam and at Ijmuiden, north of The Hague in the Netherlands. The E-boat Force established its operational headquarters at Scheveningen, a suburb of The Hague, with a back-up headquarters at Wimereux near Boulogne. As France and Belgium surrendered, the German Navy constructed other bases for their coastal forces at Ostend, Boulogne, Dieppe, Le Havre, Cherbourg, and St. Peter Port on the Island of Guernsey. In so doing, they ringed all of the British East and South Coasts from Lowestoft near The Wash in the Northeast down around Ramsgate and the Cliffs of Dover all the way past the Solent, Lyme Bay, and Devon to the tip of Cornwall in the Southwest. With their extended range, the E-boats could stage out of their harbors and attack British coastal shipping in the Narrow Sea and the busy channels of Britain's major estuaries. They were aided by the establishment of German coastal radar stations and radio listening posts that swept the Channel and the lower North Sea to detect convoy traffic. At this early stage of the war, cooperation between Luftwaffe and German naval forces, although hardly ideal, was good enough to provide useful aerial reconnaissance for potential targets for both services. The senior officer for both T-boats and E-boats, Kapitän zur See Hannes Bütow, established a good working relationship with his able Luftwaffe opposite, Gen. Hugo Sperrle, and his VIII Fliegerkorps, later Luftflotte 3.[3]

Apparently aware for the first time of the potency of their new coastal forces, the German Navy established three flotillas for operations in the Western Region. They commissioned no fewer than twenty-two new E-

boats in 1940, retiring some of the aging original eighteen to training duties. In the span of just nine months—from April to December 1940—the E-
boats had sunk three Allied destroyers and badly damaged three more.
They sank a three-thousand-ton British mine destructor vessel, four
armed trawlers, and at least twenty-four merchant ships, totaling nearly
fifty thousand tons. These figures do not include mining operations in
which the E-boat flotillas were constantly active. They laid at least 10 percent of German mines in the waters around Britain and probably accounted for losses at least as large as those for which their torpedoes were
credited. The next year the E-boats accounted for more than sixty thousand tons of shipping in the west, at a time when many of their efforts
were directed east toward the Soviet Union. Since the bulk of their victims
were British coasters of lower individual tonnage than the merchant ships
sunk by the ocean-going U-boats, the total tonnage accounted for by E-
boats' was all the more striking.[4]

The tactics they used so successfully in this early part of the war were
those that they had worked out before the war. The chief method, called
Lauertaktik, consisted of establishing the convoy routes and best-
estimated schedules for coastal shipping, then going out at night to loiter
in the predicted convoy lanes. If they had an estimate of a convoy's speed
and direction, they tried to arrive at a position twenty to thirty miles in
front of the convoy. Then they broke up into two hunting groups of two or
three boats each, separated by a nautical mile or two. They coordinated
maneuvers by VHF radio contact. The two groups were widely enough
separated to allow a good chance of detecting the convoy if they had not
predicted its course precisely. Yet they were close enough to be mutually
supporting. They also had a greater chance of inflicting hits on the enemy
if the two hunting groups caught a convoy in a torpedo cross fire.[5]

Their low silhouettes and neutral gray camouflage made them exceed-
ingly difficult targets on moonless or cloud-covered nights. Depending
upon results, they could reload once for a second strike or simply return to
base. Following the attack, they often made off at high speed to avoid interception by the Royal Navy's destroyer escorts or its Coastal Forces with
their high-speed gasoline-engined MTBs and MGBs. The E-boat Force saw
no profit in dueling with enemy warships. As one successful E-boat commander, Günther Rabe, put it, "If they came, we went. When they left we
came in."[6]

Choosing their engagements carefully paid dividends. E-boat losses
were astonishingly light through most phases of the war. From the outbreak of hostilities in 1939 until the end of 1943, the Schnellbootwaffe lost

only thirty-one boats from all causes; most losses were due to mines, nighttime collisions with each other, or groundings in treacherous coastal waters rather than from overt enemy action. In 1940 four boats succumbed. In 1941 the number was only three. In 1942 five more were lost. With more boats operating in intensified combat in all theaters in 1943, including the Black Sea, Mediterranean, Baltic, and the Atlantic from Norway to France's Bay of Biscay, twenty vessels were lost, although only twelve of that total were in the West. As more and more of the bigger, higher-powered, and better-gunned boats were commissioned from late 1943 onward, losses fell again up to mid-1944.[7]

On 16 April 1942 an important event took place. On that day the Schnellbootwaffe, which had been under the control of the flag officer for torpedo boats, *Führer der Torpedoboote* (FdT) Hannes Bütow, was elevated to an independent command. Thereafter the T-boats came under the control of the German Navy's destroyers. Korvettenkapitän Rudolf Petersen became the new leader of the E-boat Force, holding the title of *Führer der Schnellboote* (FdS) and the rank of *Kommodore* (flag officer; between full captain and rear admiral). Mostly, those under his command referred to him as FdS Petersen. He served in that post until the end of the war. On Petersen's shoulders fell the responsibility for planning the E-boat construction program, training, development of new weapons and tactics, as well as ongoing operations. It was a demanding position, and the reorganization was an unspoken recognition of one indisputable fact: by mid-1942 only the E-boats could maintain offensive operations on the surface of the Channel and, as the war lengthened, in the West generally. The destroyers and larger torpedo boats could continue to serve as defensive vessels in a limited role in the coastal areas, and minelayers even grew in importance. But experience had shown that the E-boats posed the main threat to Allied shipping in the coastal waters of the West. It remained to be seen if Petersen or anyone else could successfully oversee the continuing expansion and modernization of Germany's most potent naval asset after its feared U-boats.[8]

One reason why Schnellbootwaffe losses were few, especially in the first years of the war, was the absence of any British aerial counterforce aimed specifically against E-boats. That situation began to change with the establishment in early 1942 of night-fighter squadrons to attack E-boats. Results were scanty at first. Coastal Command and Fighter Command aircraft had launched 187 attacks on E-boats by that autumn but had not sunk any of them. The E-boats were extremely difficult targets, camouflaged and moving at high speed at night. In late summer 1942, the Admiralty transferred a squadron of radar-equipped Fairey Albacore aircraft to Coastal Command. They joined two squadrons of aged Fairey Swordfish in the hunt. Built as torpedo bombers, these venerable biplanes were more effective because they were stable platforms with good visibility and endurance, and they could carry a respectable bomb load and radar. More modern aircraft were too fast, and did not yet have the capability to deliver new weaponry such as rockets at night. Through the winter of 1942–43, the aerial hunt continued. Its main effect was to confine the E-boats to nocturnal operations and alert them to the fact that they were being hunted more vigorously by Allied forces.[9]

As Allied naval forces increased in size and strength with radar-equipped Hunt class destroyers prowling the Channel and coastal forces MTBs and MGBs sprouting heavier 40-mm pom-poms, the expectation was that E-boat losses would rise. That seemed to be the case in 1943 with the sinking of a dozen E-boats in the main theater in the West. However, the Germans mounted their own 40-mm Bofors and more 20-mm Oerlikons, and in compensation for the added weight, introduced the 2,500-hp supercharged MB 511 diesels. From 1 January 1944 until the invasion, the Allies sank only two E-boats from a total of 36 missions involving 315 individual sorties carried out in the Channel and North Sea area. That represented a loss rate of only 0.06 boats per sortie, an astonishingly low loss ratio for the E-boats and one that spelled trouble for the Allies. Most of the crews and E-boat commanders were gaining invaluable experience as the time of the invasion approached. Also disturbing to the British was the fact that despite constant combats, they had not been able to capture even one E-boat for evaluation.[10]

The German Navy had good reason to be satisfied with their primary coastal vessel. The E-boats proved to be excellent performers in a variety of wartime roles and in all theaters. Although all of them employed the same advanced Lürssen hull design, some thirty-odd boats in the production series were built to smaller specifications. They were about 10 feet shorter, with a slightly shallower draft, and were propelled by 16-cylinder 1,320-hp Daimler MB 502 diesels that were somewhat downsized versions of the big 20-cylinder MB 511s used on the 115-foot boats. Their performance was slightly lower too. They were capable of "only" 37 knots, although their cargoes of mines, torpedoes, and defensive armament were just as deadly as their bigger sisters serving in the west.

Following the invasion of the Soviet Union, when naval operations in the Baltic wound down, the Seekriegsleitung (Germany's Naval War Office) ordered the flotillas of smaller boats back to the home port at Wilhelmshaven for maintenance and refitting. They had an unusual mission in mind. Engineers fitted the ten E-boats of the 3d Flotilla under the command of Flotilla-Chief Friedrich Kemnade with dummy smokestacks amidships and a fake superstructure. Then the crews sailed for Rotterdam. Starting on 7 October 1941, they proceeded up the Rhine, skirting the Lorelei and entering Strasbourg two days later. To passersby in Occupied France they looked like and were meant to look like slow, innocent, steam launches. With their bows and sterns literally scraping the ends of each lock, these miniature "steamers" entered the Rhine-Rhône Canal, which had been built under Napoleon's direction 150 years earlier. Several weeks and 167 locks later they emerged in the Mediterranean near Marseilles. Rounding the French and Italian coasts, the 3d Flotilla emerged as a combat force in December 1941 and began to make life miserable for the Allies at Malta, in the North African littoral, the Aegean Sea, the Adriatic, and elsewhere. Even when the war soured and the Germans were pushed back to the North Mediterranean and lost passage around the southern tip of Italy, the 3d Flotilla, holed up in the Tyrrhenian Sea, went north to Genoa. There the E-boats were transported by truck over the Po River Valley autostrada to the Adriatic Sea, where they continued the struggle along the convoluted Yugoslav Coast up to the last days of the war.[11]

Meanwhile another convoy of the compact class of E-boats moved up the Elbe River past Hamburg to lovely Dresden. This was the 1st Flotilla, led by Heinz Birnbacher. With engines and superstructure removed, their lightened hulls were then transported on trucks along the autobahn to Ingolstadt astride the Danube River where they were refloated. After a lengthy towing to Linz, their handlers mated the boats with their heavy diesels and superstructures again. In the spring of 1942 after the ice had melted, they resumed their odd journey down the Danube to the Black Sea where they joined the German forces in the Crimea, arriving in time to help in the spring offensive. There they proceeded to make life as miserable on the Black Sea for the Soviets as they had for the Allies in the Mediterranean. The efficient E-boat Forces mounted successful operations in all theaters.[12]

Nevertheless, it was in the West that the Germans deployed in quantity their largest and deadliest boats, known as the S-38/100 class, capable of bringing their upgraded and heavier weapons to bear all over the Channel–North Sea area. Despite their increased weight, they continued to speed along at forty-two knots with seeming impunity as winter gave way to spring in 1944. Maddeningly for the Allies, the mystery of the E-boats persisted. No one had been able to capture a boat intact. What information the Allies had came from interrogations of surviving crew members from sinkings in the fall of 1943, a useful source but no substitute for the real thing, especially in the earlier stages of the war.[13]

Cherbourg had become the favorite base of operations for the E-boats in the lower Channel area, and two flotillas, the 5th, under Korvetten-kapitän Bernd Klug, and the 9th, under Korvettenkapitän Freiherr Götz von Mirbach, liked to operate there. It was a sizable harbor that allowed rapid exiting if operation orders so demanded. The Organisation Todt had built formidable curved E-boat pens in the central harbor district. Actually, they had taken over some dry docks there and covered them with high quality steel-reinforced concrete roofs at least eleven and a half feet thick.

Other ports like Boulogne were too close to British airpower, coastal defenses, and radar. Cherbourg had plentiful and excellent flak defenses, so that Allied air power seldom ventured directly over it, and any pilot seeking E-boats did so a safe distance from the port. It had not been attacked in any meaningful way by the Allied strategic air forces up to the time of the invasion. The Royal Navy in general and British Coastal Forces in particular also respected Cherbourg because of the large coastal guns that studded the shore along the Cotentin Peninsula. The big coastal guns near the Cap de la Hague to the west of Cherbourg and the equally formidable batteries at Cap Levy slightly east of the port demanded respect and kept Allied surface ships of all sizes away. A close Allied naval blockade of Cherbourg was simply impossible. Little wonder that it was the favorite port for the E-boats, and it was no accident that the flotilla-strength force that caused the Allies such grief in Lyme Bay had worked out of Cherbourg. By contrast, Le Havre was too far from British targets to be an ideal E-boat base, although it was a convenient port of call for the fast boats transitioning from the North to the South. One of the most baffling problems for the Allies was trying to locate the elusive E-boats as they proceeded up and down the Channel Coast, constantly relocating and keeping their enemies guessing.

E-boat crews operating out of Cherbourg had permanent quarters in two suburbs. After British bombing raids in 1942 and 1943 appeared to target German naval personnel during the height of the U-boat war, the crews had dispersed to surrounding villages, thwarting Allied efforts to inflict casualties. The 5th Flotilla found quarters at Urville, a suburb about six miles south of the port. The 9th Flotilla occupied a former museum, a chateau in Tour la Ville slightly east of the town. Although socializing was not forbidden, there was little mingling with the French population. Veterans like Günther Rabe and Hans Schirren recalled that officers and crews alike preferred to get what sleep they could in daytime when they were not maintaining their boats or on watch. They felt they needed to husband their strength for the harrowing operations at night. The port itself was strictly sealed off to the public. Only skilled French maintenance and repair personnel with special passes were permitted into the naval premises, and they were closely monitored. The only occasion when suspicion of espionage surfaced was when German naval authorities arrested a Dutch national serving as a steward in the crew quarters. Known to them simply as "Piet," he had joined the E-boat Force in Rotterdam and moved with the two flotillas to Cherbourg. Flotilla Commander Felix Zymalkowski remembered Piet as an affable steward, who was eager to serve and was constantly hovering over them at the officers' mess. Sometime in the summer of 1944, after intercepting strong signals, the German naval authorities alleged that he had attempted, from the roof of the former museum, radio communication to the British about E-boat operations. The German Navy could produce no proof in the matter, but Piet was, according to Operations Officer Bernd Rebensburg, "neutralized," although in this case the term meant imprisoned.[14]

Security was not a significant problem for the E-boat Force, at least as far as the French Resistance was concerned. The latter were more successful at sabotage, especially in the invasion phase, rather than supplying up-to-the-minute intelligence. By contrast many French support and repair personnel continued to work for the Germans until the Allied conquest, a fact their fellow countrymen did not quickly forget following liberation.

Despite their light losses up until June 1944, operations for the E-boat Force on the Channel were a harrowing experience for everyone, and it required strong nerves to move out of harbor night after night. By this time Allied superiority and naval strength in the Channel area prevented all but the fastest, stealthiest, and most maneuverable German forces from operating, and they did so only at night. While minesweepers, the R-boats, were an important feature, the bulk of offensive operations were now left to the more agile E-boats with their experienced night-fighting crews. The E-boats also served admirably as fast minelayers. Typically, the E-boats left harbor in the late evening when darkness descended. By June, at a latitude of approximately fifty degrees north, that meant departure at 2300 hours, at the earliest. Typically, boats had to reenter harbor by 0430 hours or face the certainty of aerial attack, by far their most deadly peril.

Allied use of 10-cm, later 3-cm, ASV (air to surface vessel) radar made air attacks even more dangerous by 1944. Nevertheless, E-boat crews found ways to cope. Their passive FuMB devices (installed on E-boats by the winter of 1943–44) could tell them that Allied radar had detected them. Deck crews listened intently for the sound of aircraft circling. Experience taught them that as long as the aircraft continued to circle, they were safe for the time being; a circling aircraft had determined no precise location. When the sound of the aircraft settled into one direction, the deck crews knew it had determined the location of the target and was making its run. At that moment the commander altered course to throw off the pilot's aim. Although by no means foolproof, the tactic was simple, and it usually worked. Of course, the crew had to hear the aircraft first, and that was not always possible in the midst of close combat.[15]

Günther Rabe was one of the talented young E-boat commanders who had the good fortune to train under the able Götz von Mirbach, who was commanding the 9th Flotilla at Cherbourg. An E-boat commander since April 1943, Rabe, known as "the Raven," was wise to the ways of the E-boats' main naval adversary in the West, the Royal Navy's Coastal Forces. He and his fellow commanders had learned to change tactics in a changing war. "If you want to survive, then do the unexpected," he observed. E-boat commanders recognized that Allied radar was increasingly robbing them of the element of surprise. Instead of employing the *Lauertaktik*, lurking near shipping lanes waiting for merchant vessels, they used a *Stichtaktik*. They put their boats in a kind of wedge formation and, after ascertaining a gap in enemy defenses, the unit leaders announced a *Stichzeit*. This was the moment of a "sting." They moved in at high speed in several formations depending upon the number of boats, and at a given time all boats loosed their two forward torpedoes at the enemy ships. The intent was to sting as fast as possible and minimize the amount of contact time with enemy pickets. They then retreated as a unit. This demanded close cooperation and extreme vigilance by all crews to avoid collisions.[16]

The new tactics also demanded much from the diesels. From the moment they cleared harbor until breaking contact with the enemy and returning to port, the boats traveled at the highest cruise speed, thirty-eight knots. Only in emergency combat situations did they go to flank speed of forty-two knots. The Daimler engineers estimated that the engines would sustain damage if run at full power for more than thirty minutes, and the crews confirmed this. Nevertheless, it had become apparent that their superior speed gave them their main advantage over their enemy and did much to redress the Allied advantage in radar.

Rabe and all his above-deck crew wore snug leather jackets and trousers over their standard issue naval uniforms. They were desperately needed. Since they were traveling at nearly fifty miles per hour, the crew was chilled by salt spray and cold air. Eyes became reddened from staring into forty-knot winds for hours on end. The leather garments had the potential to fulfill another more desperate function. Close fitting around ankles and wrists, they acted like a wetsuit if the wearer had the misfortune to land in the sea. At most times of the year the Narrow Sea would kill a stranded swimmer in twenty minutes or less. The outer leather layer gave a man two hours, enough time for a rescue—if the victim was lucky.

Danger was always nearby, and the crew all wore regulation army helmets, the familiar coal-scuttle design. They were not ideal, especially if the wearer was using headphones, but their flaring sides did protect the back of the head and neck. Everyone in the E-boat Force remembered one helmetless crew member who was hit by a shell splinter so tiny that it scarcely drew blood. He died instantly. They wore their helmets religiously on the dangerous waters of the Channel.

Rabe always carried large 8 x 60 Zeiss binoculars for night work and was constantly scanning the horizon for targets or danger. The bridge crew were similarly equipped. By the winter of 1943–44, the boats began to receive a new radar detection device, a *Funkmessbeobachtungsgerät,* or FuMB as it was commonly called. It had developed in several variations, and the most advanced one in use in 1944 in the West, where danger from Allied air and sea attack was greatest, was called Naxos. It was passive and indicated that the E-boat was being painted by Allied radar. Unfortunately for the operator, it did not indicate where, at what distance, or in what direction the enemy craft was going.

A few boats, Rabe's S-130 among them, carried what the Germans called Hohentwiel, a crude shortwave radar set that German scientists had designed after reconstructing an H2S set from a Lancaster bomber that had crashed near Rotterdam. However, Hohentwiel was hastily improvised and even lacked an oscilloscope. Therefore, it, too, was less effective in determining the actual location of enemy ships. Worse, experienced commanders like Rabe rightly concluded that when turned on, it gave away their location to Allied ships and aircraft. They were reluctant to use it at all. S-130 was a special boat in another respect. It was the first to receive the new supercharged MB 511 diesels rated at 2,500 hp. Test runs on the mouth of the Weser River were encouraging. Despite increased weight from their shielded 40-mm Bofors cannon in the stern, wrap-around armor of the new skullcap bridge, and similar protective shields for all other gun crews, S-130 could make over forty-two knots. Better still, the MB 511 never missed a beat. Rabe's S-130 suffered no engine failures while on operations. Quickly, the engineers and crews began retrofitting similar equipment to other first-line boats, and all new craft received similar equipment as the expansion of the E-boat Force went forward.[17]

As the E-boat Force upgraded its equipment in the autumn of 1943, it prepared for more intensive operations against British coastal shipping. On 24–25 October 1943, a moonless night and calm seas presented perfect conditions for the fast boats. Korvettenkapitän Werner Lützow aboard S-88 led his 4th Flotilla from Ijmuiden to join units from three other flotillas in a mass attack of twenty-eight E-boats, the largest concentration in the war, against a British convoy off Cromer. This time, however, the Royal Navy had anticipated them. Three radar-equipped destroyers attacked, damaging S-63, and drove them away from the convoy into an ambush by a number of Fairmile D-class MTBs. The flotilla commander refused to abandon his helpless neighbor, S-63, and in the ensuing melee both boats succumbed to the withering fire. Lützow, designated successor to FdS Petersen, died at the bridge along with the boat's commander, Obersteuermann (Chief Helmsman) Heinrich Räbiger, but nineteen crew members were saved. Intensive interrogations of the survivors yielded useful information about improved performance from the newer E-boats. Of equal importance, the survivors gave their captors a hint of future operations. One of their number, according to the interrogation report, remarked "that Dönitz, as Supreme Commander of the German Navy, had recently issued an order of the day through S.O. (E-boats) that, during the coming winter, E-boats would operate in the greatest possible strength against British coastal shipping. On account of this, prisoners expected frequent mass attacks on our convoys to develop during the next few weeks."[18] The new year, 1944, was likely to see more activity, not less, as both sides braced themselves for the long-expected Allied invasion of Europe.

The crews were well informed. Barely a week after the sinking of S-63 and S-88, a surprise attack by 5th Flotilla E-boats off Dungeness in the Eastern Channel sank three freighters, followed by two more Allied ships off Cromer two nights later. Growing Allied strength in destroyers, coastal forces, and attack aircraft, all of them aided by better radar, were making the Channel area increasingly dangerous for the Schnellbootwaffe.[19] However, improved technology was not, by itself, decisive, as the Royal Navy's long-suffering Coastal Forces well knew, and the E-boat Force was showing no signs of backing down. In the end it came down to an experienced commander with a keen pair of eyes, good night glasses, and a high-performance boat and crew aggressively seeking targets. Veteran E-boat commanders like Götz von Mirbach, Günther Rabe, and Hans Schirren, along with their experienced crews, posed a continuing threat to the Allies in the increasingly crowded waters of the Channel.

Allied interrogations of captured E-boat personnel demonstrated that the members of the Schnellbootwaffe considered themselves to be part of an elite force with high morale. Interrogating officers could observe this for themselves in the names that E-boat personalities chose to use. Commanders had special call signs by which they were known throughout the E-boat Force. Some selected animals as noms de guerre, perhaps because they were associated with their family names. For example, Günther Rabe became "the Raven" and carried a raven crest on his boat. Friedrich Wilhelm Baehr was known to his comrades as "the Bear." Others simply liked the animal. Hans Schirren chose Seelöwe, or Sea Lion. The E-boat Force also had an Owl, a Scorpion, and a Monkey. A second popular affectation was the use of schoolboy-sounding names with a curious English twist: "Charlie" was common as was "Bobby." The German-sounding Felix evolved into a jauntier-sounding "Fips." Many young officers had already acquired their nicknames as officer cadets in boot camp at Dänholm, at the *Marineschule* at Mürwik, or at the Kriegsmarine's other training schools. Fanciful or otherwise, the names were an unmistakable indication of something more serious. The E-boat commanders considered themselves to be and were in fact part of a select fighting force.[20]

They had another weapon ashore: Kommodore Rudolf Petersen and his FdS staff in Scheveningen. Kapitänleutnant Bernd Rebensburg was typical of a staff that had been directing the E-boat Force for four years. Serving as its 1A, or Operations Officer, he worked closely with the frontline crews. The commander of the 8th Flotilla, Kapitänleutnant Felix Zymalkowski, observed that whenever any of his boats returned from a mission during which they recorded contact with the enemy or any kind of unusual incident, Rebensburg invariably appeared in time to debrief the E-boat commanders. He was always seeking the most detailed and current information for use in future operations. All of the E-boat Force personnel were impressed by his conscientiousness and attention to detail.[21] He also worked in close cooperation with the German decryption service, the B-Dienst, which had listening posts at Dunkirk and Jersey. By the spring of 1944 they had begun to make shrewd estimates of Allied shipping in Britain's coastal waters. Dubbed "Clever Bernd" by his friends, the half-blind Rebensburg had not actually broken the Allied naval codes, but lately he had begun to identify the prefixes used to identify major British naval headquarters such as C-in-C (Commander in Chief) Nore, C-in-C

Portsmouth, C-in-C Plymouth, and so on. Judging the volume and direction of signals traffic, the wily Petersen, backed up by experienced officers like his deputy chief of staff Korvettenkapitän Heinrich Erdmann, his operations officer Rebensburg, and proven flotilla commanders was able to vector the E-boat Force into promising areas where shipping had built up. This is what had sent two flotillas into Lyme Bay on the night of 27–28 April 1944. That plus the coordinated actions of senior commanders like von Mirbach, Klug, Zymalkowski, and Opdenhoff aboard their Lürssen-built E-boats had done the rest.

By June 1944 all the world knew an invasion was coming in the West. FdS Petersen had already ordered more E-boats into the Western Region, so that by 5 June no fewer than thirty-four E-boats had concentrated in the possible invasion area with more reinforcements to come. And unlike the bulk of the German armed forces being husbanded north in the Pas de Calais district, the E-boat Force was concentrating in Cherbourg and, for the first time, making brief stays in Le Havre. Their base at Boulogne also witnessed concentrations above normal levels. By making these unusual dispositions, the E-boat Force had bracketed the Normandy invasion area. Sooner or later the Allied invasion fleet would be coming to them, and there would be no lack of targets. Operation Neptune was about to begin, and the success of that operation turned on how fast the Allies could land their troops and build them up in the face of growing German concentrations. Crucial to that buildup were specialized ships, especially the LST, but also the smaller 1,500-ton LCT and its variations, and not least, sea-going tugs and ferries to wrestle larger conventional ships around the confined anchorages and to aid ship-to-shore unloading. Unless the Allies could control the E-boat threat, the landing ships, most notably the LSTs recently savaged at Lyme Bay, would be sailing into deadly peril.

The Allies hoped that the attacking E-boats on that memorable night at Lyme Bay had not been able to determine the full extent of the damage they had wrought. The following day German radio broadcasts made vague boasts about several sinkings. However, an extremely secret Allied organization knew better. Within the Admiralty's Naval Intelligence Division was its Operational Intelligence Centre (OIC), unknown to either the Germans or the general Allied public. It was responsible for evaluating German naval threats and establishing possible counteractions. The OIC was the recipient of Ultra decryptions, photoreconnaissance materials, and many other forms of special intelligence. After learning of the vague German claims over the air waves, the OIC could only scoff at this feigned German ignorance. As a later OIC report commented: "An interesting sidelight on German mentality was afforded by the subsequent German broadcast that three ships in convoy totalling 19,000 G.R.T. [tons] had been sunk. If this was to show ignorance of the real target, the ruse was decisively exposed by evidence from Special Intelligence."[22] The Allies knew from intercepts of E-boat Force signals that FdS Petersen and his staff were aware that they had sunk landing vessels. The question was, how much more did the Germans know? The Allies' remaining hope was that the departing E-boat crews had not understood the true magnitude of the sinkings, specifically the heavy casualties inflicted on the landing forces. They were to be disappointed on that account. Even as Allied intelligence personnel speculated about the extent of German knowledge, the FdS staff across the water at Scheveningen were busily calculating the results of the Lyme Bay engagement.

Following the return of the 5th and 9th Flotillas to Cherbourg on 28 April and armed with detailed debriefings of their crews, Deputy FdS Erdmann examined their own E-boat signals and digested the contents of decryptions of Allied messages by the B-Dienst. Using all the sources available to him, Erdmann offered his fellow staff officers a noteworthy appreciation of the action against Convoy T-4. "Our boats took advantage of their poor defenses and achieved good success. The landing group was scattered, and it drifted rather helplessly through the area," Erdmann noted. He drew a significant conclusion from that action for the E-boat Force: "We see now how rigid, clumsy, and inexperienced formations of this type are." Erdmann also appreciated the fact that the doomed LSTs had been heavily manned. Although the Germans were not reading Allied wireless traffic completely, there were strong indications from the B-Dienst intercepts that the attack had cost the lives of hundreds of Allied personnel.[23] The battle of wits continued.

Detailed new information about improved E-boat performance became available to Allied authorities in the spring of 1944, adding to the Admiralty's sense of anxiety as the invasion approached. The Royal Navy had been unsuccessful in its attempts to capture an E-boat intact, but prisoner of war interrogations were the next best thing. The problem in this respect was that the Allies had captured their most recent batch of German survivors in late October 1943, following the sinking of S-88 with Korvettenkapitän Werner Lützow aboard. Not only was the intelligence from those interrogations stale by May 1944, but the prisoners had not supplied particularly abundant information. Then the Allies had a stroke of luck. Two rare sinkings of E-boats took place on 26 April and 13 May when a radar-equipped Free French destroyer, FS *La Combattante,* engaged E-boat flotillas in the Channel from long range with its 4-inch gun. Through a combination of skill and good fortune she landed direct hits on both vessels causing the crews to scuttle them before being picked up.

S-147, under its acting commander Oberbootsmansmaat (Chief Petty Officer) Bernhard Theenhausen, was the middle boat in a three-boat element of the 9th E-boat Flotilla led by Korvettenkapitän Götz von Mirbach. They encountered HMS *Rowley* and FS *La Combattante* off Nab Tower in the early hours of 26 April. Star shells from the *Rowley* aided the French destroyer in landing a direct hit. However, it was not just excellent marksmanship that had doomed S-147. The third boat in line, S-167, had dropped astern shortly after the group detected the presence of Allied destroyers when firing began, and Theenhausen, suspecting damage or engine trouble aboard his neighboring boat had radioed the first boat in line, S-146 with 9th Flotilla Commander von Mirbach aboard, to reduce speed. Perhaps because he recalled Werner Lützow's violent demise in a similar situation the previous October, von Mirbach increased to emergency speed of forty-two knots instead and made smoke, leaving S-147 and S-167 behind. Tactically, his action was prudent since speed and maneuver were an E-boat's best defense in the presence of Allied warships. Although the destroyers had lost sight of the E-boats briefly, they reestablished contact, and it was then that S-147 suffered a direct hit. With his boat down at the bow, Theenhausen tried firing his forward torpedoes to lighten the boat, but one of them jammed. In the meantime von Mirbach reappeared. The Naval Intelligence Division interrogation report explained what happened next: "In an attempt to come alongside to find out whether 'S-147' was still seaworthy, Mirbach rammed her. The S.O. [Senior Officer] then ordered her to try to make harbour under her own power, and joined the other boats of the flotilla." In short, von Mirbach abandoned them to their fate. The report continued, "Prisoners were very indignant that their S.O. had given them no assistance whatsoever."[24]

The German Navy paid a high price for its flotilla commander's callousness, or perceived callousness. The twelve surviving crew members of S-147 provided an astonishing amount of information about the Schnellbootwaffe. Nor were they alone in doing so. Two weeks later, on 13 May, under similar combat conditions S-141 took a hit just forward of its bridge from FS *La Combattante*. The other E-boats in line immediately turned hard to port and made off into the night. Damage from that first round put her rudder out of action, but the crew were still attempting to steer by hand when a second shell landed in the engine room, causing irreparable damage. The Allies picked up only six survivors from a crew of twenty-four. Those embittered crew members added their share to the growing Allied intelligence pool.

Among the mass of detail the Allies gleaned was the fact that S-141 had carried three young officers on board, two of whom were receiving final training as E-boat commanders. One became a prisoner. The second, Oberleutnant zur See Klaus Dönitz, was the only surviving son of Grossadmiral Karl Dönitz. He was on deck manning a machine gun when the 4-inch shell struck, killing him and several other crewmen instantly. The third young officer also died in the engagement.[25]

A less personal loss, but one that was far more damaging to the E-boat Force, was the stripping away of most of the mystery surrounding that high-performance service. Intelligence gathered from the latest prisoner of war interrogations by the Admiralty's Naval Intelligence Division was priceless. In a dense, over-size report, the NID identified almost all of the characteristics of Germany's latest generation of E-boats, including their phenomenal high-speed performance. Prisoners revealed the fitting of new 40-mm cannon in the stern gun position on most boats, as well as the gun's precise characteristics. The Allies learned what color tracer the E-boat Force used in its machine guns and cannon. Survivors described the G-7a torpedoes and their various settings, the types of mines in use, as well as how and where the E-boats laid them. Prisoners compiled detailed lists of individual E-boat commanders including their nicknames and call signs. The personnel rosters listed flotilla commanders and their staffs as well as FdS Petersen and his key officers in Scheveningen. They confirmed the whereabouts and capacities of all E-boat bases in the West as well as in the Mediterranean and Baltic theaters of operations. The report described in detail the exact methods of radio communication used by the E-boat Force. Further information showed what kind of radar and passive radar detection devices the E-boats employed. The Allies learned, for example, that most E-boats did not possess radar and that the German Navy usually fitted sets to only one boat per flotilla. S-146 was the designated boat for the 9th Flotilla. Finally, the disgruntled prisoners gave a full account of E-boat tactics, describing how they used the German Navy's shore radar to locate convoys. They explained how they divided into elements of two or three boats when approaching their targets. Further, they described in detail the *Stichtaktik* that had been the E-boats' mainstay since 1943. Allied intelligence gained much better understanding of the tight control FdS Petersen liked to exercise over his flotillas when he sent them out into the Channel. In short, interrogations of willing prisoners of war on the eve of Operation Overlord provided an intelligence windfall for the Allies.[26]

Valuable though fresh prisoner of war information was, it was not in it-self enough to tip the balance against the E-boat Force. In fact, the detailed intelligence only confirmed the high performance of the E-boats and the qualities of their crews. The Allies, if they were wise, would have to take the threat of extensive and persistent E-boat attacks on their landing ships seriously. The question was how to deal with this elusive enemy force that was in the process of upgrading its equipment as June approached. Worse, it was showing signs of being alerted to the impending invasion and was fully aware of what it had just accomplished against Convoy T-4. Worse still, the Allied convoys would be approaching the French Coast, greatly simplifying the German Navy's task. Soon, the Schnellbootwaffe would find plenty of targets to choose from near its well-established bases at Cherbourg, Boulogne, and Le Havre.

Chapter **4**

The Admirals Contend

"The recent success of the E-boats against forces of this command in Lyme Bay on the night of 28 April bring the risk from this form of attack into sharp focus," wrote Rear Adm. Alan G. Kirk, USN, to the senior naval officer, Admiral Sir Bertram Home Ramsay, Allied Naval Commander, Expeditionary Force (ANCXF), on 4 May 1944. Kirk added that the disaster that befell Convoy T-4 "requires examination of means to prevent recurrence during the actual Operation Neptune."[1]

Five days after the interception of Convoy T-4, Admiral Kirk launched the opening shot in an intense debate among the senior Allied commanders on how to neutralize a threat they had ignored too long: the underrated German Schnellbootwaffe.

Inevitably, the LST disaster caused rancor between Britons and Americans, but in fact the navies of both nations were partly to blame. A rational analysis of why Convoy T-4 had suffered such heavy losses led to the conclusion that the U.S. Navy and the Royal Navy needed to significantly improve coordination and communications with each other if they were to avoid worse disasters when D-day arrived. Both services tacitly agreed that recriminations were a luxury they could not afford, especially with the invasion imminent. What was needed instead was resolution of the problem. The sheer magnitude of American losses lent additional urgency to the debate.

The Americans, as the most recent victims, were the first to propose solutions. Following receipt of reports and briefings from his subordinates, Admiral Kirk prepared a boldly worded memorandum for Admiral Ramsay with a title that emphasized the importance the U.S. Navy attached to the matter: "Aggressive Measures against German E-Boats and Destroyers—Operation Neptune."

In the light of the events that had taken place on the night of 28 April, Kirk shifted his focus away from the two German threats that had chiefly concerned Neptune/Overlord planners to date: U-boats and the Luftwaffe. Instead, he concluded, "The immediate threat on D–1 and D-Day is considered to be the E-boat, especially after nightfall."[2]

Kirk doubted that the Allies would achieve tactical surprise in the initial assault phase. The Germans were bound to react quickly, and that meant a German naval threat to his task forces in the western reaches of the Channel. "While there may remain some vestige of surprise as regards the beach fronts on which we are to land," he informed Ramsay, "by midnight he [the German Navy] will be able to launch attacks with his E-boats, and possibly with destroyers, with certain knowledge of the whereabouts of the Westernmost of our forces." Anchorages for Kirk's U and O task forces were limited because of the relatively deep draft of some of the fast attack transports, known as APAs, and because of the danger posed by German shore batteries. Plans called for the two American task forces to be in place by 0145 of D-day. At that point, Kirk stated, "Forces 'U' and 'O' will be particularly vulnerable to E-boat attack."

Kirk's Western Naval Task Force, which was responsible for coverage of the landings at Utah and Omaha beaches, was already stretched thin, he claimed. What firepower its warships possessed was needed to support landings. Force U, especially, needed to bring its big guns to bear on German positions so as to support General Collins's VII Corps in its westward advance up the Cotentin Peninsula to Cherbourg. "In consequence," the American admiral stated, "there is no factor of safety in terms of men-of-war which can be diverted to strike against the E-boats, either at their bases or when operating on the flanks of our assault forces." Furthermore, the American task force intended to bring the guns of virtually all its war vessels to bear on German batteries prior to H-hour, and inevitably, that meant leaving follow-on convoys without destroyers for escort duties. Kirk reminded Ramsay that "in view of recent experiences, very great concern is felt for the safety of the ships and troops in these convoys. There seems little reason to presume that escorts of the weak number and type, which for lack of ships are contemplated, will prevent losses—possibly losses of such magnitude as to jeopardize subsequent events." Although he did not mention them by name, Kirk undoubtedly had escorts like the fifteen-knot HMS *Azalea* or the elderly HMS *Scimitar* in mind.

Kirk reminded Ramsay that the Royal Navy's two commands at Portsmouth and Plymouth, which were responsible for ensuring the safe passage of the western-based American convoys to the assault area, had few ships available for that purpose. "Commander-in-Chief, Portsmouth, has but four (4) destroyers and some Coastal Forces to discharge this responsibility," Kirk observed. "Similarly Commander-in-Chief, Plymouth, has eight (8) destroyers, plus Coastal Forces, allotted."[3]

Up to this point Kirk was persuasive in pointing out the dangers the Allies faced, and because the Anglo-American naval leadership were well aware that Cherbourg was the most favorably located base for the German Navy's E-boat Force in the Channel area, the western flank of the invasion fleet appeared to face the most immediate danger of attack. Unfortunately, his proposals for what to do about neutralizing the E-boat threat were more controversial. "In my opinion the E-boats must be destroyed, or driven from the Cherbourg area, prior to D-Day," Kirk stated. "The only successful defense against the E-boat is to sink it before it can reach an attack position."

In order to achieve that result, Kirk proposed first of all a bombardment of Cherbourg with the heaviest naval guns or heaviest aerial bombs prior to D–1 so as to destroy that port as an operational base for E-boats and destroyers. In addition, he felt that the Royal Navy should supplement its covering forces under the Portsmouth and Plymouth commands so as to protect the cross-Channel convoys more adequately. In order to implement those actions, Kirk proposed the employment of a new bombardment force of two modern battleships with their destroyer screen, minesweeping flotillas, and air observation for spotting purposes plus appropriate fighter cover. He also proposed "a heavy bomber striking force of appropriate strength."[4]

Kirk was serious about the new battle group. He offered Ramsay the use of the USS *Nevada* and its destroyer screen as one of the two capital ships for the new bombardment group, but admitted he had no extra destroyers for escort purposes. This did not mean Kirk was content to leave defensive measures to the British. He actively considered other options. For example, his key officer in charge of the American PT-boat screen for the Western Naval Task Force, Lt. Comdr. John D. Bulkeley, informed Kirk in late May that the .50-caliber machine guns mounted in his boats' fore-castles were woefully inadequate for Channel fighting. Kirk moved quick-ly. "Am most desirous obtaining for American PT boats under Lt. Comdr. Bulkeley suitable semi-automatic gun for mounting on forecastle," he ca-bled Ramsay on 28 May. "This weapon needed to counter German stern gun on E-boats when chasing them. U.S. Army Mark IV 37-mm aircraft cannon is most suitable type known in this theater," he added. Since none were available in Europe, the request elicited an extraordinary response among the senior commanders. Ramsay transmitted the request to Eisen-hower, who promptly forwarded it to Generals Marshall and Arnold in Washington for immediate action. By the evening of 2 June U.S. Navy air-craft were airborne, carrying the first two 37-mm cannons to Bulkeley's dockyard in Portland where crews set about installing them. More fol-lowed in succeeding days. Kirk was absolutely sincere in his concern about the E-boat menace and was determined to do all within his power to coun-teract it. His 4 May memo concluded: "In my view we are faced with a crit-ical situation on D–1/D-Day in this respect and I recommend that every means be employed to overcome and crush this threat to our success."[5]

Kirk forwarded his original memorandum of 4 May to ANCXF Ramsay as well as copies to his own naval command. He also sent a copy to the of-fice of the chief of staff for the Supreme Commander, Allied Expeditionary Force, General Eisenhower. It landed on the desk of SHAEF chief of staff Gen. Walter Bedell Smith, Ike's close assistant. "Beetle" Smith wanted it be-cause he had left a standing directive to his American commanders to keep him informed of any changes in operational matters. Smith read Kirk's forceful memo on 6 May and, finding it of interest, passed it along to Lt. Gen. Sir Frederick Morgan, leader of the original planning staff for Overlord, with instructions to read and return it. Undoubtedly General Eisenhower read it too. His staff left a note that it would be discussed later.

Indeed it was. At the next meeting of the SHAEF commanders on 8 May the neutralization of the E-boat threat became a major topic of discussion. In the meantime Ramsay had read Kirk's memorandum and would have liked to discuss it with Kirk personally. He received an unpleasant surprise when Ike referred specifically to Kirk's memorandum at the 8 May meet-ing; that meant the memo had leapt the chain of command directly to the Supreme Commander. Admiral Ramsay was fastidious about the preroga-tives and rights of his Senior Service, the Royal Navy, and was obviously disturbed that Kirk, who was his subordinate in the SHAEF command structure and whose rank did not entitle him to be present at the com-manders' meeting, had, in effect, made an end run around the ANCXF.

According to the minutes of the meeting, Admiral Ramsay stated that "measures for dealing with the enemy E-boat menace were under careful consideration." However, Ramsay had no wish to be pushed into a specific course of action based on Kirk's memorandum alone. The Royal Navy had been in operation against the E-boats for far longer than the U.S. Navy, and Ramsay held a different perspective. "He expressed his opinion that this menace, while present, was in danger of being over emphasized," the minutes continued. "Admiral Ramsay stated he did not agree with the suggestion of naval bombardment against E-boat bases but favored aerial bombing of these bases."[6]

A lengthy discussion followed, at the end of which Eisenhower requested that Ramsay present him with an analysis of the E-boat situation. Furthermore, he suggested that the Admiralty consider the feasibility of transferring two additional U.S. destroyer squadrons from the Mediterranean to Operation Neptune.[7]

Ramsay's diary entry that night indicated his irritation with the discussion and with the effect of Kirk's memorandum on the highest leadership. Obviously, General Eisenhower had not been reassured by the ANCXF's initial assurances that his staff were actively considering moves to counter the E- boat threat. "Pressed further," Ramsay recorded, "I said that it was certainly a serious menace, but it would be a mistake to overestimate it." While they would try to destroy E-boats prior to D-day, Ramsay felt that a naval bombardment of Cherbourg, as Kirk was suggesting, "would be ineffective and risky. . . . Pressed further on this," Ramsay continued, "I said that I would not order a naval bombardment unless I received a direct order from him to do so."[8]

Such blunt language from Admiral Ramsay, whom General Eisenhower genuinely liked and respected, was a warning to Ike that continued discussions on countermeasures against E-boats would have to be conducted through established channels. Meanwhile, Ike was busily defusing another potential trouble spot. When Naval Chief of Staff Ernest J. King in Washington appointed the highly regarded Rear Adm. Bernhard Bieri, USN, to be naval adviser to the Supreme Commander, Ike informed King on 9 May, just a day after the tense commanders' meeting, that Bieri, if appointed, would serve as assistant chief of staff to ANCXF. In other words, he was assigning Bieri to serve under Ramsay. Ike reminded King of his reason for doing so: "Since I always carefully observe the principle of unity of command, all my naval operational advice reaches me through the naval Commander in Chief [Ramsay]."[9] Subordinate officers like Admiral Kirk had only a limited right of appeal in circumstances where exclusively

U.S. interests were involved. However, they knew well not to exercise that right except under extraordinary circumstances. Undoubtedly Admiral Kirk regarded the recent E-boat attack and its implications as just such an occasion.

When Admiral Ramsay arrived in London on 11 May to see the Supreme Commander about several issues, including the principle of unity of command, Ike was ready for him. Ramsay knew Bieri personally and trusted him. He was reassured to learn that Bieri would help out in operations as a member of Ramsay's staff. Thus, Ike effectively defused that issue, demonstrating yet again his sensitivity and his competence as a coalition leader.

For his part, ANCXF Ramsay had come prepared with a lengthy memorandum that he and his staff had completed the day before about E-boats. Following Admiral Kirk's alarmist prognostications, the ANCXF staff wished to put the matter in its proper perspective. In a six-page position paper entitled "Appreciation of E-Boat Threat to Overlord," the Royal Navy experts sought to allay some of the fears that they felt had started to grow out of proportion to the threat the German high-speed coastal craft actually posed.

The briefing paper noted, for example, that there were at most eighty-four E-boats in western and northern waters, of which nearly half were too far away in Scandinavia and the Baltic to have any immediate effect on Operation Neptune. The German Navy had built concrete shelters or pens in four North Sea ports that were too far away from the Normandy landing area for operational use and could, at most, serve as transit bases. That left four E-boat bases in the invasion area: Boulogne with shelters for fourteen boats, Le Havre with a capacity for eighteen to twenty boats, Cherbourg with pens for ten to twelve craft, and the more distant Brest where U-boat pens could accommodate E-boats as well.

The British paper carefully laid out possible and probable courses of action by the E-boat Force. Its authors were at pains to point out that the cautious German Navy was most unlikely to bring all its coastal craft south into the Channel area. Many would remain in North Sea ports awaiting Allied moves. They might send out reconnaissance patrols of E-boats following reports of sightings of an invasion fleet, but they would certainly not commit all their flotillas immediately. The boats demanded much upkeep, so that at most 60 percent would be fit for duty at any given time. They predicted a maximum of fifty combat-ready boats at any one time, although they doubted it would be even that many.[10]

Analysis of E-boat successes over four years of operations indicated that the speedy craft had obtained one hit per ten sorties along Britain's East Coast. Even if they got luckier in the ship-filled waters of the Seine Bay and improved the ratio to one hit in four sorties, their success would still be limited. The analysts estimated that at most fifteen boats would operate out of Cherbourg and Le Havre respectively. They would have to maneuver so rapidly that they would not have the luxury of choosing their targets carefully, so that hits would be spread out among the six thousand ships of the invasion fleet. If no reinforcements arrived, the analysts predicted that the E-boats might get nine hits on the initial assault and follow-up convoys. With reinforcements the figure could rise to twelve strikes in the initial invasion.

The short nights of June would limit the hours the E-boats could operate, and the appearance of the moon on most nights would further diminish their stealthiness. Intensive operations at the outset would see an immediate decrease in the percentage of serviceable boats and therefore steadily diminishing numbers of sorties in the days following the invasion. Finally, reinforcements, even if they did manage to come south, would concentrate on the eastern end of the invasion area rather than on the western flank where the American task forces and convoys would be grouped.

To counter the threat, Ramsay's staff recommended minelaying off E-boat bases and astride their likely routes of approach. Second, they suggested air attacks on the E-boat bases and on individual boats in transit to operational areas. Further, they intended to place blockading patrols of Britain's coastal forces off E-boat bases and in areas where they were likely to attack convoys. They were confident that increased escorts would help protect the convoys, and if necessary they could bombard the E-boat bases with Allied warships although that was the last option on their list.[11]

The general tenor of Admiral Ramsay's memorandum on the subject was optimistic, in contrast to Admiral Kirk's pessimistic position paper of 4 May. The British were confident that their first four recommendations—minelaying, aerial attacks on bases plus strikes on individual boats, blockade of E-boat bases by coastal forces, and convoy escorts—would in combination keep the E-boat threat under control. They were convinced that the E-boat Force would be unwilling to commit its reserves quickly or in large numbers at first, and so Allied losses would remain acceptable during the lodgment phase. As for Kirk's proposal to bombard the E-boat pens, the British analysts had some strong language. "It is not intended to bombard E-boat bases from warships either before the operation or during the assault. E-boats take shelter in the concrete pens and any that cannot do so are well dispersed about the port. The likelihood of damaging them is therefore infinitesimal, and to risk battleships essential to the assault to so little purpose would be a mistake."[12]

The final comment in Ramsay's report acted as a kind of general rebuttal for Admiral Kirk's entire position paper: "It is considered that the general threat from E-boats is not serious when compared with other risks that must be run during an operation of this magnitude." The ANCXF and his staff felt confident that their countermeasures would reduce risks from German coastal forces to safe levels.[13]

In trying to allay the Americans' fears following the Lyme Bay disaster, Admiral Ramsay and his staff may have deliberately tried to sound a more sanguine note than they actually felt. At the Admiralty's Operational Intelligence Centre, the expert staff that had been following E-boat operations closely since January 1944 had made recommendations internally and had undoubtedly influenced Admiral Ramsay's position paper of 10 May. Their chief conclusion was as follows: "It is important to hamper the concentration of 'E' and 'R' boats in the Channel by vigorous attack on their potential bases, and we should intensify our attack on the enemy with surface and air forces whenever opportunity offers." They foresaw the need to improve shore-based radar and plotting to improve interception of the German coastal craft by air and naval forces. Significantly, they called for another measure. "In addition, we must develop the system of cooperation between the various naval and R.A.F. authorities to ensure the quick action needed to take advantage of chances for attack indicated by radar or reconnaissance."[14]

The OIC staff had been tracking FdS Petersen's E-boat Force in the Channel area periodically since 1940 and intensively for six months. After extensive observation and analysis, they had reached some sobering conclusions. "By the end of March," the authors noted, "it had become increasingly obvious that being unable to compete with their speed, being unable to damage them effectively in port, being unable to rely on advance intelligence as to their movements, the only way to intercept and kill the E-boat menace was to make the utmost use of radar. Moreover, the offensive must be carried to the enemy side of the Channel."[15]

With a reorganization of Coastal Forces in Portsmouth Command on 8 March 1944, the Royal Navy had begun to put into operation a plan to use radar-equipped control ships in the Channel, which would vector groups of Coastal Forces MTBs onto the E-boats. Although the reorganization helped in some ways, such as rerouting British coastal convoys targeted by E-boat flotillas, the new countermeasures were by no means foolproof.

The OIC usually could not obtain decryptions of German operations plans in time to use them during the night for which they were issued. There were exceptions, as on the night of 24 April 1944, when evidence suggested that E-boats were out laying mines off the Cotentin Peninsula north of Cherbourg with an attack on convoys as a possible second intention. "Operations on this night are an excellent example of the extreme elusiveness of E-boats when at sea," one chronicler wrote.[16] No fewer than four patrols of MTBs tried to intercept the E-boats, two units off the French Coast and two more lying in wait south of Beachy Head and Selsey Bill respectively. Undeterred, the E-boats penetrated so close to a convoy near the British South Coast that only the vigilance of its close escort drove the attackers off. Aircraft of Coastal Command attacked them as they were entering Boulogne at 0500 the next morning, but all boats made it into harbor safely. A complicating factor for the Allies was the need to use photoreconnaissance or some other cover to enable the German forces to assume that the Royal Navy and RAF Coastal Command had used conventional methods to detect the E-boats. The OIC was a heavy Ultra recipient, and that war-winning secret had to be preserved at all costs.[17]

Another reason for their more pessimistic outlook was the unpredictability of the E-boat Force. The OIC staffers knew they had to be realistic in assessing their own ability to use past E-boat operations to predict future operations. "In spite of a close scrutiny of E-boat activity in the period between January and June 1944," they confessed, "in spite of a knowledge of the date and hour of immediate readiness of flotillas, there was very incomplete insight into the mind of the enemy. Would he use his E-boats in saturation strength or would he plan his attacks with a view to stretching our defences to the limit? Was he preparing to attack simultaneously from Cherbourg and Boulogne from the moment the objective of Operation Neptune became clear?"[18] After half a year of intensive observation of E-boat operations, the OIC staffers still had no satisfactory answers to these questions as the date for implementing Operation Neptune approached.

In spite of itself the OIC staff was lavish in its praise of the phenomenal performance of the E-boats. Following the torpedoing of two merchant ships and one of their escorts off Beachy Head on the night of 30 January 1944, the OIC analysts had given vent to their frustrations. Naval wireless traffic, photointelligence, numerous anti-E-boat patrols, and special intelligence had all failed to protect that convoy. "One point, however, should be clarified," the analysts stated. "Interception of E-boats, whose speed was considerably more than that of our MTBs, was possible, but destruction of the enemy was a much more difficult problem. This purely technical obstacle, though in part solved by the use of controlling frigates after April 1944, nevertheless constituted a grave handicap to the full use of the Special Intelligence available."[19] In other words, it was one thing to know where the E-boats were. It was quite another matter to catch them.

Later that summer, after the most intense Allied operations to date against E-boats, the OIC staff felt compelled to remind future readers of the threat the E-boats posed to the Allied invasion fleet, and they enlisted the support of Britain's hard-working Coastal Forces in describing the threat.

> In this connection, it might be as well to place on record yet again a comparison which has been made many times but cannot be made too often. The following is the first paragraph of Coastal Forces' Summary of Lessons Learnt from Operation Neptune. "The enemy demonstrated the superior speed and sea keeping qualities of his coastal craft. In calm weather there was sometimes a difference of 16 knots between the full speeds of E-boats and MTBs. In moderate weather also, E-boats were able to maintain a higher speed. But for these discrepancies, many more E-boats would have been destroyed"—a comment which shows a quality of masterly restraint.[20]

An OIC analysis of E-boat operations for the first half of 1944 was sobering. The Germans had launched 315 sorties from the Channel ports during that time. In the course of those missions only two boats had been sunk. The E-boat flotillas, on the other hand, had attacked five convoys, sinking eleven ships and damaging a twelfth. When they were successful in locating a convoy, their effective tactics and reliable torpedoes inflicted 2.4 hits per convoy interception, a high success rate. The British estimated that their own Coastal Forces and destroyers plus RAF Coastal Command had attempted to intercept the E-boats on all but one occasion in that six-month period. On average, two-thirds of the time the British forces failed to locate the E-boats at all.[21]

The OIC also calculated that in the first half of 1944 the number of E-boats operating from Channel ports doubled from twelve to twenty-four with an average strength of sixteen. Table 1 indicates the scale of E-boat activity. The OIC also noted the types of operations undertaken in that six-month period by Petersen's E-boat Force (see table 2).

The OIC analysts pointed out one particularly disturbing statistic. E-boats had attempted to attack convoys on at least fifteen occasions; they had actually succeeded in intercepting them only five times. "Of the specifically anti-convoy operations," the analysts noted, "between 65% and

Table 1
E-boat activity in the Channel, 1 January–24 May 1944

No. of maneuvers	36
No. of individual forays	315
Average no. of maneuvers per month	7.4
Average no. of forays per month per E-boat on duty	3.8
Average no. of E-boats engaged in each maneuver	8.8

Source: "Note on E-Boat Operations in the English Channel, January–May 1944," p. 1, OIC Special Intelligence Summary, S.I. 974a, Public Record Office, ADM 223/172.

Table 2
E-boat activity in the Channel (by type), 1 January–24 May 1944

Activity	*Probable no.*
Torpedo	15
Minelaying	10
Defensive	2
Uncertain	9
Total	36

Source: "Note on E-Boat Operations in the English Channel, January–May 1944," p. 2, OIC Special Intelligence Summary, S.I. 974a, Public Record Office, ADM 223/172.

75% failed to locate a target." On those operations where they did attack, they sank 2.4 ships. "The E-boats were thus limited mainly by the difficulty in contacting convoys," the OIC analysts concluded.[22] When faced by an invasion fleet of thousands of ships nearing their own ports, the E-boats would have no difficulty whatsoever in locating targets. The implications were obvious. When the E-boats were able to locate convoys, they hit hard. The Allies could not ignore the E-boat threat with impunity.

From the appreciations of Admiral Kirk and the U.S. Navy position paper of 4 May, from ANCXF Admiral Ramsay's counterproposals of 10 May, and from the heavily involved staff of the OIC, one common proposal did emerge: heavy aerial bombardment of E-boats in their bases. Too fleet and maneuverable to be caught with any regularity on the open water at night, the E-boats would have to be attacked in their own ports. That was the consensus on the eve of Operation Neptune.

Neither Admiral Ramsay nor any other party said so, but aerial attacks before D-day on the likeliest ports such as Cherbourg or Le Havre were not practicable. The Allied Expeditionary Air Force at SHAEF had prepared a carefully orchestrated bombing campaign, specially designed to drop double the tonnage of bombs on targets outside the Normandy battle zone for any target struck within that zone. Deception was one of the Allies' dearest commodities, and no one was prepared to jeopardize it, E-boats or no E-boats. To have attacked Cherbourg as Admiral Kirk had suggested on 4 May would have been tantamount to hanging an aerial sign behind a scout plane over the Normandy Coast saying Invasion This Way.

However, once the lodgment was secure, then E-boat reinforcements would begin filtering into the combat zone. It was then that an aerial counteraction might be feasible. The question that arose in this context was whether the Allies had the planes, crews, skills, and special equipment needed to catch the E-boats in their ports. Those ports had some of the world's most massive concrete bunkers. The Germans had erected huge gun batteries capable of withstanding the stoutest blows from capital ships, and far from being passive, they could deliver deadly counterbattery fire. Admiral Ramsay's refusal to launch a close bombardment by battleships was fully justified given the strength of Hitler's Fortress Europe, his concrete and steel defenses that had been under construction for years in ports like Cherbourg and Le Havre. The German-controlled ports also contained deadly rings of antiaircraft guns to repel any but the highest flying aircraft, plus numerous fortified points with rapid-fire guns to repel amphibious landings. After the ill-starred Dieppe Raid of August 1942, the Allies had vowed never to make an amphibious attack on another fortified city. Consequently, while the idea of attacking the E-boats in their ports after the landings at Normandy was an attractive one, it was not clear whether the Allies had the aerial weapon with which to check the E-boat menace. It was their best hope, however. Of the air forces deployed against the Axis in the spring of 1944, only one stood a chance of executing such a bold stroke: Great Britain's RAF Bomber Command.

Chapter **5**

Bomber Harris Prelude

Large strategic bombers and E-boats were unlikely antagonists in the Second World War. Each sought different prey. Each feared other types of predators far more, be they German flak and interceptors for the former or Coastal Command attack aircraft and the Royal Navy's MTB-destroyer teams for the latter. Nevertheless, events dictated that one day fleets of Bomber Command's four-engined Lancasters would end up stalking Germany's elusive coastal craft, a hunt that would climax at Le Havre.

Strategic bombing campaigns were a new phenomenon in war. Its architects had hoped they would be able to destroy the enemy's productive facilities and civilian morale. Specific military targets such as nimble E-boats seemed a remote possibility at the outset of hostilities. At issue was whether Bomber Command could transform itself from a bludgeon into a more precise instrument of war.

A Blunt Instrument: RAF Bomber Command, 1939–1944

Until 1939 only one country had ever experienced the effects of strategic bombing: Great Britain. Germany's Zeppelin attacks on London in 1915 followed by heavier-than-air Gotha bomber attacks in 1917 and 1918 had goaded the British into establishing the world's first independent air arm, the Royal Air Force, in April 1918. General Jan Smuts, the responsible imperial official, perceived the RAF's role as mounting a counteroffensive against Germany. Britain would wage strategic air war on German cities. From the start, motives behind strategic bombing were not strictly military. They also contained the element of reprisal, which carried with it the danger that political pressure might drive military establishments to attempt operations that exceeded their abilities.

Only the end of World War I stopped the RAF's leading bomber advocate, Hugh Trenchard, from launching Britain's strategic air offensive. This novel form of war struck the imagination of the public in the interwar years. Pulp fiction as well as more serious writings speculated on air wars of the future. Despite much public discussion, however, no military establishment had developed an air force with strategic bombing capabilities by 1939. Disciples of strategic airpower were usually honored more by admirers from abroad rather than at home. Giulio Douhet of Italy, Hugh Trenchard in Britain, and Billy Mitchell in the United States might attract press attention. But within their own armed forces, they were usually considered mavericks.

There was a practical reason for ignoring them. None of the major powers felt justified in committing the vast resources needed to create fleets of heavy bombers that always got through to the target—to paraphrase Prime Minister Stanley Baldwin's message to the House of Commons in 1932. The science of aeronautics and the technology necessary to support a strategic air force were still largely absent, as were national budgets to support so expensive a project in those financially strapped depression years.

Nazi Germany came closest to developing a coherent air doctrine before the war, but by 1936 its leadership deliberately chose to create a tactical air force in support of its mechanized ground forces rather than a strategic air arm. The Spanish Civil War reinforced the Germans' enthusiasm for ground-attack aircraft. This decision proved highly successful for the Wehrmacht and Luftwaffe in the opening campaigns on the Continent in 1939–40. Only when the Nazi leadership tried to use its tactical air force in a strategic role over the skies of Britain in the summer and fall of 1940 did it came to grief.

The British for their part had grown wary of German preparations by the mid-1930s, and discussions within the Air Ministry and Air Staff, the highest reaches of the Royal Air Force, forged a consensus. The growing German threat convinced them that they had established the wrong priorities. RAF Bomber Command, in existence only since 1936, would have to wait until plans for mass production of four-engined bombers had been realized by around 1941. The main priority went to Fighter Command and its air defense system, including radar networks, centralized telecommunications, command and control installations, high-performance interceptors, and skilled personnel, in short, the system that allowed the RAF to win the Battle of Britain. It consumed large resources and employed the best of Britain's scientific talent. And it worked.

Both major combatants tried strategic daylight offensives early in the war, and both failed. The German Luftwaffe and RAF Bomber Command suffered 20 percent losses of aircraft and crews when they attempted daylight long-range operations in 1939 and 1940, losses that would have crippled them in short order had they not broken off their respective engagements. Accordingly, both air forces switched over to the only option open to them: They bombed at night, each adopting a strategy of evasion of the other's air defenses.

The main problem associated with nighttime operations was that neither air force had the training or equipment to make the crucial transition to that difficult mode of attack. The Luftwaffe never seriously tried to overcome its deficiencies and remained largely a tactical air force. By contrast, RAF Bomber Command, backed by the resources of the British Empire, began a five-year effort to achieve a nighttime strategic bombing capability with which to defeat an entire nation-at-arms. The only other combatant that tried to do so was the United States, which also discovered, belatedly, how difficult it was to wage a successful strategic air war.

The obstacles were daunting not least because Britain's goals were not clear in the first two years of the war. There were discussions on the Air Staff and its Air-Targets Subcommittee on whether a strategic air effort should attempt to destroy enemy industrial capacity, enemy morale, enemy housing, or simply to improve domestic morale by undertaking an aggressive policy of taking the war back to the German people. The earliest plans, the so-called Western Air Plans, looked forward hopefully to the destruction of German synthetic oil production and other power sources such as hydroelectricity and transportation networks. They also eyed heavy naval units as worthy of attention. Many of these targets eventually proved to be vulnerable. However, plans for the execution of strategic raids remained vague at the outset because suitable weapons and aircraft were lacking.

Bomber Command started its campaign with small quantities of light twin-engined aircraft. It lacked adequate navigational equipment, including reliable radio communications, offensive radar, bombs and bombsights, marking aids and techniques, air intelligence, bomb-damage-assessment capability, meteorology, defensive armament, and training methods. It had a host of other technical deficiencies. And all this was exacerbated by a woeful lack of experience. In fact, they were charting unknown territory.

For two years Bomber Command aircraft strayed across German skies at night seeking targets of expedience. Their "strategic" bombing campaign put bombs outside targets, often on the wrong targets, sometimes on the wrong cities, and most frequently, on no targets at all. Crews used "astronavigation," shooting the stars with sextants as they gazed skyward in domed perspex canopies and shuddered in intense cold. Frequently crews resorted to dead reckoning, using rivers, cities, or prominent terrain features as their guides. Their primitive navigational efforts were usually in vain. Crosswinds regularly blew them off course, and they had developed almost no means of detecting or countering wind drift.

Events often overtook planning. Sometimes by accident the combatant air forces reached certain thresholds and blithely crossed them, unaware of the true consequences. Stray German bombers hit London on the night of 24–25 August 1940, and the British retaliated against Berlin the following night. In the Blitz that followed, the Luftwaffe damaged London and razed Coventry in November. Bomber Command took off its gauntlet, bombing Mannheim the next month. This process created a dynamic of its own with the public and political figures clamoring for more retribution.

As a result, cities, and by implication, city dwellers, once taboo to planners, became legitimate targets for strategic bombing. By the end of 1941 the RAF Air Staff was focusing on about forty German cities, mainly in the Ruhr District, because they were closest to British bomber bases. Cities were visible and immobile, and Bomber Command's inexperienced crews should, it was thought, be able to hit them. Urgent demands elsewhere dissipated Britain's bomber strength. The naval forces needed to use long-range aircraft for antisubmarine service and for bombing submarine pens in the Battle of the Atlantic. Other theaters of operation siphoned off squadron after squadron. However, the Nazi invasion of the Soviet Union in June 1941 reinforced Britain's general desire to do something to hurt the German war machine. Pressure increased on the RAF to carry out its strategic bombing offensive as almost the only means to continue the war against the Germans from the west. But given its severe limitations, Bomber Command was nowhere near ready for such ambitious operations. A crisis of confidence loomed concerning the future of Britain's strategic air war.[1]

Two years into the conflict, grave deficiencies emerged in the bombing campaign. Hitherto there had been no accountability for bombing accuracy, so almost no one was aware of the problem. Only slowly did suspicions arise that the bombers were not finding their targets. Revelation came haphazardly. Celebrated scientific adviser R. V. Jones recalled a BBC report early in 1941 that proudly proclaimed a major RAF attack on the giant Skoda Works in Pilsen. But friendly Czechs promptly informed British intelligence and Professor Jones that no bombs had fallen within fifty miles of Pilsen! Similarly embarrassing episodes followed.[2]

Several months later, in August 1941, Churchill's scientific adviser, Lord Cherwell, responded to mounting questions on the subject and assigned his secretary, D.M.B. Butt, to investigate the problem. An able civil servant, Butt hit upon a simple expedient. Crews were required to bring back a flash photograph, taken while bombing, of the site they had just hit. He compared hundreds of photographs with the crew's bombing reports. Analysis of the results, which were made known to selective RAF personnel, was sobering. Only one-third of all bombers were coming within five miles of the target in nearby Occupied France or the Lowlands. In raids on the more distant Ruhr District only one bomb in ten was falling within five miles of the target. Yet of all German targets the Ruhr cities lay closest to Britain's bomber bases. Results in Central and Eastern Germany were undoubtedly worse. And Mr. Butt was putting the best face on it, since he generously defined "the target" as something large like a city. The Butt Report, as it came to be known, forced Britain's War Cabinet, Air Ministry, Air Staff, and Bomber Command to accept the fact that they must improve navigation and bombing techniques dramatically in order to justify the staggering costs of Britain's strategic bombing campaign. Bomber Command's commander in chief, Sir Richard Peirse, tried to fault the report at first, but that further undermined his own credibility and helped to number his days at Bomber Command. Change was needed. At last the leadership at High Wycombe, under considerable pressure from the highest echelons in the British government, began a sustained program to improve Bomber Command's performance.[3]

Identifying the problem did not bring about quick solutions. But the shock of the Butt Report had wider salutary effects. It fundamentally altered the mind-set of Bomber Command's leadership. As Professor R. V. Jones explained: "Up to this time it had been difficult to persuade Bomber Command to take science seriously. The contrast with Fighter Command had been remarkable." Jones noted that if he, a scientist, visited Fighter Command Headquarters at Bentley Priory, everyone from front-line pilots up to the most senior staff bombarded him with questions. By contrast, the staff of Bomber Command at High Wycombe struck him as being as complacent as if they were on operations back in prewar days.[4] Mr. Butt's report changed all that. The harnessing of skilled scientists and quick-witted airmen that had saved Britain in 1940, was about to be repeated in Bomber Command's strategic bombing campaign.

Thereafter, a steady stream of innovations and improvements developed that gradually transformed Bomber Command from a minor irritant for the Nazis in 1941 into a major worry by 1943. In the interim, Bomber Command remained a blunt instrument, engaged in area bombing of cities because that was virtually the only target the British could hope to find and bomb at night. Daylight remained the bomber's enemy. With much of Germany's air strength directed against the Soviet Union in the summer of 1941, Peirse and the Air Staff had launched a series of daytime "Circus" operations, sending along fighter escorts for limited numbers of bombers to attack pinpoint targets. They still sustained high losses. The escorts were too short ranged to penetrate German territory, and the Germans refused to react if the targets were in occupied nations. The British were stuck with night operations and that meant area bombing of cities. Sir Charles Portal and the Air Ministry ordered it in February 1942, along with a change in leadership at Bomber Command. Lord Cherwell rationalized city-killing to Prime Minister Churchill and the War Cabinet a month later by claiming they could de-house the German workers living in the cities, thereby undermining public morale and industrial production. The rationale was that Britain would at least weaken the Germans sufficiently to allow a renewed ground campaign in the West. Some air strategists even predicted they could win the war entirely from the air. As events proved, Lord Cherwell's estimates proved to be hopelessly optimistic; nevertheless, they helped sustain the strategic air offensive when doubts were mounting about its efficacy.[5]

The large four-motored bombers, on the drawing boards since 1936, were beginning to appear at last. The underpowered Stirling went operational in January 1941, as did the more robust but trouble-plagued Halifax two months later. Britain finally found its victory bomber with the advent of the mighty Avro Lancaster, which came into service in March 1942. Each of these aircraft, especially the latter two, could carry many times more bombs than the old twin-engined aircraft they replaced. The Lancaster proved in the long run to be the premier heavy-lift bomber in the air war over Europe. The new heavy bombers were complemented by the high-performance wooden-construction Mosquito in May 1942, which proved excellent for long-range reconnaissance, marking, diversionary attacks, and many other purposes in support of the heavy bombers. However, improved aircraft were not enough by themselves.

Of equal importance were the growing array of navigational aids and equipment to find and hit targets. The British started where the German Luftwaffe had left off with its abortive strategic bombing campaign of 1940: navigational radio beams. The German beams had failed because they were complex, narrowly directed, easily detected, and quickly jammed. Out of the partnership of scientists and Bomber Command emerged a new radio navigation system called Gee. In contrast to the German system, Gee was simple, universally broadcast, difficult to recognize, and hard to jam. It was at Britain's secret Telecommunications Research Establishment (TRE) at Malvern that scientists and active military officers gathered informally at "Sunday Soviets" to talk about developments and possibilities. From those discussions of scientists and users emerged Gee.

The British erected three linked transmitting stations on their East Coast at hundred-mile intervals. The master station continuously broadcast radarlike pulses 360 degrees. The two linked stations picked up its pulses and reradiated them at a precisely known time interval. Aircrews detected the pulses with an on-board receiver. Using a Gee chart, they could then estimate their position to within a mile or two on the basis of slight variations in the timed intervals with which the receivers detected incoming pulses from the respective stations. It was a kind of universal triangulation system. Gee was everywhere and nowhere—its pulses did not have to be aimed in one direction as the old German beams had been. It was so successful that after the war its American equivalent, Loran, became a standard maritime navigational aid for civilians and military alike.

After a lengthy gestation period, Gee received its operational baptism in March 1942, on a Bomber Command raid against elusive Essen in the Ruhr District. Invariably, Essen, home of Krupp armaments, lay under cloud or industrial haze, and previous missions had missed the city entirely. This time Gee brought the bombers unerringly over the city. Alas, the attack was scattered anyway because of the perennial industrial haze, and the new navigational aid was by no means accurate enough to provide target marking. However, the novel system showed promise. Bomber Command's newly installed commander in chief, Air Chief Marshall Arthur Harris, realized that it alone could direct masses of bombers over the target and that there was safety in numbers. His thousand-bomber raid on Cologne on 30 May 1942 was Gee-equipped, and its success stemmed in large part from the fact that all aircraft followed an exact bomber stream using the new aid. Moreover, it allowed tremendous concentration of numbers, which could overwhelm German defenses. Raids that once had taken hours to execute over the target were eventually compacted into twenty minutes or less. Gee and the Cologne raid revived Bomber Command's flagging morale as well as its public image. German defenders were slow to detect the importance of the elusive pulses and they found them difficult to jam at first. Although countermeasures did materialize, Gee remained a useful tool throughout the war, and many a crew found its way back to base despite the clouds that so often shrouded the British Isles. Scientists had helped rescue Bomber Command with Gee, and their catalogue of innovations had just begun.[6]

Harris's elevation to C-in-C Bomber Command in February 1942 was a positive development at a time when the entire future of Bomber Command was under discussion. Harris husbanded his forces, unlike his predecessor, and chose his targets carefully, seeking optimum weather conditions and biding his time to allow crews to gain more training and experience until new devices had time to mature and to improve shaken morale. The Cologne raid was only one of many tactical successes under his energetic command. Following deliberate pauses for buildup and analysis, his forces would attack targets of maximum opportunity, trying out new tactics—as when for the first time experienced crews, using Gee, led inexperienced main force crews to the Billancourt Renault Factory in early March 1942. The veterans dropped flares, which helped the fledgling main force destroy the assembly halls in an attack of unprecedented accuracy. A few weeks later they did the same at Lübeck where the first-wave veterans used incendiaries to turn the wooden timbered Old Town into a fire beacon for the newcomers in an increasingly ruthless air campaign.

Under Harris the application of science to war received a warmer reception. Radar signals were proving to be useful, so the TRE's Sunday Soviet produced a second navigational system called Oboe that was so accurate that Bomber Command could use it for blind-bombing. This was no small advantage in the haze and cloud over Germany. Oboe required two stations, Cat and Mouse, situated like Gee some distance apart on Britain's East Coast and tied to each other by land cables. Cat was a tracker station that emitted 1.5-meter radar signals that directed an aircraft, usually a high-flying Mosquito, hundreds of miles away on a wide circular track designed to bring it in precisely over the target. The Mosquito reradiated the pulse, allowing Cat to determine the aircraft's exact position. Mouse measured the Mosquito's ground speed and altitude and plotted its precise distance from the target. Calculations showed at what point the bomb release should occur, and at the right instant Mouse beamed out a second inter-secting radar pulse, automatically triggering the plane's bomb release. Op-erational experiments with Oboe over Ruhr targets in January 1943 con-firmed its accuracy, with aircraft hitting their targets despite 10/10ths cloud. Hitler was furious and claimed that such a feat was impossible.[7]

That January surprise was no fluke. In March 1943, almost one year to the day after Gee first brought its bombers over Essen, Oboe-equipped Mosquitoes returned to the hazy home of Krupp, leading a main force of 440 bombers. Whereas Gee had placed them generally over the city in 1942, Oboe dropped markers and bombs right on the target in 1943. The center of Essen as well as Krupp took heavy damage for the first time in the war. A repeat raid launched one week later produced even more dam-age at the armaments works. The heartland of German industry was invio-late no longer.[8] Under proper conditions Oboe could place bombs within 680 yards of the target through the thickest cloud cover.

Oboe was not, however, ideal. It operated in line-of-sight, so the curva-ture of the earth limited its range to about 250 miles, and unlike Gee it could direct only a limited number of aircraft. Better by far would be an aircraft with its own radar system that scanned German terrain and found its target without the limitations of a distant ground station. But the cum-bersome long-wave radars currently in use made that impractical. A bril-liant scientific breakthrough made shortwave radar possible. Physicists John Randall and Harry Boot, working at the University of Birmingham, produced a cavity magnetron, a cylindrical block with six resonator cavi-ties drilled into it surrounding a cathode. Crudely put, when they housed the magnetron in a vacuum and ran a strong magnetic field and high volt-age between the cathode and the cylindrical block, the stream of electrons swirled, or resonated, in the cavities and emerged as powerful 10-cm radar pulses capable of outlining images miles away. Later, they reduced it to 3 centimeters. It was one of the premier scientific achievements of World War II and put the Allies firmly ahead technologically of the Axis powers. In the variation that applied to Bomber Command, centimetric radar evolved into an airborne apparatus called H2S. As a ground scanner, it picked up return echoes from objects like buildings, whereas water and flatlands gave little or no return. H2S operators could "see" cities, espe-cially ports, on their oscilloscopes. It also proved to be an excellent naviga-tional aid.[9] A significant feature about H2S was that British scientists had worked directly with the Bomber Command squadrons that would use it, and they installed the elaborate apparatus in operational aircraft within one month of its completion, an astonishing feat. With time, other navigational and marking aids such as G-H appeared, but the first three—Gee, Oboe, and H2S—were crucial in reviving Bomber Command's fortunes.[10]

In combination, they succeeded in significantly increasing the ability of Britain's nighttime strategic bombers to find and hit targets. There were many other innovations, some scientific, others organizational. Just as vital was the improvement in staff work to make the various parts of Bomber Command function better, to identify targets, to develop bombing tactics more effectively, and to foil the enemy's growing air defense measures.

Finding targets and assessing bomb damage became an exacting sub-specialty in the air war. Two related organizations were developed in the RAF: a Photographic Reconnaissance Unit (PRU) for collecting, and a Photographic Interpretation Unit (PIU) for intelligence evaluation. PRU was based principally at Benson, where it sent out special crews and aircraft to photograph targets and after-action results. It was the brainchild of an unorthodox Australian, Sidney F. Cotton, who in prewar days had built a quasi-civilian photographing organization that gathered better materials than the RAF. Using innovative cameras and long-range "business" aircraft, they paved the way for PRU, clandestinely mapping and photographing militarily sensitive targets all over Europe on the eve of the war. With the outbreak of hostilities, Cotton helped boost the RAF's PRU into the first ranks of photoreconnaissance organizations. The information collected by PRU pilots, often at great personal risk, was fed into PIU at Medmenham some miles up the Thames from London. Years of intensive operations and evaluation of millions of aerial photographs had turned PIU Medmenham into the premier photographic interpretation organization in the world, a boon for the Americans when they began serious air operations in 1943.[11]

The size of Bomber Command rose dramatically in the midwar period. Despite the success of Air Marshall Harris's thousand-bomber raid on Cologne in May 1942, the feat was something of a one-time stunt. Bomber Command had scraped up bombers and crews from operational training units and elsewhere to achieve that sensational number, and much of the equipment consisted of older two-engined bombers like the Wellington. They dropped fourteen hundred tons of bombs, little more than a ton per aircraft. By the spring of 1943, when Harris began a sustained campaign against the cities of the Ruhr, he could put six hundred four-motored bombers into a raid on one town like Dortmund, and they dropped more than two thousand tons of bombs with greater accuracy.

A major reason for improved performance was the reorganization of Air Staff's forces. With more and more crews and aircraft becoming operational, the need for specialized navigational aids and for improved target marking to help novice crews increased. Unfortunately, the increasing destructiveness of Bomber Command's raids had alerted the Germans to their own danger, and the resulting improvement in German night-fighting capability meant sustained operational losses for Bomber Command of over 4 percent. This painful attrition had an ominous impact. Most crews were not surviving their tours of duty, and the level of experience within Bomber Command did not expand commensurately with its size. Several ideas had been circulating since 1941 about using experienced crews in a more sustained role to help lead the newcomers to the target, similar to the informal arrangements used on the Renault works and Lübeck in March 1942. Group Captain S. O. Bufton, a veteran pilot promoted to the Air Ministry after lengthy tours of duty, circulated the idea of a specialized Target Finding Force, a bomber group composed of crews with a proven record of finding targets, to lead the main force. Harris disliked the idea of forming an elite unit within his command, preferring to keep the experienced crews among the inexperienced flyers in each squadron. Ultimately, the matter was resolved with the creation of a compromise Pathfinder Force (PFF), a force comprising standard squadrons donated from existing bomber groups to form a new 8 Group under Australian Donald C. T. Bennett, an outstanding navigator and pilot. Pathfinders began operating as squadrons in August 1942 and were elevated to the status of 8 Group in January 1943.[12]

Starting from scratch, Bennett's Pathfinders began to experiment with new marker bombs, packing incendiaries and inflammable materials around conventional bombs to create "Pink Pansies" over the target for follow-on crews. By early 1943 Pathfinder crews, with the help of prewar fireworks manufacturers, were preparing special target indicators (TIs), which they dropped on aiming points. These 250-pound bombs, loaded with pyrotechnical flares that came in distinctive greens, reds, and yellows, were highly visible and difficult for the Germans to imitate when they attempted to misdirect bombers with flares of their own. A barometric fuse deployed the flare at a predetermined height over the target, and the lit candles drifted slowly down over the target. The creation of a master bomber, an experienced bomber pilot who orbited over the target area and updated incoming crews on which indicators to use, added considerably to Bomber Command's ability to accurately mark and concentrate its attack. There were other innovations. Marker aircraft could also drop so-called spot fires directly onto the ground at the aiming point. Finally, white illumination flares dropped by back-up crews would light up large ground areas, making it easier for main force crews to locate targets. To avoid dazzling the crews, they suspended the blinding flares under black miniature parachutes. Despite Air Marshall Harris's best intentions, Pathfinders became an elite force, specializing in ground, high-altitude, and blind marking.

Recognizing that wind drift was a continuous problem for crews, Bomber Command enlisted the services of a meteorological flight to determine winds on the way to and from targets. Using the new navigational aids, they could determine wind drift with considerable accuracy and radio the information back to group headquarters with periodic updates for rebroadcast to target bound crews. Main force navigators, using Gee, Oboe, and H2S, could do the same on the way to the target. A serious commitment to determining wind drift helped correct the most common reason for crews losing their way in the hostile skies over Europe.

Finally, Bomber Command established an Operational Research Section with representatives at each group to collect information and statistics after each operation for transfer to scientists who specialized in operations analysis. They performed in more sophisticated fashion what Mr. Butt had done in 1941 and passed their information along to Air Marshall Harris, the Air Staff, and Air Ministry.[13]

By spring 1943 all these developments added up to a strategic bombing campaign that was beginning to hurt the Germans. However, despite tremendous progress, Bomber Command could still attack only at night, and its targets were still cities. Main force bombers could successfully engage only in area bombing in hopes of destroying urban industrial plants, weakening German civilian morale, de-housing workers, and slowing the growth of industrial production. The outstanding example of this heavy-handed technique came with the fire-bombing of Hamburg on the night of 28–29 July 1943. Bomber Command's catalog of innovations, including for the first time the jamming of German radar with "window" (strips of aluminum), had allowed hundreds of heavy bombers to drop several thousand tons of bombs onto the center of a tinder-dry city suddenly stripped of its defenses. The combination of incendiaries and high explosives in drought conditions led to a conflagration that burned out the old Hansa town and killed as many as fifty thousand civilians. However, given the special conditions that led to the firestorming of Hamburg and the temporary blinding of German radar, Bomber Command could not repeat itself. The war continued.[14]

Despite all the innovations, main force could bomb to within 700 or 800 yards of their target only if everything was working right, which it often was not. Gee, which the Germans were jamming more and more, could be used only in friendly skies. Oboe reached 250 miles, out to the cities of the Ruhr and no farther. H2S was still crude, hard to read, and its sets tended to break down with annoying regularity. Nevertheless, a start had been made, and cooperation between scientists and Bomber Command, once a haphazard relationship outside of aeronautical design and engine development, was now accelerating. One of those scientists, a brilliant innovator, would do the most to create an elite fighting unit within Bomber Command by solving a tactical problem for the strategic campaign. His name was Barnes Wallis.

Chapter **6**

Barnes Wallis and the Giant Bomb

One of Britain's most accomplished engineers, Barnes Wallis thought and acted more like a creative scientist than the cautious engineer of popular imagination. Between the wars he was an early pioneer in the use of geodetic construction, first for lighter-than-air ships such as his high-performance R-100 dirigible, which flew from Britain to Canada and back with ease. Then, sensing the shift in focus in technological developments, he turned to heavier-than-air craft, where his innovative geodetic construction methods produced such notable aircraft as the long-range Wellesley and then the famous Wellington bomber, affectionately known as the Wimpey. The Wellington's performance was so phenomenal for the time that it soldiered on through most of the Second World War, long after its prewar hangar mates had been retired.

When war broke out in September 1939, Wallis the scientific visionary, as opposed to the engineer working for Vickers Armstrong, turned his considerable talents in a new direction. Convinced that the war would be long and that strategic bombing would play a central role in it, he turned his attention from aircraft design to the payloads that the bombing fleets would be dropping on their enemies. Existing ordnance was inadequate. Until

1940 British bombs comprised mainly 250- and 500-pound bombs, and improvements materialized slowly. For example, ordnance designers had not begun development of a 1,000-pound GP (general purpose) bomb until mid-1938, and it took two years to reach mass production. Even that bomb was inadequate for the requirements Wallis envisaged. He concluded that industrially advanced Nazi Germany was peculiarly vulnerable to certain types of attack. Its modern industries depended heavily on power output. He concluded that what was needed was a huge bomb, accurately dropped on energy-related targets in order to cripple the German war economy and war machine. The destructive effects of one large bomb would, if accurately delivered, be far greater than the effects of many smaller bombs.[1]

Wallis bided his time, busying himself with other urgent projects at Vickers Armstrong while the war went from bad to worse for Great Britain. Finally, on 19 July 1940, he succeeded in meeting Britain's minister for aircraft production, Lord Beaverbrook, to discuss technical matters such as ground defenses against airborne landings. However, the subject quickly turned to what Wallis called a "Victory Bomber" to deliver his unusual bomb. Lord Beaverbrook was intrigued, asked him to return for more discussions the next day, and then urged Wallis to prepare a report on the subject. Profiting from intelligence provided by government agencies and his own research, he labored on it intensively through the Battle of Britain, the Blitz, and on into the winter, submitting his results to Beaverbrook and the Ministry of Aircraft Production in March 1941. It was forwarded to a hastily established Aerial Attack on Dams Advisory Committee where eminent scientists like Henry Tizard read it. Copies also made their way to 10 Downing Street, where Lord Cherwell also digested Wallis's proposals.

Wallis outlined the results such a bomb could achieve and how it could be built in "A Note on a Method of Attacking the Axis Powers" (which was more than a note; it was actually a 117-page treatise of closely reasoned prose, including 30 complex tables and 20 pages of appendices). He posed an intriguing thesis. Axis industrial output demanded enormous energy use. Power generating stations; hydroelectric plants, refineries, coal mines, and storage areas for hydro and fossil fuels were all bottlenecks in the flow of industrial power. They were usually concrete installations imbedded in earth or surrounded by water. Either medium would conduct bomb-induced shock waves—Wallis called them pressure pulses—through the structure far better than a bomb's blast effect through air. What was needed therefore was a huge bomb capable of releasing its energy in the water or earth surrounding the target. One giant bomber with its special bomb could destroy these strategic targets far more effectively than an entire squadron of bombers like the Wellington.[2]

No one could accuse Wallis of thinking conservatively on this project. A bomb exploded in water could be thin-skinned, like a depth charge. Not so the earth borer. Wallis proposed constructing a Victory Bomber capable of carrying a steel-encased ten-ton bomb to forty thousand feet so that gravity would hurl its awesome captive at supersonic speeds through the earth beneath the target. The ensuing shock waves of the explosion would travel up into the foundations of the target, where its rigid concrete construction, lacking flexibility, would actually work against itself. He emphasized the "camouflet effect" of such a bomb. Its subterranean detonation would create a large underground cavity into which earth and structures would collapse, forming a crater. Later, the public would know it as an earthquake bomb.

Unbeknownst to Wallis, the Air Staff of RAF had been considering future targets in Germany since 1937, and their Western Air Plan 5 had also looked at potential targets related to power output or storage. They concluded in the prewar years that such targets were impractical because Britain possessed neither the weapons nor the aircraft to deliver them to the target. Torpedoes, rockets, and other existing ordnance were either too puny or else impossible to deliver properly. As a civilian employee, Wallis had no clearance for such classified information, and unaware of the Air Staff's discouraging conclusions, he developed his own ideas independently.

The effect of his "Note" was to rekindle interest in strategic targets that the Air Staff had abandoned years before. Most who read the paper were intrigued. However, they were also discouraged by the performance specifications of the future Victory Bomber and doubted the destructive power of the proposed earthquake bomb. Tests on scale models of concrete structures with miniature bombs suggested that the camouflet effect might be weaker than predicted. Moreover, at that time government ministries were inundated with a bewildering array of war-winning schemes by well-meaning citizens. In May 1941, the Air Staff rejected Wallis's project, bomb and bomber alike. In the course of that summer, they had even greater cause to hold back from so bold an enterprise. The Butt Report revealed the appalling inaccuracy in Bomber Command operations; the building of an expensive bomb that had only a remote chance of hitting its target seemed pointless. Wallis was not privileged to read that report either. It remained a closely guarded secret. He could only conjecture about why his proposal was rejected.[3]

A tenacious fighter for his beliefs and one who had confronted government bureaucracies before, Wallis refused to give up. Wisely, he changed his approach and concentrated on one select aspect of his scheme, one that would demand fewer resources and materials to produce. He began to examine underwater explosions. In a moment of inspiration Wallis turned his attention to a thin-skinned bomb that could explode underwater against its target. Initially, he viewed it as a weapon to be used against naval targets but quickly realized that such a bomb might be effective elsewhere. Wallis contemplated and experimented some more, then had another inspiration. Borrowing his daughter Elizabeth's marble collection, he began ricocheting them across the water in a backyard tub with a hand-built catapult. At the proper angle they bounced twice, clearing a taut string before landing on a table. His children recorded the results. In May 1942, a year after the rejection of his initial proposal, Wallis submitted a second paper to Tizard's committee. This time he proposed the construction of a bouncing bomb designed to destroy one of the most massive structures imaginable, a hydroelectric dam.[4]

In the meantime, reevaluation of scale model tests had demonstrated to various government officials that the kinds of bombs Wallis was proposing possessed greater destructive power underground or underwater than they first supposed. Although delays occurred, and some officials like Lord Cherwell remained skeptical, Wallis received permission to conduct tests with his bouncing bomb–depth charge, and by February 1943 results proved that an airplane could bounce one across water. A crucial experiment on the Nant-y-Gro Dam in Wales confirmed the weight of charge required to breach the Möhne Dam. The Welsh dam served well as a large-scale model. Its configuration conformed to the German dam but was only a fifth its size, and its location posed no hazard to anyone. The water released by its destruction simply escaped into a larger dam. Explosives experts carefully calculated the charge they wanted and placed it in contact with the dam wall. The subsequent explosion confirmed the weight of charge needed to breach the much larger Möhne Dam, assuming, of course, that a skilled pilot could place it accurately. Film cameras recorded those crucial tests.[5] At about the same time Wallis submitted another paper, "Air Attack on Dams," to the appropriate agencies, outlining its possibilities, especially against dams in the Ruhr area.

Buttressed by Wallis's paper and the spectacular films, the idea of air attacks on dams gained credibility. Lord Cherwell relented. Various officials in the Air Ministry, Air Staff, and Bomber Command warmed to the idea. Sir Charles Portal, chief of the air staff, became an advocate and convinced a skeptical C-in-C Harris to listen to Wallis. Despite an extremely frosty reception at High Wycombe, Wallis made his point, and by the end of February the project finally received approval. The planners estimated that they had only a couple of months in which to build the necessary bombs, prepare the aircraft, and develop the tactics that would allow them to destroy Ruhr dams in the spring when water levels were highest. From this point events moved with bewildering speed. Chastened by the daunting challenges and terribly short deadline, Wallis quailed at the realization that his project, barely off the drawing board, would now be translated into a military operation with young men's lives at risk. Like those scientists who had produced H2S in record time for Donald Bennett's Pathfinders, Wallis became intensely involved with the squadron that would fulfill his scheme.

On 21 March 1943, Bomber Command put together a mainly volunteer squadron to deliver the dams bomb in a special mission they dubbed Operation Chastise. Reflecting its late arrival and unsure status, the squadron received a high number—617—but there was hope that in the course of the spring its able young leader, twenty-four-year-old Wing Commander Guy Gibson could ready its aircrew for the demanding assignment. Eleven weeks of intensive preparations and training followed.

On the night of 16–17 May 1943 in bright moonlight, nineteen heavy Lancaster bombers carried their four-ton cylindrical bombs toward the Möhne and Eder dams near the Ruhr and dropped the rapidly reverse spun bombs from an altitude of exactly sixty feet onto the waters behind the dams. The bombs skipped like huge stones hurled flat across the water and after leaping over torpedo nets, they slowed, struck the containment wall, then sank to a depth of thirty feet where hydrostatic fuses detonated them. Enormous water pressure focused the resulting shock waves and added punch to the ensuing explosion. The result was two wrecked dams, extensive flooding, and loss of industrial water supplies for the Ruhr industries. It also caused heavy loss of civilian lives. The third dam, the Sorpe, used different construction techniques, and the British were less confident of breaching it. The two broken dams were gravity dams, whereas the Sorpe was an earthen dam with a smaller core supported by two earthen banks on either side. The attacking aircraft had to fly parallel to the Sorpe on the watery side, keeping its port wing over the dam and aiming at the center of the dam, which was approximately twenty feet from the dam wall. The Sorpe required no bouncing bomb—a conventional bomb would do—and the two crews able to locate it in a valley obscured by mist dropped their bombs perfectly on target. The dam held anyway.

Despite much official trumpeting of this undoubted feat of arms, the senior British political and military leadership were privately worried by the prospect of a German retaliation. And the direct effects of the successful bombing raid were relatively short-lived. The Germans shunted other hydro- and steam-generated electric sources into the Ruhr power grid and repaired the breached dams. Heavy rains filled them again by the autumn of 1943 and the Germans hurriedly increased defenses around all their hydroelectric sources. The dams raids were never repeated.[6] Other effects of the raid were longer lasting. The young aircrew who had developed the skills needed to deliver their lethal cargoes with such pinpoint accuracy were not dispersed back to their old units. Despite fearsome losses on the dams raid—eight of the aircraft failed to return—617 Squadron had earned such fame that disbanding it was out of the question. It became exactly the kind of select unit that C-in-C Harris had wanted to avoid, and it took on a life and role of its own.

Paradoxically, after the dams adventure there was a hiatus in big-bomb development. The dams bomb had been a unique device, perfectly cylindrical and thin-skinned, like the depth charge it was. There were proposals to build modified bombs using the same principle against capital ships and possibly canals. Those projects, called Highball and Baseball, resulted in further tests, but the Royal Navy wisely decided it was too dangerous for an aircraft to approach enemy vessels with such an unwieldy cargo.[7]

For the moment, at least, Wallis was forced to cool his heels as the senior Air Ministry officials, Air Staff, and Bomber Command leaders pondered their future moves. He would have been flattered by what happened next, but civilians were not privy to the results of staff meetings at High Wycombe. On the very morning following the Dams Raid, C-in-C Harris recalled the other proposals in Wallis's 1940 "Note" and concluded that the scientist's earthquake bomb was not so farfetched after all. By early June, staff discussions, featuring a proposal by 5 Group's Air Vice Marshall Ralph Cochrane, centered on the idea of a twelve-thousand-pound bomb with a delayed fuse to be dropped deep into terra firma. Wallis had begun to make more converts at Bomber Command.

The famed raid of 16–17 May 1943, although never repeated, was proving to have other far-reaching effects. Not least, it acted as a powerful morale-building tonic for all of the RAF Bomber Command, which had endured growing losses without commensurate gains for their efforts in that period of the war. Like Harris's thousand-bomber raid on Cologne in May 1942, the Dams Raid had captured the imagination of the public.

Of no less importance within RAF Bomber Command was the existence of its specialist squadron with a new bomb, new equipment, new tactics, new skills, and, not least, new leadership. It had seen an unusually intense meshing of the skills, hardiness, and raw courage of twenty-year-old airmen with the scientific ingenuity, drive, and perseverance of Barnes Wallis. He had, in fact, unofficially become the 617 Squadron "boffin," although no one would have dared address so distinguished a scientist in that fashion. Added to the dynamics of this newly famous squadron was the fact that the specter of formidable new German targets began looming on the horizon in the summer of 1943.

The quickening pace of Germany's secret V-weapons development gave new urgency to Wallis's ideas on big bombs as scientific intelligence committees met secretly in London in June and July 1943. By then, British intelligence had at last awakened to the danger of impending attacks by liquid-fueled rockets and pilotless aircraft, the V-2 and V-1 respectively, plus other secret weapons that threatened a renewed German onslaught on Britain's cities.[8]

Almost as ominous was the steady growth of hardened, steel-reinforced concrete batteries, bunkers, and pens that Hitler's engineers and labor battalions were building for their Fortress Europe scheme and for their U-boat war. Suddenly, a deep penetration earthquake bomb no longer seemed a remote need. By July, Wallis received permission to proceed with the new generation of giant bombs he had been advocating since 1940. In his notes he referred to them always in capital letters as TALLBOY. The appellation "Tallboy" became the generic term for all of Britain's earthquake bombs of which there were three sizes. They called the 4,000-pound design Tallboy S (for small). The 12,000-pound bomb became Tallboy M (for medium). Tallboy L weighed an awesome 22,000 pounds, but it did not go into production until the early spring of 1945. When it did it was called, appropriately, Grand Slam.

The targets for Wallis's new bombs—whether industrial power plants, hardened coastal-defense structures, or underground rocket-launching sites—proliferated in 1943 and 1944 as total war saw a quickening of offensive and defensive weapons on both sides. "These targets are unfortunately of the most massive nature," he had already written in 1940, "and are practically invulnerable to attack by existing aerial methods. They are, however, concentrated in character, and cannot be moved or dispersed."[9]

A central principle in the dams bomb's success had been the concentration of shock waves by water. Shock waves in the denser medium of earth are commensurately greater, especially when occurring deep underground. Wallis predicted that the camouflet effect of the Tallboys would work better as a near mass rather than as a direct hit on a hardened site, and would make the crew's task easier. Burrowing a hundred feet underground before exploding, the bomb's pressure wave would strike upward into the foundations instead of having to penetrate the hardened roof from above in the less conducive medium of air. Near misses had the added advantage of creating an underground cavity into which structures could tumble.

The dams bomb had been a fat cylinder dropped from sixty feet; Tallboy was intended to be slender and streamlined in order to attain supersonic speeds before impact and to burrow more efficiently. Trials in December 1943 with the four-thousand-pound test bomb, Tallboy S, showed that when dropped from twenty thousand feet, it became ballistically unstable as it approached Mach 1 and tumbled far off the target. The casings on other test bombs tended to disintegrate upon impact, so that no deep penetration occurred. Therefore the designers had to construct tougher heat-treated casings and devise a way to stabilize them in flight. The final product, they realized, was going to be an expensive, even exotic, weapon. However, the testing served its purpose, and in the spring of 1944 series production of the Tallboy M began.[10]

Measuring twenty-one feet in length with a diameter of just over three feet, its newly thickened steel nose shielded the contents from destruction. With characteristic ingenuity Wallis solved the instability problem. He designed new fins that were offset with a five-degree right-hand helix to impart a rapid spin to the streamlined casing. This simple solution provided the necessary ballistic stability as it approached Mach 1 and made Tallboy extremely accurate.

This six-ton missile carried torpex, a combination of 40 percent TNT, 42 percent RDX, a powerful new explosive, 18 percent aluminum powder plus a small amount of desensitizer. TNT was stable. The Research Department Explosive—RDX, also known as Cyclonite (cyclo-trimethylene-trinitramine) —was half again as powerful as TNT but too sensitive to use alone. When mixed nearly half and half, however, it so enhanced the older TNT that the weapon's explosive power attained 99 percent of the strength of a pure RDX bomb. The aluminum powder finished this powerful explosive by boosting heat levels enormously. Originally designed in the Royal Navy's laboratories at Woolwich for torpedoes—as its name implies—torpex was perfectly suited to Tallboy. The mix was carefully heated and stirred in a batch, loaded into the massive steel casing, and then sealed under pressure in order to magnify the blast effect. In fact, it produced a higher blast level than any other standard explosive of World War II, and it was a proven product. Torpex had already performed superbly in the dams bombs.[11]

In July 1943 plans for Tallboy were advanced enough that Wallis could negotiate details with the senior official in charge of Lancaster production, Roy Chadwick, over the future payload for Britain's heavy lift Lancaster bomber. Like two wary merchants haggling over precious goods, the two finally compromised on fitting aircraft for the initial twelve-thousand-pound bomb for use in 1944. It was to be followed later that year or the next by the awesome twenty-two-thousand-pound Grand Slam. Tallboy would just fit inside the modified bomb bay of a Lancaster with slightly bulged doors. Grand Slam was so large it would have to be carried externally.

Once plans were established, the project proceeded rapidly. Wallis had a prototype ready for Chadwick's inspection on 12 September 1943. However, given Britain's overtaxed war economy, some exotic components such as the high-strength steel casing would have to come, at least in part, from the United States. Fifty-five percent of Tallboy's total weight was devoted to steel and the rest to torpex, a measure of just how strong the steel casing had to be. Serial production of the giant bombs began in the spring of 1944 and even then only in limited quantities. The English Steel Corporation in Sheffield produced the first batch of high quality casings, then shipped them to a Royal Ordnance filling factory to receive their deadly charges.[12]

More precious than anything else in the West's arsenal, the new bombs could not be area dropped. They had to be delivered with pinpoint accuracy to their targets. Only one squadron in the world had the expertise needed to drop them where it counted. In late May 1944 large trucks shrouded with heavy tarpaulins began arriving at the bomb storage depot at Woodhall Spa airfield. Unaware of what was under those bulky covers, the members of 617 Squadron went about the business of preparing for the invasion. They were about to be joined up with a new instrument of war.

The Maturing of 617 "Dambuster" Squadron

Having created a new squadron capable of unusual tactical exploits, C-in-C Harris and the senior echelons at Bomber Command seemed unsure at first how to employ it to best advantage as the air war continued. Guy Gibson, who had gained such fame leading the Dams Raid, stepped down as squadron commander shortly afterward. In July 1943 his successor as C.O., Squadron Leader George Holden, led a dozen crews on shuttle missions to bomb transformer stations for the electrified railway system in Northern Italy and then on to landings in North Africa. They bombed the harbor of Leghorn on their return flight to England on 25 July. Several nights later, following their return to home base, they sped south of the Alps again on the night of 29 July 1943 to drop propaganda leaflets over North Italian cities. Although the missions were justifiable, given Italy's wavering commitment to the war, they hint at a certain lack of direction in Bomber Command's utilization of some of its ablest crews. A less charitable judgment is that those missions represented a dissipation of effort. Misfortune soon followed.[13]

On two succeeding nights, 14–15 and 15–16 September 1943, eight Lancasters led by Squadron Leader Holden attacked the Dortmund-Ems Canal, hoping to repeat their successes on a vital target that involved breaching a body of water. They were lugging large bombs, but the bombs were of conventional design for surface detonation. The attacks failed disastrously. Fog canceled the first operation, but it cost the lives of one crew. Five more crews died on the second night including Holden and his crew. The canal escaped unharmed. Shortly after the survivors returned to base, Air Vice Marshal Cochrane, Air Officer Commanding, No. 5 Group, arrived at Conningsby to find out what had happened.

He received an earful from one of the few surviving dambuster veterans, Flt. Lt. Mick Martin. Unfailingly honest, the junior-ranked Martin from Australia told Cochrane exactly what he thought of the fruitless raids. They had experienced poor visibility all along the route, and the immediate target area had been covered in dense fog. Six Mosquito fighter-bombers had accompanied the 617 Squadron aircraft to suppress the numerous light flak defenses the Germans had concentrated along the canal. Poor visibility hampered the Mosquito crews, and the Germans poured murderous fire into the larger, slower Lancasters. That, combined with the bombers' need to loiter low over the area searching for the target, had spelled the doom of six fine crews in just two nights. That tragedy plus Martin's blunt words had their effect. Normally a taciturn commander and inured as much as any human can be to the loss of young soldiers' lives, Cochrane heard Martin out in shocked silence. Once he had finished, Cochrane appointed Martin acting commanding officer on the spot. He also put an end to operations requiring the large Lancasters to make low-level attacks on defended targets. From that moment forward, 617 Squadron began retraining as a specialized high-altitude bombing unit. A turning point in its operational career had just occurred.[14]

The effective working relationship that had evolved between 617

Squadron members and Barnes Wallis now produced further beneficial effects. One of Wallis's frequent partners in discussions was Mick Martin. Martin was a highly skilled pilot. In fact, Leonard Cheshire and others considered him to be the finest pilot ever to emerge in Bomber Command. One talent that had earned Martin such respect among his peers was his ability to maneuver his heavy four-engined bomber at its maximum speed at extremely low altitude. That skill had undoubtedly been his salvation during dangerous missions such as the Dams Raid and the attack on the Dortmund-Ems Canal. With his Tallboy bomb accepted and a prototype under construction, Wallis could now inform Martin of its characteristics and the absolute necessity of lifting it to high altitude and then dropping it with unprecedented accuracy. His imagination struck by what he learned from Wallis, acting squadron commander Martin became a convert to high-altitude precision bombing. His conversion ushered in a new era. The battered squadron developed an obsession for accurate high-altitude bombing at Conningsby. That zeal, combined with Martin's low-level flying skills for marking targets and his ability to impart those skills to others, produced dramatic results within a short time.[15]

The key to accurate bombing lay in technological innovation as well as skillful crews. In the case of 617 Squadron the equipment breakthrough lay with the introduction of a remarkable new instrument. Tom Bennett, one of 617 Squadron's leading navigators, ascribed near mystical qualities to it: "The 'magic wand' in this," he wrote, "was the Stabilized Automatic Bomb Sight [SABS], which was hand-built by craftsmen and never mass produced. 617 was the sole squadron so equipped and total destruction of their SABS was the premier requirement of any 617 crew 'in trouble' over enemy territory."[16] It was imperative that the enemy never recover one intact.

SABS was similar in performance to the American Norden bombsight, and British engineers had been working on it in secrecy since 1941. It included a telescopic sight with which the bomb aimer acquired his target. The sight was mounted on a gyroscopically stabilized platform in the nose of the Lancaster. Bomb aimers had to master the challenge of feeding accurately all the necessary variables into the bombsight, which in some ways anticipated the computer. The SABS generated aiming corrections automatically as long as the bomb aimer held the sight on target. This placed heavy demands on the crew. In fact the level of performance expected was sufficiently great that no thought was ever given to mass production of SABS for Bomber Command's main force. It remained a 617 specialty. "This bombsight demanded to be flown at the true height and true airspeed of the attacking bomber," Bennett continued, "with NO deviation from course."[17]

Wallis had taken special pains to design the casing for his earthquake bomb so that it was, ballistically speaking, extremely accurate. Other bombs might tumble or wobble during free fall; that was acceptable for bombs dropped on an area target. It was unacceptable in the scarce and expensive Tallboy. An indication of how precisely the great bomb was expected to fall can be gleaned from the fact that crews had to calculate more than just true airspeed and height. They also had to know the exact outside air temperature at the moment of release. Air temperature was directly related to air density. Wallis had calculated that an error in temperature reading of just one degree centigrade at twenty-thousand feet would result in a bombing error of twenty-one feet. A three-degree error stretched it to twenty-one yards, which fell below Squadron standards for the specially contoured and highly accurate Tallboy.[18]

Experience showed that the usual thermometers attached to the Lancaster were unreliable. Higher inside cabin temperatures affected them, as did friction-produced heat from the strong air flow streaming over the bulb that protruded from the aircraft. Even deflectors failed to solve the problem completely. The greater the velocity of the bomber, the greater the temperature reading error. Baffled, Mick Martin approached the specialist equipment designers at Farnborough, headed by Arnold Hall. Rising to the challenge, they produced a special thermometer that was calibrated in such a way as to take airspeed into account. Thereafter, each bomber carried two thermometers. Bennett recounted how they used the new information: "The squadron navigators were furnished with a formula with which they balanced the two thermometer readings to arrive at the precise outside air temperature for use in compiling the vital SABS settings."[19]

Once the navigator had calculated this temperature reading, he then turned his attention to the other factors. Bennett described the procedure: "This result was then set appropriately on the scale of the navigator's Dalton computer, against the 'indicated' height on the pilot's cockpit altimeter, allowing the TRUE height to be read off and fed into the SABS. Similarly, the TRUE airspeed could be deduced against the 'indicated' airspeed. Once these two factors had been fed in, the SABS was charged."[20]

Accurate bombing was truly a crew effort. "The navigator would offer the drift and ground speed to the bomb-aimer, who would feed these into the sight before the actual bombing run commenced," Bennett recalled. "But," he added, "these two latter 'elements' bore no relation to the crucial height and airspeed 'feed-ins,' for the bomb-aimer could manipulate the sight to correct for drift and ground speed from his visual observations through the sight and verbal instructions to the pilot."[21] Needless to say, a successful mission required intense concentration by pilot, navigator, and bomb aimer—and long hours of practice.

If air temperature readings were central to success, it followed that the squadron aircraft had to reach their predetermined bombing height as early in the mission as possible in order to minimize the variations in outside air temperature occurring at different altitudes. Therefore, once they climbed away from base, the bombers gained altitude quickly in order to adjust to conditions at the necessary altitude. Although accurate, the SABS was not a flexible or forgiving instrument. Pilots had to fly their aircraft to their initiation point, a considerable distance from the target where they would begin the crucial bombing run. "A long steady run-up, often of five to seven minutes duration, dependent on the weather conditions, with no deviation from course, was a fact of operational life that 617 captains had to accept," Bennett observed. "Thus, there was a very real danger from the accurate, predicted German 'flak' during this period." In other words, it was a time for steady nerves and placed heavy demands on even the most stout-hearted of crews.[22]

As acting commanding officer of 617 Squadron, Mick Martin screened prospective replacement crews carefully to see if they accepted the radically different demands of SABS in addition to the procedures needed for accurate high-altitude bombing. Many did not, an understandable reaction in volunteer crews who had already survived perilous night missions and who were used to weaving and evading enemy defenses as they approached their targets with the more forgiving Mark XIV Bombsight. Given 617 Squadron's recent losses, many RAF personnel viewed the company as the equivalent of a suicide squadron. Nevertheless, volunteers did arrive, and they gave every sign of accepting the challenges of the revolutionary bombing techniques. "Soon the whole Squadron was totally absorbed in mastering the intricacies and demands of the SABS," Bennett stated.[23]

Although an extraordinary pilot and an innovative tactician, Mick Martin was a junior officer without prior command experience and had agreed to take over such duties only temporarily. Fortunately for 617 Squadron, Air Vice Marshal Cochrane found a worthy replacement in Wing Commander Leonard Cheshire, who sought and accepted a demotion in order to be able to return to flying duties. Cheshire took command of 617 Squadron on 10 November 1943 and his extraordinary personality began to be felt immediately. He immersed himself in all the activities of the squadron, visiting aircrews, ground crews, and support personnel alike until he knew everyone and they knew him.[24] He found it to be an extraordinary unit with the most dedicated men and women, be they senior flight crews or the newest clerks. Cheshire fully agreed with the primacy of the squadron's new role as a tactical unit able to deliver bombs on pinpoint targets. Tom Bennett reconstructed the kind of pep talk Cheshire gave to all incoming volunteers: 'ALL squadron crew need to develop a fetish about bombs and bombing accuracy, no matter what their aircrew calling! Pilots TAKE bombs to targets. Navigators FIND targets for bombs. Bomb-aimers PUT bombs on targets . . . and gunners PROTECT bombs to target—it's all about BOMBS!"[25]

Cheshire's remarks were not mere theatrics. All crews had to prove themselves before performing a mission. They had to carry out at least three practice exercises at the RAF bombing range at Wainfleet, dropping six bombs at a time. Typically, they were expected to drop their conventional ordnance from about fifteen thousand feet and place at least four of the eighteen bombs within fifty yards of the target, a more generous margin of error than the twenty-yard allowance permitted for Tallboys. The Squadron's bombing leader kept a Bombing Error Ladder in his office, and crews advanced or fell behind on that ladder depending on their performances at practice exercises.[26]

Since a crew's position on the bombing ladder depended upon the average of all of its Wainfleet exercises, the squadron members took them as seriously as they did live runs over enemy targets. The competition was ferocious and nonstop. Any crew, be it ever so famous, was only as good as its last practice run. The squadron had to practice other flying skills too such as low-level flying and mock combat against friendly fighters, which they called fighter affiliation. Tom Bennett neatly summed up the squadron's priorities: "617 air training hours were overwhelmingly confined to bombing practice with 'fighter affiliation' really a poor second feature!" Those crews who rested—uneasily to be sure—on the top rungs of the bombing ladder were permitted to carry to the target large single bombs such as the twelve-thousand-pound high-blast "cookie" for block-busting (as opposed to the deep penetration Tallboy, which was not yet in service). Those lower down the ladder carried as many as fourteen thousand-pounders. Crews that failed the fifty-yard standard for conventional bombing at Wainfleet twice in a row were relegated to secondary duties rather than participating in active bombing missions until they proved themselves anew. It was a pitiless system and demanded that crews constantly do their best.[27]

As the Squadron gained proficiency in pinpoint bombing in the winter of 1943–44, it joined operations where targets were marked by Pathfinder Force, often called PFF. At this point it became obvious that the marking techniques of PFF were inadequate for this special operations squadron. PFF used the new radar and navigation techniques of Gee, Oboe, and H2S, plus high-level marking to attain an average error of seven hundred yards, not bad for a main force that had been unable to place bombs within five miles of the target only a year or two before.[28] However, it was not nearly good enough for a tactical precision squadron. In addition, there was some rivalry between 8 Group Pathfinders, under the forceful AVM Donald Bennett, and the equally self-assured AVM Ralph Cochrane at 5 Group. Sometimes open criticisms of each other's performance erupted.

On the night of 16–17 December 1943, nine 617 Lancasters attacked flying-bomb sites in a forest at Flixecourt near Abbeville. A Pathfinder Mosquito, using Oboe radar to fix the location, dropped its markers with considerable accuracy by the standards of the time. Nevertheless, the markers were off by 350 yards. All nine Lancasters dropped their twelve-thousand-pound bombs within 100 yards of the marker. But because of the initial error, the net result was no damage to the enemy. Several nights later, on 20–21 December, the results were even worse. Eight 617 Lancasters and eight PFF Mosquitoes flew against an armaments factory near Liége. The bombers could not find the Mosquitoes' markers beneath the thick clouds and had to return to base without attacking. One Lancaster was lost.[29]

This pattern of failures continued when, on the night of 30–31 December, the Pathfinder Mosquitoes marked within two hundred yards of some more flying-bomb sites. Once again the 617 Lancasters struck within yards of the markers, and once again the site emerged undamaged.[30] Understandably, frustrations began to build.

At a tense meeting in Bomber Command Headquarters at High Wycombe in early January 1944, Leonard Cheshire stated to the assembled leadership that 617 Squadron required a marking accuracy of twenty yards to match its finely honed bombing skills. The Pathfinders' AVM, Bennett (no relation to Tom Bennett), openly scoffed at such a request, claiming that it was totally unattainable. "Not if the marking is done at low level," Cheshire replied, and he described the low-level marking techniques that he had learned from Mick Martin and from his own dogged efforts to improve such tactics. C-in-C Harris mediated among the strong wills of his outstanding officers. Bennett remained openly skeptical, and the best that Cheshire could obtain in concession was permission to mark targets from twenty-five hundred feet. Out of the ensuing discussions, AVM Cochrane acquired a few independent targets at lightly defended areas for 617 Squadron.[31]

During raids on flying-bomb sites in the Pas de Calais area on the nights of 24 and 25 January 1944, Cheshire and Martin tried marking from HQ Bomber Command's prescribed altitude of twenty-five hundred feet. The effort failed completely. Ignoring orders not to fly lower, the skilled Martin zoomed down over the target, closely followed by Cheshire. This time they marked it with great accuracy, and the rest of the Lancasters dropped their bombs right onto the target. Like truant schoolboys, Cheshire and Martin told Cochrane what had happened. Far from berating them, Cochrane decided to exercise his considerable influence at High Wycombe. He finally obtained official permission for low-level marking by 617 personnel, and the stage was set for a memorable experiment.[32]

On the night of 8–9 February a dozen 617 Lancasters led by Cheshire attacked the Gnome-Rhône aeroengine factory at Limoges. Located near dense civilian housing, it was lightly defended, primarily because the Germans assumed the Allies were reluctant to inflict large loss of life on the French population. Until that night they had been correct. Diving his huge Lancaster to less than a hundred feet off the ground in bright moonlight, Cheshire buzzed the factory and got an accurate fix on its layout. In fact, he buzzed it three times, and the French factory workers, well warned by this time of an impending attack, fled from the threatened site.

On his fourth run, at a height estimated to be only fifty feet, Cheshire dropped a load of thirty-pound incendiary bombs directly onto the factory roof. One after the other the eleven remaining Lancasters made their high-level run over the site using SABS and dropping the high-blast twelve-thousand-pound cookies. Ten of them made direct hits, completely devastating the factory. Amazingly, no French lives were lost, and all twelve of the 617 aircraft returned safely to base.[33] It was a textbook example of what the squadron had been striving for and augured well for the future.

Hindrances remained. Martin and Cheshire's marking methods were extremely risky, especially in a mighty four-engined Lancaster. Down drafts and low-level turbulence were always a possibility. By 1944 the Lancaster was beginning to fall into the category of slower aircraft and was increasingly vulnerable to light flak. The factory at Limoges was nearly undefended and was, therefore, atypical. Against stoutly defended targets like flying-bomb sites, E-boat and U-boat pens, and German-held targets generally, a marking aircraft like Cheshire's Lancaster would have had little chance of survival. After several more missions of varying success,

Cheshire received a temporary leave from 617 Squadron to familiarize himself with the high-performance twin-engined Mosquito fighter-bomber. A hundred miles an hour faster than the Lancaster, the all wooden "Mossie" was a much better marker aircraft. Cheshire liked it from the start.

By 5 April Cheshire was ready for operations again, and that night 144 Lancasters from 5 Group, paced by 617 Squadron, and led by Cheshire in his solitary Mosquito, attacked an aircraft factory in Toulouse. No Pathfinder aircraft were present. This time the target was heavily defended. Undeterred, Cheshire made two passes at high speed over the factory. Once again the workforce had time to evacuate, and on his third pass Cheshire dropped his markers squarely on the factory. Two follow-up Lancasters from 617 Squadron dropped their flares from high altitude directly onto Cheshire's markers, and the rest of the bombing force ran in over the target. The result was once again sheer destruction as the bombers achieved the highest concentration of bombs on a target to date in the war. C-in-C Harris was delighted, and in return for a promise that 617 Squadron would use its new skills to bomb Munich, he allocated three more Mosquitoes to them for marking. For good measure he also returned two Lancaster squadrons (83 and 97) from Pathfinder Force, 8 Group, to their original 5 Group. Finally, Harris detached 627 Squadron from PFF to 5 Group to learn 617 Squadron's new marking technique. Significantly enlarged, 5 Group now had permission to undertake operations independently of PFF. Unamused by the downsizing of his Pathfinder Force, AVM Bennett referred to 5 Group thereafter as "The Lincolnshire Poachers." However, acceptance by the highest levels of Bomber Command for its marking methods gave the crews at Woodhall Spa much satisfaction. The squadron had just put one of the final pieces of the puzzle together to make it a true tactical squadron capable of bombing with pinpoint accuracy and for preparing the target for a huge punch from the main force arriving overhead.[34]

Like Harris, Cheshire was a man of his word, and on the night of 24–25 April he and his squadron mates proved that the attack on Toulouse had been no accident. A sizable bombing force of 234 Lancasters and 16 Mosquitoes, almost all of them from 5 Group, attacked Munich as they had promised Harris they would. Once again the Mosquitoes marked precisely despite intense flak, and the high-altitude main force put their bombs directly into the center of the city. Much of beautiful Munich turned into rubble that night as the war ground pitilessly on.[35]

The new marking tactics had unavoidable limitations. The risk to the low-diving aircraft in the vanguard was considerable, especially if the pilot was brave enough to make multiple passes as Cheshire did. The technique required visual acquisition of the aiming point and accurate marking in a steep dive. If weather in the target area deteriorated, a common occurrence in the cloudy skies over Europe, then the attackers had to abort the mission. Bad weather caused 617 Squadron to cancel several operations in the winter of 1943-44 and again in the summer of 1944. Pathfinder Force had labored hard to develop all-weather techniques. PFF employed Oboe as far as the Ruhr District and with sufficient accuracy to satisfy area bombing needs. Outside Oboe range its newer tools, H2S and G-H, provided alternate marking. When the weather was clear enough to allow visual bombing, PFF could drop its target indicators onto the aiming point. If the attacking bombers confronted a cloud cover over the target, they dropped bright flares instead, which produced distinctive colors, so that the supporting main force could aim its bomb loads on a specific aiming point in any weather. Oboe, H2S, and G-H never attained sufficient accuracy for pinpoint bombing, but they did meet the requirements for area bombing. However, when conditions were right, the 617 Marker Force, backed up by the formidable accuracy of the squadron's SABS-equipped Lancasters and further enhanced by the heavy bombloads delivered by main force squadrons, could produce awesome and concentrated devastation. But 617 Squadron now faced a new challenge that had nothing to do with bombing.

With the Normandy Invasion only five weeks away, C-in-C Harris detached 617 Squadron from its normal tactical bombing role to prepare for D-day with "Operation Taxable." This was a huge deception plan, coordinated with several other plans, to fool the Germans into concentrating their forces elsewhere than in Normandy. The challenge for 617 Squadron crews was to fly precise "open-elliptical" advancing orbits, dropping "window" at precise intervals on a precise course and to keep it up for two hours. Using aircraft flying at 160 knots, the effect was to impose on German sea-scanning radar screens the impression of a vast naval armada approaching the Pas de Calais coast at a speed of 8 knots. The operation demanded superb flying, and the Squadron practiced hard, using captured German radar to test and hone their skills. They met the challenge and perfected the techniques, which the Squadron navigators had personally developed, in time for D-day.[36] A great achievement. Operation Taxable helped pin the entire German 15th Army in the Pas de Calais at the very moment Allied armies were storming ashore in Normandy. Once Operation Taxable was completed, 617 Squadron returned to combat operations as a special striking force. The hour for the contest between Bomber Command's foremost tactical unit and Germany's high-performance Schnellbootwaffe was fast approaching.

After standing down for a few days after the invasion, 617 Squadron received its first tactical mission in direct support of the Normandy Invasion. Belatedly, the Germans were sending armored forces into the Normandy area over French railways from the South. If stopped, their absence from the battlefield would save lives and buy the Allies precious time in building up their forces to counter German armor. A tempting target to accomplish that goal was a crucial railway tunnel emerging at the Loire River near Saumur. In great haste Bomber Command ordered 617 Squadron to load up the first Tallboys that had been stockpiled in great secrecy at Woodhall Spa. On the night of 8–9 June, twenty-five Lancasters, preceded by three of their Mosquito marking aircraft and four flare-dropping Lancasters from 83 Squadron, attacked the tunnel. Conditions in the clear night sky were favorable, marking was perfect, and twenty-three Lancasters dropped their Tallboys for the first time in the war. Some dropped directly on the markers at the mouth, causing great damage. However, pilot Joe McCarthy, an American on service with the RAF and a Dams Raid veteran, dropped his Tallboy seventy-five yards up the mountain side, a near miss. What happened next fully confirmed Barnes Wallis's theories. The bomb penetrated ninety feet of rock and earth and exploded directly over the tunnel ceiling. Ten thousand tons of mountain cascaded onto the tunnel. The Germans were still trying to dig it out nearly three months later when the entire battle front swept over them. The tunnel delivered the railway line immediately onto a large bridge across the Loire. Two Lancasters from 617 Squadron and the 83 Squadron "illuminating Lancasters" attacked that bridge with one-thousand-pound bombs at the conclusion of the Tallboy attack. This attack within an attack effectively destroyed the bridge and denied German reinforcements in Southern France the use of this strategically important rail line to Normandy. The feared armored division finally arrived in Normandy piecemeal and with worn equipment, having suffered breakdowns and aerial attacks along its wide detour. The Tallboys had been tested, and they had worked.[37]

It sometimes happens that a lack of experience or the introduction of a new factor in a plan upsets the entire scheme, and the participants have to rethink their original plans. This was not the case in the raid that took place over Le Havre. The forces of Bomber Command had assembled one by one the various components that would play a role in that unusual operation. The dropping of Tallboy was the last piece in the puzzle. Again 617 Squadron stood down, waiting for its next tactical assignment in support of the Normandy operations. That opportunity would come on the evening of 14 June 1944.

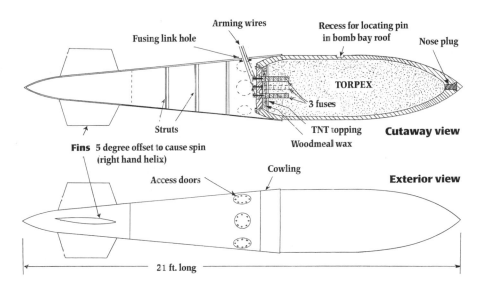

Fig. 5. 12,000 lb. MC deep-penetration bomb—"Tallboy"

Chapter **7**

Operation Neptune: Opening Moves

Nighty-Night

At 2059 hours on the evening of 5 June 1944, Admiral Theodor Krancke, commander in chief at the German Navy's Marine Gruppe West headquarters in Paris issued the code word *Körbchen*–literally translated as "little basket," but usually baby talk for "nighty-night"–to all his units on the coast from Boulogne at the narrowest part of the Channel up to Zeebrugge in Belgium. In other words, on that Monday evening the commander in chief of the Kriegsmarine in the West told a major part of his forces to lower their war readiness from condition two to condition three. They were to stand down. With an Allied invasion expected all during the glorious, sunny weeks of May, the German High Command had not bidden their forces "nighty-night" often that spring. However, the weather over Western Europe had been so violent since the previous weekend that Krancke felt they could relax a bit. After all, no one can remain forever vigilant. No doubt FdS Petersen and his staff in Scheveningen as well as crews from the E-boat Force in Boulogne, Rotterdam, and Ijmuiden chuckled at receiving beddy-byes from the Naval Commander in Chief West.[1]

At 0415 hours on the morning of that same day in an English trailer camp buffeted by sheets of rain, the Allied Supreme Commander, Gen. Dwight David Eisenhower, having heard all the arguments for and against the invasion, paused for a second, then said: "O.K. We'll go."[2]

With that final command, over 200,000 troops, loaded onto 6,000 fully manned ships, plus 12,000 aircraft and their crews, were set in motion toward the mainland of Europe. Operation Overlord and its gigantic naval tandem, Operation Neptune, had begun. They were not moving toward Boulogne in the Pas de Calais district, as might have been expected. They were aiming for the more distant beaches of Normandy where the forces of Hitler's Fortress Europe waited in fewer numbers and with fewer guns. Krancke's stand-down signal had not applied to the defenders in Normandy, and ostensibly at least, they remained at a higher state of readiness.

Darkness came, and despite sporadic German radar plots of surface ships out on the waters off the Normandy Coast, confused radio signals of sightings by German minesweepers, and scattered reports of parachute landings inland, the German operations rooms in Cherbourg and elsewhere did not issue an invasion alert until 0130 hours of 6 June. As late as 0328 the German Sea Defense Commandant of the Seine-Somme district at Le Havre was informing his colleague, the Sea Defense Commandant for Normandy, that the situation was "confused."[3] Even as he spoke, the first Allied boats were setting down on their designated beaches. Thousands of paratroopers were already scrambling over the ancient peninsula, forming up units against the German Wehrmacht. Against all odds the Allies had achieved tactical and strategic surprise. The liberation of Europe had begun.

The Spout

Planning staffs for the vast Operation Neptune, the naval operation that would shepherd SHAEF's forces across the Channel from British ports to the Far Shore, were determined to minimize the risks from German air and naval counterattack. They had organized themselves to provide maximum security against the Germans' once-dreaded U-boats, from their once-vaunted Luftwaffe, and now, following the disaster at Lyme Bay, from the Schnellbootwaffe, the German Navy's formidable E-boat Force. Therefore, plans for the disposition of the invasion fleet, intricately laid out by ANCXF Ramsay and his staff, had had a lengthy and intensively discussed evolution.[4]

From all the ports, estuaries, and coves on the South Coast of England, and even from ports as far away as Scotland and Northern Ireland, the ships emerged. The assault troops, concentrated in the South of England, would be taking the shortest sea voyage in order to avoid unnecessary risks. Lines of LSTs, LCTs, transports, warships of all sizes, tugs, ferries, and thousands more seacraft filed out of Plymouth, down the River Dart, from Brixham, Torquay, Exmouth, Portland, Weymouth, and Portsmouth, down the Solent past Southampton and around the Isle of Wight, out from Newhaven and the Nore and a hundred other places, all heading south. Instead of sailing individually or even in normal-size convoys from those many harbors directly across the Channel to the widely separated Normandy beaches, they organized themselves into a precisely delineated, carefully orchestrated sealink that required promptness, exact navigation, and excellent seamanship.

Moving along swept channels off the English coast, the giant convoys converged on "Point Z," a circular area of five sea miles thirteen miles south of the Isle of Wight. Point Z was also called "Piccadilly Circus," an apt name given the incredible volume of sea traffic that started to pass through it on the night of 5 June. Operation Neptune called for minesweepers to sweep five lanes through this crucial choke point, one for each of the task forces assigned to bring the troops to their respective beaches from west to east: Utah, Omaha, Gold, Juno, and Sword. The lanes broadened out slightly half way across the Channel into two lanes each, one for fast and the other for slow convoy traffic. They dubbed this passage across the English Channel "the Spout." The vulnerable Allied ships were under orders to stay within the Spout at all costs. As the ships approached the Normandy Coast, the swept lanes diverged again as each task force spread out, the Americans heading west, the British and Canadians east toward their assigned beaches. Task Force U, the Americans' westernmost advance, would proceed up to an invisible defensive line drawn through the waters just north of Utah Beach and called the Mason Line. Destroyers and coastal forces would patrol it constantly. Another line, which stretched eastward from it across the waters north of Omaha Beach and was called, predictably, the Dixon Line, was for Task Force O. The British task forces were doing the same. Some staffer, an exuberant angler no doubt, had designated their easternmost shoulder, over forty miles away from Utah off the mouth of the River Orne, the Trout Line. To the best of their ability the warships of the Western Naval Task Force from the American and Royal navies and the Eastern Naval Task Force of the British and Canadians would defend the invasion fleet in its passage from the English ports, through Piccadilly Circus, down the Spout to the beaches and back again while other warships pounded strongholds on the hostile shore. It was a system designed not for convenience or rapid passage but to deliver firepower at the sharp end and to ensure survival for the vulnerable transport vessels that shuttled back and forth across the Narrow Sea. The Allies' first priority was to achieve their lodgment on hostile soil. That accomplished, they had to achieve a rapid buildup of strength in Normandy. That, in turn, meant they had to secure the sealink that would allow the Allied Expeditionary Forces to gain strength faster than the Germans in the lodgment area.

Time was critical. They had to beat the Germans in the race of the buildup within a matter of weeks. If the Allies won the buildup, then they could force a breakthrough of German lines followed by a breakout into a Second Front. If they did not win, there would be no Second Front. The future of Europe and of civilization as the Allies knew it was riding on Neptune/Overlord. SHAEF and every member in the gigantic invasion effort, with the prayers of their respective nations behind them, had been concentrating hard in the months and weeks preceding its execution to make it work. The achievement of tactical and strategic surprise on 6 June was a promising first victory. Now, with the establishment of that vast sealink, they had to prepare for the inevitable German counterattack.

Initial Counterattacks

The first reaction by German naval units to the invasion came even later than that of the land forces. At 0348 and at 0352 hours the 5th Torpedo Flotilla and the 15th V (*Vorposten,* or picket) flotilla at Le Havre received signals from Marine Gruppe West ordering them to attack landing craft to the west off Port en Bessin and Grandcamp. Reduced in numbers by mines and bomb damage during the previous weeks, only four ships were combat ready: *Möwe, Jaguar, Falke,* and T-28 under T-boat Flotilla Commander Korvettenkapitän Heinrich Hoffmann. They passed the outer mole of Le Havre at 0442 on 6 June heading west toward the mightiest invasion fleet the world had ever seen. In what must have been one of the loneliest missions of the war, the nine-hundred-ton torpedo boats, which more closely resembled small Allied destroyers than torpedo boats, steamed westward from Le Havre undetected and enveloped themselves in a giant Allied smoke screen in the Seine Bay. When they emerged on the other side, the little flotilla immediately confronted a breathtaking sight: at least two capital ships, dozens of cruisers, scores of destroyers, and uncountable landing ships. Hoffmann radioed this information back to port, identifying the Allied fleet as concentrating off Ouistreham. Wasting no time, the German flotilla leader gave the command to fire at 0535. Wisely, the Germans dispensed with gunnery and loosed all torpedoes immediately. This was no puny gesture. They filled the area with eighteen of the deadly G-7a torpedoes, several of which narrowly missed battleships HMS *Ramillies* and HMS *Warspite*. Amazingly, the only casualty was a Norwegian destroyer, the *Svenner*. Struck amidships by one of the German "eels," she sank quickly. The German attackers had no time to observe the results. Harassed by a storm of heavy Allied naval shells that raised huge geysers all around them, Hoffmann's torpedo-boat flotilla prudently reversed course and headed back at maximum speed into harbor. From the first moment of contact with the enemy, German antiaircraft guns fired incessantly, beating off wave after wave of aerial attacks. In sixty minutes of frenzied action, they had expended all torpedoes and all ammunition. Miraculously, the 5th T-boat Flotilla passed back into Le Havre's great port unscathed. It was the German Navy's only combat on the first day of Operation Neptune.[5]

Meanwhile at Cherbourg, the E-boats of the 5th and 9th Flotillas received a signal from FdS Petersen to reconnoiter off the Cherbourg peninsula. Radar plotting had failed for the most part, and Petersen could offer no specific locations for his boats to search. Leading the 9th E-boat Flotilla, its sharp-eyed commander, Korvettenkapitän Freiherr Götz von Mirbach, looked around at his sleek boats. He was uneasy about the well-being of his neighbors, the seven boats of the 5th E-boat Flotilla. Usually commanded by an outstanding ace of the E-boat Force, Korvettenkapitän Bernd Klug, the 5th had a mint new commander now, Kapitänleutnant Kurt Johannsen. After four years of full-time operations at sea, Klug had finally conceded that his nerves were shot and that he could lead from the front no longer. With FdS Petersen's blessing, Klug departed that same day for duty on Petersen's staff at Scheveningen. Changing the guard at this moment with an invasion alert on was hardly ideal, but von Mirbach knew that Johannsen was an able officer and the men liked him. After a final check with the shore authorities he gave the command: *Seeklar.* They were ready to put to sea. A deep rumble of diesels filled the air, and at 0430 fifteen sleek E-boats arranged in two columns passed out beyond Cherbourg's outer harbor into the rough waters of the Channel, the 5th Flotilla heading northeast, the 9th northwest. Forewarned of reports about a huge invasion fleet, they immediately began looking for signs of the enemy.

Commanders Günther Rabe and Hans Schirren, veterans of many an action in the Channel during the previous two years, were among the files of E-boats departing Cherbourg that morning. They were troubled by the timing of this mission. Dawn was coming up, and while it was true that normally the nocturnal E-boats would be passing Cherbourg's digue, its outer breakwater, at about this time, the direction they were heading was wrong. They should be reentering harbor, not starting out. However, their orders were specific. FdS Petersen wanted a reconnaissance of the waters off Cherbourg, and he wanted it immediately. All serving members of the E-boat Force revered their senior officer. They knew that Petersen was not reckless and that he would not risk their lives needlessly. They repaid loyalty with loyalty this day. They also kept a sharp watch.

Despite their misgivings, the veteran E-boat crews at Cherbourg cruised peacefully off the Cotentin Peninsula for an hour and a half as teams of spotters on the bridges joined their commanders and scoured the skies and waters around them. To their surprise it was as if they had the ocean to themselves that morning. Not even the sharpest lookout encountered a single boat or ship on the water anywhere during the reconnaissance. The skies from which they feared sudden attack by their old nemesis, Coastal Command, remained empty. The horizon held no destroyer vectoring Britain's sea greyhounds, its MTBs, onto them. Baffled, but also relieved, the crews of the two flotillas turned south again, those of the 5th Flotilla passing under the guns of Battery Hamburg, the imposing coastal fort to the east of the city, bristling with four 280-mm cannons. By 0600 they were reentering Cherbourg's inner port, their unusual reconnaissance completed.[6]

That was the extent of German naval action on D-day, 6 June 1944. The Allies had truly caught the Germans by surprise. The OIC commented on the Cherbourg-based E-boat experience during the first crucial hours of the invasion. "Obviously they were searching blindly, and their return as early as 0600 was in keeping with the thoroughly abortive nature of this their first invasion sortie."[7] It was a stroke of luck that kept von Mirbach and his E-boats to the north. Had the two flotillas rounded the Cotentin Peninsula to the east and south that morning, they would have encountered Admiral Don Moon's Task Force U in full daylight. Such an encounter would have placed the E-boats in a hopeless tactical position. Allied naval and air power would have made short work of the German Navy's thin-skinned coastal craft, which depended almost exclusively on speed and the dark of night in order to survive.

On D+1 a second naval engagement amply demonstrated why the larger German war vessels were not the main naval threat to the Allies. At 0621 on 6 June Marine Gruppe West had ordered its heaviest surface units to make ready for a run to Cherbourg via Brest. These were the German

Navy's destroyers stationed in ports in the Bay of Biscay at Royan and at Bordeaux, and they included the Z-24, Z-32, and the ZH-1, formerly the Netherlands Royal Navy destroyer *Gerard Callenburgh,* but captured and refitted by the German Navy. Within one hour of that first signal, an Ultra message went out to the pertinent Allied naval and air commands alerting them to the destroyers' intentions. That afternoon the Bletchley Park listeners, keepers of the Ultra Secret, intercepted the word *Lebensfrage,* "matter of life," a codeword for a plan that the Allies knew meant a coordinated movement of destroyers from the Brittany ports and torpedo boats from Le Havre, probably with the intention of concentrating at Cherbourg. Subsequent intercepts fed the Allies with valuable information on the course and speed of the destroyers, and Coastal Command flew reconnaissance patrols in the designated area so that a "chance" sighting by aircraft would protect Ultra.

Using that alternate intelligence, burly twin-engined Beaufighters attacked destroyers Z-24 and ZH-1 forty miles south of St. Nazaire, causing light damage and slowing the destroyers' advance. This initial engagement demonstrated that Allied interception of larger, slower surface ships even at night was feasible. The two enemy destroyers entered Brest at 0415 on 7 June and spent the rest of that day repairing damage. There they were joined by the hastily repaired Z-32, which had slipped out of Bordeaux at a later time. At this point another development, later revealed by prisoner of war statements, showed how much importance the German Navy placed on this mission. The destroyers were conducting a second mission besides offensive operations. They were carrying supplies for the E-boat flotillas. ZH-1, for example, had a store of torpedoes for the E-boats. While some work parties labored to repair battle damage, other crews were distributing the scarce torpedoes among the three destroyers, four to each ship, as well as lubricating oil for the increasingly beleaguered E-boats at Cherbourg. The Germans had to be desperate, the Allies knew, if they were forcing their sleek destroyers to double as supply ships.

Another series of German naval signals proved that the three destroyers plus an 850-ton "Elbing" torpedo boat, T-24, would make their final run to Cherbourg that night. The orders were detailed and precise, and by 1911 hours that same evening the Allied command had read them all. Spotter aircraft "just happened" to pick them up off Ushant and vectored the Royal Navy's 10th Destroyer Flotilla from Plymouth onto the unsuspecting German ships. HMS *Tartar, Ashanti, Javelin,* HMCS *Eskimo, Haida,* and *Huron,* and Polish destroyers, ORP *Blyscawica,* and *Piorun* steamed south. During an intermittent night action from 0130 until nearly 0500 on 9 June, the Allied destroyers sank ZH-1. Z-32 ran aground and subsequently fell victim to aerial attack. It was not a one-sided victory. Flagship HMS *Tartar,* with Commander B. Jones, RN, aboard as senior officer, received heavy damage in the fierce engagement. Her crew suffered considerable casualties.[8]

The destroyer battle made one point clear. Germany's conventional warships could not complete their mission to Cherbourg. The undamaged Elbing and Z-24 retreated to Brest at 0610, the latter suffering from major damage that kept her in port until 16 June. Subsequently, they retreated to the Gironde where both ships finally succumbed to aerial bombardment on 24 August 1944. No German destroyer ever reached Cherbourg again. Even when making passage at twenty-seven knots, these larger German surface units were unable to operate even at night in the face of the Allied warships gathered to protect Operation Neptune. Trying to pit the strength of main force units against the Allied armada was obviously a losing proposition.[9]

The other significant naval arm that the Allies feared, German U-boats, fared almost as poorly as its destroyer force. A total of nine *Schnorchel* boats, U-boats fitted with snorkel devices for underwater breathing, had departed from the Bay of Biscay following the invasion, a move carefully monitored by the listeners at Bletchley Park and the OIC trackers at the Admiralty. Fully alerted to the danger, by 10 June the Allies' intense air and naval searches had sunk one U-boat. Two more limped into Brest badly damaged. Yet another had turned south again toward the Biscay ports with major damage, and one lonely U-boat entered St. Peter Port on the Isle of Guernsey with empty batteries on 13 June. Only one U-boat actually reached its assigned patrol station off the Isle of Wight by 15 June; another attacked a target of opportunity well south of its patrol area, sinking HMS *Blackwood* off Cap de la Hague on that same day. But that same German submarine sustained such heavy damage in the counterattack that it immediately retreated to Brest. That one action and the sinking of an American LST off Cap Barfleur, also on 15 June, were the sole U-boat accomplishments during the first three weeks following the invasion. Any boats that made it into the area were so constantly and intensively harassed by Allied antisubmarine forces that they were forced to retreat within hours or days back to the Atlantic ports. Under any conditions, the shallow, confined waters of the Channel were unfavorable for submarines, and Operation Neptune increased the risks enormously. No other U-boats, coming in from the Atlantic or from other points, were able to enter the Channel again until 25 June, and when they finally did, the Allies were ready for them. While the German Navy had nonsnorkel U-boats in the

Biscay ports, it did not try to employ them even in its moment of desperation, knowing that such a gesture was suicidal. The ineffective U-boat response was roughly comparable to the Luftwaffe's efforts, which consisted of dropping some mines at night.[10]

The Luftwaffe of June 1944 was a wraith. While German responses to the Canadian raid on Dieppe had demonstrated German dominance of the skies over the Continent in 1942, its virtual nonappearance over Normandy in June 1944 was the product of an intensive and lengthy Allied aerial campaign that had already cost the lives of thousands of young Allied airmen. Now the effects of that campaign were clear. With most of its airfields in Western France interdicted and the bulk of its experienced pilots killed, wounded, transferred inland to defend the Reich, or shipped in desperation to the Eastern Front, the Luftwaffe could barely operate. Its daytime fighters mounted a few isolated strafing runs over the Normandy fleet and then disappeared. German records for Luftflotte 3 claimed to have mounted 250 sorties, but most German troops on land were adamant in claiming afterward that they never once saw their own aircraft overhead. Even the respected night fighters failed them. Elaborate Allied deceptions lured them hundreds of miles away to the north, far removed from the fleets of vulnerable glider tugs and troop transports concentrating over two special places on the Normandy battlefield, the Orne River north of Caen for the British 6th Airborne Division, and the Cotentin Peninsula for the American 82d and 101st Airborne Divisions. From the opening minutes of the invasion, the Allies achieved air supremacy, an accomplishment that General Eisenhower had predicted and one that lay at the heart of his conviction that Operation Overlord was a sound military undertaking. The tepid response of the Luftwaffe on D-day fully confirmed Eisenhower's assumptions.[11]

The Land Battle, 6–26 June 1944

The Allies were surprised to learn from survivors of the destroyer clash of 8–9 June that the German Navy had tried to run supplies of torpedoes and lubricants for E-boats into Cherbourg aboard its destroyers. Were they already running low on critical stores? If so, why were they resorting to chancy waterborne supply runs instead of using overland routes into their strategically placed naval base, a base they knew to be the most effective launching platform for operations for the E-boat Force?

The American command's preoccupation with the Cotentin Peninsula was not hard to discern. They badly wanted its deepwater port, Cherbourg. Recognizing its importance for the rapid buildup of supplies for the invasion forces, Generals Eisenhower and Bradley had decided relatively late in their planning to enlist the aid of an experienced corps commander who had made a name for himself in the Pacific as a dynamic leader who reached his objectives in a hurry: Lt. Gen. J. Lawton Collins. "Lightning Joe," as his loyal troops called him, was fresh from victories in Guadalcanal; following his temporary leave in Washington in December 1943, he had been transferred to Europe at Eisenhower's request. The move had required the approval of General Marshall. Collins arrived in England to take command of his soon-to-be famous VII Corps in January 1944 and immediately set about intensively training his troops. Now, six months later, he stood with his men at a rail aboard Adm. Don F. Moon's command ship, the USS *Bayfield,* when at 0220 hours on D-day the anchor chains of Task Force U's transport rattled onto the ocean floor off Utah Beach. Admiral Moon and General Collins gave the order for their shipborne forces to prepare to land three hours later. They hoped the assault waves would quickly link up with the eighteen battalions of paratroopers who were already ashore. No one had received any word of their fate throughout the night of 5–6 June. Collins could only pray that they were safe and accomplishing their mission.[12]

While it was obvious that Cherbourg, nestled between hills on the northernmost coast of the peninsula, was the prize that made an expedition so far to the west in Normandy worthwhile, the problem was how best to capture the large port quickly, with the least casualties, and without dangerously dividing the invading forces from their respective beachheads. The Dieppe disaster two years earlier had taught the Allies not to attack a fortified coastal town frontally. It was better to try the oblique approach. The Americans would land on a weakly defended coastal stretch somewhere else and take Cherbourg from the rear. SHAEF's planners had devoted considerable attention to this problem in the months preceding Operation Overlord. They studied the Cotentin Peninsula closely in relation to the other beachheads being planned for Normandy proper, stretching eastward to Caen. Then they made some crucial decisions.

The Cotentin Peninsula is a broad neck of land jutting north from Normandy out into the Channel, with some odd geographic features that could limit military operations. At its base, thirty miles south of the northern tip, two small rivers, the Douve and the Merderet, converge from the west and north, respectively. Once joined, they flow eastward through Carentan, at that time a small town and a desirable communications hub. East of Carentan the Douve becomes a tidal estuary that bends gently north again, flowing into the waters of the Seine Bay and forming a natural boundary between the Cotentin Peninsula and the rest of Normandy. The land that abuts the two streams is flat and unwooded. To the west and north, the bottomland rises gradually into hedgerow country, those remarkable, eccentrically shaped fields first formed by Normans a thousand years ago out of mounded up earth and hedges with which they and succeeding generations fenced livestock and tamed the constant westerlies that sweep in from the sea.

From the air the bocage, as the French call it, looks like a patchwork quilt. To Allied soldiers on the ground it posed awesome military obstacles. German soldiers complained about the bocage too, but its hedges significantly strengthened the German defense. Hedgerows predominate in the middle of the peninsula, but the outstanding feature of the southeastern base of the Cotentin is its many marshes. In the spring of 1944 the German occupiers had flooded the marshy river valleys as a precautionary measure; bands of shallow water as much as a mile wide and five or six feet deep inundated the river valleys for many miles. Those water barriers were just as formidable as the hedgerows on dry land. Even less promising from the Allied point of view, similar marshy areas closer to the east coast largely separated the beaches from the mainland; only a series of narrow causeways linked them to solid ground. The tidal estuary of the Douve effectively cut off the Cotentin Peninsula from the rest of Normandy, a potential threat for the Americans, who hoped to link up their two beachheads quickly before that skilled opportunist, Erwin Rommel, could pour a counterattack into the gap. Although it looked broad at its base, fully half of the Cotentin Peninsula of 1944 was taken up by these soggy geographical features. Given the land's peculiarities, German military surveyors had good reasons for considering the southeastern beaches of the Cotentin Peninsula to be unpromising terrain for an Allied landing.[13]

Precisely for that reason the SHAEF planners had given meticulous attention to a surprise attack on a weakly defended stretch of sand on that selfsame coast. A successful lodgment there would require quick action by shipborne troops on the beach to race inland. However, there were sharp limits on what even the fastest invaders could accomplish from the seaward side. Rather than allowing the German defenders several hours to block the crucial causeways, the SHAEF planners decided to drop two full divisions, 13,600 men of the 82d and 101st Airborne divisions, several miles inland. These troops were to secure the causeways and seize bridgeheads over the Douve and Merderet rivers. They would wrest a precarious hold until relieved by the heavier units of the VII Corps rolling in from the shore. The plan seemed workable, but it needed seasoned troops to execute it. That was why General Collins had worked his VII Corps so hard at Slapton Sands and elsewhere. That was why the Americans had engaged in the expensive and exhausting amphibious exercises in Lyme Bay even though the practice beaches and adjoining waters lay in an active war zone. As Collins well knew, a tragic consequence of that calculated risk had been the loss of 749 soldiers and sailors, most of them 4th Infantry Division soldiers, drowned off Slapton Sands.

Now, five weeks later, that same division, reinvigorated and safely transported by Rear Admiral Moon's Force U, stood off Utah Beach waiting for H-hour. Led by Maj. Gen. Raymond O. "Tubby" Barton, the division comprised VII Corps' spearhead on that fateful morning. They were about to place two battalions of troops on Utah Beach at 0630 hours.

The seas that morning had scarcely had time to calm following the storm. Conditions were especially rough to leeward from the eastern coast, and the troops aboard the small landing craft had to endure six-foot waves. Two special craft, with navigational equipment that was expected to position the incoming waves accurately, foundered in the heavy chop. Such incidents, seemingly trivial in themselves, often precede disaster. This time the results were fortuitous. Strong currents and winds thrust the assault troops two thousand yards to the south of their intended landing spot, and smoke from the air and naval bombardment limited visibility. The task force's miscalculation in navigation set the landing force down on a lightly defended stretch of beach, a mile south of a German stronghold that contained many more mines and obstacles. Prior to the invasion, the planned beachhead had looked more promising to invader and defender alike. By sheer chance on this morning the Americans sideslipped it.[14]

Among the soldiers in the first wave was an arthritic assistant division commander, Brig. Gen. Theodore Roosevelt, son of the former president and, at age fifty-seven, an unlikely figure to be leading twenty-year-old assault troops. Limping ashore under German shelling with his famous cane, Roosevelt looked around the chaotic scene along with the youngsters around him. They were baffled as they surveyed the unfamiliar features of the beach. Ignoring the confusion all around him, General Roosevelt searched with glasses for familiar landmarks, probed his memory as well, and then concluded—correctly—that they were about a mile south of the original landing site. Then he made a snap decision. A veteran of the North African and Sicilian landings in which far more confusion had reigned, he knew that the first wave had landed in good order. That was a major accomplishment in itself. He also knew that it would take precious time to reboard and move north. Besides, delays could cause chaos among the follow-on troops, stacked up in wave formations out on the water. The 4th Infantry Division and the VII Corps behind it would, Roosevelt concluded, begin the liberation of Europe from the spot where they had just landed. Roosevelt's cool reactions and sober judgment were exactly what were needed at that moment as the green troops milled about in the sand and anxious senior commanders waited uncomprehendingly offshore. Soon, waves of troops, engineers, and heavy equipment began pouring in on "Utah Beach South." The results bore out Roosevelt's decision. Force U suffered only two hundred casualties that entire day, including twelve men killed. If good fortune had abandoned the American 4th Division on Lyme Bay, it put in a timely appearance five weeks later on an obscure shore of the Cotentin Peninsula.[15]

From the outset, General Roosevelt's sound tactical decision set the tone for the entire campaign by VII Corps under its able commander. Lt. Gen. Joseph "Lightning Joe" Collins had earned his moniker in the Pacific. He was about to validate its pertinence in Europe. He was an aggressive, hard-driving leader who held the confidence of his men as well as his superiors. Those were exactly the qualities Generals Eisenhower and Bradley were looking for. The sooner Collins and his VII Corps took Cherbourg, they reasoned, the faster the buildup phase would proceed.[16]

The question was, once ashore would the 4th Division be able to advance over the constricting causeways west of the beach? Or would they be confronted by four killing zones dominated by the German Wehrmacht? The German Army was always a stout enemy on defense, and its leaders had sound military reasons for assuming an Allied landing would take place elsewhere.

It took several hours for the initial waves to organize themselves for an advance and to accumulate armored vehicles and assault guns. Engineers frantically cleared mines and bulldozed access ramps out of the sandy beaches and through the sea walls, linking the invaders to the roads. By noon, under "Tubby" Barton's impatient gaze, they moved westward, facing whatever destiny awaited them on the bare, coverless causeways flanked by brackish water on either side. Neither Barton nor anyone else from the landing party had had any radio communication with the airborne troops. No one could predict what kind of reception was awaiting them half a mile to the west.

Barton had chosen his ablest officer, Col. James Van Fleet, and his well-practiced 8th Infantry Regiment to be the point for his spearhead in the amphibious assault. As the troops and vehicles ventured out onto the cambered ribbons of road, the soldiers slogged in front of and alongside

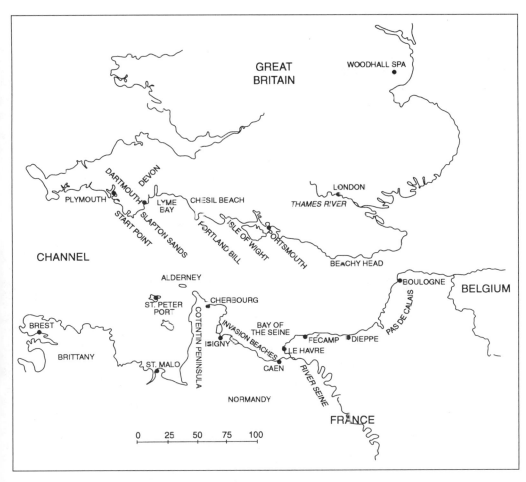

Map 2. Neptune/Overlord area of operations

their vehicles, while mechanized crews peered from turrets and through slits. They were waiting for the telltale flashes of German guns across the marshes to the west. Those flashes would translate seconds later into high-velocity shells exploding in their midst. Some troops began to run forward.

To general amazement, Van Fleet's infantrymen poured over all four causeways unopposed. No one spotted German infantry, and enemy artillery fire was distant and desultory. Instead, on the opposite side troopers of the 101st Airborne Division were there to greet them. It was the same on all four causeways. The VII Corps linkup had begun, and the Utah beachhead was off to a propitious start as Van Fleet's forces, reinforced by further infantry and mechanized units of the 4th Infantry Division, surged onto solid land, looking for airborne pockets to the west and to the north where the widely scattered troopers of the 101st and 82d Airborne divisions had descended the night before.[17]

Until that moment there had been great concern about the wisdom of dropping two full divisions of lightly armed paratroopers onto the water-streaked Cotentin Peninsula, but General Bradley, hardly known as a butcher of men, had been adamant. Even if the young troopers took heavy casualties, he felt, their sacrifices would save many thousands of lives if the Allies could get inland across those dangerous choke points that looked so much like the causeways the troops had come to know on the English South Coast. Even so, for troops facing combat for the first time, Slapton Sands must have seemed a lifetime away.

Although taken by surprise, the German defenders quickly realized that the Americans had landed on the Cotentin Peninsula in strength. They also grasped immediately that the invaders' goal was to seize Cherbourg. Counterattacks were not long in coming. By turns Hitler, Rommel, and Krancke had all felt uneasy about Normandy and its northernmost peninsula. They had already positioned two static divisions, the 709th Infantry in the east and the 243d Infantry in the west, then added the more mobile 91st to the list of defenders, reinforcing it with tough young soldiers from the 6th Parachute Regiment, which they placed in Carentan. The German high command also ordered in the 206th Panzer Battalion and organized a Seventh Army Sturm Battalion to operate as an armored reserve in addition to several other detachments. If the Americans secured a lodgment on the shore, these large forces of the German Seventh Army could be expected to offer a vigorous response.[18]

Given the Germans' increased troop concentrations, the allocation of the 82d Airborne as a blocking force to the west and north, plus the 101st as a link to the causeways with blocking forces to the south, proved to be a wise precaution. Bradley's decision also carried with it great sacrifice. The fighting that followed was bloody and desperate, but the actions of the paratroopers, alone and in small groups, achieved their goal of speeding the advance of VII Corps. The paratroopers landed in sufficient concentration at the right places to confuse the German defenders and disrupt their counterattacks long enough for VII Corps to link up and generate offensive power.

Throughout the dark early hours of 6 June, on into the first full day of the invasion, and then into a second night, paratroopers, reinforced here and there by gliderborne assault troops, pulled themselves together. Despite the wide scattering of units over many miles of the Cotentin Peninsula, despite scores of watery deaths, despite the loss of most of their heavy equipment and virtually all of their radios, the surviving airborne and glider troops fought off disorientation and loneliness. Men without officers and officers without men formed themselves into scratch units and struggled toward their objectives. Rigorous conditioning and training, including a premium placed upon self-reliance, helped them cope with the dangers all around them. One of their improvisations was a toy metal cricket issued to each soldier, which he could click and receive two clicks from fellow parachutists in return. That night, in a scenario made familiar to later generations by a film re-creation, the crickets sounded softly but repeatedly throughout the landing zones as knots of men stumbled together, recognized each other's distinctive signals, and moved out to secure their objectives.

They outfought their enemy. Scores of confused and deadly night actions found them seizing the initiative. Whether they encountered the static forces, more mobile units like the 91st Division, or the fearless seventeen- and eighteen-year-olds of the German 6th Parachute Regiment, the American airborne forces fought them to a standstill, and then pushed them back.[19]

A Wehrmacht officer acting as commander of the 6th Parachute Regiment while his superiors were in Rennes attending a war game was Oberstleutnant Baron Friedrich von der Heydte, a tough professional soldier and decorated veteran who had seen extensive service in all theaters including the Eastern Front. Baron von der Heydte was a formidable leader in combination with his youthful soldiers. Intelligent, aggressive, and experienced, he was just the kind of old hand in charge of fearless teenage troops whom the Allies most dreaded during their first tentative hours ashore. Alerted early on to the danger of invasion, von der Heydte had mounted a motorcycle and ridden north from Carentan to the picturesque little village of Ste. Marie du Mont near the coast. With the coming of dawn he clambered up the village's tall church steeple and gazed out toward the coast. What he saw made him draw in his breath. Hundreds of Allied ships dotted the horizon, and scores of landing vessels were shunting back and forth conveyorlike from ship to shore. Von der Heydte lowered his gaze. There, snaking its way toward him was one of the crucial causeways. Only days earlier artillerists had sited a battery of four cannon about a mile away at a place called Brécourt Manor to deny the Americans that very causeway, but all was quiet around him. Hurriedly, he climbed down, raced back to Carentan, and ordered a battalion of his own troops plus artillerymen toward Ste. Marie du Mont as well as to the battery of four 10.5-cm guns. They would force the Americans back onto the beach and pound them mercilessly.

Unbeknownst to Oberstleutnant von der Heydte, a few scattered Americans, including Lt. Richard Winters and nine enlisted men of Company E, 506th Regiment, 101st Airborne Division, were taking cover behind a hedgerow a few hundred yards from that same battery. When its guns started firing, a company officer appeared and informed Lieutenant Winters that their battalion was scattered and it needed to consolidate in order to guard against the counterattacks that were sure to come. There were no men to spare, he said. Winters and his improvised squad would have to silence the guns without help even though the Germans had them fully manned and defended by fifty of von der Heydte's parachutists. Armed with two light machine guns, a 60-mm mortar, some grenades, rifles, and an odd assortment of their usual infantry weapons, the untried troopers set to work.

With Winters in the lead, they divided themselves into three teams and used the fire and maneuver tactics taught them since the beginning of their airborne training. Eschewing heroics, the soldiers placed covering fire for each other. One element, after creeping up under cover, inundated the closest emplacement with grenades. Meanwhile another component poured in rifle fire from another direction, and within minutes the newly initiated squad had knocked out its first cannon. Having penetrated the Germans' protective trenches, the soldiers from Company E continued their advance using the same tactics. A second gun fell as its surviving crew fled. Then another succumbed and in short order another. In the end, all fifty of the 6th Regiment defenders and the artillery teams had either fled, fallen wounded, or died in the engagement, defeated by an attacker less than a fourth their strength. The tiny unit took its losses too: four dead and two wounded. But their actions ensured that the soldiers of the 4th Infantry Division rolled with minimal losses off Utah Beach, over the causeways, and onto the solid ground that allowed them the maneuvering room to prepare their forces and mount their attacks.[20]

Such small unit actions were the rule in those first crucial days of the invasion. Two other actions epitomized the effort and the cost needed to expand the landing zones into a genuine front: the assault over the La Fiere Causeway and the taking of Carentan at the base of the Cotentin Peninsula where a crucial linkup occurred between the American VII Corps from Utah Beach and the American V Corps from Omaha Beach.

With communications often lacking and coordination impossible, the green American forces seized bridgeheads, abandoned them, then returned only to find them in determined German hands again. Confusion characterized both sides, but it was the Americans who gained the tenuous footholds that counted most. Forced by the unfavorable terrain into frontal assaults over bare roads with swamps on either side, the lightly armed troops took their casualties by the hundreds, and they inflicted them by the hundreds on the stout German defenders. Despite fierce fighting, including counterattacks that occasionally saw hand-to-hand fighting with the bayonet, the American land forces on the Cotentin Peninsula survived the hundred miniature battles on the causeways and among the hedgerows and forced the Germans back. They blocked counterattacks from the north and south and maintained their bridgeheads over the Douve and Merderet rivers.[21]

As a result of their efforts singly and in small groups, they held vital territory long enough for heavier armed units from the sealift to come inland in good order. General Barton's 4th Infantry and Gen. Manton Eddy's battle-hardened 9th Infantry divisions, followed by newer, untested divisions, the 79th and 90th, used the airborne troopers' springboard to undertake further advances. Nevertheless, conditions tested all of the combatants severely. The poorly prepared 90th Division performed so badly that General Collins withdrew it from the front for retraining under new leadership. Eventually, it became an excellent division, but its initial failure on the Cotentin Peninsula demonstrated the ferocity of the fighting with which only well-trained troops could cope.

By 10 June the forces on Utah Beach were beginning to contact units from the American V Corps from Omaha Beach. They had established a solid linkup by the evening of 12 June when airborne and infantry units finally drove the stubborn 6th Parachutists out of Carentan. This feat meant a contiguous Allied beachhead all the way from the Cotentin to Caen. By seizing Carentan, they set the stage for further moves south and west and made German counterattacks much more difficult. All around the perimeter, VII Corps reinforced the paratroopers' bridgeheads. By 13 June the Americans on the Cotentin Peninsula under General Collins were ready to jump off in three directions, two of which could easily spell the doom of Cherbourg as a German base.

Individual initiatives taken in the first hours of Operation Overlord later proved strategically significant. Long before the VII Corps began its exploitation phase from the initial landings, the first troops on French soil made gains that had a direct bearing on the naval war, which continued unabated out on the Channel. One site in particular, Ste. Mère Eglise, which the Allies had chosen as a key center for the initial 82d Airborne Division landing, proved in the hours and days following the invasion to have a significance far beyond what the Allies had anticipated.

In the early hours of 6 June, Lt. Col. Edward Krause, commanding the Third Battalion, 505th Regiment of the 82d Airborne, landed a mile west of Ste. Mère Eglise in the exact field assigned to him—a rarity that night. He assembled his men quickly and with the help of a friendly, if tipsy, Frenchman, they learned that the German occupiers of the village were now transport troops rather than frontline infantry. Maintaining silence, the paratroopers advanced along hedgerows into the town, which had witnessed a fire earlier that night. In its glow the German garrison had slaughtered a number of American paratroopers during their descent and assumed they had beaten back a raid. Amazingly, the Germans had gone back to bed. As dawn approached, all was peaceful in Ste. Mère Eglise. Krause detached six patrols and posted them around the town. When everyone was in place, he crept alone into the village at first light and found a utility building near the central square. Aware that the newly liberated village was a main conduit for communications, Krause spotted a large line emerging next to a building. He had located the central cable connections that ran through the town. Raising his spade, the airborne officer swung it down onto the central cable point, which parted quickly. That blow cut off all land lines between Cherbourg and the rest of France. FdS Petersen in the Netherlands never knew of Colonel Krause or vice versa. But the latter had just dealt the former a heavy blow. If the German Navy or any other forces in Cherbourg wanted to communicate with their higher commands, they would have to use radio communication thereafter, unaware of the listeners at Bletchley Park two hundred miles away who were busily taking down five-letter groups of signals as the German High Command desperately tried to maintain control of its forces. Colonel Krause's singular act marked the beginning of Cherbourg's doom as a base of German operations.[22]

Starting with the same airborne assault at 0115 hours, other American forces fell astride the only first-class road in the Cotentin Peninsula, the hard-surface Route Nationale 13, which connected Cherbourg with Normandy and the rest of France. They set up road blocks. Troopers from the 82d and 101st also landed in sizable numbers on top of and beside a raised railroad embankment that snaked through the watery areas of their landing zone. The raised railway attracted them like a magnet because in some places it was the driest spot for miles. This was no rail spur. It was, in fact, the main double-trunk line of the national railway that also stretched north from Carentan up the Douve and Merderet river valleys to Cherbourg. With both the railway and the auto route under their control, the two airborne divisions put a halt to German traffic over those two crucial transportation arteries even as they interdicted the Germans' previously secure landlines. There were a few small roads to the west and a rambling light track that meandered that way too, but the main transportation arteries that led through Normandy to Caen and on to Paris were permanently lost to the Germans. That had not been the troopers' main concern upon landing, but the interdiction, so soon in the battle, of vital communications links proved to have far-ranging results.

As VII Corps hastened up the Cotentin Peninsula in the vain hope of gaining an intact port, it unwittingly began denying use of that port to the Germans. Although not obvious at first, critical supplies, including naval stores, mines, torpedoes, ammunition, fuel, and spare parts ceased flowing overland to Cherbourg from the opening moments of Operation Neptune/Overlord. The German Navy was finding it increasingly difficult to operate from what had been the main base of operations for the E-boat Force. The German High Command was determined to deny the use of Cherbourg to the Allies, but two could play the same game.[23]

The Americans paid a high price for their efforts. The troopers and infantrymen of VII Corps suffered nearly three thousand men dead and another ten thousand wounded, captured, or missing. Most of the latter found watery, unmarked graves in the marshes and inundations of the Cotentin Peninsula. Stalled temporarily in its northern drive, the VII Corps under its able commander cut through to the west, sealing off the Cotentin Peninsula at its base by the morning of 18 June. That move ended any hope of retreat for the Germans caught north of the new battle lines. Without pause the VII Corps veterans wheeled north; their advance was relentless. A week later, following an old-fashioned naval bombardment by U.S. battleships, cruisers, and destroyers on Cherbourg's outlying coastal guns, they captured the port on 26 June and took thirty-nine thousand Germans prisoner. The 4th Infantry Division concluded its part in the bloody campaign by surrounding Battery Hamburg and silencing the three giant guns that had survived the naval bombardment. Unfortunately, no miracle attended Cherbourg's deliverance. Obeying Hitler's personal orders, its military commanders, Gen. Karl von Schlieben and Adm. Walther Hennecke, supervised the systematic destruction of the great port.

Nevertheless, the Americans' arrival warranted a victory celebration. A day after his arrival in Cherbourg, VII Corps Commander Collins strode up the steps of the Hotel de Ville and turned in front of the commanders of his airborne and infantry divisions. Speaking in rusty but passable French, he presented a tricolor made from paratroopers' silk to Mayor Paul Reynaud as the citizens of Cherbourg mingled with American troops drawn from throughout the victorious VII Corps including the triumphant 4th Infantry Division. German shells dropped near them, but no one moved. With dignity Mayor Reynaud thanked General Collins as hundreds of Cherbourgeois wept openly and unashamedly. They had good reason. Cherbourg was the first major city of France to be liberated.[24]

That happy event was the culmination of weeks of hard fighting that had already begun to influence developments on the water well before General Collins's gallant gesture on the steps of the Hotel de Ville. It was the strangling of Cherbourg's lifelines on the Cotentin Peninsula, a process that had begun within the first minutes of D-day, that had destroyed its usefulness to the Germans. Within days German naval prisoners, survivors of the destroyer duel, revealed to their captors the German Navy's desperate efforts to resupply its E-boats by water. Increased German signals traffic began to show unmistakable signs of trouble for the feared 5th and 9th E-boat flotillas at the western end of the Channel as well. Long before the besieged Germans at Cherbourg surrendered, they had begun to feel the effects of the land battle to the south. The Americans on land had helped break off one of Germany's naval pincers and in so doing had added greatly to the defense of the Normandy Invasion Fleet.

On the afternoon of 14 June 1944, RAF ground crews began loading Tallboy
bombs into 617 Squadron Lancaster bombers for a rare daylight raid on Le Havre.
(Imperial War Museum)

This is probably S-63 on a training mission with the E-boat Force *Schulflottille* in the Baltic Sea. (Bibliothek für Zeitgeschichte in Stuttgart/Hans Schirren)

Günther Rabe, "the Raven," commanded S-130. He led it and two other E-boats on a miniature "Channel dash" on the night of 24–25 June 1944. (Courtesy of Günther Rabe)

Hans Schirren usually commanded S-145, but on 14 June he was in temporary command of S-144 when debris trapped it under a floating dock. Schirren and his crew steered the neighboring S-167 out of Le Havre's harbor as the second Allied raid began. (Courtesy of Hans Schirren)

The Royal Air Force attracted volunteers from throughout the British Commonwealth, as well as from the United States. Big Joe McCarthy's 617 Squadron crew assembled for this photo at RAF Scampton in June 1943. *Left to right:* George Johnson, RAF, bomb aimer; Don McLean, RCAF, navigator; Ron Batson, RAF, mid-upper gunner; Big Joe McCarthy, American in RCAF, pilot; William Radcliffe, Canadian in RAF, engineer; Ron Eaton, RAF, wireless operator. Rear Gunner David Rodger, RCAF, was absent. (Courtesy of *London Daily Mail*)

Navigator Tom Bennett *(left)* and Pilot Gerry Fawke stand in front of their 617 Squadron Mosquito marker aircraft at Woodhall Spa in the summer of 1944. (Courtesy of Tom Bennett)

Pilot Nick Knilans volunteered for the RCAF, transferred to the RAF, then by special arrangement became a USAAF lieutenant while serving with 617 Squadron for the duration of the war. (Courtesy of H. "Nick" Knilans)

In 1926 the German Navy tested "Bodo," an experimental fast boat. It was often commanded by Reservist Eduard Rabe, whose son, Günther, occasionally joined him on board. Later, Günther Rabe joined the E-boat Force, assuming the moniker "the Raven." (Courtesy of Günther Rabe)

These prewar E-boats had the Lürssen Yard's fast planing hull and "effect" rudders. Their bows and superstructure, an older, less successful design, were replaced from S-26 onward with a higher forecastle and covered torpedo tubes. (National Archives)

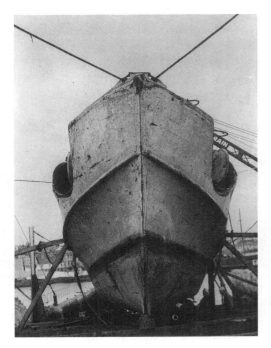

This front view of a prize E-boat, soon to be sent to the USSR, shows its displacement-like hull. It was photographed on 14 May 1945 at Devonport Yard. (Bibliothek für Zeitgeschichte)

This rear view of an E-boat details the main rudder and the two "effect," or side, rudders in relation to the boat's three screws. (Bibliothek für Zeitgeschichte)

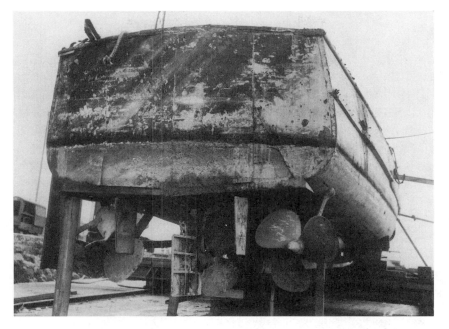

This rear view of an E-boat details its flat hull in the stern, in addition to its triple rudders and screws. (Bibliothek für Zeitgeschichte)

Right: Two S-26 class boats at den Hoofden, the Netherlands, 6 May 1941. At the stern of each are mines. (Bibliothek für Zeitgeschichte)

Two 1944 boats with rounded skullcap bridges in a Channel or North Sea port, 26 March 1944. (Bibliothek für Zeitgeschichte)

A late-war E-boat, S-201, displays the armored skullcap bridge that became standard in 1944, as well as the mount for the forward 20-mm Oerlikon cannon between the torpedo tubes. (Bibliothek für Zeitgeschichte)

In 1941 MTBs from Britain's coastal forces severely damaged S-111 and boarded her; however, she sank under tow. Note RN battle ensign. (National Archives)

On 13 May 1945 this late-war E-boat pulled into Felixstowe to surrender and to provide minefield charts. Several staff officers, including Operations Officer Bernd Rebensburg, were on her bridge. (Imperial War Museum)

Accompanied by coastal forces MTBs, this late-war E-boat crossed the Channel on 13 May 1945 for internment. (Imperial War Museum)

LST 507 crossing the Atlantic with an LCT piggy-backed aboard. LST 507 was the first ship in Convoy T-4 attacked by E-boats in Lyme Bay on the night of 27–28 April 1944. (National Archives)

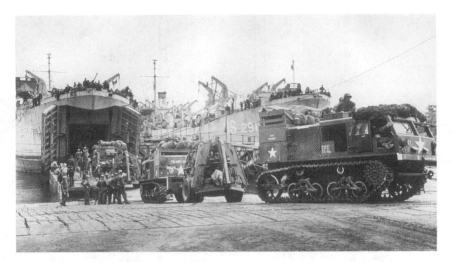

LSTs with flat bottoms, clam-shell doors, and steel-reinforced decks proved they could receive heavy combat equipment in British ports, roll it off on open beaches in France, dry out on a falling tide, then refloat for another voyage. (National Archives)

LST 283 enters the Channel at the mouth of a river for exercises in the spring of 1944. The Allies had to conduct their practices in an active war zone, and the Americans aboard three LSTs paid a high price off Slapton Sands on 28 April 1944. (National Archives)

Two LSTs carrying barrage balloons enter the Channel for amphibious exercises leading up to the Normandy Invasion. (National Archives)

Badly damaged by the E-boat attack in Lyme Bay, LST 289 limped back into port under tow by her two LCVPs. Thirteen men died at their stations on the 40-mm gun pan on her stern. (National Archives)

LST 289 rests in Dartmouth harbor after being attacked in Lyme Bay. (National Archives)

Wounded and dead from the Lyme Bay disaster are offloaded from an LST at one of the Channel ports on 28 April 1944. (National Archives)

Every port, fishing village, cove, and estuary on Britain's South Coast looked like this on the eve of the Normandy Invasion. The Germans would have plenty of targets on D-day. (National Archives)

Rear Adm. Alan G. Kirk, USN, on the bridge of his command ship, USS *Augusta*, before the Normandy Invasion. He called attention to the E-boat threat and pressured SHAEF to do more to protect the invasion fleet. (National Archives)

View from a Mulberry, or artificial harbor, onto Omaha Beach. The Allies expected it and the British Mulberry at Arromanches to ease off-loading, but they proved vulnerable to the weather. (National Archives)

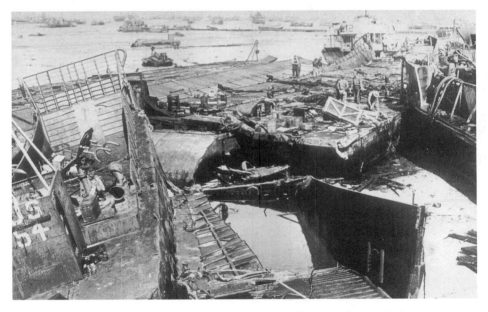

The gale of 19–22 June 1944 wrecked this American Mulberry and severely damaged the British one. With harbors like Cherbourg and Le Havre demolished, the Allies were heavily dependent on LSTs and other landing vessels to place cargoes on open beaches. (National Archives)

U.S. soldiers taking German prisoners at fortresses around Cherbourg on 26 June
1944. Cherbourg's capture eased Allied efforts to defend the invasion fleet.
(National Archives)

This secret prewar German photograph of Le Havre, taken by German photoreconnaissance expert Theodor Rowehl in 1938, details all targets of military value. The Allies referred to such representations as "Dick Tracy" photographs. (National Archives)

RAF 542 Squadron took this aerial reconnaissance photograph of Le Havre on 3 February 1943 when pens on its Mole Centrale neared completion. Other features included a floating dock in the Bassin Theophile, the Gare Maritime at top, and the prewar wreck *Paris* lying on its side. (National Archives)

By midwar, Allied photoreconnaissance and photointerpretation surpassed German efforts. This targeting photograph shows Le Havre with completed pens on the eve of the invasion. (National Archives)

This bomb damage assessment photograph shows Le Havre at low tide on 15 June 1944. A giant crater below the pens marks a Tallboy impact. Left of the smoke pall, a coastal craft has been thrown up onto the quay, evidence of a violent wave. The floating dock is half submerged. (National Archives)

An enlargement of the 15 June 1944 bomb damage assessment photo details the floating dock with a trapped S-144 displaying its irregular bow curve and crescent-shaped skullcap bridge. (National Archives)

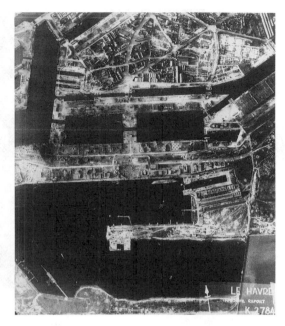

Tallboys nearly obliterated the Gare Maritime where Germans had stored munitions, mines, and torpedoes. The central hangars in the pens caved in after a mysterious explosion on 25 July 1944. (National Archives)

This view of the smashed bunker at Le Havre was probably taken from a crane by Allied inspectors in October 1944. It shows two Tallboy impacts, one on the right corner, the other on the apron adjoining the Mole Centrale. (Imperial War Museum)

A view from inside the destroyed bunker at Le Havre shows the ten-foot-thick steel-reinforced ceilings of the structure. (Imperial War Museum)

The open hangars of the Le Havre pens faced onto the outer tidal basin. Two Tall-boys landed there. The massive construction hints at what would happen to vessels inside if a tidal wave surged inward. (National Archives)

By 12 September 1944 when the Allies entered Le Havre, thirteen thousand tons of bombs had devastated the town—the same explosive power that destroyed Hiroshima a year later. (National Archives)

Le Havre from the ground, October 1944. (National Archives)

American troops disembarking at Le Havre saw numerous mutually supporting
batteries. After the Dieppe disaster in August 1942, the Allies avoided amphibious
assaults on fortified towns. (National Archives)

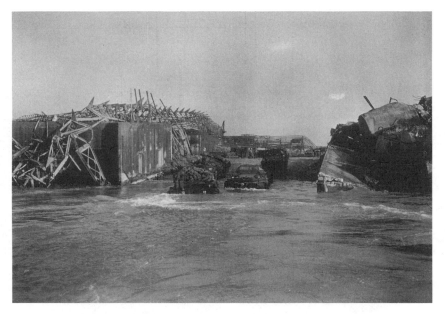

In overcoming the effects of German demolitions at Le Havre, the U.S. Navy employed amphibious vehicles to shuttle cargo from ships to shore. (National Archives)

The Americans worked frantically to revive Le Havre. Port discharge was crucial to Allied advances. (National Archives)

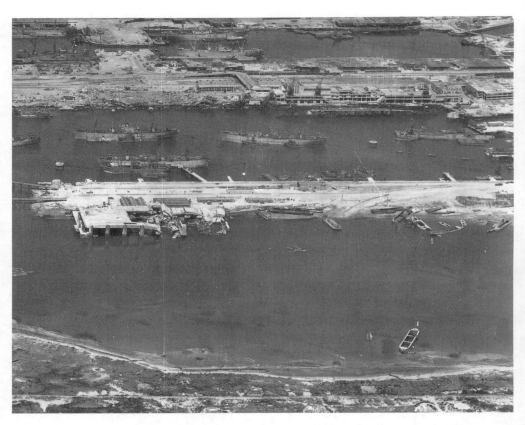

Le Havre on 18 June 1945. Allied bombing, possible French sabotage, and German demolition have done their work. (National Archives)

Boulogne, 17 June 1944. Photointerpreters outlined possible Tallboy impacts on the E-boat pens in this bomb damage assessment photograph. (National Archives)

Boulogne, 25 September 1944. On the eve of the Allied takeover this magnified aerial view shows the effects of Tallboys from the 15 June raid and demolition by retreating Germans. The pens at Rotterdam and Ijmuiden met a similar fate. Note scuttled naval craft blocking access to the sea. (National Archives)

This ground-level view of Boulogne's E-boat pens reveals their massive construction. The RAF airman at upper left is standing on the twelve-foot-thick reinforced concrete roof. (Imperial War Museum)

Chapter 8

The Sea Battle, 6–13 June 1944

If the German Navy, like its landward counterparts, was caught off guard by the invasion, it began to recover quickly. Although threats from destroyers and U-boats either failed or were delayed, the same could not be said of the Schnellbootwaffe. All around the southern rim of the Channel, E-boat flotillas began nighttime operations as D-day waned. Signals also indicated that FdS Petersen had alerted reinforcements to start making their way westward from the Low Countries into the invasion area. Any hope that Germany's coastal forces might be intimidated by the sheer size of the invasion fleet vanished. The forces at hand immediately swung into action.

From Boulogne, four E-boats set out to explore the waters between Le Treport and Dieppe on the evening of 6 June. This may have been in response to Operation Taxable, the Allies' giant ruse the night before, when aircraft from RAF Bomber Command's 617 Squadron had dropped aluminum strips for the benefit of German radar, mimicking a seaborne convoy in progress toward Dieppe at eight knots. No sooner had the boats departed Boulogne than Allied radar detected them HMS *Obedient* locked onto the four E-boats at 0115 on 7 June forty miles south of Beachy Head and vectored MTBs against the diminutive force. In a move that foreshadowed a week of move and countermove, the German craft sped off at forty-two knots and easily evaded their would-be attackers. A Wellington bomber of Coastal Command reported a sighting of E-boats seventeen miles off Dieppe that same night and attacked, claiming hits. Ultra signals did not confirm this. All four boats reentered Boulogne unharmed.[1]

With Cherbourg fully intact, the Allied navies had to worry about both flanks of their sea bridge. All but one of the fifteen boats based at Cherbourg returned to sea that same evening following the invasion, departing at 2256 hours and maneuvering in concert with the forces from Boulogne. Flotilla commanders von Mirbach and Johannsen led from the front at their fastest cruising speed of thirty-eight knots, heading east and south along the Cotentin Peninsula to a coastal region around Marcouf where, FdS Petersen wired them, "there are constantly worthwhile targets in the area." Ultra intercepts had alerted the Allies earlier that evening to the impending E-boat mission, and the task force defenders adjusted their forces accordingly. HMS *Retalick* picked up the Cherbourg flotillas and directed several MTBs against the German attackers. Despite forewarnings from Ultra, a series of inconclusive engagements continued through the night hours. Displaying audaciousness, the E-boat Force pressed on, and at 0050 on 7 June one of the Cherbourg boats torpedoed an LCT, which sank two hours later. The Germans also claimed to have sunk LST 715 in the same night action.[2]

A young Royal Navy officer, Lt. Robert Loveless, was serving as executive officer aboard a neighboring vessel, LCT 921, as they returned that same night from a run into Omaha Beach. "We were making what appeared to be a normal passage into the night . . . when suddenly there was a hissing sound and then an almighty bang, followed by lashings of water. I was knocked out and on coming to was surprised to find myself lying quite whole and flat on the bridge duck-boards. All was silent, the engines stopped. The skipper too was just recovering consciousness and had opened a confused eye." Surviving crew prepared to abandon ship, but at the last minute decided that their LCT was not foundering. The rest of the flotilla had gone on in compliance with orders, so the damaged LCT 921 limped back to port alone. "The inquiry held on our return," Loveless explained, "established that it was an E-boat which had torpedoed us—we were lucky that it hadn't come in and finished things off with its guns while most of us were knocked out. Our sister vessel had been sunk without trace over to our starboard."[3]

Germany's fast fighting boats could not, however, operate with impunity. Allied minelayers had been busy laying their deadly charges off Cherbourg. Two E-boats, S-139 and S-140, ran over this newly laid Greengage Field on their return to port. Both blew up with heavy loss of life. With their demise, the post–D-day attrition of Germany's Schnellbootwaffe had begun. But to engage in speculation about a rapid destruction of the E-boat Force would have been premature. Ultra decrypts that same night confirmed the westward passage of several new E-boats along the Dutch and Belgian coasts. Reinforcements were already starting toward the Normandy battle area.

On the night of 7–8 June the tempo of operations increased when Korvettenkapitän Kurt Fimmen's Boulogne-based 4th E-boat Flotilla moved out into the Channel in strength. Royal Navy destroyers HMS *Obedient* and *Thornborough* engaged them briefly but lost contact. Allied aircraft on patrol over the Channel repeatedly attacked E-boats during the course of that night and, like the destroyers, claimed to have damaged or sunk boats. Ultra usually did not "break" fast enough to vector Allied units to exact interception points, but this form of special intelligence did offer valuable estimates of operational strength for individual flotillas. It also provided a valuable check on Allied claims of damaged or sunk E-boats. Typically, intercepts listed the number of E-boats departing a given harbor for their mission. They then recorded the number of boats returning from that mission to the same or another harbor. In this instance, all seven E-boats of the 4th Flotilla entered Le Havre as ordered by FdS Petersen on the morning of 8 June. Allied claims notwithstanding, Petersen's fast fighting boats were demonstrating that despite the awesome numbers of warships and aircraft on and over the Channel, they could continue to operate. This meant, in effect, that the E-boat Force was almost alone in carrying the fight to the Allies on the Channel.[4]

The mission from Boulogne was indicative of two other noteworthy facts. First, the E-boats inflicted no damage to Allied shipping that night. If they, themselves, were not caught, Allied vigilance was preventing them from accomplishing their mission. Second, the Ultra decrypts, even though delays in breaking them prevented same-night use, were allowing the OIC to build a history of E-boat operations that could establish patterns and allow them to observe the shifting concentrations of boats in the Channel ports under German control. The OIC's specialists in tracking the German Navy's small-craft movements continued to monitor the situation closely. At the moment, they decided, the bulk of the boats were to be found in Cherbourg in the west and Boulogne to the north and east. However, events might change that pattern.[5]

The solutions proposed by Allied naval authorities in May to counter the E-boat threat were by no means foolproof. Sometimes one Allied initiative worked against another. Both Admiral Ramsay and Rear Admiral Kirk had recommended the use of minelays athwart E-boat bases. Greengage Field off Cherbourg was one of them. It had indeed claimed two E-boats, but the following night the small-craft tracking team at the OIC observed to their consternation that it was having another, undesired, effect. Eleven E-boats had sortied on the night of 8 June to attack convoys of the Western Task Force. MTBs engaged them, but the British boats had to tread water carefully because the mines were no respecters of nationality. Similarly, British coastal forces dared not approach too close to the Western Task Force at night because of trigger-happy Allied gunners. Already by the second night after the invasion, the E-boat Force had made its measure of the Allies' new minefield. As the OIC commented: "The available sea area between this and the approach routes of the Western Task Force was insufficient for the successful routing of E-boats, and several actions had to be broken off. It was obvious that once the delimitations of the Greengage Field became known to the enemy, it served to protect rather than deter him."[6]

Difficulties beset both sides. One of the E-boat commanders making nightly forays from Cherbourg against the invaders was Hans Schirren, skipper of S-145. He recalled that conditions were hardly ideal as they attacked the Western Naval Task Force. "Our E-boats often had to launch torpedoes at a great distance against the big warships and destroyers, and we had many fights with the MTBs. The cover for the approaching invasion fleet by destroyers and MTBs was too heavy for us to come into good shooting range, and there was no control [verification] possible with respect to torpedo hits."[7] Both sides tended to exaggerate the effectiveness of their attacks, and inflated claims were common following the confused night actions.

Another E-boat commander who participated in the nightly missions from Cherbourg was Günther Rabe, commander of S-130. Rabe's boat was one of the first to be fitted with the upgraded MB 511 engines the previous autumn, and his powerful boat was equipped with Hohentwiel, one of Germany's first shortwave, centimetric radar devices. S-130 also carried one of the first upgraded passive radar detectors, called Naxos. Rabe preferred to use Naxos over Hohentwiel, which, he was convinced, tended to give away S-130's position to Allied radar detectors. Like Schirren, a highly experienced commander and veteran of many a fight on the Channel, Rabe pressed on night after night following the invasion, undeterred by the Allies' superior numbers. In fact, the OIC small-boat trackers monitored him and his activities with special care. To them he was known as "The Raven," a direct translation of his family name but also a tribute to his abilities. Rabe observed that despite constant monitoring of his boat by Allied radar, which he could usually detect, the sheer speed of his boat plus its low silhouette and effective gray camouflage paint made S-130 a difficult target.

Stealth and speed alone, however, were not enough. Although willing to repeatedly engage the enemy, Rabe and his crew found it discouraging, to put it mildly, to have to fight in conditions where the E-boats were constantly and vastly outnumbered. Moving at speeds of thirty-six to thirty-eight knots during the entire mission and sometimes at full emergency speed of forty-two knots, they would loose their two torpedoes—there was no time for a reload—and turn immediately for port without being able to verify fully what effect their attack had had. On one night after an attack, Rabe and the deck crew watched silently from the bridge while S-130, its torpedoes expended, filed past a convoy of at least eighty Allied ships. The E-boats' cannon were primarily for defense against Allied aircraft and warships like MTBs and were not heavy enough to sink large transport vessels. Therefore, they held their fire as they slipped silently down the long columns of LSTs and other ships. "Everyone reported the same conditions," he said of those exhausting nights. Still, they fought on.[8]

With land lines down all over Western France, FdS Petersen was forced more and more to use radio signals to address the E-boat Force. Therefore, the OIC could dispatch information to Allied units night after night, informing them of impending operations with such details as from which harbors the E-boats would issue, whether the mission was for torpedoes or minelays, and to which harbor they would return. For the night of 8–9 June, for example, the main activity appeared to be minelaying, and HMS *Trollope* vectored two MTBs onto E-boats of the 4th Flotilla operating from Le Havre and apparently laying mines off Cap d'Antifer. Despite this timely warning, Britain's Coastal Forces could not catch their elusive enemy.

On the same night, signals to the 5th and 9th flotillas at Cherbourg indicated that they were to lay mines at certain locations off the Cotentin Peninsula where Allied battleships were known to be operating. The E-boats were carrying two torpedoes each plus six sea mines. They were directed to attack targets of opportunity outward bound, and then on the return journey they were directed "to attack everything."[9] Forewarned, Allied ships and coastal craft assigned to the Western Naval Task Force assembled for an interception. The OIC recorded what happened next, even with foreknowledge of German intentions. "In spite of this, E-boats managed to avoid waiting patrols, and two convoys, E.T.C.I and E.T.M.IP were attacked. LST 314 and 376 were torpedoed and sunk in position 49 deg. 50'N, 00 deg. 52'W. From W/T reports made on their return and duly intercepted, it is clear that the mining programme of 5th and 9th E-boat flotillas was undertaken against extremely heavy opposition."[10] The OIC analysts doubted that the minelay had been effective because the Allies were alerted to it. However, an ominous threshold had just been crossed. The E-boat Force claimed its first multiple LST victims since the events on Lyme Bay the previous April.

When asked many years later if E-boat crews had a preference for attacking LSTs, Günther Rabe replied, "Every time!" But despite their slow speed and relative lack of maneuverability, they were not, he admitted, the easiest targets for E-boats. At five thousand tons displacement, LSTs were big ships, but they were short vessels nonetheless, decreasing the chances of a hit. They were extremely shallow draft vessels intended to land on a beach. Therefore, if the E-boat commander were not careful, his torpedoes would run harmlessly under the LST without exploding, as happened several times in Lyme Bay. Unfortunately for the Allies, the German attackers appreciated that problem and fitted magnetic pistols to the torpedoes. This gave a much better chance of detonating under a ship's hull. The loss of two landing ships on 8–9 June proved that point emphatically.[11]

Although they were down two LSTs when dawn came on 9 June, the Allies could see danger signs for the E-boats operating in the Channel. The 5th and 9th flotillas at Cherbourg had operated with fifteen boats on D-day; after three nights of intensive operations they were down to eleven boats, and signal traffic from Cherbourg indicated that four of those eleven were barely operational. If that was a hint from his flotilla commanders for FdS Petersen to stand down for a day or two to recover and refit, it failed of its purpose. Petersen ordered the remaining boats out.[12]

The remorseless expenditure of men and equipment was not the only new development detected by the OIC. By D+3 OIC plots indicated that the relative positions of E-boats in the Channel ports had begun to change. A check of signals since 6 June showed that whereas there had been 15 boats at Cherbourg initially, 1 in transit at Le Havre, and 14 in Boulogne, by 9 June the figures had changed. By D+3 there were 13 at Cherbourg (if damaged or refitted boats were included), 8 at Le Havre, and 6 at Boulogne, with another 6 in transit from Ostend. Reinforcements continued to come in but none had been able to reach Cherbourg yet. The E-boat Force was finding it could advance from the east only as far as Le

Havre. Cherbourg was looking more and more isolated.[13] On the evening of 10 June, four boats from the 2d E-boat Flotilla went out from Boulogne intending a torpedo run followed by a dash into Cherbourg. It was not to be. Intercepted signals showed them entering Le Havre the following dawn.

Other evidence of the increasingly desperate circumstances in which the E-boat Force found itself began to accumulate. Supply personnel at Cherbourg sent a statement of requirements to the torpedo inspectorate of the Kriegsmarine in Kiel revealing a desperate shortage of torpedoes. The OIC listeners reported the results: "This statement revealed a very low ebb with little prospect of improvement as it was mutually agreed that under present circumstances 'transport by rail was out of the question.' On the 8th of June some improvement in the Cherbourg position was anticipated since thirty warheads and impact pistols had that day been dispatched by road from Brest to St. Malo." The ill-fated destroyers had attempted to carry extra torpedoes for the E-boats but without success. Finally, on 12 June naval C-in-C West, Admiral Krancke, ordered five M-class minesweepers at St. Malo to carry the thirty torpedoes the rest of the way into Cherbourg. Supplies were becoming increasingly tenuous as the Allied stranglehold on land and sea tightened around the Cotentin Peninsula.[14]

Still, the E-boats continued their nightly prowls. Eleven boats from Cherbourg filed out past the breakwater, at 2230 hours of 9 June, heading east to the southern end of the Spout. Using their high-speed *Stichtaktik,* they lanced through the defenses and launched all torpedoes before turning about for a high-speed run back to port. All eleven boats filed back into Cherbourg again at 0500 on 10 June. "The E-boats proved extremely elusive," the OIC chroniclers admitted, "and no definitive engagements with our MTBs were reported." Nevertheless, that short sharp action left death and destruction in its wake. Despite close escort from HMS *Cottesmere,* two British ammunition coasters, SS *Dungrange* and SS *Brackenfield,* went down at the southern end of the Spout at 0300 and 0315, respectively. Only two men from the *Brackenfield* survived, none from the *Dungrange.*[15] The Allies discontinued sending convoys southward from the Isle of Wight "during the hours of darkness," the OIC recorded, "owing to the risk of E-boat attack at the southern end of The Spout."[16] Despite their own severe supply headaches, the German E-boat Force was starting to disrupt the flow of supplies for the Allies. The situation was not serious yet, but the E-boats were proving to be tenacious opponents.

The relevant naval code for E-boats, Dolphin, which the OIC had been reading regularly and which had broken quickly enough at times to have same-night application, witnessed an inexplicable delay for the night of 9–10 June. The OIC staff did not read the message until 1210 hours on 10 June, so it was of no operational value. However, Dolphin for 10–11 June broke only three hours later. The Allies had an understanding of the coming night's operations by 1720 of 10 June, followed by additional information half an hour later.

Twelve E-boats from the 2d and 4th flotillas were ordered out from Le Havre to lay mines in the Eastern Seine Bay. They were to engage in torpedo operations before setting in at Boulogne on the morning of 11 June. One significant fact the OIC derived from the intercept was an order from FdS Petersen for boats without torpedoes to make for Boulogne immediately following the minelay. In other words, some of the E-boats were operating without torpedoes. The Allied analysts deduced that Cherbourg was not the only port experiencing supply problems. There was a scarcity of torpedoes in Le Havre too.[17]

Joy among the OIC staff must have been brief. However few torpedoes the E-boats sallying forth from Le Havre possessed, they made good use of them that night. Several boats encountered a convoy hauling components for one of the vital artificial harbors, the British Mulberries. In a few hellish minutes the convoy's escort, HMS *Halstead,* had its bow blown off and had to be towed back to Portsmouth. Another German "eel" sank an unnamed merchant ship. Two fleet tugs that were towing large units for the Mulberries, called Whales, suffered hits. Tug *Sesame* received two torpedo hits and sank with the loss of eighteen men. Tug *Partridge* sank ten miles off shore. Only forty-five of her seventy-nine crew members survived. Forewarned, a radar control ship, HMS *Trollope,* had plotted the incoming E-boats, and HMS *Wensleydale* gamely opened fire as did several MTBs. It was all to no avail. The E-boats escaped. Sometime later, additional signals gave only one slight cause for satisfaction by the Allies. Instead of entering Boulogne as ordered, all twelve E-boats had again retreated to Le Havre.[18]

Far to the west, the eleven boats remaining from the 5th and 9th flotillas were ordered to repeat the previous night's operations. They attacked Force U off Utah Beach in groups of two and three boats and this time achieved penetration of the defensive perimeter. Ninth Flotilla Commander Götz von Mirbach aboard S-138 succeeded in torpedoing a destroyer, the USS *Nelson.* (At first he believed he had sunk a cruiser.) The *Nelson,* minus its stern, somehow made it back to Portsmouth, another casualty of the stubborn war waged by the E-boat Force. LST 538 dodged one torpedo only to be struck by another. She managed to beach, unload, and then retract after making emergency repairs.[19]

Another ship out on the water on 11 June was LST 496, one of the survivors of the Lyme Bay disaster. She had been fitted out with a third deck for the evacuation of wounded and had already made one trip across the Channel to Omaha Beach, ferrying men and equipment onto the beaches and evacuating casualties. The big landing ship made another crossing to the Normandy shore a few days later, this time carrying U.S. Army Rangers, tanks, and other heavy equipment destined for Omaha Beach. Aboard her were PO Bill Gould and ten other crewmen who had survived the sinking of LST 507 and who were now serving on their second landing ship. As dawn approached they began to see the faint outline of the French Coast some miles away. Gould described what happened a few minutes later. "By this time it was the morning of 11 June, and we were nearing the French Coast. I was on deck near the stern, and I think it was around 6:00 a.m. [0600 hours], in full daylight, when we hit a mine. . . . The force of the explosion knocked me clear off the deck, and I was unconscious for a while. It caused a lot of damage, and the ship went down fast. We lost a lot of crew and Rangers. The captain of LST 496, Stanley Koch, was killed in the explosion too. I was wounded but got into the water. . . . I was the only survivor from the group from LST 507 that had been transferred to LST 496. All the others died."[20]

There was no way of determining what kind of craft had placed the mines that destroyed LST 496 or other Allied vessels crowded into the invasion area. The Luftwaffe was able to drop a few during night sorties, but the bulk were laid by German R-boats, the 125-foot minelayers, and by E-boats. Their mines were suitable for waters less than twenty-five fathoms, which was where LST 496 met its fate. The OIC and the naval commands were well aware that the German Navy's minelaying flotillas were based in Le Havre. Their destructive cargoes were a constant source of concern as the architects of Operation Neptune worried about their finite supply of landing ships, LCTs, fleet tugs, and ferries, all of which had to operate in those shallow coastal waters. At this time the German Navy began using its new oyster mines, which detonated when activated by the pressure wave of a passing ship. There were no effective countermeasures at the time except for ships to slow down to four knots in coastal areas. This new headache gave the Allies an additional reason to carefully monitor German naval activity in and out of Le Havre.[21]

If the early hours of 11 June were costly to the Allies, the E-boats quickly discovered that their luck, which had been considerable up to that point, had also begun to turn. Given the intense level of operations, casualties were bound to occur, and the only surprise was that a change in fortunes took place so late. One E-boat, S-112, had been damaged earlier, and although repairs had restored her somewhat, her steering gear was still defective. The fact that FdS Petersen had ordered S-112 out at all was a measure of the desperation the German Navy felt at this critical stage. Shortly after midnight on 11 June the damaged boat broke down completely, and at that moment Allied destroyers and MTBs attacked. HMS *Duff* vectored two British boats onto the E-boats at 0030, and at close range MTB 448 and S-136 dealt and received lethal blows. Both eventually sank. The rest of the E-boats, including S-112, which had been successfully defended, retreated westward.[22]

At 0206, boats of the 5th Flotilla created a diversion by deliberately attacking the destroyer screen off Barfleur, an unusual move since E-boats normally avoided contact with warships. In the meantime two boats of the 9th Flotilla broke through the Spout and headed east, arriving safely in Le Havre the next morning. The 9th E-boat Flotilla Commander, Korvettenkapitän von Mirbach, later explained that they succeeded in making the breakthrough by carrying the fight close in shore among several groups of Allied destroyers and accompanying MTBs.[23]

Off Cherbourg at 0327 hours, the remaining E-boats had taken off six surviving crew members from the heavily damaged S-136 and were setting a fire to scuttle her. A few minutes later, RAF Coastal Command Albacores attacked. Those slow, sturdy biplanes, using state-of-the-art ASV (air to surface vessel) centimetric radar, had located the stopped boats. In the attack that followed, near misses showered Kapitänleutnant Günther Rabe's S-130 with deadly bomb splinters. Rabe was on the bridge at the time and recalled that there was no warning whatsoever of the impending attack. He and several men topside were wounded. Later, back in port, repair crews counted at least two hundred splinter holes. Rabe's steel helmet had undoubtedly saved his life during the attack. However, he had to use the fingers of one hand to plug a gaping wound in his forehead as he steered with the other. The wounded crew were in the hospital for several days while repair crews used anything, including iron rails from railroad stores, to plug S-130's many splinter holes.[24]

Rabe's crew had incurred especially bad luck. Other E-boat personnel such as Korvettenkapitän Felix Zymalkowski, commanding the 8th E-boat Flotilla, and Radioman Ernst Benda recalled the Schnellbootwaffe's tactic for avoiding aerial strafing by radar-equipped Allied aircraft at night: Listen carefully for engine noises. When Albacores and similar attack planes circled overhead, they had not yet pinpointed a target. However, when crewmen heard increasing engine noise coming from one direction, it meant only one thing. The pilot was entering his strafing run. That was the moment to take fast evasive action. The tactic was by no means infallible. Wind, water, nearby engines, or battle noise might form an unwanted sound curtain, or urgent demands such as the rescue of crews from damaged boats could deflect attention for a fateful few minutes, as happened to Rabe and his crew. E-boat operations had become increasingly perilous, and everyone knew it.[25]

Despite their losses on that June night, from the E-boat Force's perspective they had been successful. They had inflicted mounting losses on Allied convoys. Two E-boats, S-144 and S-146, penetrated right through the Spout, and sped safely into Le Havre before dawn the following morning. Among the escaping 9th Flotilla crew on board S-144 was Kapitänleutnant Hans Schirren, whose own boat, S-145, was laid up in Le Havre undergoing engine repairs after a hit the previous night from an American PT boat. From prisoner of war interrogations, the Allies knew that the 9th Flotilla Commander, Korvettenkapitän von Mirbach, usually used S-146 with its advanced radar and radar detectors as his command ship. He shared the bridge with its current skipper, Kapitänleutnant Ullrich Roeder. The passage of a flotilla commander aboard a specially equipped E-boat from Cherbourg to Le Havre was noteworthy, but what did it portend? Certainly the ability of the E-boats to pierce through the heavily defended Spout was a worrisome development for the invaders. Roeder later explained how they had continued to maintain mobility despite dense Allied defenses. "The German E-boats retained temporarily a certain advantage in tactical maneuvering despite the buildup of U.S. and British radar organizations at sea," he observed. They did so, he added, "because the E-boats could turn on the spot and were capable at times of evading the radar command system easily. We had the impression that British coastal forces and U.S. and British destroyers had to get onto the blower [radio telephone] and could not react immediately to our movements."[26]

Penetration of the Spout was hardly the Allies' only worry that night. Stung by the Germans' successful attacks on artificial harbor components, the Allied leadership called off the transiting of Mulberry convoys except during daylight. Once again, the E-boats were proving to be formidable opponents.[27]

The mounting strain, however, was beginning to reach intolerable levels for the E-boats at Cherbourg. Dolphin, the pertinent German cipher, was slow to break for the Allies again on 11–12 June, so they were unaware of certain telltale developments. On that night only six E-boats set out from Cherbourg, passing the breakwaters at 2315, and the Allies noted with some alarm that the German coastal batteries were particularly active this time. Inevitably, a gap opened in the Allied naval defenses, and two more E-boats escaped through it unseen, heading eastward like their predecessors the night before into Le Havre. The four boats remaining in western waters returned safely to Cherbourg.[28]

Meanwhile the E-boats that had been concentrating in greater numbers at Le Havre were also active. Twelve E-boats from the 2d and 4th flotillas, reinforced by two boats from the 9th Flotilla, emerged from the Seine port on the night of 11–12 June and immediately ran into trouble with HMS *Melbreak* and *Tanatside* off Cap d'Antifer. Intercepts from German wireless traffic suggested that two E-boats received damage. However, the seagoing tug *Allegiance,* which was towing a Phoenix unit for the British Mulberry, was relieved of its burden when a torpedo sank the heavy component.[29] Despite the E-boats' success against a key Mulberry unit, information from an Ultra decrypt the following evening revealed a new operational development for the Allies. Although the twelve E-boats from Le Havre that had attacked Mulberry components were supposed to proceed to Boulogne by dawn of 12 June, and intercepts claimed they had done so, such was not the case. The new decrypt revealed that all twelve boats had returned instead to Le Havre. Whether from desperation or by design, the E-boat Force appeared to be concentrating more and more in the eastern Seine port.[30]

Other significant developments were taking place to the west. By nightfall of 12–13 June, the four remaining operational E-boats at Cherbourg obeyed orders for a torpedo run and filed out of harbor with three heavily gunned harbor launches to stiffen their firepower at the start of the mission. The tactic succeeded. No fewer than four destroyers engaged them. HMS *Vidette* and *Onslow* attacked first at 0015, but without result. Almost an hour later at 0110 in a more easterly position, the Canadians had their chance. HMCS *Camrose* and *Baddeck,* corvettes drawn from Canada's transatlantic convoy escorts, were protecting Mulberry units that night. Suddenly, they, too, recorded E-boat attacks but claimed to have repulsed them. Perhaps the Allies' luck would change if they could intercept the Germans on their return to Cherbourg. It was not to be. The four E-boats on their mysterious mission never returned westward. As on the two previous evenings, the fast boats from Cherbourg continued their passage eastward, penetrating the Allied defense and emerging unscathed in Le Havre.[31]

Operations might be scaling down at Cherbourg, but they continued to build at Le Havre, which only a few days before had been considered merely an emergency base for E-boats. This time no fewer than fourteen boats participated in a night action. Dolphin had broken early this time, and the Allies issued warnings to the appropriate Channel forces based on an Ultra decrypt at 2149 hours on 12 June. As a result, escorts HMS *Melbreak, Wensleydale,* and *Bassenden* successfully defended the western wall of the Spout against the large E-boat force. Operation Neptune suffered no losses on that shoulder despite the most concentrated E-boat attack since the beginning of the invasion. The intercepts indicated that boats of the 2d Flotilla were to make for Boulogne upon completing their mission rather than returning to Le Havre. The Allies arranged their forces accordingly. Concentrated attacks by Coastal Command aircraft lurking off Boulogne finally achieved results. Marine Gruppe West conceded the loss of two E-boats sunk that night trying to make Boulogne.[32]

By the evening of 13 June, the OIC had accumulated conflicting reports about the concentrations of E-boats at the various Channel ports. However, a suspicion was growing that the large port at the mouth of the Seine was now accommodating far more E-boats than it had ever before done. Analysis indicated that there were 6 boats at Ostend, 5 at Boulogne, 15 at Le Havre, and only 4 remaining at Cherbourg.[33]

That same evening Dolphin proved difficult once again, not breaking until 0850 the morning of 14 June. OIC could issue no useful information to Allied units, but this communications lag proved to be harmless. The weather had deteriorated by the evening of 13 June, and information recovered the next morning simply confirmed that FdS Petersen had canceled all operations the previous night because of heavy seas. However, OIC's analysis of distribution patterns led to a heightened sense of excitement as suspicions grew about the concentration of coastal craft at Le Havre.

"The distribution of E-boats at this time must have been a source of concern to the Germans," the OIC final report concluded. "Obviously there were too many E-boats in Le Havre and too few in the peripheral bases of Cherbourg and Boulogne. Further reinforcements west of Calais would be dangerous until redistribution had taken place." In other words, the bulge of forces at Le Havre was beginning to look suspiciously like a bottleneck in the flow of the one German naval arm capable of carrying the fight to the enemy. The OIC report continued: "Le Havre was an emergency rather than an operational base and as such could not be allowed to become overcrowded." With rising excitement, the chroniclers noted what consequences might yet flow from the high winds on the Channel. "The fact that weather intervened and precluded E-boat operations on the night of

13th June incidentally guaranteed the existence of a uniquely significant target for the saturation air attack on Le Havre on the following day."[34]

While such an air raid looked promising, there was no assurance at the OIC or anywhere else that night that the wily Kriegsmarine would be content to let its surface units continue to crowd into Le Havre, good weather or bad. In five years of war they had learned to be unpredictable, and to date no Allied air raid had ever caught them in appreciable numbers in any Channel or North Sea port.

Retreat

Subsequent decryptions of FdS signals that broke on 14 June told another story about E-boat dispositions that was significant. FdS Petersen informed the senior naval officer at St. Malo that the baggage for the 5th and 9th E-boat flotillas was to be transferred from Cherbourg to St. Malo. This was to coincide with the return passage of boats from Le Havre to Cherbourg. The few boats still in Cherbourg were to prepare for another torpedo operation that same night, and the still damaged S-112 was to hold itself in readiness to join the operational boats in flight. Petersen commanded all remaining 5th and 9th flotilla E-boat forces to prepare for permanent transfer westward on the night of 15–16 June.[35] Despite the threat they had posed to the Allies from Cherbourg, Petersen had his reasons for making the change. "Obviously Cherbourg was finished as an E-boat base," the OIC observed, "on account of the pressure exercised from landward in the north of the Cotentin Peninsula." In words that would have warmed the hearts of General Collins and the forces of the U.S. VII Corps, the navy-oriented OIC spelled out the consequences of the Americans' irresistible pressure on the Germans at Cherbourg: "In spite of repeated E-boat sorties from the port during the first week of Operation Neptune, the land situation behind Cherbourg had early been recognized as critical. The thorough destruction of Cherbourg Harbour had been ordered by C-in-C West [Admiral Krancke] as early as 1230 on 10th June." Faced with the inevitable, the German naval leadership was looking toward the destruction of Cherbourg as a viable harbor for the Allies. In essence, by 10 June they had written it off as an E-boat base.[36]

The fast-boat trackers at the OIC, who for many months had closely followed the activities of Germany's Schnellbootwaffe, could not hide their admiration for what they had witnessed through the intercepted signals and other special intelligence as the Germans prepared to blow up their most effective naval port. "This background of imminent dissolution allied with the punishment of our own forces, the inhuman use made of men and material and the fact that between A.M. on 6th June and A.M. on 12th June, E-boats from Cherbourg had completed approximately thirty-four operational hours without a twenty-four hour respite forms a sterling tribute to the morale of the E-boat crews."[37]

Although the Allied authorities knew that the E-boat Force had fought a clean fight in the war, with no hint of atrocities or deliberate cruelty, they also knew that Germany's fast fighting boats and their seasoned crews were a dangerous enemy. Admiration aside, if they could place their skilled opponent within their grasp, they would not hesitate to crush him. An examination of E-boat activities for the week following the invasion provided some sobering statistics (see table 3). Landing vessels, including the LSTs, which composed only 4 percent of the Normandy Invasion Fleet, were taking a disproportionate share of the losses. Even more telling was the OIC table indicating which types of German forces were inflicting the casualties (see table 4). The OIC analysts admitted that the figures might have to be modified later, but it was obvious that the E-boat Force had attained an extraordinary level of activity in the first week following the invasion (see table 5).

Table 3

Allied losses due to enemy action (by class), 5–12 June 1944

Class of vessel	No. of vessels		
	Sunk	*Damaged*	*Total*
Cruisers and above	0	0	0
Destroyers, frigates, corvettes	7	4	11
Minesweepers	2	3	5
Light coastal forces	2	0	2
Landing ships	5	12	17
Landing craft	8	7	15
Merchant ships	7	11	18
Grand total	31	37	68

Source: "Note on Operation Neptune–First Week," p. 1, S.I. 978a, Public Record Office, ADM 223/172.

Table 4
Allied losses due to enemy action (by cause), 5–12 June 1944

	No. of vessels		
Cause	*Sunk*	*Damaged*	*Total*
Mines	10	15	25
E-boats	12	6	18
Destroyers	0	1	1
Aircraft	2	5	7
Shore batteries	4	1	5
Torpedo boats	1	0	1
U-boats	0	0	0
Uncertain	2	9	11
Grand total	31	37	68

Source: "Note on Operation Neptune—First Week," p. 1, S.I. 978a, Public Record Office, ADM 223/172.

Table 5
E-boat effort and results, 5–12 June 1944

Average no. of E-boats on duty	31
No. of maneuvers	20
No. of individual forays	170
No. of Allied ships sunk	12
No. of Allied ships damaged	6
No. of E-boats sunk	3

Source: "Note on Operation Neptune—First Week," p. 2, S.I. 978a, Public Record Office, ADM 223/172.

Losses to date had been acceptable as far as the Germans were concerned. In fact, given the disproportionate Allied strength, it was surprising that E-boat losses had not been far greater. The OIC also observed that the casualties inflicted by the E-boat Force were solely from torpedoes (see table 4). OIC could not estimate the Allied casualties caused by E-boat minelaying activities. The sheer intensity of operations was, they admitted, impressive. "In effect, every serviceable E-boat operated every night," the OIC analysts concluded. However, such a pace was not sustainable indefinitely, they predicted: "On the basis of past experience, it would be surprising if this effort could be maintained for much longer."[38]

Yet there were certainly no guarantees that the Schnellbootwaffe's efforts would slacken. If the current pace of operations continued and if the cunning FdS Petersen succeeded in feeding in more reinforcements—and those reinforcements were already in motion southward from the Baltic and elsewhere—then sooner or later the threat posed by E-boats to the invasion fleet would become deadly. Existing Allied countermeasures such as minefields, increased surface patrols, and intensified aerial sorties were helping to keep the E-boats at bay, but only just. A month earlier, both Admiral Ramsay and Admiral Kirk had concluded that what was needed was a heavy bombing raid on the E-boat Force's primary base of operations. However, the Schnellbootwaffe had learned the art of deception well. A difficult question confronted the Allied leadership on that evening of 13 June 1944, Where would the E-boats be on the following day?

Chapter 9

Bomber Command Target: E-Boat Pens

The Shell Game

With the dawning of 14 June, D+8, there was mounting concern in the OIC about the whereabouts and activities of Germany's elusive E-boats. Operation Neptune had settled into a routine, and planners could see that the pace of E-boat operations continued to quicken during that first crucial week after the invasion. With German coastal forces pecking around the edges of the invaders' centralized shipping spout down the center of the Channel, Allied trackers feared that the E-boat Force might yet pull off a coup against the convoys, especially the precious LSTs. The E-boat tracking team at the OIC pondered through the dawn hours a problem that had preoccupied them for months: how to predict the pattern of attacks and how to pinpoint their center of operations for an Allied counterattack. Having assembled in force at Le Havre on 12–13 June, would the E-boats disperse to Boulogne, Ostend, or Cherbourg as they had so often done before, darting at first light into the hardened ports along the Channel coast like the proverbial peas in a carnival shell game? Or had they altered their pattern this time and decided to remain in Le Havre? It was a maddening problem. The German Schnellboot-waffe was so unpredictable.

As sometimes happens in such operations, luck entered the picture in the guise of Mother Nature. June had ushered in rough weather in the Channel area, confounding longstanding meteorological trends, and although the weather had calmed somewhat after 6 June, high winds and heavy seas returned a week after the initial lodgment. On at least one night the FdS had canceled operations for one or several E-boat flotillas. Then a broader weather disturbance developed. Knowing that his E-boat Force was nearing exhaustion, FdS Petersen radioed all units on the evening of 13 June: "All departures canceled because of weather."[1]

Outwardly, it might seem strange that Petersen was being so choosy about weather conditions with a mighty invasion effort on and possibly the fate of the war hanging in the balance. But he had his reasons. Operations for his thin-skinned craft were risky enough even under normal sea conditions in the Channel. By this time the E-boats' tremendous flank speed, which consistently outperformed that of Allied naval craft, had become almost their only guarantee of survival in the crowded, radar-swept waters of the Channel. It would have been reckless for Petersen to risk the lives of his crews for no gain against the increasingly dangerous protective screens if bad weather slowed his greyhounds and threw away their sole remaining advantage. Larger Allied warships by their very nature could keep a steeper sea and still fight. The E-boats could not. Rudolf Petersen was not a reckless man. Neither was he a fanatic. He decided to husband his forces until sea and weather conditions favored his E-boats and not the vessels of the enemy. It was the prudent thing to do.

The problem with Petersen's prudence was that the Allies, thanks to Ultra, were listening. The lingering question on that fateful 14 June was whether the naval forces assembled in Le Havre for operations the previous night had been ordered by Petersen to disperse again or simply to remain in place. It all depended on how quickly the decryptors could "promulgate," that is, break, the relevant German code known as Dolphin. An OIC report described what happened next: "Dolphin for the . . . 13th and 14th did not break until 0850 on the 14th, with the result that operational intentions for the night 13th–14th June could not be promulgated in time to affect Channel surface dispositions."[2] While disappointing, such delays were not unexpected. Of far greater worth was the fact that the Allies knew in timely fashion from this crucial decryption that the forces gathered at Le Havre had not gone operational on the thirteenth. This was priceless information. But they would have to act with dispatch if they expected to profit from it. There was the distinct possibility that the forces the Germans had assembled in Le Havre, numerous enough to be cumbersome, might out of sheer expediency have remained in harbor with the intention of trying again the next night. Because of delays in promulgation, succeeding Ultra decryptions could not tell them the Germans' next move in time. The moment had come to unsheathe another weapon of war.

A Lonely Reconnaissance

On the morning of 14 June 1944, Flt. Lt. P. J. Kelley, a veteran photoreconnaissance pilot from 542 Squadron and leader of its B Flight received word that he would be flying a dangerous mission that day. Nine pilots had already lifted off from a special airfield early that morning, but the weather was unfavorable, with heavy cumulus buildup and occasional showers over France. Most of the returning pilots reported that their intended targets were obscured. The weather improved by late morning, and Kelley made ready for a rapid departure. In preparation for this reconnaissance the pilot's briefing staff had produced an exact flight plan and precise map coordinates for the target area rather than calling for photo "takes" of specific objects like E-boats. There was little mystery about the target this time. One glance at the coordinates told Kelley that the port of Le Havre was the main target they had in mind. His was an exacting job, which was why the RAF selected only its finest aviators who had great navigational skills for such work. Following the briefing, Kelley inspected his aircraft, Spitfire XI, RM.638, a typical model of the squadron's specially modified, unarmed Spitfires produced for the RAF's top secret Photo Reconnaissance Unit base at RAF Benson. This PRU collecting center was situated near Wallingford, fifty miles northwest of London. It lay in close proximity to Britain's even more secret Photographic Interpretation Unit at Medmenham on the Thames, where some of the war's unsung heroes, photointerpreters (PIs), were waiting for the results of Kelley's efforts.

Following his takeoff at 1245, Kelley rapidly gained altitude over the Channel, looking for flying-bomb sites over the Pas de Calais while en route to Le Havre. This secondary target proved to be an unsuccessful effort because of heavy cloud, and Kelley wasted no time looking for gaps. Heading almost due south by this time, Kelley proceeded in accordance with his flight plan, which carried him directly to Le Havre where the weather was rapidly improving. His payload consisted of two of the RAF's big F.52 aerial cameras with 36-inch focal-length lenses placed just aft of his cockpit and aimed straight down to take split vertical images. The technique had evolved from the pioneering efforts of a swashbuckling photoreconnaissance innovator from prewar days, Sidney Cotton. An Australian with an unorthodox way of doing things, Cotton and his organization had taught the RAF how to collect aerial photographs, legally and otherwise in peacetime, efficiently and expertly in wartime. They taught the world that speed, evasion, and stealth far excelled the older techniques of cannon and brute force in collecting aerial intelligence.[3]

On this day Flight Lieutenant Kelley would need all the skills and specialized equipment he could muster in order to obtain detailed photos of ground targets from six miles up. Some aircraft had forward-facing or side-facing cameras for oblique angles, but not this one. Oblique takes required diving to low altitude and making extremely dangerous runs beside the target. "Dicing with the devil," the pilots called the practice. To have ordered such a "dicing run" over the port of Le Havre in June 1944 would have been tantamount to issuing a death sentence to the highly experienced leader of B Flight. Verticals were what were needed now anyway. This mission was intended to provide prestrike intelligence of ship concentrations, as opposed to other PRU functions such as identification of unfamiliar weapons or objects of military importance. Bomb damage assessment was another vital photoreconnaissance objective. Because this photographic mission had primarily one target in mind, the ground crews loaded in relatively short spools of film in order to save weight and to avoid waste. Other missions might require reconnaissance of several target areas and therefore more film, but today's mission was special.[4]

Visibility improved steadily as Kelley passed over the mouth of the Seine, approximately forty-five minutes into his flight plan by now. Despite the relative safety of thirty thousand feet, he experienced increasing tension as he neared the primary objective. Alone in clear skies, Kelley knew he would have to contend with a strong reaction from heavy flak and possibly from German interceptors as he flattened out his aircraft, adjusted for wind drift, and held to a precise course along the map coordinates detailed in his flight plan. With his powerful lenses mapping an extremely narrow swath, there was no room for error. Kelley would have to run the exact flight path prescribed. Fortunately, ports were one of the more identifiable targets for high-flying recce pilots.

A flashing light on his controls assured him that his cameras were operating properly, with warm air from the engine passing over the lenses to keep them clear and electrically driven shutters opening and closing as the 7-inch spools of film advanced in precise 8.25-inch increments over the focal plane. Holding his aircraft at the same altitude throughout the run was imperative. It meant high resolution photographs of uniform size and angle, hopefully with 60 percent image overlap from one frame to the next. This in turn translated into a stereoscopic viewing effect for the PIs back at Medmenham. It also meant that they could establish an exact scale for the photographs, and that was important for the PIs when it came time to measure the size of objects. PRU pilots carried a special card giving the time interval (TI) needed between each photo take. Computing altitude, ground speed, and the camera's focal length, they adjusted the interval between takes so as to achieve the 60 percent overlap. The pilots at Benson had developed a near mania for precise measurement. For this mission Kelley had to adjust his TI for fairly rapid takes since the 36-inch focal length of his lens covered a small area of ground, even from an altitude of six miles.[5]

All PIs had to see stereo. Stereoscopic quality conferred a tremendous depth of field to the viewer, and psychologically it heightened the PI's sensitivity to black-and-white images. For reasons that are still not entirely clear, this special effect made it likelier that PIs would evaluate their target information more accurately. Some of the RAF's finest PIs were women, of whom Flight Officer Constance Babington-Smith, investigator of the V-1 site at Peenemünde, was only the most famous. It had taken these PI specialists months, sometimes years, to develop the skills needed to evaluate aerial photos and to see stereoscopically as they lined up two consecutive photos in a series and positioned their viewing scopes over the prints. Some PIs became so proficient with the technique that they did not need the scope. Knowing the dangers involved in approaching Le Havre, they silently wished the pilot success. Kelley had other reasons to perform up to PRU's exacting standards. A successful run this time meant that neither he nor another squadron mate would have to return to the dangerous port again soon.[6]

As soon as he reached the Channel, Kelley began craning his head constantly, his eyes searching for telltale contrails from enemy interceptors. His lightweight Spitfire XI had no armament whatsoever. Its tools of trade were its exotic, heavy cameras. The additional weight of aerial cannon would only have slowed him down and made him more vulnerable to interception. Speed was his best ally, and the ground crews had labored for hours polishing the aircraft's surfaces. They even sanded the surfaces around rivets and filled them before polishing. The speed advantage of an extra ten or twenty miles per hour might prove crucial. In the summer, as now, aircraft left contrails at altitudes higher than thirty thousand feet depending on temperature and humidity levels. By flying just below that boundary layer, a smart recce pilot would leave none, forcing his would-be attacker to stream a telltale white plume behind him as he descended. In the winter Allied pilots reversed the technique, flying above twenty-three thousand feet and scouting low for contrails coming up. Attentive pilots learned such tricks quickly. Either that or they played sparrow to a German sparrow hawk.

As the port loomed up under his leading edge, the moment of truth came for this veteran reconnaissance pilot. As part of his strategy, Kelley had located a prominent feature in the target area, such as the pens or the floating dock. Flying at a maximum cruising speed of 380 mph he dropped a wing vertically to port, followed quickly by a reverse bank to starboard. Having located the same feature alongside the same point of his wing tips in twin vertical banks, he went horizontal again. While crude by later standards, this maneuver satisfied him that he was directly over his target and was not crabbing sideways because of winds. Running straight and level onto his photographic "leg," Kelley thumbed his camera button, and the camera light began blinking near his left knee. Suddenly, the optical equipment came to life, shutters blinking at the surface far below as the spools of sensitive film stuttered past the high-resolution lenses.

There was good reason to be tense now. In broad daylight approaching straight and true over the Seine port, Kelley had lost any element of surprise. The enemy knew exactly why he was there and what course he was flying, namely right toward them. Knowing what his mission portended, they would do all they could in the next few moments to down this unwanted intruder. It was a naked feeling. Scores of reconnaissance pilots before him had come to grief at this crucial phase of the mission. More than a dozen Allied recce aircraft had been shot down during the previous week alone in the dangerous skies over Normandy. It was a hectic time. In fact, Kelley's squadron was in the process of breaking all records for the intensity of its operations during June 1944. They ended the month by flying more missions than at any other time in the war. The pilots of 542 Squadron flew twenty-nine out of thirty days that month, and its A and B Flights accumulated 225 operational sorties. Every pilot and every serviceable aircraft was in action. Fatigue had become a fact of life for pilots and ground crews alike.[7]

Making Kelley feel even more conspicuous this time, his Spitfire was sporting prominent new black-and-white stripes over the powder blue camouflage paint of its polished fuselage and wings. These were the famed Normandy markings, obligatory for all AEAF forces since the eve of the landings. Allied aircraft could not confuse his Spitfire with a German plane. Unfortunately, neither could the Germans.[8]

Alerted minutes earlier by his solo approach, the German gunners in Le Havre raised the barrels of their rifled cannon and watched through their superb optical range-finders and hooded radar scopes, waiting for the order to fire. As he monitored his instruments and swiveled his head constantly around the horizon, Kelley probably hoped against hope for some kind of lapse by the flak defenses. If so, he was doomed to disappointment.

Up rose a terrifying box barrage from the Luftwaffe's rings of heavy batteries that encircled the port. These were large 8.8-cm Flak 41 or even larger 10.5-cm Flak 39 cannon capable of piercing winged aluminum cocoons and their contents at thirty thousand feet. That was approaching their maximum upper range, but on this day they had only one target upon which to register. The guns lofted 21- and 33-pound projectiles, respectively, each with a muzzle velocity faster than the bullet leaving a soldier's rifle. Because of them, Le Havre's airspace had achieved considerable notoriety among Allied pilots. A good place to avoid, the veterans all said. Timed to explode at thirty thousand feet, the big shells took approximately thirty seconds to achieve height and detonate, creating orange balls that were immediately shrouded by black puffs. Those on the receiving end could not see the deadly splinters that showered from the bursts, although survivors of near misses talked of hearing a sound akin to a dog's bark.[9]

Buffeting from near misses in the morning air forced Kelley to concentrate on steadying his fragile aircraft as the camera light continued to wink. At least he did not have to worry much about aerial interception at this phase in the mission. German pilots respected their own flak. The photographic run lasted only a minute. It must have seemed much longer. Kelley was nearing completion of the run over the designated coordinates, and by some miracle he was still airborne.

On this particular morning not everyone on the ground stared up with hostile intent. French writer Georges Godefroy, a native of Le Havre, was keeping a diary of the war years that he and his fellow Havrists endured under German occupation. Well aware of the proximity of invasion forces just thirty miles away, the civilians were alert to new developments. The firing of heavy guns around the city around midday was a break in routine and captured everyone's attention. Was it the prelude to another landing? With evident relish, Godefroy paged to the end of his journal notations and began recording the special event: "In the morning [it was actually midday] a visit by a reconnaissance plane which the Flak attempted to bring down—in vain; then complete calm reigned until the evening."[10]

Six miles up, the twin cameras reeled to the end of their spools, and Kelley banked sharply to port. Nosing over into a shallow dive, he gathered even more speed and set course north over the Channel again, pulling steadily away from the danger zone. Amazingly, no German interceptors had attacked on this flight, more evidence that the Allies were maintaining air supremacy over the Normandy battlefront. Recce pilots generally kept radio silence during a mission, but upon nearing the English South Coast and knowing that British radar would be tracking him, Kelley broadcast the agreed-upon password. "Backwash" was typical. Radar controllers and air defense personnel knew that a friendly aircraft was returning to base.

At 1415, a scant ninety minutes after he lifted off, Flight Lieutenant Kelley touched down at Benson. Alerted by his one-word message over the coast, ground crews were waiting by the hardstand. They hurriedly detached the film packs from his aircraft's cameras and handed them to two special couriers from PIU Medmenham, fifteen miles away. This country mansion, poised on bluffs overlooking the Thames, with its sprawling grounds dotted with prefabricated huts, had evolved into the world's most expert photointerpretation center. Hundreds of British and American PIs had learned their secret trade here, and the PIU organization had assembled a vast system of advanced equipment and trained personnel for their work. The couriers rushed the newly landed twin spools into the PIU film processing laboratories, having marked them for immediate processing with the highest priority. This was a hot item, and the senior brass were waiting impatiently for the PI experts to exploit the latest intelligence from Le Havre for impending operations.

Soon technicians were developing and fixing the twin spools of 100 ASA film in chemical baths, and images began to appear as large negatives. Speed was essential here. Even before the emulsion had finished drying, they placed clear cellophane strips over the exposures and began making giant black-and-white contact prints directly from the negatives. Already, the photointerpreters were gleaning information from the reverse black-and-white images on the negatives and soon would move on to the prints. Long practice had made them efficient in reading the images either way. Loss of quality from the rapid processing was minimal, and speedy interpretation more than made up for a minor loss of detail. Stereoscopes at the ready, they waited for the dual overlapped prints of Le Havre's port. The question was, what did these aerial photographs, obtained at such risk in human life, tell them?[11]

On that day the hard-won images told Medmenham's PIs a great deal. Years of monitoring Le Havre and other sites of military value in Occupied

Europe had allowed them to build up extensive files in the PIU library, re-
plete with sequences of images and banks of information about targets.
They called this bank of information about a target its "base line." First-
phase photointerpretation was satisfied with identifying hot items, in this
case E-boats. Second-phase work, usually performed by the same PI on
the same day, required looking at all the frames from the mission for new
or more comprehensive information. Sometimes vital new intelligence
emerged from takes where the PIs were evaluating completely different
objects. Using special intelligence, Professor R. V. Jones had deduced solid
evidence for Germany's rocket and other V-weapons programs in the summer of 1943, and PIs were put on the alert. Flight Officer Babington-Smith
discovered a V-1 flying-bomb (not Jones's rocket) on a stereo pair taken
over Peenemünde on 23 June 1943 and reviewed by her on 13 November
1943. She placed that intriguing evidence in her base line. Several weeks
passed. Then on 1 December while looking at the first frame—therefore
without the benefit of stereo imaging—on a long roll from another photographic run over Peenemünde made on 28 November, Babington-Smith
spotted a second miniature airplane poised on a ramp. She concluded that
it was a V-1 about to be launched. The expert pilot making the photoreconnaissance run, Squadron Leader John Merifield of 541 Squadron, also
based at Benson, was simply photographing an airfield, and only good luck
had allowed him to capture an image of the nearby ramp on the coast.[12]
Babington-Smith's photointerpretive skills and methodical persistence did
the rest. Making the connection between the V-1 and its launch requirements, the Allies systematically bombed the telltale ramps which in the
meantime had begun to appear in Occupied France. By delaying Hitler's
V-1 attacks on London by six months, the effort saved thousands of lives.
Second-phase PI was well worth the effort.[13]

Third-phase photointerpretation entailed a different dimension. As important as identifying objects of military value, changes in target information were the desirable product now, and Medmenham's specialist PIs who
knew the target's history intimately were waiting to perform this demanding work. It was a mark of their importance that they also had access to
sanitized versions of Ultra and to other forms of intelligence as part of the
base line with which to gauge target information. These specialists possessed intelligence, phenomenal memories, and imagination, although
they had to temper that last trait and not assume too much from the images they analyzed. All of them could see stereo and could concentrate on
minute detail.

By June 1944 the Allies had trained hundreds of PIs who had honed their skills to a fine edge preparing for the invasion. Over a hundred of them alone were concentrating on the V-weapon sites. Some specialized in transportation networks. A few found their niche in ports and naval targets. Third-phase PI could take days, sometimes weeks, of analysis. On this particular day several specialist PIs began poring over one site, the port area of Le Havre. With files from previous missions over the harbor at the ready, they looked for the new and unexpected. This form of analysis was and still is an arcane science, and it was the unknown specialists at Medmenham who had become its masters in World War II, outstripping the Germans in sophistication and technique two years earlier.

The PIs had good reason to be excited by Flight Lieutenant Kelley's work. The photos did not lie. Le Havre's harbor was chockablock full of German naval craft! It had never been so crowded before. Moreover, the Bassin Theophile had the heaviest concentration of boats. This was a tidal basin in the outer harbor with direct access to the Channel. The PIs noted that the craft were tied up in such a way that they could put to sea rapidly. The inner basins, which could be reached only through locks, were far less crowded because, depending on the phase of Le Havre's twenty-foot tides, vessels at war readiness might be caught like fish in a barrel if an air raid materialized over the city. Forewarned by this evidence, RAF planning staffs could confine the target to a specific part of the port. Best of all, the eccentric bows and fanlike skullcap bridges of the E-boats were prominently displayed in one particular area of the Bassin Theophile. Using the film's known scale and their own practiced measuring skills, the PIs determined that the craft were about 115 feet in length, just as they should be. They were moored in quantity alongside the Quai Johannes Couvert, which in turn lay astride the sprawling Gare Maritime. That placed them just to the west of another prominent feature, the old prewar passenger liner *Paris,* now a wreck and lying on its side next to the quay. There were several more E-boats nearby, including two tied up beside the huge floating dock. Undoubtedly several more were inside the enormous pens, they thought. The sleek coastal craft had plenty of company too: four of Germany's 900-ton torpedo vessels, the so-called T-boats; numerous R-boats, that is, the German Navy's 125-ton minelayers; minesweepers; VP-boats, or picket boats; auxiliary craft; tugs; and harbor defense launches. Small craft of every description were tied up to the quays. There was scarcely an empty space anywhere in the entire outer harbor.

The E-boats held the photointerpreters' closest attention. Their distinctive vertical profile with interrupted bow curves made them leap out of the newly made prints. Why were the Germans concentrating so many light naval units in one place? Perhaps they assumed that the formidable air defenses of the large port plus the presence of hardened pens would deter the Allies from attacking. It was also likely that the Germans were basing their dispositions on the assumption that Bomber Command, if it came, would, as always, attack in the safety of darkness. By nightfall, as had happened so often in the past, the speedy E-boats and the dangerous minelaying R-boats would be out on the open water, stalking Allied shipping or laying their explosive charges in the shallow waters around the invasion fleet. Come the next dawn, they would slip into a different port, and the maddening shell game would begin again.

These striking aerial photos told another story as well. Crowded into Le Havre, the German naval dispositions posed an imminent threat to the Eastern invasion fleet only thirty miles away. With so many specialized coastal forces concentrated in the tidal basin, and poised as they were for rapid deployment, the German naval flotillas were obviously being readied for a massive sally that same night. For the moment at least, the Germans dared not move. Allied air superiority had them trapped there for the duration of daylight hours, with no hope of exit until 2300 hours at the earliest. The Allies had perhaps eight hours to react to this unmistakable threat. Using long-established telecommunications links, the PIs passed along their evidence and their conclusions to the appropriate commands including SHAEF and representatives to SHAEF from the AEAF, the Admiralty and its OIC, and Bomber Command Headquarters at High Wycombe. Confronted with this timely intelligence, the Allied leadership was faced with a series of crucial decisions that same afternoon.

Alert

First, ANCXF Admiral Ramsay, who was in overall charge of Operation Neptune, evaluated the evidence with his staff. They quickly reviewed the history of E-boat operations, especially since D-day, considered the Ultra decryption that revealed cancellation of the previous night's operations, reviewed the OIC's analysis, and absorbed the import of the reconnaissance mission and PI findings just in from PIU Medmenham. Aware of how difficult it was to intercept the E-boats on open water and remembering their conclusion that attacking the E-boats in port was their best recourse, Ramsay decided that the time had come to act. Raising a telephone receiver, he took the unprecedented move of "requesting" a mission directly of C-in-C Bomber Command Harris at High Wycombe. As Ramsay recorded in his concluding report on Operation Neptune, "By 14th June there was considerable concentration of enemy E-boats in [Le] Havre, and at my request Bomber Command carried out a heavy attack in the port just before dusk with the object of immobilizing the enemy craft."[14]

As naval commander in chief and therefore subordinate only to Eisenhower, Ramsay carried a tremendous responsibility for the safety of Operation Neptune. At this crucial moment in the war he wielded the highest authority, including the selection of bombing targets. A month earlier, in early May 1944, Ramsay, Rear Adm. Alan Kirk, and their respective naval staffs had determined that the Allies would require a heavy bombing raid at short notice on E-boats in connection with the invasion. Likely targets were the ports of Boulogne, Le Havre, Cherbourg, or possibly Brest. Now they knew the shell game had ended at Le Havre. Such targets had stout concrete bunkers, but Ramsay had also warned that the E-boat Force had started dispersing its coastal craft around each harbor. Fully briefed by the OIC, Ramsay and his staff were able to offer valuable operational details to Bomber Command Headquarters. For example, given the short nights of June on the Channel, E-boats would not depart until 2300 hours. He left it for Bomber Command to solve the tactical needs for the impending raid. Warned weeks in advance, C-in-C Harris and his staff were well prepared for Ramsay's request. The mission they envisaged would require a combination of tactical precision bombing for hardened sites and concentrated area bombing for the large port.[15]

Bomber Command HQ at High Wycombe immediately sent out orders to the various group headquarters under its command. At 5 Group, AVM Cochrane and his staff issued their orders in turn to 617 Squadron at Woodhall Spa and to many other all-Lancaster squadrons of 5 Group. This was a major effort encompassing squadrons from several Bomber Command groups: 1 Group, 3 Group, and several squadrons of Pathfinder Force at 8 Group, as well as the independent 5 Group. Because of SHAEF's unusual request, Le Havre, and specifically its concentrations of German naval craft, had suddenly become the highest priority air target. Years of operational planning and execution had honed Bomber Command's many elements into a smoothly functioning machine. That afternoon preparations got under way for a major raid involving several hundred bombers. Special photographic multiprinter machines at Medmenham spewed out hundreds of duplicate prints of the port of Le Havre. Air staffs for the participating squadrons prepared mission briefs outlining flight plans, targets, including specific aiming points, bomb loads, markers and flares, flak concentrations, meteorological reports, and all of the minutiae associated with a major raid.

At Woodhall Spa, navigator Tom Bennett recalled that the pace of preparation was deliberate and businesslike rather than frantic. His squadron had not seen action since the Saumur Tunnel episode on 8 June, so the aircrews were well rested. All over Lincolnshire and East Anglia alerts were going out to the Lancaster squadrons of the various bomber groups plus the Pathfinders. Le Havre was a shallow penetration of German-occupied territory, in contrast to remote and dangerous targets like Berlin or Munich. Even so, the timing of this raid was anything but normal, and it set the aircrews to wondering.[16]

Something rare was about to happen to the Bomber Command crews. For the first time in the war they were going to raid en masse in daylight. Apprised by ANCXF Ramsay when the German naval units were likely to put to sea, High Wycombe had issued orders setting H-hour at 2230 hours that evening. Since the Allies were on "British Double Summertime daylight saving time" in the spring and summer months for the duration of World War II, they had set their clocks two hours ahead of Greenwich Mean Time. This adjustment, known as "Baker Time," meant they would be starting the raid at the peacetime equivalent of 2030. Since Le Havre was virtually on the Greenwich longitudinal line and close to fifty degrees north latitude and the calendar was within one week of the summer solstice, the bomber force could expect the sun to be just setting as they approached Le Havre. There would be plenty of daylight to mark and bomb their targets.

What could account for this remarkable change in tactics? Commander in Chief Harris himself had decided to make the shift. A conservative when it came to tactical innovations, he had voiced the opinion as late as April 1944 that "it would be unprofitable and uneconomical to change over to day bombing." However, with the coming of the invasion and the achievement of Allied air superiority over the Normandy battlefield, Harris recognized that the situation had fundamentally changed. As noted in an RAF summary of events for that period:

> After D-Day . . . it became evident, that, in spite of all expectations to the
> contrary, enemy day fighters were unwilling to react against strong fighter
> cover. At the same time, owing to the short nights at that time of the year,
> it became impossible to undertake any deep penetration by night into en-
> emy or enemy occupied territory, and the degree of darkness was such
> that a high casualty rate was to be expected on all night operations. The
> C-in-C [Harris] decided, therefore, that it might be less costly to undertake
> deeper penetrations into enemy occupied territory by day with good
> fighter support than to operate by night during the short dark period.

Arrangements were made for fighter cover to be provided by Spitfires of No. 11 Group . . . and the first large scale daylight operation since May 1943 was carried out on the evening of the 14th June 1944, against the Dock Area of Le Havre. Fighter opposition was practically nil, and this Command subsequently carried out frequent day attacks against targets in France and the Low Countries, fighter cover being provided by No. 11 Group in every instance.[17]

In short, the raid on Le Havre marked a turning point in RAF operations. Despite his innate conservatism, one week after the invasion and in the aftermath of the most intensive air campaign to date, Harris felt he had compelling reasons for making the change. It was a credit to his tactical flexibility that he reversed himself so quickly and completely. Now it remained for his aircrews to discover whether Harris's decision had been well advised. The raid was unusual in another respect. Unlike the spring raids that had seen the maturing of 617 Squadron's bombing and marking tactics exclusively within 5 Group, the raid on Le Havre entailed the use of Bomber Command's main force. Squadrons from at least four groups were involved. The attack would involve 234 aircraft including 221 Lancasters arranged in three waves.[18]

As it had done in the experimental spring raids 617 Squadron was going to head up this aerial armada with three special marking Mosquitoes led by Leonard Cheshire. They would be followed by twenty-two Lancasters with a special assignment in the overall mission. Each would be lugging just one bomb, a twelve-thousand-pound Tallboy. The twenty-two crews that had reached the top of 617 Squadron's bombing ladder had won the right to throw the largest missile in the Allied armory.

All afternoon, ordnance specialists had been preparing the giant bombs. They performed this demanding work away from the ground crews and aircraft on the perimeter of the field at a bomb dump whose earthen berm walls would deflect blast upward in case of an accidental detonation. Inside those thick walls, crews were assembling the two major components of the new Tallboys. First, they inspected the torpex-filled nose section for any faults and then inserted three fusing pistols, containing the time delay mechanisms, into the bomb's three exploder pockets. Three fusing wires led from the pistols, one per pistol, out of the bomb housing through a fairlead opening for external attachment. After attaching the pistols, the armorers joined a light alloy tail fairing to the heavy nose, completing the streamlined shape of the bomb. By this time the fusing wires were protruding from the bomb, ready to be inserted into the jaws of a fusing attachment in the bomb bay roof once they had raised the monster into the aircraft. This way the awesome bomb remained inert until its aircrew chose to arm it. They inspected the entire housing to be sure the components were correctly aligned and there were no unintended nicks, dents, or scratches to disturb its ballistic qualities.

Assembly completed, they lifted the bomb with a heavy Ransome Rapier crane onto a special trolley, then connected the RAF's workhorse David Brown tractors to it and hauled the Tallboy under the open bomb bay doors of a waiting Lancaster. They had to position the bomb precisely under the aircraft. The trolley was fitted with four winches that lifted an integral cradle, carrying the bomb slowly up into the specially modified bay. Normal bombing up procedure was to attach winches inside the aircraft after which the crew fed winch cable through the floor for attachment to the bomb, but the heavy Tallboys placed too much strain on such a system. In addition, the Lancasters had strengthened bomb beams to cope with the heavy load. Now the crew raised the bomb gingerly until a dowel pin fixed to the bomb bay roof could be inserted into a recess in the bomb casing. With the payload now in place, the crew took two metallic link strop arms dangling from the aircraft on either side of the bomb and lifted them up, joining them under the belly of the bomb with an electromechanical release slip. Then they took up the slack in the strops, tightening their port and starboard attachment points inside the aircraft. Finally, they adjusted steadying crutches fore and aft to complete the securing of the bomb. These precautions held the Tallboy firm against vibrations and the slipstream. On a wartime mission the Lancasters might encounter bad weather and heavy turbulence. Enemy interceptors, flak, and searchlights might demand even more violent maneuvering although there was a limit on how much strain the aircraft could take from a six-ton bomb no matter how well secured. Crews simply had to endure the risks. Satisfied that the bomb was secure, the armorers inserted the three fusing wires into the jaws of the fusing unit fitted to the bomb bay roof. Later, during the mission, the bomb aimer would select a setting marked Bomb Fused, and the jaws would clamp the wires securely, allowing the ends inside the bomb to pull clear from the pistols when the Tallboy dropped.[19]

Meanwhile other ground crewmen were feeding ammunition belts, performing last-minute maintenance, polishing perspex canopies, and attending to all the other duties that would bring the great bombers to a state of readiness. It was no accident that the squadron had few mechanical breakdowns and a correspondingly low early-return rate. There were good reasons why the aircrews respected the ground crews at Woodhall Spa and vice versa. By early evening all was in readiness.

The Raid Begins

It was a strange experience for the aircrews to be flying so early that evening. For the first time they were manning their aircraft for an operation in which the crucial strike phase would take place in broad daylight. At exactly 2010 hours the first bomber left the ground, led by Flt. Comdr. Les "Smiler" Munro, a New Zealander. In rapid succession the others followed, and within fifteen minutes all twenty-two aircraft were airborne. Following long-established routine, they assembled over Woodhall Spa at fifteen hundred to two thousand feet, keying on each other visually, with each successive aircraft cutting off the wide curve of the formation as it turned over Lincolnshire. With the last bomber aloft, the squadron was formed.

They then arranged themselves into a row of V-shaped subformations with three or four aircraft forming each "Vic." The big bombers flew with a lateral clearance of two hundred feet, and each Vic assumed a slightly different, or "staggered," altitude, the first Vic forming up at the highest altitude and each trailing Vic assembling a few hundred feet below the one in front. Sometimes they worked it in reverse so that the first bombers flew lower than those following.

Once the squadron had approached its initiation point (the leg of the flight plan that led directly to the target) it would adjust its position slightly for the actual bombing run. The aircraft would then move out of the Vic and draw abreast of one another while continuing to fly at slightly varied heights. They would also maintain the staggered altitude and distance between each line. This was 617 Squadron's "gaggle" formation for final approach to the target and was used by all Bomber Command squadrons. They had devised it so that each aircraft could fly individually onto the target and bomb with the greatest accuracy. It also made spotting and aiming by German flak crews more difficult since no single bomber was at the same altitude as another. The net result was that they offered no horizontal or vertical plane for the Germans' heavy caliber guns.[20]

The Lancasters gained altitude as rapidly as their heavy loads permitted. Because penetration of German-defended air space to Le Havre was shallow, the bombers were carrying less than full fuel tanks. In fact 617 Squadron's 12,000-pound Tallboys were not as heavy a load as that being hefted by the other Lancaster squadrons. Some of their aircraft were carrying fourteen 1,000-pounders, while others had loaded up a mix of 1,000-pounders and 500-pounders. A few bombers from main force were carrying 4,000-pound high-blast blockbusters, which the crews sometimes called cookies. The smaller bombs would be effective in throwing splinters across docks, quays, and the surfaces of ships. The lighter bombs also functioned as antipersonnel bombs. Somehow a rumor had circulated among the 617 Squadron crews that the Tallboys weighed 14,000 pounds, and they assumed on this raid that their payloads were identical to those of other squadrons. In practice the 2,000-pound difference between assumed and actual weight made little difference. There was room for only one Tallboy in the specially modified Lancasters anyway.[21]

There was another reason for 617 Squadron's slightly lower fuel load. They wanted to attain the highest practicable altitude in order to give their new bombs maximum velocity when they "put" them onto the target. Thus the twenty-two Lancasters attained altitudes that varied anywhere from 19,100 feet down to 15,500 feet depending on their position in the gaggle. Soon they were leading a bomber stream of 221 Lancasters from the various groups plus several Mosquitoes from 8 Group (PFF) who would join in the target marking started by Cheshire and 617 Squadron. All three of the Pathfinders' navigational and marking aids would serve them well on this raid. Gee remained unjammed over the Channel. Oboe's Cat and Mouse stations easily reached Le Havre, and the centimetric radar of H2S worked best when scanning ports.

Cheshire's primary aiming point was to be the concrete bunker, which he would attack at low level, using the 5 Group marking method that he and Mick Martin had pioneered. Once marked, the bunker was to receive half of the Tallboys. Other 5 Group squadrons in main force were to follow up with large numbers of conventional bombs with which to saturate the area surrounding the bunker.

The second aiming point, to be marked by five Oboe-equipped Pathfinder Mosquitoes with green flares for main force, was about six hundred yards north and east along the quays and docks that formed the upper end of the tidal basin, the Bassin Theophile. This second aiming point was centered alongside the Gare Maritime where photointelligence from that day's mission had indicated the heaviest concentrations of naval craft including the valuable E-boats. Like the pens, this second aiming point was selected to receive eleven Tallboys.[22]

Above and ranging in front of the huge bombers were Spitfires from 11 Group, forming a protective shield against would-be attackers. Aided by daylight and clear weather at height, the mission proceeded according to plan as the gaggles swept across the summer sky. It was yet another display of the Allies' emerging supremacy in the air as the bomber force thundered overhead, crossing central and southern England.

It was an unusual sight for onlookers accustomed to glimpsing mostly American aircraft flying combat missions in broad daylight. Of late the Americans had begun to dispense with camouflage paint, and the formations of new aluminum aircraft sometimes glinted like schools of silver fish as they floated in box formations high above the English countryside. By contrast that evening, the Lancasters' dull black camouflage paint silhouetted them boldly in the sunny evening light as they headed for their rendezvous point. Their darkened appearance, huge throbbing engines, and prominent twin tails gave the big bombers a sinister look. The modified 617 Squadron Lancasters had an added feature: a pronounced bulge amidships where modified bomb bay doors hinted at the special payloads inside.

The raid that was about to begin was unusual not only because of its unorthodox timing, weaponry, and target selection but also because of the meshing of its strategic main force squadrons with tactically precise components of 5 Group, especially 617 Squadron. For the first time they would be attacking the same target simultaneously. Whatever the outcome, it promised to be a memorable evening.

Chapter **10**

The Witches' Cauldron

A scant six hours had elapsed between PRU confirmation of German naval concentrations at Le Havre and the moment when 221 of Bomber Command's Lancasters approached the edge of friendly air space, making their way to the Bay of the Seine. It was a measure of the huge strength Bomber Command had accumulated at this stage of the war that two other bombing forces, each larger than the Le Havre raiders, were assembling hurriedly for attacks later that night. One force of 337 aircraft, including 223 Lancasters, 100 Halifaxes, and 14 Mosquitoes, was hastily preparing to strike German troop concentrations. Allied army reports had just that day located them at Aunay-sur-Odon and Évrecy, and the heavy bombing force hoped to trap them there before they could reach Normandy. Yet another force of 330 bombers, mostly Halifaxes, was preparing to attack railway centers at Cambrai, Douai, and St. Pol, thus isolating the Germans in Normandy even more.[1] However, the main attention at High Wycombe was centered on the special force winging its way south this evening. So much was new about the impending raid on Le Havre that anticipation within C-in-C Harris's staff was keen.

The flight plan, worked out weeks in advance, carried them southward, well away from the East Coast, Bomber Command's operations staff having charted a course far enough away from Occupied Europe to avoid German radar plotting. The bomber stream droned along farther west, crossing the South Coast at Beachy Head. By this time the stream was heading almost due south, crossing the widest part of the English Channel and heading for the Bay of the Seine. Plans called for the bomber force to attack from the southwest with the sun at their backs, and once over the Channel they would not make landfall again until they came in directly over the harbor of Le Havre. Since the bomb aimers needed at least seven minutes and preferably ten from the initial point of the bombing run into the target, they would begin their run well out in the Seine Bay, passing directly over the invasion fleet, north of the Normandy beaches.

One piece of luck stayed with them: the weather. While the mission had started in clear skies in the north, the attacking squadrons had encountered thick cloud over much of southern England, and the question in many minds was how the raiders would fare over the target. The records of 100 Squadron indicated how the problem resolved itself. "Between 8 and 10/10ths cloud was encountered en route as far as the English coast, with tops up to 10,000 feet," a squadron meteorologist reported, and then added, "over the target the weather was clear with excellent visibility."[2] The Germans, many crews felt, had often benefited from bad weather over targets. If so, fortune deserted them this time. Watching the sparkling waters far below reflect the sunset, the bomb aimers knew that soon they would be able to see the targets perfectly.

Three miles above the Channel and approximately twenty minutes from the target, the 617 Squadron bomb aimers began preparing for the drop. They switched on the SABS and fed preliminary settings, such as height above target, into it. The target on this mission was at sea level. The SABS provided for the ballistic characteristics of the type of bomb being dropped, and so each bomb aimer dialed a bomb-class letter into the instrument that defined the trail and time lag for the Tallboy. The navigator, having calculated the precise outside air temperature, deduced the aircraft's true height and airspeed with the aid of his Dalton computer. He passed the information by intercom to the bomb aimer, who carefully set the readings into his sight. Then the navigator calculated wind velocity and the exact course the aircraft was maintaining on the bomb run in order to update the bomb aimer on drift and ground speed. The bomb aimer entered those readings into the sight, aligning the aircraft as accurately as possible. All calibrations up to this point were basically an initial guide to the bomb aimer as the Lancaster approached the target. The most intense phase would begin as the bomb aimer manipulated his bomb sight controls and, along with the pilot, brought the aircraft to the point of release.[3]

With preliminary computations completed, the navigator advised his pilot of the time and distance to a crucial threshold in the bombing mission, the Identification Point (I.P.), also known as the Initiation Point. The pilot made a rated turn onto the I.P., which was an easily identifiable point approximately twenty to thirty miles from the target. In this instance it might have been a prominent feature on the nearby Normandy Coast or some feature of the invasion fleet, such as the British Mulberry off Arromanches. As each bomber in the stream passed this point, the pilot opened the bomb doors and trimmed the aircraft to the required height and airspeed. At this point the navigator called on the bomb aimer to read back the vital settings he had made on the bomb sight. Methodically, the navigator checked off each setting as the bomb aimer read from his instruments, ensuring that they were in agreement on all the variables.[4]

One crucial factor that had to be established in order to ensure precision bombing by main force squadrons was wind direction and strength. The RAF called it wind-finding. Using Gee and, if available, Oboe or H2S, plus another instrument called an air plot indicator, Lancaster navigators could fix their positions precisely and determine the exact wind directions as the bombers drifted from the flight plan and their crews brought their aircraft back on course. They constantly upgraded their information on wind drift and were particularly concerned with it over the target. Radio operators from observation aircraft sent wind-finding information back to Group Headquarters by wireless telegraphy as the British called it, tapping a telegraph key to transmit the information with greater reliability than voice transmission. On the receiving end, each Group Headquarters made their computations accordingly. They then issued a final "bombing wind" to the attacking aircraft of main force just two minutes before H-hour, in time for the bomb aimers to feed this fresh information into their Mark XIV bombsights.[5]

This information was so vital to accurate main force bombing that 5 Group had a second system. Lead aircraft could drop markers about a mile upwind of the target. Then, one or more of the Mosquito navigators measured the markers' wind drift with his air plot indicator and the Mark XIV bombsight used by main force bombers to measure wind direction and velocity. The crew radioed that information by voice to a link aircraft, which passed it back to 5 Group Headquarters for processing and redistribution in the same way as the first method.[6]

It was approximately one hour after the big bombers departed from

Woodhall Spa that 617 Squadron's three Mosquitoes lifted off from base at 2120 hours and sped south, rapidly overtaking the bomber stream. Their special job was to mark the target for 5 Group, and like the Lancasters, they flew in a Vic formation. Wing Comdr. Leonard Cheshire and his navigator, Flt. Lt. Pat Kelly, were in the lead aircraft. On their left another expert marking pilot, Squadron Leader Dave Shannon from Australia and his navigator, Flying Officer Len Sumpter, flew in the number two position, while Flt. Lt. Gerry Fawke and his navigator, Flying Officer Tom Bennett, completed the Vic. Cheshire had by far the most dangerous task of the entire undertaking: diving low to drop red spot fires directly onto the concrete pens in conformance with 5 Group's novel marking method. Big though the pens were, 550 feet by 250 feet, they presented a comparatively small target from on high, especially since it was around the Mole Centrale that the Germans had concentrated their fiercest antiaircraft defenses. If Cheshire's markers were off or if he were shot down, the backup crew of Shannon and Sumpter would have to try it. Fawke and Bennett had the dubious honor of making the third effort to penetrate the hornets' nest if that should prove necessary.

Everyone seemed to have been struck by the novelty of Bomber Command's first mass raid in daylight. "It was a beautiful, cloudless, sunny evening," navigator Tom Bennett recounted. He added with tongue firmly in cheek: "Both navigators Sumpter and Bennett took advantage of the unusual circumstances (the Mossies generally operated independently on normal missions) to enjoy a flight free of navigational duties. They made sure that Pat Kelly in the lead aircraft was aware of their 'holiday' by lying back in their seats, with both hands behind their heads, sun-bathing in the warm sunshine that filled their cockpits. It was obvious from Pat's chagrined 'fist-waving' that he'd got the message! Of course, both navigators were surreptitiously map-reading and checking position regularly."[7]

This seeming light-heartedness from crews with an average age of twenty-two belied the fact that 617 Squadron and the main force were approaching the danger point in their mission, and everyone knew it. "The heavy accurate flak defences were well known by the more experienced aircrew," Bennett wrote, "and the port was always given a wide berth on normal Bomber Command operations."[8]

The Mosquitoes could afford a late departure. Making 380 miles per hour at 6,000 feet, they cruised more than 100 mph faster than the heavily loaded Lancasters; they sped through the evening, rapidly overtaking the black silhouetted gaggles that sailed along two miles higher up in the sky. "The flight went well," Bennett said, "and, right on schedule, the Vic of

Mosquitoes wheeled over the Bay of the Seine and headed for the target some minutes ahead of the Zero Hour for commencement of bombing, approaching from a south-westerly direction at a height of 6,000 feet." At that height, and keeping their distance, the Mosquitoes could escape the worst of the light flak from the port area, and there were no German aircraft to be seen as yet. They chose that height deliberately because of a gap in the German antiaircraft defenses. Above 3,000 feet light, quick-firing weapons began to lose their effectiveness. Below 10,000 feet the big guns had trouble traversing fast enough to catch up with targets, especially fast aircraft like the Mosquitoes. The veteran marking pilots of 617 Squadron were well aware of this gap in the German air defenses. Allied air defenses faced exactly the same problem.[9]

At 2229 hours and without fanfare the preliminaries to the attack began. "Going in!" Cheshire radioed tersely, as Bennett watched, "and his Mossie disappeared from the forward view of the accompanying aircraft, both of which immediately broke formation to port and starboard."[10]

As his wing mates resumed a horizontal flight attitude, standing off the port city, they had an excellent view of what happened next. "I failed to pick up Cheshire's aircraft," Bennett continued, "until suddenly the harbour area sent up the most concentrated curtain of light flak and tracer that I had ever seen! . . . or ever was to see! This creeping curtain was milliseconds behind the Mosquito as it broke across the harbour at very low level. It seemed as if every gun on every ship was firing at it!"[11]

Months of intensive training, development of effective marking techniques, and trading the Lancaster for high-performance Mosquitoes paid off. Cheshire dived to less than a hundred feet above the water, making well over four hundred miles per hour, and placed his red markers, or spot fires as they were called, directly onto the roof of the concrete pens. "I think I almost sobbed with relief when I saw that the markers had been accurately laid," Bennett wrote, "at least 'accurately' from my standpoint, which did not mean that they would meet the approval of Chesh and Dave." Awed by what he had just seen, Bennett listened intently to the radio conversation that developed between Cheshire and his number two, Dave Shannon. "Would you like me to back those up, sir?" he asked. "No thanks, David," was Cheshire's clipped response. "I think they are OK." After what the crews of the two orbiting Mosquitoes had just seen, their commanding officer's words came like a reprieve from a death sentence. "Cheshire gave the order to commence the bombing of the pens," Bennett recounted, as the three Mosquitoes circled above the city, maintaining altitude at six thousand feet, "and . . . we had a grandstand view of magnificent bombing." Cheshire remained in charge, functioning as master bomber.[12]

With the initial markers well and truly placed, and with additional green target indicators accurately dropped on the second aiming point from a higher altitude by Pathfinder Mosquitoes from 8 Group, the twenty-two Lancasters of 617 Squadron led off the bombardment. Half the aircraft vectored over the pens. The other half headed for the offset markers six hundred yards to the northeast near the Gare Maritime. Because the 617 Squadron aircraft were all dropping the rare and expensive Tallboys and because they needed to drop them with the greatest possible accuracy, it was imperative that 617 Squadron unload first before spray, smoke, and fire obscured the target area.

One of the lead bombers was piloted by Squadron Leader "Big Joe" McCarthy, a physically imposing American volunteer who had trained with the RCAF in Canada before serving with the RAF in Europe. McCarthy was one of 617 Squadron's old hands, a survivor of the Dams Raid in 1943. He was flying alongside the overall squadron commander for this mission, New Zealander Les Munro. McCarthy and his crew navigated conscientiously in the front of the aerial armada, leading their gaggle along the prescribed flight path and putting the formation in the optimum position for attack. "On the Le Havre raid," he recalled, "after turning east to run up to the pens, at least three of our aircraft were almost abreast as we came up to the aiming point."[13]

With a precision and concentration born of months of intensive training and operations, the crew turned to their respective functions. They were at seventeen thousand feet, and the run had been a good one. Using Gee, the only radar navigational aid employed by 617 Squadron, McCarthy's navigator, Flying Officer Donald A. McLean, had plotted the exact course and heading to get them to the aiming point. The radio operator, Warrant Officer Len Eaton, received the latest wind information sent out by radio telegraphy from 5 Group Headquarters.

At this critical phase in the mission the crew's bomb aimer, Flying Officer W. A. "Danny" Daniel, assumed the central role. During the prebombing phase he had given verbal instructions to his pilot to line up on the bombsight's graticule, its fine aiming hairs on the optical glass in the shape of a sword with its blade thrust forward. The graticule's cross arms, its handle and blade, did not actually intersect but left a small clear area instead. On final approach, the target appeared to move down the blade, entering the circular clear area. This was what Danny Daniel saw as he adjusted two wheels on his SABS, a range control wheel and a line control wheel, keeping the graticule on the middle of the target. The latter wheel was connected to a bombing directional indicator (BDI) on Pilot Mc-Carthy's instrument panel that indicated the fine flight corrections needed. On the final run up to the target, pilot and bomb aimer required no verbal communication. They monitored their instruments instead, making adjustments as needed. A few seconds before release a warning light appeared on McCarthy's BDI and Daniel's SABS simultaneously, signaling that a drop was imminent. Two electrical contacts built into the bombsight did the rest. Once the variables lined up, the circuits closed, triggering the release automatically, and the warning light went out. Daniel did not have to press a button. With the French shoreline looming up, he watched transfixed as a large concrete bunker slid down the blade of his graticule.[14]

At exactly 2232 hours the big aircraft lurched. The bluish grey metallic finish of a Tallboy glinted in the fading rays of the sun as it emerged from the oversized bomb bay doors. In the bomb bay roof, three arming wires dangled free, having ripped out of the casing's fairlead, cocking the fuse pistols inside. This in turn began the process of transforming the inert payload into a live bomb. Gravity did the rest as the giant missile nosed over and, gathering speed, hurtled more than three miles through its trajectory onto the target below.

Simultaneously with its release, the subtly offset fins began to kick the big bomb around its longitudinal axis. Within seconds it began to spin like an elongated football, and as the missile's speed increased, its outlines became a grey whir. By the time it struck, its builders estimated that it would be spinning at over five hundred revolutions per minute. The time lapse from release to impact would be on the order of thirty seconds, and it would strike its target with a terminal velocity approaching the speed of sound. The armorers had made an unusual setting this time. The giant bombs were fused to explode a half second after impact on a solid surface. They would bury themselves in mud or man-made structures, making penetration, but not too deep. Scientists, technicians, and crews had done their best with the technology of the 1940s in hopes of placing the deadly Tallboy on target.[15]

"I had no time to watch the bomb dropping," Big Joe McCarthy recounted later, "and had to depend on . . . my bomb aimer for comments." Bomb aimers and rear gunners had the best visibility of the ground, and the former, especially, took a keen professional interest in seeing where their missiles landed. In this instance, however, they met an unexpected complication. The three lead aircraft in the gaggle, although they were making their bombing runs independently, had, unbeknownst to each other, released their bombs at virtually the same instant. That fact spoke well for the reliability and standard performance of the SABS, the crews, and the Lancaster as a stable bombing platform. However, as the seconds ticked by and the three bombs fell into view, none of the three crews could say with certainty which bomb had dropped from which aircraft. McCarthy, still relying on Bomb Aimer Danny Daniel to observe the results, continued: "I know he mentioned that three bombs hit the pens almost together. Naturally, it might have been a second or two between each explosion, and they were spaced one in the center with a second just slightly back and to the right. A third hit the E-boats, and by then I peeled off and headed back to base."[16]

McCarthy was right in turning away promptly. Le Havre or any other target was no place to loiter or sightsee. Follow-up crews could observe and report on subsequent developments.

Navigator Bennett, on the other hand, with a ringside seat at six thousand feet in his orbiting Mosquito, could observe the results much better. "The pens area disappeared in a cloud of dust and debris as some Tallboys struck home," he noted, "whilst huge boiling circles in the water indicated near misses before the missiles exploded and added their waves and spray to the view."[17]

The Operations Record Book (ORB) for 617 Squadron recorded the suddenness and concentration of the attack. The ORB was a composite of the observations and experiences of each crew. For this night it showed the first bombs dropping at 2232 hours, and the last at 2234. Within seconds conventional bombs were also falling in quantity from 1 Group and 5 Group squadrons as well. As Flying Officer Bennett observed: "The Tallboy bombing of the harbour area was concentrated across the whole area, and much of the bombing of the supporting Main Force squadrons aligned itself into the confines of the target."[18]

In order to achieve maximum effect from their new bombs, 617 Squadron crews had performed as instructed and divided their bomb loads between the two aiming points: "Eleven Lancasters were to bomb the harbour anchorage," Tom Bennett remembered, "whilst others were briefed to aim their bombs at the 'E-boat' pens in the more easterly area of the port complex." The results looked promising. "Subsequent recce photos and reports indicated two direct hits on the pens," he wrote, "but Dr. Barnes Wallis said that 'near misses' were the correct way to deliver his 'earthquake' bombs against such targets since the tremors would undermine the foundations and cause the tremendous concrete roofs to become a liability rather than a protection."[19]

Like a gigantic aerial conveyer belt, the two hundred bombers of main force came thundering in across the mouth of the Seine and made their separate runs, keying on the instructions of the master bomber. Despite the size of the attack, its duration was surprisingly short. Years of practice had taught the British to concentrate their bomber stream, and with an all-Lancaster force, they were making 260 mph. From the moment of Cheshire's daring descent over the pens until the last aircraft had unloaded its bombs, scarcely twenty-one minutes elapsed.[20]

It was a raid they all found unforgettable. Normally terse, almost reticent in recounting a night's mission, this time when they reached the ground the crews enthusiastically filled their squadron ORBs with vivid descriptions of what they had seen.

Those bombing earliest had the least opportunity to observe what happened, while, logically, crews in the following aircraft were able to see the handiwork of their predecessors. "Bomb seen to fall in water near A/P [aiming point]," McCarthy entered in the ORB. He had bombed at 2232 from seventeen thousand feet. "One other bomb seen to fall near ours. Several sticks from 1 Group bombing seen to fall on the jetties."[21]

RAAF Flying Officer Ross Stanford, with his British-Australian crew, was piloting their 617 Lancaster at 17,200 feet. They were trailing the lead aircraft by five miles and bombed a minute later. "Several bombs fell at the same time along the water front where the E-boats should be," he entered in the ORB. "Also at least 3 direct hits were seen on the submarine [sic] pens. A good deal of smoke came up which might have been a smoke screen. The concentration of the bombs on the targets was very good indeed." Nearby and flying 800 feet higher in the gaggle, Squadron Leader Smiler Munro also had an excellent view. "Our own bomb fell right on the aiming point," he wrote. "The Squadron bombing on our own aiming point was very good, at least two direct hits were scored. Only one bomb was seen to go down on the northern aiming point, and it was also extremely accurate."[22]

Also flying at 18,000 feet and dropping his Tallboy at 2233 hours, Flt. Lt. A. W. Fearn and his crew had an unobstructed view of what happened. "Saw red spots on offset marking point," he reported. "Own bomb would fall about 150 yards off eastern corner of dock and near dockside which was the A/P given. About four bombs burst on dock edge, near E-boats, and 1 or 2 bombs burst just near the pens. Bombing was very accurate. At 2236 two terrific explosions [occurred] with lightish red glow on the dockside near the A/P given (E-boats)."[23]

Other squadron members saw much the same thing. "Three direct hits" seen. At 2235 a large crimson explosion," stated Flt. Lt. J.E.R. Williams. "Large explosion seen at 2236 (to East of target)," wrote Flying Officer M. Hamilton. "Saw red spots on marking point," entered Flt. Lt. B. W. Clayton. "At 2233.30, one bomb was seen to burst on the corner of the pen and just afterward one near miss in the water. On the other A/P, at least four bombs were seen to burst near the dockside in the water. Large explosion was seen on dockside approximately 600 yards N.W. of the pens." Another American volunteer, Lt. H. C. "Nick" Knilans, released his bomb at 2232 from 17,900 feet. His crew had a good view of what happened. "Several bombs fell in the harbor, causing enormous explosions," he wrote. "Many hits were observed on the sub. [*sic*] pens. Bombing was very well concentrated on the target area."[24]

Continuing the intense pounding, the rest of the attacking main force flew up to the target with their cargoes of conventional bombs and, with the benefit of excellent markers and plenty of daylight, dropped them squarely on the aiming points. Their bomb aimers were equipped with the less accurate but nevertheless efficient Mark XIV bombsight to put their smaller bombs literally by the thousands into the targeted area. While the main force kept it up for only twenty minutes, for those on the receiving end it must have seemed like an eternity.

The ORB reports bore a striking similarity to one another in their essentials. Virtually all the pilots spoke of seeing the target clearly and of seeing their own and other bomb loads falling directly onto the marked areas around the pens and around the basin to the northeast. Most main force pilots stated afterward that they had located the Pathfinders' green target indicators with no difficulty, and they could verify that the marking aircraft had dropped them squarely on the aiming point. Those who followed after the lead squadrons also saw the secondary effects of the giant bombs as well as the immediate results of their own.

"One orange explosion at 2246 1/2 followed at 2250 by a spectacular colossal one like golden rain," wrote Flying Officer J. B. Starr of 12 Squadron. A wing mate, Flying Officer H. A. Vernon agreed. "Bombs straddled the aiming point," he wrote; "large orange flash for 40 seconds at 2238 hours." Flying Officer L. Pappas and his crew had a more harrowing mission than most because of an engine malfunction. As a result they were forced to fly lower than was desirable, approaching the target at 13,500 feet. They were also among the last to bomb, so that visibility was becoming a problem. "Aiming point was obscured by smoke up to 13,000 feet," he observed. "Explosion north east of Bassin de Marce [Theophile] at 2246. Fires seen." Pappas could not help adding a sobering detail to his report: "From base after take-off to landing, the air crew flew on three engines."[25] Pappas and his men embodied the "press on" spirit that characterized the great majority of Bomber Command crews.

Many of the aircrew toward the rear of the main force reported seeing the same thick column of smoke. Canadian Flying Officer R. T. Banville, piloting a Lancaster for 166 Squadron recorded: "Big explosions seen at 2244 and 2246 hours with black smoke rising to 15,000 feet." Fellow 166 Squadron pilot Flying Officer J. W. Blanchard agreed. "Saw large orange explosion at 2249 1/2 hours with much black smoke," he wrote. Many speculated that it was an oil fire from the storage tanks in the harbor.[26]

Whatever the cause of that towering column, the results of the raid seemed to impress all the participating crews. One of the later 166 Squadron aircraft to bomb, piloted by Flying Officer N. C. Petty, dropped its load from twenty thousand feet. "Reported fires could be seen up to 10 miles from the English coast on the return journey," he wrote.[27]

Flying Officer H. H. Reid from 100 Squadron agreed. He, too, bombed later, at 2248 hours, from twenty thousand feet. "Reflection of fire seen 100 miles away," he recorded as they made their way back to the English coast. Squadron Leader A. F. Hamilton was also impressed. "Whole harbour was boiling with bombs," he wrote. "Town seemed to escape." Other 100 Squadron pilots were equally enthusiastic. "Perfect delivery on the docks," wrote one. "Every stick of bombs straddled the Aiming Point," recorded another. "Very concentrated attack," stated yet another. "Very concentrated indeed. All in the dock area," confirmed another enthusiastic squadron mate.[28]

Results for the evening were summed up by 100 Squadron: "Markers were reported to have been excellently placed, although most of the bombing was visual. Results were excellent, and many large explosions were observed with the smoke rising to a height of 10,000 feet." Another group, 103 Squadron, reported similarly. They, too, had encountered cloud over southern England but "it dispersed towards the target and visibility over the area was very good." They found the timing to their liking too: "As this was a daylight attack, the aiming point was identified visually, and from all reports it was a very accurate and successful attack, several crews reporting very large explosions."[29]

By 2251 the attack was over. The 221 heavy bombers, still under escort by Spitfires from 11 Group wheeled to port and flew back across the Channel, making landfall over Pevensey Bay and dispersing from there to their respective bases in England. For them it had been an exhilarating evening, bombing in daylight and achieving one of the most concentrated attacks they had ever witnessed. Remarkably, all aircraft returned to base safely. There had been no casualties at all, almost unheard of in an attack on a heavily fortified port. Inevitably, there had been close calls, not necessarily caused by the enemy. Midair collisions were always a danger to crews in the crowded bomber stream although none occurred on this mission.

Mechanical failures were also a reality for Bomber Command crews. High-performance piston-driven engines such as the Rolls Royce Merlin that powered virtually all the aircraft on this mission were bound to experience failures. Few occurred on this raid. Another surprising aspect of the raid was apparent in the crews' ORB debriefings: few crew members mentioned flak coming up from the target area, and under the vigilant gaze of 11 Group's Spitfire escorts no one had reported enemy aircraft attacks. Le Havre was well known as one of the most heavily defended ports in Occupied Europe; it was vital to Hitler's Festung Europa plans and could always be expected to vigorously defend itself. There was a mystery here, but it would be a long time before the returning bomber crews unraveled it. The main thing was that they had completed another mission successfully. Jubilantly, the crews finished their debriefings. Some prudently drifted off to bed. Other high-spirited crews took advantage of the reopening of the bars in the officers and sergeants messes to celebrate what they were convinced was a tremendously successful operation.

The View from the Ground

E-boat Commander Hans Schirren had little reason to feel elated on that evening. With his crew he was aboard an unfamiliar boat, S-144, moored alongside the huge floating dock at the eastern end of the Bassin Theophile. Normally, he commanded S-145, but it had been damaged several days earlier in an engagement with a U.S. PT boat in the Western Channel and was in dry dock in Cherbourg being fitted with new engines. Knowing their lives depended on a reliably operating vessel, Schirren and the crew were going over S-144 carefully, inspecting engines and weapons and making ready for a night action. They had ample time for such maintenance. Unknown to the British, FdS Petersen had signaled an order that evening from Scheveningen, warning that they might have to cancel T-boat and E-boat operations for the second night in a row because of unfavorable weather.[30]

They were dwarfed by the high-walled floating dock that had sat in the middle of the outer harbor since prewar days, nestled almost equidistant from the Gare Maritime three hundred yards to the north, the Mole Centrale a like distance to the south, and the dry docks a hundred yards to the east. It lay at an oblique angle across that section of the Bassin Theophile, pointing northwest and creating, in effect, a kind of sheltered minibasin for S-144. Built for the French Navy, the seven-hundred-foot dock could accommodate cruiser-size ships and was a prominent feature in the harbor. Less desirable from the German point of view, it could also serve as a convenient reference point for the attacking force. Even less fortunate from the German defenders' point of view was the fact that of all installations in a naval port, the most vulnerable to aerial attack was, so said Grossadmiral Dönitz himself, a floating dock.[31]

It was just about 2230 hours in clear skies with the sun sinking below the horizon when light flak from other craft around the harbor began to go off. A single aircraft zoomed low overhead dropping red flares. Looking up from his armored skullcap bridge, Schirren immediately ordered his crew to open fire. They needed little prompting. With the barrels of their flak guns already upturned, the experienced crew joined in the cacophony of antiaircraft fire. Their large 40-mm Bofors gun in the stern was joined by the lighter twin 20-mm Oerlikons amidships and in the bow. At first nothing happened. Then suddenly the bombers came into view. As they approached overhead, bombs came whistling down all around them, and the resulting explosions added to the incredible din in what a few seconds before had been a peaceful harbor.

Given their location at the eastern side of the tidal basin, it seemed to Schirren and his crew that the bombs were falling everywhere and at once. Because of the intensity of the bombardment and because the light flak all around them was going off, they were not aware of the true nature of the deadly Tallboys.[32] Because they were moored under the walls of the floating dock, the isolated E-boat crew benefited at first from its shielding effects as the explosions and shock waves ripped across the waters of the basin.

Among the first crews to react to the attack, firing as they did from the protective shadows of the high wall, the occupants of S-144 seemed to have enjoyed unusual luck in the opening moments of the raid. Then suddenly they found their fortunes taking a turn for the worse as the heavy bombardment intensified. One bomb, probably a thousand pounder, blasted a section of wall loose from its adjoining segments. Like an enormous hinge, the top of the heavy steel plate pitched out over the water with its base still secured to the dock. Even as its shadow loomed across the stern of the fragile E-boat, Schirren's 40-mm gun crew continued firing away. Then as the heavy metal slab continued its lazy arc over and away from the dock, the flak gunners had just time to scramble to safety before it pinioned the stern of the boat. Immediately, everyone set about trying to wrench their craft free while all around them the air attack continued.

They struggled in vain. The heavy section of dock, said Schirren, "had caught the starboard stern of S-144 and would not let go, like an angry dog."[33] It weighed several tons, and there were no floating cranes to be had, especially in the midst of an intense bombing raid.

Meanwhile, other desperate activity was going on all around the harbor. For some the fourteenth of June had been a day of celebration. Newly installed as commander of the 5th E-boat Flotilla, Kapitänleutnant Kurt Johannsen was a happy man. After a week of intense operations, he had just that morning been awarded the Knight's Cross, Germany's highest category of decoration for gallantry. In the same ceremony, Korvettenkapitän Götz von Mirbach, commanding the 9th E-boat Flotilla, already a recipient of that coveted award, had received Oak Leaves to his Knight's Cross for his actions. With formalities completed, 5th T-boat Flotilla Commander Kapitän zur See Heinrich Hoffmann had graciously welcomed all the T- and E-boat flotilla commanders on board his nine-hundred-ton torpedo boat, *Möwe,* moored along the Quai Floride, several hundred yards from the assembled E-boats. Fourth E-boat Flotilla Commander Kurt Fimmen joined them. For such a special occasion Hoffmann had prepared a rare toast of French champagne. The assembled T- and E-boat officers had much to be grateful for. Their respective flotillas were still intact, and they alone among the German armed forces were in a position to carry out offensive actions against the newly lodged invasion fleet just off the nearby Normandy shore.

No sooner had the assembled commanders drunk their toasts than light flak began to erupt all around the harbor. Shortly, the ominous sound of heavy motors droned overhead, and at that moment complete panic broke out. Officers and men ran wildly from the torpedo boats onto the quays, some heading for their own boats, others simply seeking shelter. The first bombs began to land, and for those on the ground and in the harbor it must have seemed like hell on earth. A brave man, von Mirbach had found partial shelter in a doorway on the exposed quay and looked around, wondering how to help his comrades. Kurt Fimmen ran to join him. Then, with bombs exploding everywhere, Fimmen grabbed a passing soldier and pulled him in with them into the shallow depression. At that moment tragedy struck. Splinters from one of 1 Group's small bombs pierced the unfortunate soldier, killing him instantly. Von Mirbach was luckier, taking splinters in the legs and in his neck. He was destined to be in a hospital for a month. Miraculously, Fimmen emerged unscathed.

Kurt Johannsen, newest flotilla commander and a rising young star of the E-boat Force, was not so lucky. No survivor actually saw what happened, but apparently Johannsen was blown by the force of a bomb blast into the water and killed instantly. They listed him as missing until the next day when rescue crews located his body and his comrades-in-arms were able to identify him. All mourned his death. He had served for one week as a successful flotilla commander and had had just two hours to enjoy the honor of receiving his country's highest military decoration for valor. Fully as valuable as the E-boats themselves, the senior E-boat commanders were taking a terrible beating at Le Havre on that fateful fourteenth of June.[34]

Absent from the group of senior officers who had gathered on Hoffmann's torpedo boat for the evening celebration, 2d E-boat Flotilla Commander Hermann Opdenhoff was exhausted from the intense pace of operations since 6 June. Slightly older than the other commanders, he had decided to retire early to the Officers' Quarters, a villa on the hills above Le Havre near the Fort de Tourneville. It offered an excellent view of the harbor, and it was from there that Opdenhoff saw the attack developing. Within moments it became obvious that the port area and everything in it were taking a terrific pounding. It was also likely that communications out of the naval base had been severed by now. Accustomed to taking the initiative, Opdenhoff placed a call from the villa to FdS Headquarters in Scheveningen. The time was 2245.

The 1A, or FdS Operations Officer, Kapitänleutnant Bernd Rebensburg answered. Excited, Opdenhoff rapidly explained the situation to him and to Petersen's chief of staff, Korvettenkapitän Heinrich Erdmann, who came on the line too. The two senior officers had ample grounds for believing their fellow officer. "We could clearly hear the sound of the bombs detonating in the background while Opdenhoff spoke," Rebensburg recalled. The headquarters staff rated Opdenhoff as a highly competent, unflappable leader. If he was telling FdS Headquarters that the situation was serious, then it was.

They discussed the raid and possible reinforcements for several minutes while Opdenhoff updated them on the disposition of their naval forces around the complex basins of Le Havre. By now towering columns of smoke were beginning to obscure his view of the harbor. With only this one call from the officers' quarters, it was obvious that no one in the harbor was able to get through to the outside. Rebensburg asked Opdenhoff for more information from his vantage point above the city when it became available. With the din of the bombs still ringing in the earpiece, they heard Opdenhoff ring off. There was little anyone at headquarters could do now except await developments.[35]

In another part of the city, just off one of the main thoroughfares, the Boulevard de Strasbourg, author Julien Guillemard listened from his apartment to the frightening din in the nearby harbor. "It was 2230 hours when the air raid sirens launched their mournful cry into the air," he wrote of that day, "and bombs fell by the dozen into the port, in large measure upon us, a massive bombardment." Despite what Bomber Command pilots saw, damage in Guillemard's part of town around the city theater, within the district of St. Joseph, and around its church had been considerable. Two bombs landed within 120 feet of Guillemard's apartment building, damaging its upper floors, blowing out windows and the front door, and killing one tenant. This, the seventh raid they had endured to date, was by far the worst, he judged. Yet frightening though the evening attack was, Guillemard and his neighbors knew that it was the harbor district and not their residential area that was taking the brunt of the bombs. They almost felt pity for the Germans who, they were convinced, were dying by the hundreds in the port area.[36]

Another French eyewitness, diarist Georges Godefroy, also remembered the scene vividly. "At about 2230 hours a formation of 18 Mosquitoes arrived from out of the northwest," he recorded. "One of them detached itself from the rest, dived, and pulled out in a strafing run over the Rue Félix-Faure, firing his machine guns. The Flak fired off a torrent of tracers up into a second formation of 35 Lancaster bombers that, accompanied by escorts, were deploying for the attack. It was a bombardment of an intensity which we had never experienced before. The flak died out rapidly as the bombs continued to rain down."[37]

Godefroy and his fellow citizens of Le Havre had just witnessed Leonard Cheshire's incredible feat of marking. Those Havrists who dared continued to look on in fascinated horror as the Lancasters of main force, backing up 617 Squadron and its deadly missiles, delivered their knockout blow against what minutes before had been a formidable naval fleet.

Twilight deepened within the twenty-minute duration of the raid, and thick smoke from oil fires, munitions stores, and wrecked ships added to the gloom over the port area. As the last of the bombers flew off and one by one the antiaircraft guns ceased firing, emergency crews emerged from wherever they had been hiding, and along with the ships' crews and harbor personnel they set to work containing the conflagrations and doing what they could for the wounded and dazed survivors. Bombs had fallen everywhere; the docks and quays were a shambles. Smoke continued to billow up from the greasy oil fires, sharply reducing visibility. At least one of the large nine-hundred-ton torpedo boats was on fire.

By 2300 hours night had finally descended, further hampering the Germans' repair and rescue efforts. The bombing had knocked out all electricity, and it was hard to determine the extent of the damage. But no one doubted that they had been badly hurt. Fires still raged in several parts of the harbor. Periodically, new explosions erupted, throwing flashes of orange light onto scenes of utter devastation. Some were secondary explosions. Others resulted from delayed-action bombs, intended to hamper fire and rescue operations.

Out in the harbor Hans Schirren and the crew of S-144 gamely continued their efforts to free their trapped vessel from the debris of the floating dock. Time dragged by, and without heavy lifting equipment their task was beginning to look hopeless. Ominously, the huge dock was showing signs of foundering, and if they did not detach S-144 from its clutches soon, it would drag her down too. Despite their predicament they were distracted by a curious apparition that emerged through curtains of smoke during the periodic flashes from explosions: ghost ships. A curious knot of four E-boats floated silently in the Bassin Theophile, trailing thin wisps of exhaust smoke, which indicated that their small auxiliary engines were still running. They were crewless. To Schirren they appeared to be completely undamaged. Farther across the water, visible periodically through the pall of smoke, another clump of three boats was still tied up at the pier, abreast of the Gare Maritime.

It was the first group of boats that caught Schirren's attention. "The four S-boats [lashed] together by ropes with running auxiliary engines had come loose from the quay where the inner boat had been fastened," Schirren wrote. "They were sound and healthy and had sustained no damage, but the crew and commanders were missing. They had apparently left the boats for shelter and had been partly hit by exploding bombs on the quays."[38] Given the magnitude of the bombing, the sight of unmanned E-boats floating helplessly in the harbor was, perhaps, not so strange after all. All agreed that this night had seen one of the most hellish raids any of them had ever experienced.

Even so, isolated groups like Schirren's scratch crew aboard S-144 refused to panic. Veterans of many a battle, they expected to carry on somehow in the dawn of the next day. Soon they would secure the valuable E-boats and set about the business of restoring some semblance of order. They had their work cut out for them. The outer port was one vast ruin. The fall of the bombs around the pens and Gare Maritime had been intense. All of the quays, docks, moles, and various installations around the tidal basin had sustained hits. And the repeated explosions and fires that continued long after the bombers departed told them that ships and installations were still succumbing to the blows that had started at 2230 hours.

Although they could not know it, the crews of the lead bombers in 617 Squadron had observed the fall of the first three Tallboys accurately. One had impacted about seven feet inside the northwest corner of the huge structure, completely penetrating the roof, which was nearly ten feet thick, and severely fracturing the seven-foot thick west wall and the nine-foot thick north wall for a distance of thirty-five feet on either side. It had left a crater sixteen feet in diameter. Now the heavy roof perched uneasily on its displaced walls, which had been knocked askew by at least six inches, an ominous development as structural engineers well knew. Several conventional bombs had also struck the concrete roof. Later photographs showed numerous shallower craters. They also proved that the four antiaircraft positions atop the bunker were abandoned. The fate of the crews, exposed so pitilessly to the rain of bombs, had undoubtedly been a harsh one.

The northwest section of the pens, site of the first Tallboy impact, had two floors divided by a twelve-inch thick reinforced concrete slab. With its short half-second fuse delay, the bomb had detonated while burying into the thick roof. Midway along its passage through the reinforced concrete, the huge bomb had exploded with a terrifying roar. The ensuing blast completed the penetration, hurling chunks of concrete and steel the rest of the way through the stout roof and devastating both floors. It killed eight German guards instantly.[39]

Another Tallboy crashed through the north central portion of the apron that surrounded the pen. It completed its trajectory by boring into the adjoining Mole Centrale. The ensuing blast demolished a thirty-five-foot section of the thick apron and blew through a three-foot thick concrete shed on the mole as if it had been a cardboard box. The shed had housed the giant bunker's air conditioning plant, which immediately disintegrated, and the same blast severed all electrical cables between the pens and the rest of the harbor. Power, lights, and communications ceased abruptly in the opening seconds of the raid.[40]

Of great concern to the Germans were two Tallboy detonations south of the pens out in the lower half of the tidal basin. One exploded approximately 150 yards in front of the open pen doors and another perhaps 350 yards away to the southeast in the shallower mud flats. As a result, one R-boat had foundered directly across the mouth of the only deep water channel into the pens, effectively blocking access. Both explosions had sent walls of water surging toward the open bays where boats had been loading up inside. With all communications severed for the time being, no one knew what was happening within the protective pens, but they feared the worst.[41]

At the Gare Maritime on the Quai Johannes Couvert 600 yards to the northeast, the situation was scarcely better. Eleven of the 617 crews had put their bombs on this second aiming point, and several had hit in the immediate vicinity. Fused like the others to go off a half second after impact, those Tallboys had likewise produced a tremendous blast effect on the surface rather than burrowing below. Looming over the Gare Maritime and visible throughout the harbor was a handsome 180-foot-tall clock tower. In happier days, disembarking ship passengers had glanced at it as they hurried to plush train compartments for the rail journey to Paris. At 2233 that evening the clock's hands disappeared in a blinding flash of light. Just one blast—undoubtedly the work of a Tallboy—toppled the entire brick, steel, and concrete structure headlong onto the ground. The entire high-ceilinged railroad terminal, measuring 630 feet by 250 feet, collapsed in ruins. Within its 5.4 acres the Germans had stored hundreds of tons of mines, torpedo heads, and other explosives. It was those stores that accounted at least in part for the massive secondary explosions that had caught the attention of the bomber crews high above.[42] By 2251 hours the Gare Maritime was no more. Scores of naval personnel had died there.

The Germans estimated that at least seven major fires were burning simultaneously in the harbor by this time plus several more in the city itself. Bridges, ramps, and other traffic arteries were down all over the harbor, as were repair depots, thus hampering fire and rescue operations. The entire Quai Johannes Couvert was blocked by wreckage. The stunned survivors knew they had witnessed one of the most concentrated attacks ever carried out by Bomber Command. But as midnight came and went, it was hard to tell the true extent of the damage because of the dense smoke and the darkness of night that shrouded everyone and everything.[43]

Hardened by years of war, the German naval forces and other military personnel pulled themselves together. Singly and in small groups they emerged from shelters and unscathed places around the harbor and began helping fire and rescue crews contain the damage. While unarmed civilian French forces, the Défense Passive, battled the flames in their beloved city, German armed forces from the surrounding area began straggling in to help their fellow sailors and soldiers in the stricken port. It had been a horrible raid, but now the moment had come to bind up wounds, take stock of the situation, and carry on with the war.

Chapter **11**

E-Boats' End

Long experience had taught the staff of Bomber Command that it could not expect to eliminate German military targets in one raid no matter how concentrated. The ability of their tenacious foes to recover or at least to improvise the essentials needed to carry on was a fact with which Allied planners simply had to contend. Germany's armed forces had proved their powers of recuperation consistently through five years of aerial warfare. Therefore, planning at High Wycombe frequently called for a series of attacks at varying intervals in order to hinder or eliminate Axis recovery and to do it in such a way as to be unpredictable to defenders on the ground or in the air. The evening attack of 14 June 1944 in full daylight had been one such tactical innovation, and it had caught the German defenders at Le Havre by surprise. The question now was, when would RAF Bomber Command choose to follow up on that unusual raid?

The Other Shoe

Although fires still raged in several areas around the port as night deepened, and bombs with delayed fuses detonated periodically on land and under water, something approaching calm set in as the seasoned troops went about their wartime routine of fire-fighting and rescue work. The darkness, made more pronounced by billowing oily smoke, seemed to wrap the port in a protective shroud as midnight came and went. Many waited eagerly for dawn, which came at 0430 hours during this, one of the shortest nights of the year in Northwest Europe. Perhaps the lifting of darkness would raise everyone's spirits a bit. For the moment however, there was no choice but to keep at their jobs of tending comrades in need, fighting fires, and salvaging what equipment they could. The night wore on.

A little over two hours had passed since the last of the heavy bombers had turned for home, when a subtle change in the atmosphere caused men all around the port to look around and up. They could see little, but some felt a slight vibration in the air. It was shortly after one in the morning as the bleary-eyed survivors stumbled about their work. Acrid smoke continued to issue from oil fires and from stricken ships as naval personnel filtered back by ones and twos to their boats and stations. Suddenly, out of the blackened sky brilliant green and red flares erupted and began to descend over the stricken port, casting an eerie glow over everything and everyone. For the uninitiated it might have appeared a beautiful sight, just like a fireworks display. After five years of war there were no uninitiated. In horror, officers and men stared up at the flares as they floated down over the outer basin. Simultaneously the vibrations increased sharply in intensity. Everyone knew what would happen next. The British were returning for another air attack.

The German defenders had good reason to feel dread. Overhead another 119 Lancasters were fast approaching Le Havre, and although it was dark at ground level, the defenders knew their attackers would have little trouble locating targets. Fires from the first raid were serving all too well as navigational beacons.

Nevertheless, the advance guard started off with the usual rain of brilliant markers and illuminators. This second phase conformed more closely to Bomber Command's routine night operations. It was a routine that had evolved from years of experience. First, two of the Oboe-equipped Mosquitoes dropped green target indicators, and three more followed with red flares. Back-up aircraft would run in with brilliant illumination flares, being guided to the target by Oboe and H2S. The master bomber, orbiting over the target, would replenish the markers periodically as he managed the main force bombers over the target. It all followed an exacting sequence. This second H-hour at Le Havre was timed for 0115. The first marking aircraft dropped their flares at H–5 to H–3 minutes. The illuminators started exactly one minute after the first marker at H–4 and continued until H+1. The main force would then commence bombing at 0115. The last bombs were expected to fall at 0121, compressing the 119 bomber-stream over the target into a deadly six-minute pulse. By June 1944 Bomber Command had developed incredible proficiency. The attack that followed adhered closely to the plan outlined by the briefing staff. Although the entire sequence began one minute before the designated time, at 0109, that deviation from the schedule had no impact whatsoever on the outcome.[1]

The German forces could not know it, but the target this time was a little different. The initial attack had concentrated on the concrete pens but had also included harbor installations such as dry docks, the floating dock, the Gare Maritime, warehouses, jetties, and quays. The second attack aimed for different prey: ships and men.[2]

"On the approach three large buildings were on fire," commented Flt. Lt. M. C. Wakefield of 7 Squadron. "The Green T.I. [target indicator] fell at 0109 hours followed by a Red. Three more Green T.I.s fell at 0110 hours right on the aiming point. The Master Bomber instructed the Red and Green T.I.s to be bombed. Our own bombs released accordingly." And so it began all over again. "Bombing appeared well concentrated around the aiming point," Wakefield added, "and the Master Bomber made a favourable comment to this effect. Visibility good."[3]

Bomber Command was dropping the other shoe, and for the German defenders at Le Havre whatever luck they might have had seemed to have deserted them.

The master bomber sat in the cockpit of his darkened Lancaster, circling the stricken city and giving detailed instructions to his marking aircraft and bombers. He updated them constantly on which markers to aim for. Sometimes, as happened on this night, a stick of bombs would extinguish the marking flares. When the greens winked out, the master bomber radioed one of his "backers up," a waiting Lancaster from 8 Group, to renew the marking. These specialized aircraft carried mostly target indicators plus some bombs to allow the crew the satisfaction of knowing they were inflicting damage on the enemy. But their main function was to maintain accurate marking for main force. Periodically, as old markers died out or were snuffed out, the master bomber ordered a replenishing TI drop from Pathfinder backers up. In order to confuse the enemy, who often tried to imitate the markers, he could also order a shift to yellow target indicators or white ones as he did that night.

The 119 Lancasters, mostly from 3 Group, were carrying loads of four five-hundred-pound and ten or eleven thousand-pound bombs in addition to hooded illumination flares. The flares floated under blackened umbrella-like parachutes in order to avoid dazzling the crews above. No Tallboys fell. They were not needed. This second wave sought out the thin-skinned craft in harbor and the thinner-skinned humans who manned them. Le Havre was the last port left to the German Navy that could be of any use in the fight against the Normandy fleet, and the British were determined to render it unusable, even as the Americans were making Cherbourg untenable. A grim catalog of horrors unfolded as the crews of the attacking squadrons dropped their bombs, saw what they saw, and returned to base to tell about it.

The stream of aircraft bombed from an altitude of anywhere from twelve thousand to sixteen thousand feet. The weather remained clear, and many of the crews remarked on the excellent visibility of the target and how ineffectual the antiaircraft fire was. Among the first to attack were seventeen Lancasters from 514 Squadron. A squadron chronicler summarized his unit's experiences. "The dock area was illuminated by fires started in the northern part of the harbor earlier in the attack, and by numerous explosions which lasted throughout the attack; bombs were seen falling in the dock area. Flak was negligible and confined to light tracer. . . . Very good attack. Explosions and fires seen 70 miles from target." Many pilots from the participating squadrons noticed the strange absence of heavy flak. One great fear for bomber crews was to be "coned" by several searchlights, making it easier for the gunners to target the aircraft. That night the searchlights were far less aggressive. Crews counted only four of them, and their efforts seemed feeble and half-hearted. No aircraft reported being coned that night. The squadrons of the second wave were having no trouble navigating across the Channel to their target. Squadron Leader H. Tilson of 622 Squadron explained why: "Fires from the first attack seen when crossing the English coast," he wrote. Like a giant beacon, the destruction at Le Havre was drawing the heavy bombers unerringly to it.[4]

Some of the 514 Squadron pilots clearly saw individual ships burning in the harbor below, and they told of seeing bombs falling all along the quays. "Perfect attack," wrote Flying Officer R. Langley, who bombed from fifteen thousand feet at 0115. "No troubles," he added. Others were less fortunate. A wingmate, Flt. Lt. M. Dodds, bombed from the same altitude and almost at the same time. "Attack good," he wrote but added, significantly, "had combat with Me. 110." In fact, four of 514 Squadron Lancasters had running battles with German night fighters a few minutes into the attack. Afterward, they claimed one downed and two damaged. Two minutes behind the lead aircraft, Flt. Sgt. A. F. Prowles released thirteen thousand pounds of high explosive on the port at 0116 and then reported, "Big area of fire in docks and town to the North." He was also witness to a unique event that night: "One aircraft seen shot down." Prowles witnessed the destruction of the only bomber, a Lancaster, lost in the two-phase attack. Given the noticeable absence of heavy flak, it had probably fallen to the guns of one of the German night fighters. After years of heavy losses, this respite for Bomber Command in action over Le Havre was entirely welcome. It was proving to be an extraordinary raid against a port that had instilled the fear of its defenses in every Allied pilot's heart.[5]

Many crews reported renewed explosions about twenty minutes after the second attack began, listing the times variously from 0132 hours to as late as 0153. They continued to report tremendous secondary detonations far out over the Channel while steering back to friendly territory. Pilot Officer H. W. Thomson of 7 Squadron summed it up. "Big explosions observed at 0134 hours and 0136 hours, and the second explosion was very big and visible from a few miles off the English Coast."[6] Other pilots reported the same phenomenon.

With the exception of that lone Lancaster and its luckless crew of seven, which Prowles had seen going down, the remaining 118 heavy bombers descended without mishap to their bases in England, most of them landing at about 0230 with some stragglers coming in as much as an hour later.

The two raids together had dumped 1,800 tons of high explosives on Le Havre, delivered by 353 aircraft in the span of a little over three hours. Besides the 22 Tallboys, they dropped 4,500 of the smaller bombs. In the past, Bomber Command had hit other targets with more aircraft and more tonnages than had descended on the hapless port city that night. Nonetheless, the 14 June raid was a special one because of the extreme accuracy of the marking through all phases of the raid, the initial use of what was at that time the world's most destructive bomb, and the sheer concentration of the strike against a well-defined target. The stakes were high too. The Allies had finally caught up with their worrisome nemesis, the E-boat Force.

A Time of Surprises

Unfortunately, some of the secondary explosions were not emanating from military targets. Pillars of smoke and explosive flashes were coming up from civilian areas of the city adjacent to the port. As the chronicler for 635 Squadron put it, "Most of the bombing was well concentrated although one stick fell across the town." That one stick was by no means the only errant set of bombs to fall. Flt. Lt. A. J. Craig of 7 Squadron, who had seen the green markers inadvertently extinguished by bombs early in the attack and had received orders from the master bomber to aim for the red markers instead, admitted that not all the bombs were finding the target. "Large amount of bombs seen to fall around the aiming point," he wrote, "but also evidence of bad bombing in the town and sea." One contributing factor to the inaccurate bombing later in the attack was a tremendous increase of smoke in the target area. The very success of the raid was making it more difficult for the bomb aimers at the rear of the bomber stream.[7]

One of the bright fires the crews reported seeing was a large civilian factory in the city proper. "During the two bombardments, or shortly after, we regarded with sadness flames coming from the Manufacture des Tabacs [tobacco factory] only 250 meters from our house," wrote Julien Guillemard. Undoubtedly its fires created confusion for bomb aimers in succeeding aircraft, and the conflagration attracted even more bomb loads on what the bomb aimers thought was a legitimate military target. The Nôtre-Dame district closest to the port area received considerable damage. Fortunately, the city authorities, knowing that air raids on the port would likely strike it, had evacuated the civilians at an earlier date. Nevertheless, the damage had spilled into other areas of the city. Ultimately the raid cost the lives of 76 citizens, injured another 150, and destroyed no fewer than 700 houses and commercial structures. Local civil defense, the Défense Passive, firefighters, and youth organizations did their best to limit the destruction. Havrists were paying a high price for their impending liberation.[8]

For every bomb that strayed into the city, a dozen more found their mark in the harbor. Hans Schirren and his crew had struggled valiantly to dislodge S-144 from the floating dock, but despite their best efforts they were not successful. A second boat, S-167, was alongside, and they discovered that its commander had been wounded in the evening raid. When the green and red markers began to descend at 0109 hours, they, like the others, stood transfixed for a second, but quickly went into action. "I decided when the second attack started not to be the subject of another event like with S-144," Hans Schirren recalled with notable understatement, "and got a mixed crew together and left the harbor, steering to compass readings . . . because of smoke all over the place."[9]

As S-167 steered blindly through the dense fumes toward the outer reaches of the harbor, it passed close by another boat, S-146, commanded by Kapitänleutnant Ullrich Roeder. Strangely, the boat was drifting in the outer harbor, its engines stopped but with its crew still aboard. With a raid still in progress it was hardly the moment to come about and ask questions. Schirren and his crew continued steering S-167 doggedly through the inky blackness of the port, praying that they could avoid the hail of bombs that continued to whistle down around them. Later, they learned that Roeder's chief machinist had depressurized the diesels' compressed air bottles during the first raid. If bomb splinters had struck them, the machinist cautioned, then the brittle steel cylinders would have blown up, killing everyone below decks. Undoubtedly they regretted that decision now, adrift, and lacking the vital compressed air needed to start their heavy diesels in the midst of another aerial attack. Later, Roeder observed ruefully "that the fate of many a boat depended upon whether or not the boat's command . . . had released its compressed air (as was done foolishly on my boat), or not (as was wisely the case with Hans Schirren). . . . I was pinned down, that is to say incapable of starting engines—and lost our boat."[10]

By some miracle, Schirren's newly commandeered S-167 made the breakwater to the northwest and left harbor undamaged. They decided that their best recourse was to head out into the Channel some distance and wait for dawn to approach before reentering Le Havre. If the port was no place to be that night, the Channel was no place for one lonely E-boat to be when daylight returned. Rumors still persisted that the Allies intended to land at Le Havre, but after clearing harbor and escaping the smoke, Schirren knew otherwise. The Channel waters off Le Havre were empty. After what they had just endured, their lonely presence in the dangerous coastal waters seemed almost peaceful.

For others, the pace of events was picking up. Far to the north, the phone rang at 0115 at FdS Headquarters in Scheveningen. Bernd Rebensburg picked up. It was Hermann Opdenhoff on the line to say that the British had returned to Le Havre. Scarcely believing their ears Rebensburg and the FdS chief of staff Erdmann heard the familiar sound of bombs detonating in the background as they listened to the flotilla commander's vivid description of further damage being inflicted. Given the dense smoke and confusion, no one was certain what their losses were at the moment, but Opdenhoff assured them that the tally would be very high. That was enough for Rebensburg. With Petersen's permission he immediately donned cap and great coat, and dashed to a waiting car. A military chauffeur drove him nonstop through the night until they reached Le Havre the following morning at around 1000 hours.

After ringing off, Opdenhoff went down to the port area to see for himself what had happened. Mercifully, the RAF bombers had left for good this time. Like the first attack, the second had been brief, lasting a scant six minutes. By 0430 dawn began to come up over the port and the pale light revealed for the first time the true extent of the night's devastation. Opdenhoff and the surviving E-boat personnel could only shake their heads as they surveyed the scene. Not a quay was still intact. Scarcely a boat was still above water. The huge floating dock was half submerged now, having carried the slender hull of S-144 partway below the surface of the Bassin Theophile. Some of the boats, or more accurately pieces of them, were actually up on the quays. The Germans asked themselves how this could have happened.

American volunteer pilot Lt. Nick Knilans, safely back at Woodhall Spa, could have told them. He recorded the night's events in his operational log: "Dropped a 14,000-pound bomb [the 12,000-pound Tallboy] along with others. Created a tidal wave in the harbor. Carried thirty torpedo E-boats up onto the quay and smashed them and many harbor installations."[11]

One boat had survived. Shortly after 0430 as dawn began to come up, outlining the continuing pall of smoke over Le Havre, Hans Schirren and the crew aboard S-167 had decided that they faced fewer perils in port now, and steered their solo course from the Channel back into port. It was with a sense of weary pride that they presented S-167 to a wide-eyed flotilla commander, Kurt Fimmen, the only flotilla commander still fit for duty. Theirs was the only combat-ready E-boat left in Le Havre. In fact, at that moment it was the Germans' only combat-ready war vessel left in the Normandy combat zone.[12]

A different fate had awaited the others. Barnes Wallis's Tallboys had performed in a way no one had predicted. Augering into the tidal basin and surrounding docks, they were fused to explode a half second after impact. At that instant those that had landed in the basins exploded their five thousand pounds of high-blast torpex, creating a kind of epicenter. Milliseconds later powerful shock waves coursed through the confined shallow waters, building up into pressure waves that crashed against hulls and waterfronts. Confidential German reports admitted afterward that there had simply been no empty space left at the quays on the evening of 14 June with boats and auxiliary vessels tied up everywhere. It was no exaggeration to say that at the moment of detonation the hapless harbor had been choked with vessels. When the first Tallboys hurtled into the basin, at more than seven hundred miles per hour, they were probably invisible to the defenders. Then, seconds later out of the giant columns of spray emerged the destructive waves that raised the boats closest to the quays out of the water, smashing them against the stone and concrete quays and against each other. Some waves actually lifted a few boats entirely out of the basin and up onto dry land. Either way the force of the shock waves had smashed them and the other craft in harbor as if they had been children's toys. What the German officers saw before them in that gray dawn was kindling wood.

With difficulty they picked their way around the blasted remains of the Gare Maritime out onto the Mole Centrale to the enormous concrete pens. Surely the bunker's stout walls and ceilings would have protected the boats inside. The ceilings were nearly ten feet thick, poured of the highest quality concrete with stout steel reinforcing.

From the outside, the pens seemed to be intact. They had withstood bombing before. Surely they would do so now. True, two bombs had struck, one on the roof and another on the northern edge where the bunker joined the quay. In each instance it left a neat three-foot cylindrical hole. Yet the structure looked whole. When they entered the pens, however, they were in for a surprise. Opdenhoff and Rebensburg confronted scenes of devastation comparable to what they had just seen on the quays. Like the craft outside, the boats in the bays had been smashed to little pieces. How had this happened?

They learned from survivors that one of the Tallboys, a near miss that had landed in the water of the tidal basin several hundred feet in front of the open doors of the pens, had created a pressure wave. The resulting wall of water had surged through the doors, simultaneously raising boats and smashing them against the high ceiling of the bunker. Because of the twenty-foot tides along this section of the coast, the Germans had, of necessity, to build the structures high. In fact, the bunker had been built to a height of forty feet, and the resulting gap had allowed the surge of water plenty of room to give the craft added momentum. Now they, too, lay broken on the watery bunker floor. Two boats, caught in the open at the entrance to the bunkers, were now underwater wrecks, one of them partially blocking access for the others.[13]

Staring at the mess, Opdenhoff and Rebensburg totaled up their losses. Rebensburg estimated that there had been twelve craft in the pens. They were all gone. However, he knew something the Allies did not. None of them were E-boats. Allied intelligence had misunderstood the true purpose of the powerful concrete structure. It was, in fact, an R-boat pen for

125- to 150-ton minelaying vessels. The E-boats entered it only when they were being fitted out for minelaying missions, which had been infrequent up to now. On the night that Bomber Command struck there were no E-boats at all inside.

It was just as well that photographic evidence had shown E-boats elsewhere in the confines of the Bassin Theophile. The decision to expend half the rare Tallboys elsewhere than on the pens had been a prudent one. Fusing the monster bombs for a half-second delay had paid off too. The second saturation attack on the boats in the tidal basin had also proved to be a wise move. The double pounding from the air had finished off the rest of the craft still afloat, except for Schirren's scratch crew on S-167 making their blind cruise out of harbor. There was no denying that the Allies had dealt Germany's coastal forces a body blow this time. The only issue remaining for the inspecting naval officers was to assess their losses.

For the numbed survivors on the ground and even more so for the relieved aircrews safely back at their stations in England a puzzling question remained: Why had the flak been so ineffective? Why had only one Lancaster been shot down out of 353 aircraft dispatched? Le Havre's defenses had a fearful reputation at all levels, as Flt. Lt. P. J. Kelley, the recce pilot of 542 Squadron, had found out that morning. Those who had watched Leonard Cheshire's incredible feat of courage in the initial marking dive had remarked that the tracer that followed him was the heaviest they had ever seen, or were ever to see. Yet when the main attack began most pilots observed surprisingly little flak, and comparing it to other raids they were not particularly impressed. It was a mystery.

A few German officers knew what had happened to the flak of Le Havre that evening, and it was an event that pointed out grave flaws in their military organization, flaws that were worse than any of the Allied blunders that had culminated in the Lyme Bay tragedy six weeks earlier. From his headquarters in Paris the Luftwaffe commander of Luftflotte 3 had issued a "no shoot" order to the big antiaircraft batteries in Le Havre to take effect at 2230 hours on 14 June 1944. The reason was simple. He intended to send several German attack aircraft with experimental radio-controlled bombs on low-level flights across Le Havre that evening so that they could assault the Allied fleet off Normandy only thirty miles away.

The heavy flak installations were part of Reichsmarschall Hermann Göring's fiefdom, and they followed their own chain of command, in this case a Flakführer for the Port of Le Havre. The Luftwaffe's inventory included many of the fearful radar-predicted 8.8-cm and 10.5-cm guns that had given the high-flying PRU Spitfire such a hot reception twelve hours earlier. This Flakführer had absolute say over the shooting of cannon in harbor. At 2135 hours he received the fateful no-shoot order from Luft-flotte 3 and reissued it at 2205 hours to all units in harbor including all naval units: no flak and no searchlight illuminating permitted after 2230. The senior naval officer present was disturbed by this blanket order and telephoned the Flakführer command post immediately. Surely the order did not apply to his boats in harbor or at sea, the naval officer demanded of his Luftwaffe opposites. The Flakführer, who was out at the moment, returned the senior naval officer's call, according to a later German report, and repeated the order, which, he assured his naval opposite, was "absolutely mandatory for naval combat units too."[14] Thus, when the actual attack began at 2232, the entire air defense system was already under orders not to shoot. Independently, the battery commanders sought permission from another rung in the chain of command, Flak Regiment 100, which did give permission, but the stubborn Flakführer immediately counter-manded that order.

The net effect of the Luftwaffe decision was devastating for the German defenders at Le Havre. One minute after Cheshire's solo marking run at 2229 hours, the *Flakverbot,* or no-shoot order, for the big guns went into effect. As the guns fell silent, the flak crews heard the thunder of the Lan-casters approaching. Then, perfectly visible in the evening sky, with their four large engines, sinister fuselage, and distinctive double-ruddered tail section sharply silhouetted in the sun's dying rays, the Lancasters sailed in from the Channel in their unique gaggle formation. No one on the ground could mistake them for anything other than what they were: a heavy British bomber formation.

The naval report criticizing the Luftwaffe's interference at this critical juncture explained the situation in stark, angry terms. "At the time of the attack on Le Havre it was still light. The enemy formation, stretched over a length of 20 kilometers, was easily recognizable and not to be confused with our own aircraft." Furious at what happened, the naval reporting officer finished with a salvo of his own. "It is absolutely imperative that local commands should in such circumstances have a completely free hand in using their weapons."[15]

Impatient with their own leadership's irrational no-shoot order, a few Luftwaffe gunners had fired anyway. The naval report on the incident expressed warm approval of the Luftwaffe crews' independent actions. "If . . . several of the lighter flak units had not fired despite a lack of permission, then the air raid alert for all units afloat, whose crews were mostly on board and within half an hour of 'seeklar' [putting to sea], would have come only with the fall of the bombs. Given the severity of the attack, this would have resulted in a several-fold increase in the number of casualties."[16]

Despite the Luftwaffe's blanket order, navy gunners on the boats had felt fewer constraints than the soldiers in the flak batteries, and they fired as best they could, mostly with 20-mm Oerlikons and, in some instances, with the larger 37-mm flak or 40-mm Bofors guns. However, with the bombers cruising at least three miles high, their light flak had little effect. Since the bombers had targeted harbor installations such as the pens, quays, and jetties first, their carpet of bombs effectively silenced the more dangerous Luftwaffe batteries early in the attack. Then, in the second phase that began at 0114 hours, when the no-shoot order had lapsed, it made little difference. Many gunners had been wounded or killed, or their emplacements had been damaged. The result was that once again the Lancasters encountered light or ineffective flak.

By chance or miscalculation the double raid on Le Havre resulted in a great victory for the Allies and a stunning defeat for the Germans. The fortunes of war had smiled on the E-boat flotillas that had planed into Lyme Bay on 28 April, and Allied ineptness had compounded the tragedy that ensued. Now, six weeks later a similar fate awaited the attackers and the attacked, but with one important twist: this time the losers wore German uniforms and the winners wore RAF blue.

What They Accomplished

Delighted by what their pilots were reporting, Allied intelligence authorities hoped to find out the true results of the raid quickly. But smoke and confusion on the ground the next day made photoreconnaissance more a game of guesswork than scientific analysis. As an OIC report indicated, "From subsequent reconnaissance photographs, virtually unable to distinguish between E and R boats, it would have been impossible to assess the losses sustained in E-boat strength and personnel."[17] Fortunately, they were able to turn to a reliable source for their answers: Rudolf Petersen. With land cables down, the E-boat Force had to resort to radio transmissions in their "secure" naval code, *Offizier M*, known to the cryptographers at Bletchley Park as Dolphin. The listeners at B.P. were getting the information almost as quickly as Marine Gruppe West in Paris or Dönitz's Seekriegsleitung Headquarters in Berlin, and they were forwarding it to their frequent customers, the OIC at the Admiralty in London. What the naval officers on the spot had to report was incredible. The British had the great advantage of comparing their own estimates with those of the enemy.

Unaware of the actual strength of the Bomber Command force that had attacked, and impressed by the ferocity of the bombardment, the Germans estimated that 500 to 800 aircraft had hit them, not the 234 that had actually attacked in the first phase. Their overestimation was understandable given the accuracy and concentration of the attack. After all, the British calculated that two-thirds of the 1,200 tons of high explosives dropped on Le Havre had struck within 400 yards of the aiming points during the daylight raid. Except for the twenty-two Tallboys, all the rest were 1,000- or 500-pound bombs; the calculated density of high explosive was eight tons per acre in the target area. The second, nighttime attack, which had used Oboe marking, placed one ton per acre on target. However, its many smaller bombs had had a disproportionately disruptive effect on rescue and recovery operations. By British estimates the Germans had lost 38 vessels sunk outright with another 31 to 34 ships damaged.[18]

German naval estimates were comparable. The raid had sunk outright three of the T-boats, *Falke, Jaguar,* and *Möwe.* Another, *Kondor,* lay helpless and damaged in dry dock. A T-35-class T-boat, T-28, had also received damage and was unfit for operations. The Schnellbootwaffe had lost ten of its first-line E-boats, sunk outright by direct bomb hits. Three more were heavily damaged and permanently out of action, one of them, Roeder's S-146 beached, another, S-150, with its bow completely blown off. Another was barely capable of movement. Only Schirren's S-167 was combat ready. In addition, the Germans lost dozens of other war vessels: three of the valuable R-boats, including one blocking the pens, dozens of smaller minelayers, minesweepers, patrol vessels, trawlers, harbor defense launches, tugs, and the giant floating dock lying half submerged in the oily waters.[19]

Despite the stark facts listed in the Ultra decryptions, even the British were not fully aware of what happened because of the German Navy's need to condense radio signals as much as possible. Because special intelligence had not garnered any information from German sources about a tidal wave effect, the OIC analysts were inclined to discount it as a factor in the damage that occurred. However, other sources contradicted their cautious estimate. Operations Officer Rebensburg and other senior E-boat Force personnel had personally inspected the concrete pens the following morning and reported tremendous damage to R-boats. Bomb damage assessment photographs taken on 15 June showed evidence of boats strewn around the edge of the Bassin Theophile, with at least one hull fully out of the water on the Quai Johannes Couvert. Although special intelligence had not been able to gather such evidence from its usual German sources, that did not mean it had not happened.[20]

Meanwhile Petersen's staff were listing in additional communications further estimates of the damage inflicted. They reflected a magnitude of naval losses unprecedented in the long war. Perhaps even more sobering was the fact that the pens, built at such heavy expense with scarce labor and resources, were no longer inviolate. Two bombs—the Germans rightly called them two of the heaviest they had ever seen—had penetrated the R-boat bunker. The smaller bombs had destroyed numerous heavy flak positions and searchlight batteries. The attack had flattened warehouses, blown over virtually all the cranes in harbor, blocked roads and causeways all around the port, and wrecked the one and only torpedo-loading facility in the port. Worse, the raid had burned out the entire store of preciously hoarded torpedo warheads that the navy had collected with such difficulty in the preceding weeks. Just as grave a loss was the destruction of their store of sea mines. Personnel losses were also heavy. The bombs and shock waves had killed more than two hundred naval officers and men. Another one hundred were seriously wounded. Among the fallen were twenty E-boat ranks, virtually the equivalent of one boat crew. Although those numbers appeared moderate, given the nature of the raid, they failed to reflect the toll in veteran commanders. Among the dead were the able Kurt Johannsen whose remains were finally identified. Two of the T-boat commanders, the skippers of *Falke* and *Jaguar,* had died aboard their ships. Götz von Mirbach was out of the war for a month, at a time when his experience and inspired leadership were sorely needed.[21]

As the staff of trackers at OIC absorbed further information from Bletchley Park decrypts, thereby hearing the Germans themselves describe the situation as "catastrophic," they had reason for self-congratulation. "It was a disaster of the first magnitude," the OIC monitoring staff concluded, "and in reality brought to an end the effective E-boat opposition in the Channel." Knowing themselves to be anonymous backroom warriors, the OIC small-craft trackers felt compelled to leave to posterity an accounting of what it had taken to make Bomber Command's raid possible: "The spectacular achievement of the Le Havre raid must not blind the observer to the laborious, unspectacular and unremitting efforts of analytical study whereby the story revealed in intercepted naval W/T [wireless traffic] was digested, pieced together and promulgated often under conditions of great strain and tension. Those efforts forewarned and forearmed those responsible for protecting our cross-Channel convoys, allowed for tactical redisposition, attack, and finally destruction. It was no mean achievement."[22] Looking back from the perspective of fifty years, we can only agree.

The OIC analysts produced several tables of statistical evidence in assessing progress in the war on E-boats. More than sheer numbers of German vessels lost, they demonstrate the true impact of the raids on Le Havre and on Boulogne in the Allies' long war against the E-boat threat. First, they gave an overview of the classes of Allied vessels from the Normandy Invasion Fleet that had become casualties (see table 6). Of concern was the fact that landing ships and landing craft had taken a disproportionate percentage of the casualties. The OIC's second table compared casualties suffered by the Allied invasion fleet in the first and second week following 6 June (see table 7). Statistics for the second week show a sharp drop in ships sunk or damaged. The next table detailed shipping casualties according to cause (see table 8). The results were striking and the OIC's analysts were in no doubt about the results: "The drop in casualties from E-boat attack and from mining is thus mainly responsible for the reduced scale of loss in the second week." They observed that Allied efforts to locate German minelays and wider-searched channels in the second week were partly responsible for lower casualties, but the sharp reduction in E-

Table 6

Allied losses due to enemy action (by class), Operation Neptune (first fortnight)

	No of vessels		
Class of vessel	Sunk	Damaged	Total
Cruisers and above	0	2	2
Destroyers, frigates, corvettes	10	7	17
Minesweepers	3	7	10
Light coastal forces	2	3	5
Landing ships	7	18	25
Landing craft	13	9	22
Merchant ships	9	15	24
Grand total	44	61	105

Source: "Note on Some Enemy Reactions to Operation Neptune, First Fortnight," S.I. 980, p. 1, Public Record Office, ADM 223/172.

Table 7

Allied losses due to enemy action, Operation Neptune (first fortnight)

	No. of vessels		
	Sunk	*Damaged*	*Total*
First week	36	38	74
Second week	8	23	31
Grand total	44	61	105

Source: "Note on Some Enemy Reactions to Operation Neptune, First Fortnight," S.I. 980, p. 1, Public Record Office, ADM 223/172.

Table 8

Allied losses due to enemy action (by cause), Operation Neptune (first fortnight)

	No. of vessels		
Cause	*1st week*	*2d week*	*Both weeks*
E-boats	18	0	18
Mines	31	13	44
Shore batteries	7	6	13
Aircraft	8	6	14
U-boats	0	2	2
Destroyers, T-boats	2	0	2
Minor enemy surface craft	0	3	3
Uncertain	8	1	9
Grand total	74	31	105

Source: "Note on Some Enemy Reactions to Operation Neptune, First Fortnight," S.I. 980, p. 2, Public Record Office, ADM 223/172.

boat activity made the real difference. Their next table compared levels of E-boat activity from one week to the next (see table 9). Once again the statistics demonstrated a sharp drop in activity between the first and second weeks. The OIC conceded that with the sheer passage of time a reduction in the scale of effort by E-boats was inevitable given the abnormally high levels of activity in the first week. In fact, that initial level of performance had been nothing less than phenomenal being six times greater than ever before recorded. A falling off in performance was only to be expected. But the other primary cause was directly attributable to Bomber Command's strategic air raid on Le Havre and to a second one the next evening on Boulogne although the latter did not destroy any E-boats. The OIC analysts produced a final table outlining the cause for a such precipitate drop in E-boat effectiveness in the second week following the invasion (see table 10).

The figures in table 10 are, if anything, too benign. The OIC staff was being conservative in its assessment of the raid on Le Havre and did not include the three heavily damaged E-boats or the disruptions caused by casualties among military personnel, destruction of naval stores, pens, or other installations. For example, German salvage teams devoted much effort in the following weeks to raising equipment from the wrecks littering the basin floors. E-boat diesels were especially prized as were the Enigma machines each boat was carrying. Even so, the statistical evidence demonstrated how crucial the air raid had been in turning the fight against E-boats in the Channel.

Bomb damage assessment photographs taken over Le Havre on 15 June while the tides were out confirmed the mounting evidence of mass destruction, which the Allies had already begun to glean from Ultra decrypts. Delighted by the results, C-in-C Harris sent a signal on 16 June to all the crews of 1, 3, 5, and 8 (PFF) groups: "The attacks on Le Havre were magnificent. You have virtually destroyed the entire German naval forces there. This was the most important naval force opposing our invasion traffic and comprised some 60 . . . vessels."[23]

Encouraged by their success at Le Havre, Bomber Command renewed its onslaught against the E-boats by attacking the port of Boulogne the very next evening. Bad weather and the Germans' usual pattern of dispersal prevented it from being as mighty a blow as the Le Havre raid. Only eleven of the Lancasters were able to drop the devastating Tallboys. However, this time they were fused to explode far deeper. The rest of the bombers returned to base lugging the precious bombs with them. Nevertheless, the deep penetration near misses cracked the pens and destabilized them. Follow-on raids by nearly three hundred main force Lancasters also blanketed the port area. Once again the small units in the harbor, especially the useful R-boats, were sunk in quantity. The OIC estimated thirty-one ships sunk and nine damaged.[24] This second raid gave notice to the Germans that their coastal forces would always be at risk when found in concentrated numbers. Furthermore, for all practical purposes, Boulogne was finished as a transit point for German coastal forces. Ominously, the pens, far from protecting them, were themselves becoming a liability. Within a twenty-four-hour period, Bomber Command destroyed the E-boat threat in two of the most vital ports in the Normandy Battle Zone.[25]

The twin raids were almost unique in the annals of Bomber Command, dependent as they were upon the liberal use of special intelligence. The Tallboys were at that moment among the most secret weapons in the Allied arsenal. Therefore, when C-in-C Harris signaled congratulations to his crews again on 19 June, he labeled it top secret: "The attacks on Le Havre and Boulogne succeeded in virtually destroying the entire German naval forces in those harbours," he wrote. "Nearly 100 Naval and Naval Auxiliary craft were sunk or destroyed and the proportion sunk, at least 60, being remarkably high." Harris regretted the cloak of secrecy he had to place upon the victorious raids but felt he had no choice. "For security reasons," he continued, "not too much was made of this greatest of air-sea victories, but crews can be satisfied that their efforts have altered the entire aspect of the naval war in the Channel."[26]

The British were not alone in concluding that the raids had produced fundamental changes in the sea war off Normandy. A German naval summary for June 1944, written by Naval Commander in Chief, West, Adm. Theodor Krancke, admitted that the two raids, especially the attack on Le Havre, marked a turning point. Specifically, he interpreted the latter as a backhanded compliment to the German Navy's E-boats. By this time the naval leadership were aware that the Allies had deliberately sought out their prized coastal vessels and destroyed them. "The great raid of the enemy against the port of Le Havre, which they had left alone up to then, is to be understood as a consequence of the successes our naval forces achieved in the first week following the invasion," Krancke concluded. "Those heavy losses completely put an end to our offensive operations in the second week following the invasion."[27]

FdS Petersen also assessed the critical period of operations when the Allied invasion fleet was freshly assembled at Normandy and professed to see certain advantages for his forces. First, the Allies had not attempted to take Cherbourg or Le Havre immediately, "so that the E-boats had bases

Table 9

E-boat effort and results, Operation Neptune (first fortnight)

	1st week	*2d week*	*Both weeks*
No. of maneuvers	20	14	34
No. of individual forays	170	84	254
No. of Allied ships sunk	12	0	12
No. of Allied ships damaged	6	0	6
No. of E-boats destroyed	5*	10	15
Average no. on duty	31	25	28
Average no. of sorties per week, per E-boat on duty	5.5	3.5	4.5

*On the basis of more complete information, the OIC raised its initial estimate of 3 E-boats sunk in the first week to 5 destroyed in the same period.

Source: "Note on Some Enemy Reactions to Operation Neptune, First Fortnight," S.I. 980, p. 2, Public Record Office, ADM 223/172.

Table 10

E-boats destroyed, Operation Neptune (first fortnight)

Probable cause	*No. of E-boats*
Air attack on Le Havre	10
Air attack on E-boats at sea	2
Mines	2
Surface craft (destroyers and MGBs)	1
Total	15

Source: "Note on Some Enemy Reactions to Operation Neptune, First Fortnight," S.I. 980, p. 3, Public Record Office, ADM 223/172.

close to either flank from which they could operate against the Seine Estuary," he wrote. Moreover, the Allies had been forced, initially "to operate with large surface forces and transport units in a narrow area without any regular convoy rhythm, so that there were always worthwhile targets in the area." He noted further: "Enemy defense systems were not fully worked up, so that in the early days they were reasonably easy to break through." A final factor favoring the German forces related to experience. "The enemy had many new units," Petersen observed, "especially American units which were neither used to the area nor to E-boat warfare, and which were therefore easier targets for E-boats than the experienced British Channel destroyers."[28]

Against those factors, Petersen listed the operational disadvantages with which the forces under his command had had to contend: "(1) the small number of E-boats compared with the size of the Allied forces, (2) the short nights and consequently short operational time, (3) the necessity for constant change of bases with consequently unfavorable effect upon the length of operations which were particularly conditional on the insufficient supply of torpedoes in Le Havre."[29] Always, the decisive factor seemed to lead back to the raid on the leading Seine port.

At Marine Gruppe West, Admiral Krancke hoped that his coastal forces could still recover from the double blow at Le Havre and Boulogne. However, by the time they began to filter replacement boats back into Le Havre, the Germans discovered that the Allies had instituted such effective radar nets around the mouth of the Seine and concentrated so many anti–E-boat units that offensive torpedo operations in flotilla strength by the fast boats were now out of the question. Once fixed by radar, the E-boats could be tracked and their position passed along from hunting group to hunting group. It had become as perilous as operating along the English Coast, the German naval leadership concluded. The Germans had entirely given up attacks along the British South Coast after their success at Lyme Bay six weeks earlier because of intensified British radar. Boats might still operate individually or in groups of two from the French harbors. They could still lay mines. However, Krancke admitted that for all practical purposes the game was over. He concluded: "These are the reasons why the E-boats achieved no further successes that month, except for a few mining operations. Even the weather was unsuitable for their operations."[30]

In desperation, the German Navy carried on in the weeks following the raid, using the E-boats as platforms for launching experimental long-range zigzag torpedoes called *Dackel.* However, they had to fire them just off Le

Havre and the strange weapons made their way independently thirty miles down to the Normandy anchorages at nine knots where they began their zigzag pattern. Surprise netted them a few hits the first night, but Allied torpedo nets and other countermeasures rendered *Dackel* completely ineffective thereafter. Aimed torpedo attacks by the E-boat Force, traditionally their most effective type of mission, were fast becoming a rarity for the surviving flotillas on the Channel. Faced with an Allied supremacy on the sea to match its supremacy in the air over Normandy, the Kriegsmarine began to look to even less orthodox weapons and tactics.

In July and August, for example, the Germans accumulated scores of navy volunteers to ride bubble-topped launch vehicles that looked like torpedoes mounted atop armed strike torpedoes for night launchings from land. These strange piggyback weapons, called *Neger,* were part of the Germans' last-ditch *Kleinkampfverbände,* or small combat units. The *Neger* were soon followed by a deeper diving cousin called *Marder* (wood marten), but it, too, was ineffective. The commitment to what amounted to experimental craft proved to be a wasteful gesture that cost the lives of dozens of youthful sailors for meager results. The Allies erected more torpedo nets and alerted the invasion fleet's bristling perimeter defenses to the unorthodox attackers. The painfully slow units made easy targets, and the Neptune defenders made quick work of them. Finally, in desperation, the Kleinkampfverbände employed manned miniature power boats laden with explosives called *Linse* to attack the fleet. Once again the element of surprise scored some damage to a few craft, but rigorous countermeasures put a halt to *Linse.* The net sum of such operations was that they were almost uniformly unsuccessful, and they demonstrated that the small combat units had joined the E-boat Force in becoming a phantom threat.[31]

Meanwhile the Allied buildup continued. The big LSTs shuttled back and forth between the English ports and the open beaches, off-loading their vital cargoes of men and materiel, indifferent to the Germans' wrecking of the port of Cherbourg and unaffected when die-hard troops transformed other harbors into fortresses as they did at Le Havre. The ships and crews of Operation Neptune plied relentlessly back and forth across the Channel, defending their sealink regardless of whether storms broke the Mulberries or the ports remained out of reach. The Allies went on to win the vital buildup phase of the invasion, and starting on 25 July 1944, weeks before any port came into use, they transformed the invasion into a breakthrough followed immediately by a breakout into the Second Front. There would never be a German transportation plan in reverse worked by the E-boats. The Le Havre raid saw to that. But because of the incredible pace of events and the subtle nature of that operation, the public was only dimly aware of its significance. Frustrated by the nearly complete secrecy he had to invoke on the harbor raids, Arthur Harris was heard to mutter afterward when no accolades for his forces were forthcoming: "If the Navy had done that, it would have counted as a great sea victory."[32]

It was a great victory, and its architects were many. It was achieved through the intelligence and determination of the keepers of the Ultra Secret, equal perseverance and skill by the staff of the Admiralty's Operational Intelligence Centre, imaginative and precise work by the pilots and photointerpretation personnel of PRU Benson and PIU Medmenham, constant pressure by the determined crews of the Royal Navy's destroyers and Coastal Forces plus the crews of RAF Coastal Command, the fruits of Barnes Wallis's creative mind in combination with the dedication, inspired leadership, and highly developed skills of Bomber Command's 617 Squadron and the determined crews of Bomber Command's main force. Not least among the victors were the fighting American divisions of VII Corps, including the paratroopers of the 82d and 101st Airborne divisions, the reinvigorated 4th Infantry Division, the veteran 9th Infantry Division, the quick-learning rookie 79th Division, and even the neophyte 90th Division, all of which had isolated Cherbourg and forced the German naval forces into a trap, the witches' cauldron of Le Havre. Those who had fallen in Lyme Bay played a role too. Their tragic deaths had alerted the Allies to a danger they could no longer ignore. Six weeks later in the waters of another bay the hunters had become the hunted.

Chapter **12**

Retreat and Pursuit

Despite the incredible pounding that Germany's Schnell-bootwaffe and other naval forces took at Le Havre on 14 June 1944 and again the following evening at Boulogne, the survivors did not give up. A remarkable aspect of the war at sea in the European Theater of Operations from this point forward was the determination shown by the Kriegsmarine to continue the fight by any and all means left to it, despite the high cost in human lives and a drastic decline in its effectiveness. Therefore, although their defeat at Le Havre was decisive in the sense that it suspended the German Navy's ability to conduct offensive torpedo operations with E-boats in flotilla strength, the Allies had to reckon with a tenacious fighting retreat of the Schnellbootwaffe and other coastal forces as the Allied Second Front liberated first France and then the Lowlands. Even more serious, from landward the Germans in defeat obeyed Hitler's orders to defend all major ports, so that the stubborn defense of Cherbourg, followed by its destruction as a major entrepôt, was repeated again and again as the front swept over the other Channel ports. Shipping and supply problems for the Allies, exacerbated by the lack of a large, well-placed, and undamaged port, remained one of the chief obstacles to a continued advance. Those difficulties go far in explaining why World War II in Europe ended in May 1945, rather than in the autumn of 1944.

Strategic Retreat at the Water's Edge

The retreat of the E-boats exposed long-existing tensions between the Schnellbootwaffe and the leadership of the German Navy, but it also revealed how resourceful the crews were. A tug-of-war ensued between FdS Petersen and the Seekriegsleitung (SKL) concerning how best to utilize the remaining E-boats at Cherbourg and points west following the raid on Le Havre. The small-boat tracking staff at OIC listened in fascination as the naval authorities in the Cherbourg and Brittany ports ordered an evacuation to St. Malo to escort coasters to the Channel Islands, while FdS Petersen called for a fighting retreat eastward back to Le Havre and other centers of German naval activity that were still able to carry on the struggle. For a time the issue simmered as E-boat Commander Günther Rabe and his "Raven" boats transported wounded personnel, critical supplies, and in one instance even female entertainment personalities on night runs out of Cherbourg to St. Malo, returning to the surrounded port with medicines and ammunition.

Matters finally came to a head on the night of 23–24 June when the SKL authorities ordered all remaining boats out and approved the demolition of the last remaining harbor facilities. At 2300 hours that evening Rabe headed S-130 and two other boats out of Cherbourg Harbor for the last time, trading distant shots with an American Sherman tank as they passed the Gare Maritime. Torn between conflicting orders from FdS Petersen and the convoy officer in St. Malo, the tiny group initially moved east, then reversed course to westward under the heavy coastal guns. Replenishing fuel at St. Malo, the Raven's three boats moved north again to the Channel Island of Alderney. There they awaited FdS Petersen's final orders. The OIC described what happened next. "At 1503 on 25th June S.O. E-boats [FdS Petersen] ordered the RABE group to transfer from Alderney to Le Havre—probably one of the most formidable directives ever given the Channel E-boats." Accordingly, Rabe's S-130, accompanied by S-168 and the hastily repaired S-145, set course north northeast on the evening of 25 June, heading directly toward an invasion fleet of six thousand ships. Unbeknownst to Rabe, Dolphin broke early, at 1904 hours that evening, alerting the entire Royal Navy to his intentions.[1]

Individual initiative and experience plus the quality of their vessels saved Rabe and his crew. True to his own dictum to do the unexpected, Rabe moved far out into the Channel, close upon the English South Coast where he was least expected. In the darkness he almost collided with a surprised British destroyer. The OIC small-boat tracking staff monitored Rabe's passage. "At 0107 on 26th June, HMS *Tanatside* contacted two E-boats one of which crossed her bows and passed close on her starboard side. The E-boat, though under Oerlikon fire, was unscathed as 4 inch and pom-pom [40 mm] could not depress sufficiently to bring to bear on her." Rabe and his crew, with S-168 following, pressed on. The third boat, S-145, had suffered a recurrence of steering gear problems and turned back. "By this time the E-boats had merged with the mass of cross-Channel shipping," the OIC report continued, "and all radar control of their movements was brought to an end." As the Portsmouth diary commented: "Once again the superior speed of the E-boats prevented us from effective action." This miniature "Channel dash" occurred in weather sufficiently rough that not even the hardy MTB crews of coastal forces had dared to venture out into it. As dawn approached, the Raven at the bridge of S-130, with S-168 alongside, pulled into Dieppe. Their arrival in damaged and only partially serviceable boats was mute testimony to the resourcefulness of commanders and crews and a stark reminder of the seakeeping qualities of E-boats even in the moment of defeat for the Schnellbootwaffe. A few days later, S-130 limped northward under escort and by stages reached safer ports where she underwent extensive repairs.[2]

At Le Havre the surviving naval forces continued to mount operations, however shakily. Replacement E-boats and R-boats proceeded out of harbor singly or in groups of two. The E-boats would stand off the port entrance to launch special long-range T3a *Dackel* torpedoes thirty miles across the mouth of the Seine at an economical nine knots where they began their zigzag search pattern. On nine separate nights in July, they tried these bizarre weapons, sinking one coastal vessel on the first night with the aid of surprise. Thereafter, Allied countermeasures such as torpedo nets made further deployment of the slow-moving *Dackel* a waste of time, as a disgusted FdS Petersen well knew.

Le Havre's giant E- and R-boat bunker, the cause of so much attention earlier, continued to see its luck decline. On the night of 5–6 July a newly installed torpedo depot in its central hangars blew up under mysterious circumstances and inflicted heavy loss of life. At least forty-one torpedo heads detonated, causing the massive roof, already weakened by Tallboy impacts, to cave in, further reducing the effectiveness of the bunker. German naval reports stated that the source may have been a sailor whose carelessly discarded cigarette ignited a gasoline storage facility, which in turn engulfed the torpedo depot. Later, a French master electrician in the employ of the Germans, Maurice Leboucher, claimed to have wired a charge to the torpedoes and, using a telephone circuit, detonated the heads by placing a call from a safe distance. French authorities claimed afterward that 117 German military personnel died in the explosion and fire. No matter what caused the explosion, the German Navy and its "impregnable" bunker were having a rough time of it as the summer of 1944 wore on.[3]

Finally, at the end of August, as the remaining E-boats and other coastal craft evacuated the port, the Germans blew up the last usable hangars at the eastern end of the pens, so that it was thoroughly wrecked by the time the advancing Allied armies closed in on Le Havre from the land side during the last weeks of August. The German Navy evacuated all remaining forces from Le Havre on 24 and 25 August.

The OIC small-boat trackers declared the cessation of German naval activity in the Seine port to be a major turning point in the sea war on the Channel. "Perhaps the most striking feature of a study of E-boat dispositions in the Neptune area is the pivotal role of Le Havre," the OIC staff reported. "The fall of Cherbourg as an E-boat base may have appeared catastrophic, but the fall of Le Havre virtually entailed the collapse of operations from Boulogne as well. Boulogne was a peripheral base, and by the time E-boats had been withdrawn so far, they had really ceased to play an integral part in Channel warfare. This is in some measure borne out by the fact that barely a week elapsed between the evacuation of Le Havre and the planned destruction of Boulogne."[4] By 3 September the Germans were forced to demolish their facilities at Boulogne and Calais. Within a few days not one E-boat remained operational west of the Hook of Holland. The sea war off Normandy had come to an end so far as the Schnellbootwaffe was concerned.

This unheralded victory hardly meant that the Allies were on the verge of concluding the war at sea or on land. FdS Petersen fed in more E-boat reserves up to the moment the evacuation from Le Havre commenced, and thereafter the Allies had constantly to reckon with forty boats operating in the North Sea and along the Dutch and Belgian coasts. The OIC had carefully observed the activities of the Schnellbootwaffe under Petersen's direction in the weeks following the pulverizing raid on the Seine port. "Reviewing the activity from Le Havre during the last two and a half months," the OIC trackers wrote, "it is impossible not to admire the manner in which S.O. E-boats [FdS Petersen] not only surmounted great obstacles in the matter of supply and maintenance, but also . . . the way in which he operated the E-boats under his command. . . . The tactical han-

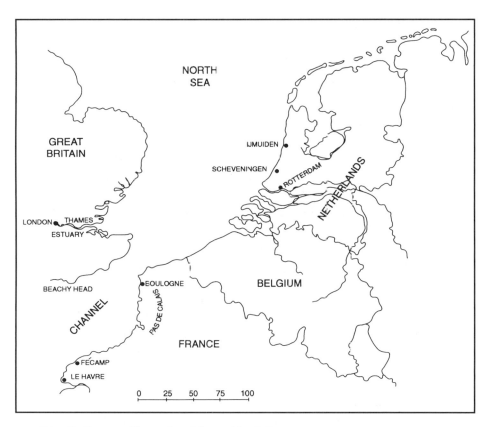

Map 3. Eastern Channel and lower North Sea

dling of sorties was masterly." For example, they cited the ability of the E-boat Force to feint with isolated torpedo attacks in one direction to bait Allied destroyers and MTEs while groups of E-boats seeded Germany's deadly oyster mines elsewhere.[5]

Although they could operate in flotilla strength less frequently now, E-boats continued to sow mines in the Schelde Estuary, the North Sea, and even on occasion off the Thames Estuary. Given Allied preponderance on the water, increased attrition among the E-boat Force was inevitable, but the quality of surviving and replacement crews remained surprisingly high down to the end of the war. Although no longer capable of threatening the Allied sea bridge across the Channel, the E-boat Force nevertheless remained a stubborn foe, one that required constant monitoring by special intelligence personnel and vigilant patrolling by destroyers, MTBs, and Coastal Command aircraft to the last days of the war.[6] Eventually, Bomber

Command felt compelled to take a hand once again as the war crept north and east.

German resistance on the landward side of the water's edge could only be described as tenacious. As they had done elsewhere, the remaining German troops and naval security forces turned Le Havre into a fortress and while defending it against besieging British and Canadian troops, they wrecked those sections of the port not already in ruins. They also took care to sow numerous oyster mines in the harbor and its approaches for which the Allies had no effective countermeasures. So formidable were the strongholds manned by the eleven thousand German defenders that British 1st Corps Commander, Gen. Sir John Crocker, called upon RAF Bomber Command to soften up the German positions. Meanwhile the 15-inch guns of the heavy monitor HMS *Erebus* and battleship HMS *Warspite* dueled with German guns of equal caliber at the Battery Grand Clos slightly northwest of the town. Both sides inflicted damage in the old-fashioned coastal bombardment, but it was Britain's air arm that wreaked true havoc. Working under the assumption that the French citizens of Le Havre had evacuated, RAF Bomber Command began on 5 September 1944 a series of pulverizing raids that culminated in saturation bombings of eight strongholds on 10 and 11 September. Nearly a thousand heavy bombers participated in the 10 September raid. When the last Lancaster and Halifax had departed, Canadian and British troops clambered over fields of rubble to take the surrender of the dazed Germans when the port fell the following day. As they looked around them, the words of the ancient, Tacitus, may have come to mind for troops of the 51st Highland and 49th West Riding divisions with attached Canadian brigades entering the stricken town: "When they made a desert, they called it peace."[7]

Bomber Command's September raids dumped at least ten thousand tons of bombs on Le Havre, which, in combination with the earlier summer raids, raised the total to thirteen thousand tons, the same amount of explosive power that destroyed Hiroshima a year later. At the moment of its liberation, Le Havre was no more. Vast plateaus of rubble were all that remained of a once modern city, and two thousand civilians lay dead under its ruins.[8]

For some days an eerie silence hung over the rubble. Cautiously, Allied inspection teams began probing its mine-strewn wastes. They could not linger. In pursuit of the retreating German 15th Army, Canadian and British ground troops slogged north to begin the same wearisome sieges all over again at Boulogne, Calais, Dunkirk, and along the approaches of the Schelde Estuary. However, Le Havre was too important a supply base to ignore. In early October American naval personnel began entering the city in quantity in hopes of reviving its port. Like those who had first entered the town on 12 September, the American landing parties could only stare at first. A U.S. Navy history of its activities in Le Havre described the reactions of the first Americans ashore: "All of these early contingents found a city the likes of which they had never seen before," the report began. "When the Nazis surrendered the area, they regarded it as completely destroyed. And they were not far from wrong."[9]

Allied resuscitation efforts notwithstanding, Le Havre experienced no miraculous recovery. No phoenix rose from its ashes. A year after the war, in May 1946, famed British resistance leader George Millar walked through Le Havre with a companion. They were among the first tourists to visit the great port following a harrowing entry into harbor aboard a sailboat. Wrecks still littered the approaches and every basin, but with the help of some friendly fishermen they finally settled into a narrow berth. "We asked several people to direct us to the centre of town," he wrote, "but their answers were vague." They walked inland for a time, trying to get their bearings. Millar finally asked an elderly pedestrian in a starched collar the same question. "Centre of the town?" the Havrist asked in amazement. "There is no centre. The town has been destroyed by war. . . . If you want to see where the old centre of the town was, then you are standing within two hundred metres of it." They looked around them at the mounds and hillocks of masonry and brick, then stumbled on. Le Havre's first peacetime visitors finally located a place to eat amid the ruins and then returned on foot to the only shelter available to them, their own boat. Millar described what greeted them on their way back to the port area. "The sea wind, which should have been clean and salty, blew curtains of dust and grit along the roads, curtains that sucked more dust from the rubble on either side as they passed so that far inland the air was thicker and heavier than among the ruins themselves."[10] To this day Havrists who experienced the raids of 1944 are reluctant to talk about them.

Le Havre was not alone in its misery. Both sides meted out mass destruction daily as the war ground on. Although the Kriegsmarine realized that its bunkers were threatened by new weapons, it seemed to have gained a reprieve after the heavy raids on Le Havre and Boulogne in mid-June. Bomber Command had attacked no E-boat installations per se in the months that followed. However, the resurgence of E-boat operations out of Dutch ports into the lower North Sea and crucial river estuaries such as the Schelde once again elevated Petersen's E-boat Force into a target of increasing importance in Allied eyes. The remarkable ability of his command to recover was about to receive an Allied compliment of sorts.[11]

There were few ports and protective shelters of which the E-boat Force could avail itself in its northeastward retreat at the water's edge. Among those few were Waalhaven in Rotterdam and the giant pens at Ijmuiden. Massive structures like those in the French ports, they were impossible to camouflage. At a SHAEF meeting on 5 December, the senior commanders decided that Bomber Command's special squadrons should attack the pens. Accordingly, on 15 December 1944 in the pale light of a winter's day seventeen Lancasters of 617 Squadron arrived over Ijmuiden and released their Tallboys on the E-boat pens. Unfortunately, heavy cloud obscured the results, and this time no special intelligence was forthcoming that allowed them to read German damage estimates. But one week later they received an unwelcome answer in the form of renewed E-boat operations. In fact, Petersen's next move caught them off guard, a fact reflected in a top secret priority despatch on Christmas Day which C-in-C Nore rushed to the Admiralty for SHAEF: "From the scale of E-boat attack on the nights of 22–23 and 24–25 December, it is apparent that a large number of operational E-boats are based at Ijmuiden and Waalhaven [Rotterdam]. Request bombing of these E-boat pens may be intensified at a very early date." The attack of 15 December had seemingly gone astray. For the moment at least the Allies could do little. Bad weather precluded any immediate follow-up action.[12]

Four days later, on 29 December 1944, sixteen Lancasters struck the E-boat pens at Rotterdam causing massive destruction and heavy loss of life. It was then that survivor Hans Schirren saw at close quarters the effects of Tallboy impacts. Once again his amazing luck held and he survived the raid when many of his comrades did not. Then several more weeks of heavy weather gave the German coastal forces a seeming respite. Finally, on 8 February 1945 fifteen heavily laden Lancasters returned to Ijmuiden. This time they finished the pens for good. By now the message was clear. Since the very pens themselves were beckoning Allied attack, dispersal and camouflage were the E-boats' sole remaining protection as the special squadrons of RAF Bomber Command resumed pounding the E-boat Force's last remaining strongholds.[13]

This knowledge came late to the Allies. Poor visibility and the lack of photoreconnaissance had delayed the attackers' ability to digest important evidence in a timely fashion. As it turned out, the first of the renewed attacks on Ijmuiden in mid-December had inflicted a more telling blow than anyone could have hoped for. FdS Petersen had reached a pessimistic conclusion following an inspection of the Ijmuiden pens on the morning after the December raid. Two Tallboys had penetrated the roof, he recorded, destroying S-198 and damaging six more E-boats. One crewman was killed; twelve were listed as missing and five wounded. Maintenance facilities throughout the structure were thoroughly disrupted, and six pens were now unusable. One E-boat remained undamaged, but it was entombed inside its pen, trapped by giant slabs of steel-reinforced concrete. In short, Petersen conceded, the entire 8th Flotilla was now out of action. From the 15 December raid he drew an obvious lesson. "This event brings the bitter knowledge that E-boat shelters in Rotterdam and Ijmuiden in their present form no longer afford protection against bombing and have accordingly lost their purpose. I have therefore decided not to fill the pens with E-boats any longer, in view of the character of these shelters as special targets. The boats will be dispersed in the harbours, even at the expense of other advantages. This measure is not an ideal solution, and may be subject to alteration under certain circumstances, according to air situations or the tactics of enemy day-fighter-bombers."[14]

Petersen was entirely correct that dispersal of the thin-skinned boats around harbors was not an ideal solution. On 6 February 1945 an Allied air raid on Ijmuiden, probably by Coastal Command fighter bombers, damaged those E-boats lying dispersed outside the pens while those vessels inside were protected. Two days later 617 Squadron returned with Tallboys and penetrated the pens yet again. But despite the damage to dispersed boats during the 6 February raid, Petersen had stood by his decision that boats in pens still ran the greater risk. Not one E-boat was inside the Ijmuiden pen on the follow-up raid of 8 February. Wallis's earthquake bomb, when accurately delivered by 617 Squadron, had turned the German bunkers, built at enormous cost with scarce strategic war materials, into permanent liabilities.[15]

A happier fortune awaited the Allied landing ships. Because the fate of Le Havre was typical of what happened to other Channel ports in the summer of 1944, the continued necessity for off-loading onto open beaches and makeshift ports meant that vessels like LSTs were indispensable to the maintenance of Allied momentum once the breakout occurred. The most authoritative source on Allied shipping problems after 6 June summed it up nicely: "One of the outstanding features of logistic support in the first six months of operations was the unexpected extent to which U.S. supplies and personnel were funneled through the Normandy ports. . . . The capacity of the beaches proved a godsend in view of the delayed opening of

Cherbourg. In the first seven weeks they constituted practically the only intake capacity on the Continent." Given the Germans' determination to hold onto and then ruin all major ports, the Normandy beaches continued to be responsible for off-loading a large percentage of men and materiel up to November 1944, far longer than Allied planners had ever envisaged.[16]

By 4 September 1944, with the fall of the giant port of Antwerp intact to Field Marshal Montgomery's 21st Army Group, it appeared that the answer to the Allies' logistical woes was at hand. But Antwerp lay sixty miles inside the Schelde Estuary. Perceiving an opening between the German 15th and 7th armies, Montgomery, with Supreme Commander Eisenhower's assent, husbanded resources for the airborne assault, Market-Garden, at Arnhem rather than seizing the strategic approaches to Antwerp. It was a gamble that failed. Not only was the airborne assault one bridge too far, the 15th Army blocked the Schelde for a crucial two months. The German Navy's E-boats, small combat units, and its new two-man midget submarines, along with Luftwaffe mining sorties, aided the Wehrmacht, which had reinforced the heavy shore batteries at Walcheren Island, South Beveland, and elsewhere. The total effect rendered Antwerp's fall to the Allies meaningless during a vital stage of the war. Hapless Canadians and Britons battled Germans under appalling conditions in the watery polders and approaches for many weeks. The first convoy into Antwerp did not off-load until 28 November 1944, long after Allied momentum in the West had ceased. By then the Allies in the West were butting their heads against the Siegfried Line and other stout defenses throughout western Germany and the Upper Rhine. The Germans' fighting retreat along the water's edge had paid them major dividends in purely military terms, but in the end, despite the Ardennes Offensive, it proved only to have prolonged the agony of war by another six months. Nobody won.

RAF Bomber Command

Having demonstrated the effectiveness of its precision tactical squadron in combination with main force bombers, RAF Bomber Command found many more targets for its Tallboy bombs. The 617 Squadron crews began attacking the worrisome V-weapon sites, smashing a massive concrete-covered structure in a quarry at Wizernes on 24 June 1944. A few days later they destroyed a flying-bomb storage facility at Siracourt with Leonard Cheshire marking low in his maiden trip in a high-speed Mustang, part of a batch obtained from the U.S. 8th Air Force by the Air Ministry. The Tallboys were now handsomely repaying the high cost of developing them. Next, Bomber Command attacked a huge complex of caves at St.-

Leu-d'Esserent, north of Paris, which the Germans had also turned into an "impregnable" V-weapons storage site. Tallboys wrecked the cave complex. Perhaps the crowning achievement in the fight against V-weapons came on 6 July 1944 when 617 Squadron Lancasters, led for the last time into combat by Cheshire, destroyed the massive V-3 long-range guns sited at Mimoyecques. The V-3's ultra long-range multiple barrels, five hundred feet in length, were buried in a site deep underground, and only a Tallboy had a chance of penetrating it. No V-3 ever became operational, a victory for Bomber Command that saved the lives of hundreds and possibly thousands of civilians in London and the South counties. A grateful Bomber Command ordered Cheshire as well as 617 Squadron's three senior squadron leaders McCarthy, Munro, and Shannon—all veterans of the famed Dams Raid—to cease combat operations at once. They had served long and faithfully, but enemy action or combat fatigue would claim them if they continued on operations. Others could replace them.

The tempo of 617 Squadron operations continued at high speed during that fateful summer of 1944. Other targets included submarine pens at Brest and elsewhere, although they were so robust that not even the Tallboys could destroy them. Several aircraft were lost or severely damaged on those raids because of dense German flak, an indication of what might have happened at Le Havre had the Luftwaffe not issued its *Schiessverbot* on the evening of 14 June. Other notable targets for the special bombs included the battleship *Tirpitz,* anchored in Kaa Fjord in Northern Norway. It survived in damaged condition one 617 Squadron attack from a shuttle raid out of the Soviet Union's Yagodnik airfield near Archangel but was forced to move farther south. The *Tirpitz* capsized in a 617 Squadron follow-up raid near Tromsö in central Norway on 12 November 1944, taking a thousand men down with her. During that same autumn 9 Squadron, a main force unit in 5 Group, became the RAF's second precision squadron and joined 617 Squadron in launching pinpoint attacks with deadly Tallboys on hardened targets, including the E-boat pens at Ijmuiden. Later still, the ultimate development in Barnes Wallis's earthquake bomb concept—his twenty-two-thousand-pound Grand Slam—destroyed a huge viaduct at Bielefeld in March 1945 and an enormously strong submarine pen at Hamburg in the last days of the war. By this time there was virtually no target left in Hitler's twelve-year Reich that the Allies could not destroy if they so chose. Scientist Wallis's earthquake bomb had reached its true potential. The dropping of another special bomb on Hiroshima on 6 August 1945 eclipsed the earthquake bomb. Tallboys and Grand Slams were never used again.

Chapter **13**

How Serious Was the E-Boat Threat?

It had taken an extraordinary effort to cope with the German coastal forces and especially its fast fighting boats at the time of the invasion. Yet little public attention centered on E-boats following the smashing of their most effective bases by mid-June 1944. Superficially at least, flotillas of fast torpedo boats did not seem to be life threatening to the vast invasion fleet in that same summer. Certainly the Kriegsmarine had not attempted, nor could they have attempted, a genuine sea battle in the Channel with the forces at hand. But experience showed that only the E-boats had sufficient performance to fight and survive on the surface of the sea area around the invasion front. The E-boat Force was highly specialized. It possessed decided advantages of speed and stealth under nighttime conditions, assuming moderate seas and moonless skies. Lacking armor and conventional firepower, it was a dangerous, if fragile, instrument that required special handling by naval leaders who understood its strengths as well as its limitations. Fortunately for the Kriegsmarine, it found its competent handler in Kommodore Petersen. The E-boat Force could, in common with the better-known U-boat Force, be likened to a wolf pack stalking herds of larger prey in hopes of hamstringing and felling the most vulnerable. In this case the prey were LSTs, LCTs, tugs, and ferries, which were vital to the needs of a fleet without an adequate port. Even so, the E-boat Force found itself overwhelmed by Allied naval and air strength that, combined with the use of special intelligence, struck effective blows the Germans could not withstand. Nevertheless, a question remains as to how the German Navy might have offered a more credible threat to the forces of Operation Neptune/Overlord.

Answers to that question lead directly to the problems and limitations associated with how Nazi Germany mobilized and armed itself for war. Part of the problem lay in the very quality of the coastal craft ordered by the Kriegsmarine. Germany's S-38/100 E-boat of 1944 was, if anything, too good. By comparison with British MTBs and American PT boats, it had much greater range, harder hitting torpedoes, excellent defensive armament and armor, speed, and because of its special hull, superior sea-keeping qualities. It was a different class of vessel than the coastal craft of other navies. The problem with the design was that it demanded increasingly hard-to-get materials and equipment, which limited production. It also demanded a large, experienced crew in order to extract the best performance from it. The biggest, fastest torpedo boat of World War II in any navy, the E-boat, built the way the German Navy wanted it, demanded four different high-quality woods, scarce light-metal alloys, three hard-to-build, high-performance diesels with an average service life of four hundred hours, sophisticated radar, and an array of increasingly rare antiaircraft cannon of various sizes. That was why there were only 34 E-boats in the Channel ports when the invasion came. Adequate defense demanded that the Germans have 134 or even better 234 E-boats on hand as the first or outer defense force against an invasion. Since they were first-class boats with extended range, they should have been carrying the fight to the Allies at their own ports of embarkation as well as in mid-Channel, mining and launching torpedo attacks in the crowded waters off the South Coast of England.

For all the research and development the Kriegsmarine lavished upon E-boat hull design, power plant, weapons, and defensive armor and armament, it imposed severe handicaps upon its E-boat Force by its failure to keep pace in other fields. Simply stated, the Germans failed to remain competitive in the realm of electronic warfare and the collection of various types of intelligence. The Channel E-boats needed far better centimetric radar than what they possessed in order to locate and intercept enemy shipping. They needed much better passive radar detection devices to counteract increased Allied surveillance of their own activities. At a time when Allied photoreconnaissance and photointerpretation were paying increasing dividends, the E-boat flotillas were forced to hunt Allied targets through older means. For example, they depended upon analysis of previous patterns of operations and their ability to monitor the intensity and location of enemy radio traffic through their B-Dienst. Skill and experience allowed them to wring the utmost out of such outdated methods, but they were not enough. By mid-1944 Allied superiority in electronic warfare and intelligence gathering had placed Germany's technology-dependent air and naval arms at an increasingly severe disadvantage. The German Navy's failure to modernize its weapons systems embodied in the *Schnellboot* largely negated the investment it had made earlier in the development of the world's finest coastal vessel.

It should have had access to the Luftwaffe's efficient 30-mm cannon, which hit nearly as hard as the cumbersome 37-mm or 40-mm Bofors cannon but required only two crewmen instead of seven and weighed far less. Requiring the E-boat Force to use torpedoes and mines designed for much heavier submarines and surface vessels was another indication that the Kriegsmarine had extended only half-hearted acceptance to its coastal forces. Finally, compelling the E-boat flotillas to operate without the benefit of maritime aerial reconnaissance was nothing short of folly.

Other omissions abounded. The Kriegsmarine needed a second class of E-boats comparable in size, performance, and sheer numbers to the British MTB or the American PT boat. A small, shallow-draft, simple-construction vessel with a length of eighty feet made of light metal and wood, manned by ten or a dozen men firing small, limited-range torpedoes, and operating in flotillas of dozens of boats closer to the defended shore would have posed a second major sea hazard for the Allies. This was known in the jargon of coastal forces as the "swarm-of-bees" approach. True, the German Navy had been working on a light-weight LS-boat, *Leichtes Schnellboot,* but it never went into serial production and was not a factor in the war. The E-boat Force had to work with its first-class E-boats alone, and there were simply never enough of them. Their seawater coolant pipes protruded more than five feet underwater and demanded more than a fathom of clean water to operate efficiently. This, in combination with a hull of relatively deep draft for a coastal vessel, made it difficult to operate in the smaller Channel ports where shifting tides and shoals limited the use of the larger E-boats. Had it been able to operate out of ports such as Dieppe, Fécamp, Treport, Caen, Grandcamp, Isigny, and several of the Channel Islands, the E-boat Force could have achieved genuine dispersal with a corresponding increase in difficulty as potential targets for Bomber Command.

The lack of adequate numbers of E-boats was not attributable entirely to German decisions. The Allies also played a role in limiting the quantity of E-boats available to the Kriegsmarine. The powerful Mercedes Benz diesels, first the MB 501s and 502s, and then the late war MB 511s and MB 518s, were marvelous power plants. However, they were hard to build and for most of the war only one mill with a special hammer was able to forge their crankshafts. They required special roller bearings from one factory in Schweinfurt. For all practical purposes only one assembly plant produced the diesels. That was the Daimler Benz factory at Untertürkheim, a suburb of Stuttgart. A second assembly plant at Marienfelde in Berlin produced for a short time, but in a rationalization drive led by Albert Speer, the Armaments Ministry converted it to tank engine production instead. At its best, the one remaining assembly line, geared up for full production, could turn out only ten diesels per month. The estimated life span for the high-performance diesels was only four hundred hours. Therefore, almost as much labor in a second facility was needed to rebuild and refit older diesels.

Allied intelligence noticed that the Germans had taken elaborate precautions in camouflaging the Daimler Benz plant in Untertürkheim. It lay beside the Neckar River, and the Germans had completely covered a canal that entered the river next to the factory with elaborate camouflage netting. Similarly the Germans had painted all approach roads and railroads with camouflage paint. Allied photointerpreters were skilled in detecting such precautions, and the more the enemy utilized them in the Daimler complex the more interested the PIs became. Research into prewar records indicated that the set of buildings had been a testing center for experimental high-performance engines and chassis. Allied air intelligence could not determine precisely what the complex was producing by midwar, but they had accumulated enough information at Medmenham in late 1943 to decide that the Untertürkheim facilities warranted serious attention.[1]

First, a diversionary force of 157 Halifaxes and 21 Lancasters inflicted light damage on Stuttgart and the Daimler plant while Bomber Command's main force units struck Berlin on the night of 26–27 November 1943. On the night of 20–21 February 1944, 598 aircraft—most of them Lancasters—bombed Stuttgart through heavy cloud, damaging the Daimler-Benz complex. A formation of 557 aircraft repeated the tactic on the evening of 1–2 March. Two weeks later on the night of 15–16 March an even larger force of 863 aircraft, mostly Lancasters and Halifaxes, attacked the city again. Unexpectedly heavy winds caused delays and may have upset the bomb aiming because many of the bombs fell short or in open country south of the city. However, some found their mark. As a result of the three raids, production of E-boat diesels ceased entirely for a month. Those attacks plus similar ones on the ball bearing works at Schweinfurt further impeded diesel production at a crucial time when the E-boat Force was attempting to expand in size prior to the invasion.[2]

Dismayed, FdS Petersen and his staff were convinced the Allies had deliberately planned to halt E-boat production. That was simply not the case, but through coincidence, the strategic bombing effort had had the effect of slowing E-boat production at a critical phase of the war. Hulls lay in Bremen waiting to be matched with diesels that the Daimler Benz factory had not yet produced. But the raids did prove to be a curtain-raiser for the final event. On 5 September 1944 a heavy USAAF daylight bomber attack aimed specifically for the Daimler complex with its E-boat diesels and advanced DB 603 and DB 605 aircraft engines. A postwar Strategic Bombing Survey report summarized: "This attack caused extensive damage to the building and utilities with virtual total disruption of production from which the plant never recovered."[3]

The E-boat Force had another adversary that was almost as effective in checking its growth as the Allied strategic bombing campaign: the leadership of the Kriegsmarine. Unlike the U-boats, which had already proved their potential in the First World War and which had a powerful advocate in Admiral Karl Dönitz, the E-boats had matured more slowly and were, by their nature, confined to more limited battle areas and conditions, namely coastal waters in light to moderate seas at night. For that reason and because they were more vulnerable surface vessels, their potential destructiveness was not as great as U-boats. Nevertheless, they fulfilled a valuable role in a modern navy's arsenal. Those who came to understand their potential best were younger, less senior officers like Rudolf Petersen, who rose to the relatively modest position of Kommodore, or flag officer (ranked between captain and rear admiral), in the German Navy. Whether under the leadership of Admiral Raeder or later Admiral Dönitz, the Seekriegsleitung demonstrated an ambivalence bordering on hostility to its own E-boat Force.

Several reasons account for this ambivalence. First, the E-boats were no miracle weapon, and their handlers had to understand their limitations as well as their strengths in order to get the best out of them. In the opening campaigns in Poland, Scandinavia, the West, and again in the Baltic in 1941 against the Soviet Union, the SKL repeatedly misused its E-boats. It sent them on slow patrols, used them as slow convoy escorts, assigned them as picket boats on occasion, and failed to see them for what they really were: fast torpedo platforms in confined waters. They were a genuine threat to merchant shipping entering coastal areas and, therefore, an especially dangerous threat to island nations like Great Britain. Only slowly as the crews and E-boat staff gained more experience did their potential become apparent, and even then there were still many skeptics at the SKL in Berlin and at Marine Gruppenkommando West in Paris where Admirals Wilhelm Marschall and Theodor Krancke also viewed the E-boat Force and its commanding officer, FdS Petersen, coolly.

Part of the reason for the sometimes frosty relations between Petersen and his seniors lay in his personal background. Although an extremely able E-boat commander and then at the beginning of the war as a successful flotilla commander, Petersen was by no means an enthusiastic supporter of National Socialism. To be sure, he was never part of any organized opposition to Hitler and the Nazis, and he never had any connection with the resistance. However, Petersen did have a skeleton of sorts in his family closet: his father. The elder Petersen was an Evangelical Protestant minister in Berlin-Lichterfelde and a member of the *Bekennende Kirche,* or Confessing Church, as opposed to the National Socialist–oriented German Christians, who were trying to take over German Protestantism. Even more damning in the eyes of the Nazis, Petersen's father was a close associate of Martin Niemöller and was sufficiently outspoken against the German Christians that the Gestapo jailed him on at least one occasion during World War II. The son was scarcely encouraged to greater political loyalty by the harassment of his father. That may have had a bearing on the younger Petersen's extraordinary statement on a quay on Heligoland to the six E-boat commanders and senior engineer of the 2d E-boat Flotilla on 3 September 1939: "This war is a second world war. It will last longer than the First World War, and in the end we shall lose it."[4]

That was an act of unusual civil courage that could easily have had severe repercussions. In 1941 while on patrol, a submariner and naval officer from a wealthy anti-Nazi family, Leutnant zur See Oskar Kusch, removed a portrait of Hitler from the wardroom of U-154. Other officers reported him, and Kusch ultimately paid with his life.[5] By contrast Petersen's loyal subordinates did not repeat their commander's statement at the beginning of the war outside their select circle. Nevertheless, enough of Petersen's coolness to the war and to the higher leadership slipped through to produce his frosty relations with Raeder, with Dönitz, and with his immediate superiors at Marine Gruppe West.

Further evidence accumulated. His operations officer, 1A Bernd Rebensburg, recalled that when an enlisted man from the E-boat Force reported from the Eastern Baltic that he had been pressed into a firing squad that executed civilians, Petersen immediately circulated an order forbidding all E-boat personnel from participating in future actions of that kind.[6]

Consistently during the course of the war, Petersen refused to make reckless use of his small force. Rather, he conserved it whenever possible, employing it only when conditions favored his swift but fragile boats. The notion of fanatical resistance left him cold, and when younger officers spoke warmly of an outright sea battle at the time of the Normandy invasion, Petersen adamantly refused to consider such an action, preferring to save the lives of his young officers and crews who, like those in comparable Allied forces, formed a group that in terms of education and training were an elite cadre.

Such an attitude hardly made him a revolutionary. At bottom, Petersen was socially and politically conservative and a German nationalist who was not completely indifferent to Hitler's appeal. After all, the terms of the Versailles Treaty had forced his family to leave North Schleswig after 1918 when it reverted to Denmark. Moreover, he had chosen the military as his lifetime career, and he prized the "soldierly" virtues above all others. Rebensburg recalled a trip the FdS made to Berchtesgaden in the summer of 1944, ostensibly to inform Hitler of the hopelessness of German naval resistance to the Allies. To the general surprise of the staff, Petersen returned to FdS Headquarters from his meeting full of enthusiasm, convinced that increased priorities in E-boat production and in the expansion of the E-boat Force generally would turn the situation around. His euphoria lasted only a few weeks, until the reality sank in that Hitler's promised changes were not forthcoming. Petersen returned to a state of covert resignation rather than overt action. Any incipient resistance would have incurred immediate betrayal. In contrast to Petersen's political ambivalence, several recently arrived FdS staff members were ardent supporters of National Socialism, and they would have detected any efforts by their chief to resist or oppose the war. None ever did.[7]

The destructive raid on Le Havre, which for all practical purposes spelled the doom of the E-boat Force, also demonstrated fatal weaknesses in the Germans' organization for modern war. The Luftwaffe leadership's decision to issue a no-shoot order in the harbor district on that fateful evening made the disaster complete, but it was by no means a unique event. Adm. Friedrich Ruge, Field Marshal Rommel's highly respected naval adviser in Normandy, understood the implications of that grievous decision and traveled to headquarters in Paris to discuss the matter with his naval superiors. "At Navy Group West I met with Admiral Krancke who was enraged about the events at Le Havre," Ruge recounted. The Luftwaffe flights for which the no-shoot order was issued had been few in number, he complained. "During the hours preceding the air attack, a desperate Krancke had telephoned in all directions to have the order rescinded," Ruge continued, "but to no avail." Some days later, Rommel was trying to achieve unity of command over all the armed forces in his Army Group B, no easy task given the stubborn independence their leaders had exhibited under National Socialism. "This touched on the foundations of the current autonomy of the Wehrmacht's branches," Ruge observed. Some of the liaison officers objected loudly, but Ruge agreed with his superior. "In this matter Rommel was completely correct," he wrote, "since it was absurd to have three branches of the Wehrmacht operate autonomously in such a strained situation. A good example had been the firing prohibition of the anti-aircraft guns at Le Havre, which resulted in heavy losses for our naval forces."[8]

Unfortunately for the German theater commanders but fortunately for the Allies, the scandal surrounding the debacle at Le Havre did not lead to any improvements in command unity. It could not possibly do so because of fundamental flaws in the highest German leadership. Grand Admiral Dönitz explained why. "Göring was very fond of criticizing the Army and the Navy in Hitler's presence," he stated in his memoirs and noted that Admiral Raeder had forewarned him of Göring's methods at Führer Headquarters.

> I, too, very soon became aware of Göring's tactics, which were to hasten to Hitler and be the first to report, often in quite inaccurate form, the failures of the other services. As a result, there were not a few collisions between us. The most violent . . . of these happened at a large conference into which Göring marched and announced that German E-boats had suffered heavy losses during an air raid on one of the Channel ports and that the Navy was to blame because the E-boats, instead of being dispersed and camouflaged, had been lying conveniently together in a little group.

Dönitz had assumed on the basis of Krancke's report that the Navy had dispersed its boats thoroughly and was outraged by Göring's antics. "I refuse to tolerate these criticisms of the Navy," he retorted. "You would be better advised to look to your own Luftwaffe, where there is ample scope for your activities!" A stunned silence followed. Then Hitler called his paladins to order and afterward soothed Dönitz's ruffled feathers.[9] The clash enlightened no one. At no time did the senior commanders address the glaring breakdown in interservice cooperation at Le Havre that had so worried able subordinates like Rommel and Ruge.

If the highest leadership exhibited a lamentable inability to cooperate, the same could be said to hold true within the middle echelons of the German Navy where the Schnellbootwaffe frequently found itself isolated or its operations subordinated to the needs of local naval commands or by the Seekriegsleitung. The OIC small-boat trackers had first-hand knowledge of the frictions and disagreements in the uneasy relationship between FdS Petersen and his superiors such as Krancke and Dönitz. An identical problem applied to Petersen's working relationship with naval commanding officers in the Channel ports. As the last three E-boats remaining in Cherbourg prepared to evacuate on the evening of 23 June, a series of confusing and conflicting signals ordered them to move in two different directions. The senior German naval officer in charge of western defenses ordered the boats to move west and south to St. Malo, carrying urgent supplies of antitank weapons. In direct conflict with that order, FdS Petersen signaled them that evening at 1937 hours to proceed eastward to Le Havre, making a torpedo attack en route. The E-boat crews, apparently under orders from the local naval commander, continued to load supplies for St. Malo. At 2154 hours that evening an exasperated Petersen sent a second signal asking them to "endeavor with all resources" to break through eastward. Two minutes later in a move that had the listeners at Bletchley Park and at the OIC shaking their heads in wonder, the Cherbourg-based crews radioed a request for the appropriate harbor-light recognition signals at St. Malo. Despite orders from Petersen they were preparing to go west, and, so the British thought, in all likelihood out of the war.[10]

Petersen was determined not to relinquish control of his own E-boats, and after exchanging further secure land-line communications with Krancke's headquarters in Paris, he radioed the convoy officer at St. Malo at 2204 hours that his three boats had been ordered to Le Havre with instructions from Marine Gruppe West. A half hour later, the senior naval officer for Western Defenses grudgingly acknowledged that the E-boats were under Petersen's operational control. However, he signaled, if they could not break out to the east to Le Havre that night, then they were to proceed to St. Malo anyway. And so it happened. On the following morning E-boat Commander Rabe's group of three boats put into St. Malo, not Le Havre, raising the strength of the E-boat Force in the Brittany port to four boats. In masterly understatement, the OIC staff commented: "It is unusual for intercepted W/T [wireless traffic] to throw such a flood of light on an element of conflict within the German naval High Command."[11]

The head of the last Cherbourg E-boat contingent, Kapitänleutnant Rabe, "the Raven," remembered the events of 23 June differently. He was there. The higher German command—and the Bletchley listeners—were not. With communications frequently disrupted, he could not keep FdS Petersen informed of developments regularly, and there were overriding factors that determined what he could and could not do, no matter what orders were being issued. For example, all the beleaguered Cherbourg E-boats, including Rabe's S-130 were damaged, so an offensive war patrol with torpedoes eastward to Le Havre was, he knew, out of the question. Confusion reigned at Cherbourg with respect to orders: the Americans were threatening; German wounded urgently needed evacuation; and the chances of further repairs and the possibility of better communications at St. Malo were all factors that beckoned him westward. A decisive leader, he led his group into St. Malo while the higher command debated. At no time did the doughty Rabe consider leading his boats "out of the war," a decision amply confirmed by his "Channel dash" eastward several nights later.[12]

However, Rabe's independent decision did not alter the situation at headquarters. Even more significant, the disagreement of 23 June was not an isolated incident, and a question still remained, What were they to do with the remaining E-boats located at St. Malo? It was, the OIC staff observed, "a disagreement affecting not just the destiny of four E-boats but German naval strategy in the Neptune area." It transpired that Hitler himself was responsible ultimately for the sharp disagreements and vacillations among his naval authorities. A radio communication on 22 June from Marine Gruppe West to the Navy Office St. Malo revealed the underlying reason for conflicting priorities surrounding the E-boats. "The Führer has ordered the strongest replenishment of supplies for the Channel Islands," Admiral Krancke signaled. "C. in C. West has decided that the supplying of the Channel Islands has precedence over Cherbourg." Petersen refused to give up so easily and succeeded in convincing a reluctant Krancke that other coastal vessels such as armed trawlers and coasters should resupply the Channel Islands, not his precious E-boats. On the evening of 24 June Petersen ordered his boats north to Alderney, preparatory to moving back into the invasion area, but the stubborn Convoy Office at St. Malo still interfered, requesting of Krancke that "the Rabe group be left in the Channel Islands area to tie down enemy groups and secure replenishment of the Channel Islands with most urgent supplies." Pulled back and forth by his subordinates and by Hitler's interference, Krancke finally made his decision. In the early hours of 25 June, Marine Gruppe West replied unequivocally to St. Malo's request: "No. Rabe group is urgently needed for operations against the landing fleet."[13]

A fighting retreat of the E-boat Force eastward along the Channel ports was the only militarily sound option as Allied pressure increased, but Petersen had had to fight his own naval command in order to implement it. The E-boat Force and its commander, FdS Petersen, enjoyed an uneasy relationship with their own Kriegsmarine and with Germany's highest authorities.

Those differences intensified as the war continued into 1945. Operations Officer Bernd Rebensburg and others on FdS Petersen's staff heard repeated rumors of clashes between their commander and Dönitz over tactics and the level of activity that the E-boat senior officer was willing to undertake. The younger officers bridled with indignation because sources whom they trusted informed them that Dönitz had accused Petersen, and by implication, themselves, of outright cowardice. Petersen refused to discuss those verbal exchanges with his subordinates, but given their contacts with other staff officers at the SKL, the E-boat Force staffers were in no doubt as to the seriousness and bitterness of those charges.[14]

Despite his displeasure with the E-boat Force and with its commanding officer, Dönitz felt he had to be more circumspect when stating his position in writing. In January 1945, after the failed outcome of the Battle of the Bulge, he sent an urgent communication reflecting his displeasure to Petersen. The naval commander in chief, SKL, conceded to his FdS that the E-boat Force had had to fight throughout the conflict with too few boats, but that fact had led to an undesirable result. "It has led to too great a tendency to conserve its own strength and to avoid excessive risk rather than arriving at the conclusion that desire and necessity demand: inflicting the maximum destruction on the enemy." Only actual operations would produce the opportunity to develop appropriate tactics to the changing war situation, Dönitz claimed, and the E-boats were not engaged in enough operations to know how to make the necessary changes. He ordered the E-boat Force to increase the tempo of operations and to try new tactical methods. His many suggestions showed him to be the same aggressive commander that had marked his tenure as senior officer of U-boats. They also reveal that in common with some other high-ranking officers at the SKL he knew remarkably little about E-boats.[15]

Dönitz complained, for example, that there were numerous instances when one Allied destroyer had chased away three, four, and recently even five E-boats without the latter ever firing once at their convoy targets or at the destroyer. "Is that not exaggerating the strength of one destroyer against a group of E-boats?" he asked. Dönitz also criticized E-boat commanders and crews for too frequent cancellation of sorties because one of the boat's three diesels had become unserviceable. The implication was that they could still attack convoys on just two engines. Just as bad, he noted, they broke off combat too frequently and were placing too high a priority in coming to the aid of other E-boats damaged in action. There were many other particulars, but those charges were particularly galling to serving E-boat commanders and the FdS staff.[16]

Those officers and crews who had experienced actual combat in E-boats knew something Dönitz did not. There was no percentage in pitting fragile, wooden construction coastal craft against steel-hulled destroyers with radar directed, quick-firing, four-inch guns, especially since the heavier Allied units were working in hunting teams with coastal forces MTBs and MGBs. The E-boats' torpedoes worked best when fired stealthily against unknowing merchant ships. Crews had almost no chance of aiming and firing at a fast-charging destroyer. The defensive armament of an E-boat stood up well against MTBs and afforded some antiaircraft protection. But it was simply unrealistic to expect gun crews to duel with heavier enemy warships with their far heavier firepower and significant technological advantages. Rebensburg noted later that Allied use of star shells and air-dropped flares could illuminate the battle zone long before the E-boats were in effective range for torpedoing. Once the alarm was raised, an E-boat's last remaining hope was the speed with which it could "sting" the enemy, and that *Stichtaktik* demanded flank speed.

Dönitz also revealed his unfamiliarity with E-boats by admonishing crews to operate without full use of their diesels. An E-boat functioning with two diesels could make approximately twenty-six knots. That might look impressive against transport convoys making ten to twelve knots, but by this stage of the war the Channel was teeming with high-speed destroyers, entire flotillas of MTBs and MGBs, and multiple squadrons of attack aircraft, all of them looking for E-boats. Rebensburg estimated that the stealth advantage, which E-boats once had held, ended in 1943, and E-boat losses thereafter occurred mostly in poor visibility. Increasingly, the night belonged to the Allies. By this time, the only advantage Germany's last remaining surface vessels had on their side was their remarkable speed and maneuverability. Even at the fastest cruising speed of thirty-eight knots they were finding their missions perilous from the moment they left harbor until their return. The steady attrition of E-boats in the

Channel from mid-1944 until May 1945 amply attested to that fact. To demand, as Dönitz was doing, that they operate in a partially damaged condition was tantamount to ordering suicide operations.[17] Dönitz's expectations from 1944 until Hitler's suicide were simple: all those serving under his command, including the hapless U-boat Force, were expected to sacrifice themselves ruthlessly without regard to the odds.[18]

Such an attitude was in stark contrast to the one Petersen had inculcated in the men under his command since April 1942. The E-boat veterans knew that under the conditions Dönitz found acceptable they would be sacrificing themselves with no effect on the enemy since E-boats operating with marginal performance would never reach an Allied convoy route. Radar would have bracketed the lamed attackers long before they came within range, granting overwhelming advantages to the aggressive anti–E-boat forces. Finally, the elite crews of the E-boat Force simply found it unacceptable to abandon damaged boats and leave their crews to their fate. Experience showed that since 1943 packs of MTBs regularly fell upon stragglers. Besides, there were simply too few E-boats left in the West to write off damaged craft and crews as Dönitz was suggesting.[19]

Despite these internal disagreements and bickerings, the net result was that the E-boat Force continued to function much as it intended, no matter what Dönitz and other critics thought. Petersen was too experienced and too skilled to be replaced, and he continued to serve as FdS to the last day of the war. The E-boat Force did the best it could with dwindling supplies, weapons, and fuel. Rising to the challenge, the crews husbanded diesel fuel, repaired boats, replaced lost or captured crews, and carried on the fight to the best of their ability. Results were sometimes fruitful despite Dönitz's obvious disenchantment. Mines became the Schnellbootwaffe's major weapon, a serious menace in the confined waters of the Schelde Estuary. E-boats even carried the fight back to the Allies, seeding mines once again in the mouth of the Thames Estuary.[20] Nevertheless, the scale of operations steadily dwindled as the entire German war machine ground slowly to a halt and the Allies converged from East and West to squeeze Hitler's failed Reich out of existence. Personnel losses continued. Flotilla Commander Hermann Opdenhoff died in these final engagements. It was symbolic of their sagging military fortunes that the last significant wartime role of E-boats was transporting stranded soldiers and civilians in the Eastern Baltic ports to the Western Baltic in advance of Stalin's forces.

Two noteworthy scenarios involving E-boats in the West came in early May 1945. On 13 May, on a sunny Sunday afternoon, two E-boats manned by skeleton crews and senior FdS staff members crossed the North Sea from Rotterdam heading for Felixstowe with urgently needed charts of German-laid minefields. Midway, a flotilla of ten coastal forces MTBs met them and accompanied them into port. At the bridge were Rear Adm. Karl Breuning, Operations Officer Bernd Rebensburg, and other long-serving members of FdS Petersen's staff. Petersen himself was back in the Baltic by this time at their last headquarters near Flensburg. Just before tying up, an MTB approached and an agile Royal Navy officer leaped on board. He was Peter Scott, a legendary figure from coastal forces who had fought the E-boat Force in the West for years. He accompanied the Germans ashore and introduced them to other Royal Navy officers who were to debrief these newly arrived prisoners of war. It would be misleading to describe this first meeting of officers from the two coastal forces as congenial. Rather, it savored of military correctness. Losses on both sides had been too high for too long to expect otherwise. The German officers were there to begin the surrendering of their mysterious, high-performance boats to the long-curious Allies. They were also there to provide detailed charts of German-laid minefields. As survivors of history's most destructive war, they had begun, however tentatively, the painful process of healing. Those arrangements completed, the two groups parted, the victors returning to civilian pursuits for the most part, the losers to prisoner of war camps.[21]

Rebensburg, in common with E-boat radiomen and signals personnel connected to the B-Dienst and other forms of wartime intelligence, went first to a prison at Den Helder in the Netherlands and then in late June to a high-security camp in Esterwege in the Emsland. Formerly a Wehrmacht prison for deserters and the condemned, Esterwege under British management treated its German prisoners with something less than charity. When asked why, guards informed prisoners of what their armies had found recently at Bergen-Belsen. With the passage of time the captors relented somewhat, releasing the nearly blind Rebensburg in February 1946. Thereafter, the other German intelligence personnel, singly and in small groups, returned to civilian life and to the hardships associated with eking out a living in post-Hitlerian Germany.[22]

The second scenario occurred a few days earlier, on 10 May 1945, in more northerly waters, namely the Geltinger Bay on North Schleswig's Baltic Coast. With the final rescue operation of E-boats arriving with two hundred wounded soldiers per boat from Courland, a five-hundred-mile journey westward to Schleswig, Petersen ordered a formal flag-lowering ceremony in the presence of the E-boat Force personnel. He gave a brief speech, recounting the accomplishments of that force, and ordered the men to maintain order and discipline and obey the Allied surrender terms.

The ceremony ended with the singing of the national anthem. Thereafter, the personnel resumed preparations for the transfer of boats, weapons, and equipment to British forces, and they braced themselves to enter prisoner of war status.

This final scenario involving the E-boat Force also had a cruel twist that affected FdS Petersen down to his final days. Following directives from Dönitz transmitted through him by British authorities, he kept his E-boat Force intact for a time after the cessation of hostilities in the Western Baltic ports. The victors had demanded under threat of renewed bombing attacks that the German forces retain good order and discipline and that in addition to an end to military resistance there also be no scuttling of ships, destruction of military property, desertions, or chaos. No record exists of this informal arrangement, but survivors claimed afterward that the Royal Navy eyed the E-boat Force as a potential ally of necessity if Soviet forces continued to advance westward along the Baltic, and they expected Petersen's forces to maintain military integrity beyond the final surrender on 8 May.[23]

These conditions produced fateful consequences. Four sailors serving with the E-boat Force had deserted with their sidearms in Svendborg, Denmark, on 5 May 1945. Fellow sailors admitted that the four hoped to avoid internment in British prisoner of war camps, wanting to return home instead. Danish resistance members immediately recaptured the four and handed them back over to their youthful, zealous officer who, enraged by their claims that they were deserting in order to combat the Soviets, took them under guard to Petersen's headquarters for judgment. Following a standard wartime court-martial, the presiding officers found three of the men guilty of desertion with weapons in wartime, a debatable decision given the partial surrender to Field Marshal Montgomery on 5 May. Furthermore, they found that the three ringleaders had tried repeatedly to encourage others to desert. The panel issued a lesser three-year penal sentence on the fourth sailor, a youth aged nineteen who had joined them at the last minute. The case then went to Petersen for final consideration. After a sleepless night of deliberation and fearing a general breakdown in discipline—in an unrelated incident eleven mutinous sailors aboard a minesweeper had just been executed—Petersen finally backed his officers' decision. All assumed that desertion in such circumstances could carry only one outcome: execution. Accordingly, on the morning of 10 May 1945, a few hours before the flag-lowering ceremony, the three were placed in front of a firing squad on board an E-boat support ship in Geltinger Bay, and under the gaze of hundreds of personnel were executed at Petersen's command.[24]

The irony of their deaths was not lost on the E-boat veterans who knew what Petersen's aversion to fanaticism had done for them during the war years. Petersen never recovered from that last cruel act as the wheels of postwar justice advanced remorselessly. Three lengthy trials of him and the other officers involved in the courts-martial proceedings dragged on from 1946 to 1953, during which time they, too, were periodically incarcerated. Ultimately, the federal German courts released the accused officers because it was the judgment of those courts that despite their commission of errors, such as a failure to appoint defense counsel for the accused, the officers involved had done their best to follow the German armed forces' existing code of military justice even though it was unacceptably harsh by later standards. That exoneration gave Petersen scant comfort: "A court of human beings may have set me free," he stated after the trial, "but in the eyes of God I will always be guilty." Petersen became a near recluse for the rest of his life. He appeared briefly at one reunion of E-boat veterans at Vegesack in the mid-1980s, made no public statements, and retreated into solitude again until his death in 1988.[25]

Full Circle

It appeared to most observers that the advent of atomic warfare on 6 August 1945 had brought to a close the need to employ unconventional bombs such as Barnes Wallis's Tallboy. Leading air forces concentrated in the following decades on speed and the ability to deliver atomic weaponry despite lessons from Korea, Vietnam, the Arab-Israeli conflicts, and elsewhere that precision tactical ability with conventional weapons was paramount. Then, in the mid-1980s, awareness grew that the ability of conventional forces to project power was enhanced enormously when air and ground forces truly cooperated, a lesson already learned once by the combatants of World War II. The AirLand Battle became the new doctrine, and air forces started to pay more attention to the weaponry needed to suppress the enemy in cooperation with their own ground forces.

Such was the thinking when, during the Persian Gulf War of 1991, it became obvious that Iraqi command and control centers, enormous cubes twenty feet thick all around and constructed of the best steel-reinforced concrete, were impregnable to conventional ordnance. Buried a hundred feet underground, the centers were immune to conventional bombs and missiles. Despite terrific Allied pounding of his forces, Hussein and his military staff continued to exercise command and control, a contingency few had expected once the Allies had established air supremacy over Iraq. Missiles and bombs already in the Allied inventory had proved effective against a wide array of hardened sites and vehicles on or just below the surface. No conventional weapon could hope to reach such stout targets buried so deep, and no one was prepared to use nuclear weapons.

In the midst of the aerial campaign, the U.S. Air Force Systems Command studied the vexing problem. There was no time to go to the drawing board to design new ordnance. They would have to take existing materials off the shelf in order to devise their new bomb quickly. In just seventeen days, scientists and technicians from Texas Instruments and the air force, working at facilities at Eglin Air Force Base in Florida, produced the GBU 28 bomb. First, they settled upon discarded steel cannon barrels and with computer assistance designed a new, slender bomb shape. Other team members looked to its contents. They filled the bore with a custom-made brew from the new generation of ultrahigh explosives that far exceed the power of World War II substances like torpex. The teams then fitted a smart Paveway III laser guidance system to the new bomb and rushed a test unit out to the Tonopah Bomb Range in Nevada for an air drop. Weighing forty-seven hundred pounds, the test round plunged at supersonic speeds so deep underground that they never found it again! Other test rounds fired horizontally with rocket assistance demonstrated the bomb's awesome penetration power. The slender shape could pierce the stoutest concrete walls. Satisfied with its ballistic, penetrative, and explosive characteristics, the Eglin armament staff made up more GBU 28s, and a C-141 Starlifter rushed them to the Gulf, three days into the ground offensive. Less than five hours after arrival, two F-111F fighter-bombers attacked one of Hussein's special deep-cover command centers. The first bomb deviated slightly from its objective. The second struck it squarely, boring through earth and concrete with ease to destroy a bunker with walls twice as thick as the massive pens at Le Havre had been. A few hours after detonation, Hussein and his military sued for peace, bringing an end to the Gulf War. The principles behind Barnes Wallis's deep penetration bomb, updated with the technology of another generation, had proved perfectly sound and were now a part of the AirLand Battle concept.[26]

The Iran-Iraq War of the 1980s, followed by the Persian Gulf War of 1991, demonstrated anew that the world's leading navies were ill prepared to deal with the coastal forces of small powers in confined waters. Mines and shallow-draft fast fighting boats made the Persian Gulf a dangerous place for the western powers in both conflicts, and air power by no means provided a full remedy. Risking heavy surface units in confined waters against small, expendable craft revived concern about the old "swarm-of-bees" concept of coastal warfare. The evolution of fast coastal forces has come full circle with the U.S. Navy's recent decision to build two new classes of coastal craft, the 70-foot PB Mk. V (Patrol Boat Mark Five) and the 170-foot PC 1 (Patrol Craft One). The class leader for the PC 1 is the USS *Cyclone* designed by Vosper Thornycroft. She, like S-130 and the E-boats of an earlier generation, is powered by multiple 3,000-hp diesels and combines great range with speed and reliability on a high-performance platform. Perhaps the torpedoes of yesteryear have faded as a weapon of choice for brown water navies, but mines and missiles have not.

Epilogue

The Survivors

World War II placed extraordinary demands upon ordinary people. The veterans of the respective Allied and Axis organizations who had figured so prominently in the little-known sea war off Normandy in 1944 were for the most part citizen-soldiers. As adolescents, most had entered the war for a straightforward reason: answering their nation's call to arms. At the conclusion of hostilities most dropped the soldier aspect gladly and became ordinary citizens again—as much as the daunting experience of total war would allow. What is striking about so many of those survivors is their determination to achieve positive goals in later years, to build, to reconstruct, to heal, or at the very least, to lead normal, uneventful lives. Despite many decorations for martial valor, most of them chose to build civilian careers, and many, in reflective moments, have sought to chronicle events from the war in an effort to preserve a record of what happened as they knew it. Many, if asked, might not articulate the reasons. Others see it as a warning to future generations against the dangers and the waste produced by ideological conflict and total war. That is a fundamental lesson that each generation apparently must learn for itself, but at least histories provide a record for future generations to consult on their way to seeking their own understanding of human conflict and its limitations.

Radioman Ernst Benda, caught in Norway on VE Day, helped to surrender Germany's E-boats to Norwegian and British representatives before returning with other E-boat crews to Wilhelmshaven and internment in July 1945. Following his release from POW status, the youthful Benda returned to his native Berlin where he found his family in the ruins of their modest home living in poverty, like virtually everyone else in the former German capital. Much like Rudolf Petersen, Benda had had a skeleton in his closet under the Nazis. His father was half Jewish, so the younger Benda as a quarter Jew had not been able to rise in rank despite a sterling performance as radioman and a general all-around competence that had won the admiration of skipper and crew alike. Likewise, he had been barred from university studies under the Nazis.

Ambitious, Benda decided to study law; he became a student in the Soviet-controlled Berlin University in 1946. But dissatisfaction with the communists' heavy-handed attempts to control the old university induced him in 1948 to become one of the founding students of the Free University in the U.S. sector of Berlin. The Americans identified him as a promising leader, and he became one of the first German-American cultural exchangees, studying at the University of Wisconsin from 1949 to 1955. Immediately upon his return to Berlin, he entered the political arena, heading the Christian Democratic Union youth organization and holding office first in the Berlin House and then in the Bundestag in Bonn. He also became a distinguished professor of law and was the Federal Republic's Interior Minister in 1968–69. Eventually, he rose to become President of Germany's Federal Constitutional Court in Karlsruhe and an internationally celebrated legal expert before his retirement in 1991. He is an active public figure even now and currently presides over the national congress of Germany's Evangelical Protestant Church. An avid small-boat sailor, Ernst Benda still preserves vivid, if bittersweet, memories of his service with the Schnellbootwaffe.

Navigator Tom Bennett continued to practice his specialized skills in the RAF for a time, instructing postwar trainees in Britain and serving briefly as an adviser to the Royal Hellenic Air Force. Later he became flight commander and deputy squadron commander, unusual ranks for a navigator, while serving with an RAF maritime reconnaissance squadron in Malta. He followed this with more cadet instruction in England, then left military life in 1955 to raise a family. Bennett worked as an administrator in commercial firms on the London Docks before transferring to the Port of London Authority in 1975. Upon retirement, he enrolled in evening classes to hone professional writing skills. Following six years of literary effort, Bennett achieved his goal, a well-received narrative history, *617 Squadron: The Dambusters at War*. He is now, unofficially, a historian of 617 Squadron Association, maintaining close contact with its many members and helping to organize its activities.

Leonard Cheshire ended the war as a celebrated public figure, but the experience of so many combat missions had told on him. He was Britain's official witness to the atomic bombing of Nagasaki as he stared out of a B-29 bomber at the ominous cloud ascending. Cheshire shed his uniform and entered a period of emotional crisis, becoming a recluse for a time. When he encountered a fellow RAF veteran who was dying of cancer and was in worse emotional condition than himself, he abandoned his own cares and set about nursing his fellow comrade-in-arms through his final illness. That nurturing experience changed Cheshire's life. He founded the Cheshire Foundation Homes and began systematically to care for others, concentrating at first on those who had been scarred by the emotional ravages of the war. He made it his life's work. In 1989 with his wife, Baroness Ryder of Warsaw, he founded the Ryder-Cheshire Mission for the Relief of Suffering and was created Lord Cheshire of Woodhall in 1991. On 31 July 1992, Lord Cheshire died, beloved of all who knew him.

LST 507's medical officer, Dr. Eugene Eckstam, had a brief hospital stay in Sherbourne following the torpedoing in Lyme Bay but was reassigned to LST 391 in time to help transport the American V Rangers to Omaha Beach. He also helped evacuate Allied and German wounded from Omaha Beach back to hospitals in England. After a brief return to the United States, he joined other medical crews in the Pacific, landing at Cotabato, Mindanao, in the Philippines on 17 April 1945. After the war, Eckstam returned to his native Wisconsin and continued to practice medicine for the rest of his long career. Now in retirement in Monroe, Wisconsin, he organizes reunions of survivors of Exercise Tiger and has gathered extensive published and unpublished sources for future histories of the sinkings in Lyme Bay.

LST 507 and 496 survivor Bill Gould endured a lengthy convalescence in hospitals in England and the United States before returning to active duty aboard the cruiser USS *Miami* toward the end of the Pacific War. Eventually, he became a plant supervisor in a printing firm in the lovely Hudson Valley of his native New York. Bill has amazed physicians and friends alike by his ability to survive cheerfully despite bouts of poor health. He tends his garden and landscapes extensively, enjoying the outdoor life. Like Eugene Eckstam, he stays in touch with other LST survivors, including former boatyard owner, millwright, and technical sales representative Owen Sheppard of Birmingham, Alabama. Fellow Birminghamian and former pharmacist's mate Bill Walker also left the navy at war's end. He studied law, rising to become city attorney before retiring in 1989. They and many other friends in the LST organizations journey to New Bedford, Massachusetts, on 28 April every year to attend a memorial to their fallen comrades. Although appreciative of growing public awareness of what happened to Convoy T-4 in Lyme Bay in that spring of 1944, Eckstam, Gould, Sheppard, and Walker cannot forget that for many years no one seemed to know or care about the fate of the 749 Americans who did not survive that bitter night.

Reginald Vincent Jones returned to academia and taught physics at the University of Aberdeen for many years. He liked to joke with young faculty members, assuring them with a twinkle that he had not won the war single-handedly. Now retired, Professor Jones journeyed to Washington, D.C., one autumn for a special ceremony. On 27 October 1993, he received from CIA Director R. James Woolsey the first R. V. Jones Award, named in his honor and presented to Professor Jones by the Central Intelligence Agency for demonstrating "scientific acumen applied with art to solve intelligence problems," the only time the award will be awarded publicly. Despite his advanced years, Professor Jones accepted the award in a spirited and inspiring address that credited special intelligence personnel, courageous agents, photoreconnaissance and photointerpretation experts, and many others as the people who make such awards possible.

Although scheduled to fly night fighters in the Pacific after VE Day, Nick Knilans had no regrets when Japan's surrender made his conversion to American combat aircraft unnecessary. He returned to his native Wisconsin after the war and became a teacher. After many years in the classroom, "Nicky," as his many friends know him, served for two years as a Peace Corps Volunteer in Nigeria. Like so many of his veteran friends, Knilans had seen young men die all around him, and he embraced religion as a pillar that had helped bring him through times of danger. He was convinced that God had spared him for other missions. Later, he became a champion of Mexican-American youths and was a counselor for many years in the California penal system. Nicky retired in 1978 but continues to support underprivileged youth in Mexico and California while residing part of the year in Wisconsin. Knilans stays in touch with his many friends in the 617 Association and carefully preserves all his wartime records with friends in Canada.

Big Joe McCarthy was an exception to the general rush back to civilian status. He became a test pilot at the Royal Aircraft Establishment in Farnborough after the war, flying seventy-eight aircraft types including twenty captured German designs. McCarthy returned to Canada in 1946, and during a distinguished career in the Royal Canadian Air Force continued on active flight operations up to the moment of his retirement. His many postings included testing, training, antisubmarine duties, and one stint organizing emergency air transport during the Congo crisis in 1961. Wing Commander McCarthy retired from the RCAF in 1968 and returned to his native United States to live with his family. Like Knilans and Bennett, he has made a point of meticulously preserving his log books and records from the war. Big Joe is an active 617 Association member and frequently visits his former wartime friends in Canada, the United Kingdom, and the United States.

Günther Rabe and his crew were aboard S-130 when the war came to an end, having put into Den Helder in early May. There they were taken prisoner, and in July 1945 the Allies ordered them to steer S-130 into Wilhelmshaven where many of the Kriegsmarine's vessels were being concentrated. The Raven emerged from prisoner of war status in January 1946, by volunteering for particularly hazardous duties. He joined the German Minesweeping Administration (GMSA) of the Allied occupation authorities and shipped aboard the former E-boat tender *Tsingtao,* which was now performing peacetime service tending minesweeping vessels. The volunteer crews removed mines off the South Norwegian Coast during much of 1946 and cleared the waters off North Denmark in 1947. Safely returned to dry land again in 1948, Rabe worked as an import-export salesman in Hamburg during the early years of the Economic Miracle. However, the Raven could not forsake the tang of salty air forever, and in 1956 he entered the Federal Republic's fledgling navy, the Bundesmarine. After completing a tour of duty in the Defense Ministry, he organized a flotilla of the new Jaguar-class fast boats, successors to E-boats, inculcating the training and procedures of NATO to the newly constituted crews. Rabe then joined NATO's command structure for Northern Europe, AFNORTH, in Oslo for three years as a member of its Operations Division. For his final tour of duty he returned to the Federal Republic's Defense Ministry in Bonn until his retirement in 1977. He, too, carefully preserves records, logs, and charts from his wartime experiences and occasionally grants interviews to the media about his experiences.

The Raven's faithful E-boat, S-130, having delivered up her secrets to the Allies, returned from British "captivity" in 1954 to serve as a training vessel for new crews. In the early 1960s she shed her torpedo tubes for more modern weapons of war and steamed on active service for three more decades with the Bundesmarine, teaching instructors and fledgling crews alike the advantages of fast fighting boats with clever engineering, sleek hulls, and reliable power plants. In 1988 at the advanced age of forty-six, S-130 steamed into Wilhelmshaven for her final port call. There she was broken up, the last of her breed.

Former Operations Officer Bernd Rebensburg discovered quickly that the Royal Navy had more than a casual interest in him at the end of hostilities. His Coastal Forces opposites such as Peter Scott interviewed him extensively and flew him from his initial internment at Felixstowe to Kiel, briefly, to obtain even more accurate charts for German-laid minefields. Then they promptly interned him along with B-Dienst and intelligence personnel at Esterwege. Rebensburg remained there until released in February 1946. Although a Rhinelander, he had property in Kiel, and once freed he immediately began growing crops on it during Occupied Germany's time of hunger. Occupation restrictions barred him and most other naval officers from university studies. Ever after, Bernd Rebensburg tended his garden, employing as many as ten neighbors and feeding many mouths. However, gardening was hardly the intellectual challenge his sharp mind needed. Although he remained "just a farmer," Rebensburg became a consultant to the Bundesmarine. As one of the world's leading experts in coastal force operations, he advised later generations of young officers in his special area of expertise. Like Knilans, Rebensburg embraced religion strongly, but his renewed piety had a slightly more earthly, even militant twist. He found the atheism of Marxism-Leninism—along with the rest of Soviet Communism—to be anathema. Furthermore, it was in close proximity along the Baltic shore. Rebensburg volunteered to become a "stay-behind," that is an agent-in-place for the Western Allied intelligence services in the event Soviet forces ever occupied Western Europe. With the downfall of ideological extremism in the East, Rebensburg directs his energies and formidable intellect elsewhere. He is assembling a private archive on the former Schnellbootwaffe, and he too maintains close ties with the veterans of the E-boat Force. Like so many other veterans, they assemble on 11 November, in their case at the Naval Memorial in Laboe to remember fallen comrades. On occasion they send a wreath to veterans of the Royal Navy's Coastal Forces and receive one in return. The two organizations still retain ties, and individual members pay social calls on each other from time to time.

Hans Schirren, the skipper of S-167 at Le Havre, continued on active service with the E-boat Force to the end of the war. After release from prisoner of war camp, the youthful Schirren worked as an agricultural laborer during the lean years of the Occupation. By 1948 he had entered the business world in export, and at one point was an agent for a firm selling women's clothing. By 1950 he had returned to Hamburg with an import-export firm. There he married, started a family, and became a shipbroker's apprentice in which capacity he spent half a year in the United Kingdom. By 1957 he had gained enough experience to start his own shipbrokering firm, Hans Schirren KG, and engaged in numerous shipbrokering, shipbuilding, and other maritime enterprises thereafter. The firm continues operations to the present day and is currently under the direction of his son. Ever restless, the elder Schirren devotes his considerable talents to his newest enterprise, Schirren Windenergie GmbH, an alternative energy firm specializing in high-technology wind turbines with windparks and sales all over Western Europe including Wales, Denmark, and Germany. Sobered by past political failings in German history, Schirren is frequently engaged in public issues, trying to make the mainstream political parties more responsive to public needs. Like the other veterans, he fought a hard war, and like them he hopes that healthier societies will never see the need to fight another one.

Barnes Neville Wallis pursued new frontiers in aviation after the war. He pioneered the development of swing-wing aircraft and called his invention an aerodyne. It proved to be years ahead of any other design concept and outfitted the American F-111 fighter bomber and later the swift European Tornado fighter bomber. Wallis was knighted in 1968, an honor many felt he should have received much earlier. Sir Barnes died in 1979.

Felix Zymalkowski commanded the 8th E-boat Flotilla in Dutch ports to the end of hostilities. Upon release from POW status, he returned briefly to his native Berlin, but as a former naval officer, he was banned from any further maritime service. With a young family to support, the hard-pressed Zymalkowski somehow found a way to matriculate at Kiel University, where he earned a doctorate in chemistry and pharmacy. He instructed there and in 1959 earned a professorship at the University in Hamburg. He received the call to become director of Bonn University's prestigious Institute for Pharmaceutical Chemistry in 1959. Zymalkowski completed his distinguished career in medical research there. Now in retirement, Felix Zymalkowski, as the *Dienstälteste,* eldest surviving member of his Crew 34, continues to edit the newsletter of his class of naval cadets, organize reunions, and help preserve the bonds that have held his fellow naval officers together for so many years.

Veterans of many nations, they came from ordinary backgrounds for the most part, but the war forced them to perform in extraordinary ways. For many that became a lifetime habit.

Notes

Chapter 1   The Lyme Bay Disaster

1. Interview, author with Gould, 15 September 1993.

2. See Lewis, *Exercise Tiger,* 23–30, on LST construction. See also Buffetaut, *D-Day Ships,* 25–54.

3. Quoted in Bradley and Blair, *A General's Life,* 228.

4. See Harrison, *Cross-Channel Attack,* 158–73, 269–70.

5. See Lewis, *Exercise Tiger,* 73.

6. Letter, Eckstam to author, 28 May 1994.

7. See Lewis, *Exercise Tiger,* 75–76.

8. Letter, Eckstam to author, 28 May 1994; interview, author with Gould, 15 September 1993. See also Greene, "What Happened Off Devon?" 26–35.

9. Letter, Eckstam to author, 28 May 1994.

10. Ibid.

11. Interview, author with Sheppard, 30 September 1993.

12. Interview, author with Walker, 14 September 1993; letter, Walker to author, 4 May 1994.

13. Letter, Eckstam to author, 28 May 1995.

14. The early death toll was 638 men. MacDonald counted 749 servicemen lost ("Slapton Sands," 64–67).

15. Interviews, author with Gould, 15 September 1993, and Sheppard, 30 September 1993.

16. See Lewis, *Exercise Tiger,* 110.

17. Quoted in Chandler, *Papers of Dwight David Eisenhower,* 1,389. See also Harrison, *Cross-Channel Attack,* 270.

18. See Rohwer and Hümmelchen, *Chronology of the War at Sea,* 196.

Chapter 2   Enemy Torpedo Boats

1. The origin of the term "E-boat" is obscure. Hümmelchen says it refers to the Lürssen "Effekt" ("German Schnellboote," 176). The British were unaware of that design feature at first but used the term "E-boat" starting in 1939. Veteran Michael R. D. Foot recalled that when he inquired about the name he was told it meant *Eilboot* (fast boat); letter, Foot to author, 20 January 1994.

2. See Gray, *The Devil's Device.*

3. On early E-boats, see Schmalenbach, "S-Boats," 10–25.

4. See Whitley, *German Coastal Forces,* 7–10.

5. See Fock, *Fast Fighting Boats,* esp. 11–16, 20–22.

6. Older but useful is Cooper, *The E-Boat Threat,* 13–20.

7. See Tirpitz, *My Memoirs,* 1:47–67. See also Massie, *Dreadnought,* 167. A critical account of Germany's pre-1898 navy is Leyland, "The Spirit of the German Navy Law," 151–60.

8. See Schmalenbach, "S-Boats," 12. See also Phillips-Birt, *Famous Speedboats,* 13–47.

9. On Lürssen-built FL, or *Fernlenk* boats, see Taylor, *German Warships of World War I,* 200.

10. See Fock, *Fast Fighting Boats,* 53–59; Schmalenbach, "S-Boats," 12–14; and Cooper, *The E-Boat Threat,* 19.

11. See Taylor, *German Warships of World War I,* 201; Schmalenbach, "S-Boats," 14.

12. See Schmalenbach, "S-Boats," 14–16; Cooper, *The E-Boat Threat,* 21; and Breyer, *Die Deutsche Kriegsmarine,* 2:61–62.

13. See Thomas, *The German Navy in the Nazi Era,* 41–42.

14. See Whitley, *German Coastal Forces,* 13. The officer, Eduard Rabe, was Günther Rabe's father. The son joined the E-boat force a decade later; letter, Rabe to author, 9 August 1993.

15. See Whitley, *German Coastal Forces,* 12–14.

16. See Fock, *Fast Fighting Boats,* 107–11.

17. See Hervieux, "German Torpedo Boats at War," part 1, 60–65, and part 2, 74–78; interview, author with Rabe, 29 April 1993. Rabe served on T-boats and observed that they were fast but that their engines were unreliable.

18. Rear Admiral Bey left E-boats for heavier surface units in 1939. He commanded the battle cruiser *Scharnhorst,* going down with that ship on Christmas Day 1943.

Surviving E-boat commanders praised their training under German Navy regulars; interviews, author with Rabe, 29 April 1993; Rebensburg, 1–2 May 1993; and Schirren, 3 May 1993. Zymalkowski was one of their professional officers and led a flotilla; interview, author with Zymalkowski, 10 December 1994.

19. Rabe, Rebensburg, Schirren, and Zymalkowski agreed that physical and mental demands upon E-boat commanders were heavy and even heavier on good flotilla commanders who were crucial to efficient E-boat operations; interviews, author with Rabe, 29 April 1993; Rebensburg, 1–2 May 1993; Schirren, 3 May 1993; and Zymalkowski, 10 December 1994.

20. See Fock, *Fast Fighting Boats,* 111–15. Naval architect David B. Wyman advised the author on their design; interview, author with Wyman, 1 September 1992.

21. See Teale, *Fast Boats,* 1–42.

22. Regarding British MTBs and their effect on American PT designs see Lambert and Ross, *Vosper MTBs and U.S. Elcos.* See also Cooper, *The E-Boat Threat,* 25–28.

23. Otto Lürssen died in 1932, but his design team remained intact. On hull design, see Fock, *Fast Fighting Boats,* 111–25.

24. "The Use of Special Intelligence in Connection with Operation Neptune, January 1944–September 1944," p. 167, Public Record Office, ADM 223/287; hereinafter cited as OIC Neptune Report. Charged with tracking E-boat activities, the OIC noted that "Interception of E-boats, whose speed was considerably more than that of our MTBs, was possible, but destruction of the enemy was a much more difficult problem" (p. 32).

25. See Whitley, *German Coastal Forces,* 30–33.

26. Interview, author with Benda, 8 December 1994.

27. "German E-Boats S-147 and S-141, Interrogation of Survivors," July 1944, interrogation report C.B. 04051 (104), Washington Navy Yard. British Naval Intelligence Division (NID) staff compiled many facts on E-boat construction from prisoners. See also Whitley, *German Coastal Forces,* 23.

28. See Fock, *Fast Fighting Boats,* 120–22.

29. See Scott, *Battle of the Narrow Seas.* Scott's father was Antarctic explorer Robert Scott. On Hichens's last fight, see p. 130.

30. See Whitley, *German Coastal Forces,* 35; letter, Rabe to author, 13 October 1993.

31. Interview, author with Zymalkowski, 10 December 1994.

32. On the S-26 profile, see Breyer, *Die Deutsche Kriegsmarine,* 64; see also Fock, *Fast Fighting Boats,* 189.

33. Letter, Rabe to author, 13 October 1993.

Chapter 3   Wartime Operations to June 1944

1. On wartime operations, see Whitley, *German Coastal Forces,* 41–44.

2. Another overview of early operations is Hervieux, "S-Boats at War," 270–74.

3. See Whitley, *German Coastal Forces,* 46.

4. See Hervieux, "S-Boats at War," 274.

5. Interview, author with Zymalkowski, 10 December 1994.

6. Interviews, author with Rabe, 29 April 1993; Rebensburg, 1–2 May 1993; Schirren, 3 May 1993; and Zymalkowski, 10 December 1994.

7. Interview, author with Rebensburg, 1–2 May 1993. He noted that pre–S-26 boats were transferred to Spain or relegated to the Baltic training flotilla.

8. On Petersen's responsibilities as head of the new E-boat force, see Schultz, "Die deutsche Schnellbootwaffe im 2. Weltkrieg," 16. E-boat veteran Schultz prepared this memorandum after a reunion of E-boat personnel at Bremen on 22–24 May 1987; copies are in the private archives of Bernd Rebensburg in Kiel and in the Marine Offizier Vereinigung in Bonn. The TdS stressed repeatedly to his superiors the need to expand the E-boat force (p. 8).

9. See Whitley, *German Coastal Forces,* 56, 62.

10. On E-boat losses in the first half of 1944, see "Note on E-Boat Operations in the English Channel, January–May 1944," S.I. 974a, Public Record Office, ADM 223/28.

11. See Hümmelchen, "German Schnellboote," 163–67. Friedrich Kemnade described operations in the Mediterranean; see *Die Afrika-Flottille,* 153–58.

12. See Hümmelchen, "German Schnellboote," 168–69.

13. The British and U.S. navies compiled exhaustive reports on weapons, tactics, and organization from prisoners. See "British Naval Intelligence Division (NID) Prisoner-of-War Final Reports" folder, box 2, National Archives, R.G. 38, Special Activities Branch (OP16Z).

14. Zymalkowski recalled that they called him "Piet" and that he was popular with everyone; interview, author with Zymalkowski, 10 December 1994. Rebensburg commented: "The report about the Dutch steward who was a spy is probably true. I learned it from him after the war. I had reported [then] about a spy in Cherbourg who was picked up and who was said to have radioed the departure of E-boats"; letter, Rebensburg to author, 6 October 1993. Rabe added: "We, too, had suspicions about the steward but no actual evidence. It was rather odd that he transferred with us from Rotterdam to Cherbourg"; letter, Rabe to author, 13 October 1993.

15. Interview, author with Zymalkowski, 10 December 1994.

16. Interviews, author with Rabe, 29 April 1993, and Zymalkowski, 10 December 1994.

17. Interview, author with Rabe, 29 April 1993.

18. "German E-Boat S-88, Interrogation of Survivors," December 1943, p. 5, series C.B. 04051, document C.B. 04051 (89), Washington Navy Yard; see also Scott, *Battle of the Narrow Seas*, 170–72, and Hümmelchen, "German Schnellboote," 170.

19. See Hümmelchen, "German Schnellboote," 171–72.

20. "German E-Boats S-147 and S-141 Interrogation of Survivors," July 1944, p. 18, series C.B. 04051 (104), Washington Navy Yard; hereinafter cited as NID Interrogation Report with boat designation. For the intensive apprenticeship of young officers that gave rise to such nicknames and attitudes, see Rust, *Naval Officers under Hitler*, 37–76.

21. Interview, author with Zymalkowski, 10 December 1994.

22. "The Use of Special Intelligence in Connection with Operation Neptune, January 1944–September 1944," pp. 42–43, Public Record Office, ADM 223/287; hereinafter cited as OIC Neptune Report. See also Beesly, *Very Special Intelligence*.

23. Log, FdS, Scheveningen, entry for 28 April 1944, p. 109, Bundesarchiv-Militärarchiv, RM 55/8. They knew that E-boats had damaged one ship and assumed it was an LCT. It was LST 289.

24. NID Interrogation Report, E-boats S-147 and S-141. Published editions appeared in July 1944 but the NID had distributed interrogation results immediately to appropriate Allied commands.

25. Outwardly, the presence of Dönitz's son as an officer added prestige to the E-boat Force. However, E-boat staff concluded he had no leadership potential. Unlike the midshipmen aboard S-141, he received no leadership training but manned a light machine gun instead. Rebensburg suspected that the Grossadmiral knew his younger son's limitations but let him serve anyway. No one could accuse the elder Dönitz of favoritism; interview, author with Rebensburg, 1–2 May 1993.

26. NID interrogation Report for S-147 and S-141, passim.

Chapter 4   The Admirals Contend

1. Folder, "Aggressive Measures against German E-Boats and Destroyers," memorandum, Naval Commander, Western Task Force, to ANCXF, 4 May 1944, p. 1, National Archives, R.G. 331, decimal file, 045.93; hereinafter cited as NCWTF memorandum, 4 May 1944.

2. Ibid.

3. Ibid., p. 2.

4. Ibid., p. 3.

5. Folder, "Aggressive Measures against German E-Boats and Destroyers," secret priority message, 28 May 1944 from Naval Commander, Western Task Force, to ANCXF for SHAEF, plus attached incoming and outgoing messages 29 May through 11 June 1944, SHAEF to AGWAR for Marshall and Arnold,

COMNAVEU, CNO, and Eisenhower, National Archives, R.G. 331, decimal file 045.93; NCWTF memorandum, 4 May 1944, p. 3.

6. "Supreme Commanders Conferences, Minutes of Meeting . . . 8 May 1944," p. 2, National Archives, R.G. 331, SHAEF, SGS, 337/11.

7. Ibid.

8. Quoted in Chalmers, *Full Cycle,* 211.

9. Letter, Eisenhower to King, 9 May 1944, cited in Chandler, *Papers of Dwight David Eisenhower,* 1,855–56.

10. "Appreciation of E-Boat Threat to Overlord," 10 May 1944, memorandum from Office of ANCXF, pp. 1–2, National Archives, R.G. 331, decimal file 045.93.

11. Ibid., p. 4.

12. Ibid., p. 6.

13. Ibid.

14. "The Use of Special Intelligence in Connection with Operation Neptune, January 1944–September 1944," Summary, p. 12, item 36, "Proposed Counter-measures against 'E' and 'R' boats," Public Record Office, ADM 223/287; here-inafter cited as OIC Neptune Report. See also Beesly, *Very Special Intelligence.* The key personality at the OIC was Commander (later Vice Admiral) Sir Nor-man Denning, K.B.E., C.B. OIC personnel specialized in tracking U-boats, but a central figure in tracking E-boats was Lt. George Clements, RN; see Beesly, p. 125.

15. See main body of OIC Neptune Report, p. 37.

16. Ibid., p. 40.

17. Ibid., p. 11. The OIC staff could sometimes anticipate German operations by as much as twenty hours. "But," they cautioned, "such a use of data could instantly compromise the source unless covered by photographic reconnais-sance or routine patrolling."

18. Ibid, p. 45.

19. Ibid., p. 32.

20. Quoted in ibid., p. 167.

21. See Hinsley, *British Intelligence in the Second World War,* 3:543–45.

22. "Note on E-Boat Operations in the English Channel, January–May 1944," p. 2, OIC Special Intelligence Summary, S.I. 974a, Public Record Office, ADM 223/172.

Chapter 5   Bomber Harris Prelude

1. On the air war, see Frankland, *Bomber Offensive,* 21–51.

2. Jones, *Most Secret War,* 210. The raid on Pilsen occurred on 19–20 No-vember 1940. See Middlebrook and Everitt, *Bomber Command War Diaries,* 105.

3. See Middlebrook and Everitt, *Bomber Command War Diaries,* 220–21.

4. Jones, *Most Secret War,* 210.

5. For a discussion of Cherwell's controversial claims, see Wright, *The Ordeal of Total War,* 176–82.

6. On Gee and other navigation aids, see Johnson, *The Secret War,* 84–89. See also Saward, *Victory Denied,* chaps. 20–22.

7. See Bennett, *Pathfinder,* 150–51. According to Bennett, Hitler believed there were gaps in the clouds and that the Luftwaffe was trying to hide its failure to intercept the bombers.

8. Johnson, *The Secret War,* 89–91. See also Middlebrook and Everitt, *Bomber Command War Diaries,* 362–66, 368.

9. See Johnson, *The Secret War,* 92–101.

10. D.C.T. Bennett was impressed with the intelligent work of scientists at the TRE in making H2S operational so quickly; see his *Pathfinder,* 135–38.

11. See Stanley, *World War II Photo Intelligence,* 40–43.

12. Bennett's memoirs are still useful reading; see his *Pathfinder.*

13. Bennett, *Pathfinder,* 157–58. Although skeptical at first, Bennett learned to respect the Operational Research Section when its analysis repeatedly improved performance.

14. Middlebrook, *Battle of Hamburg.*

Chapter 6   Barnes Wallis and the Giant Bomb

1. For technical information the author is indebted to Robert M. Owen, Official Historian, 617 Squadron Association; hereinafter cited as Owen with date of correspondence. On Wallis's concept of large bombs, see Sweetman, *Dambusters Raid,* 1–26.

2. See Morpurgo, *Barnes Wallis;* see pp. 229–31 for Wallis's paper on bombs.

3. See Sweetman, *Dambusters Raid,* 16–25.

4. Ibid., 28.

5. See Morpurgo, *Barnes Wallis,* 238–39; see also Sweetman, *Dambusters Raid,* 36–37.

6. Still useful is Paul Brickhill, *The Dam Busters.* Many technical features of the dams bomb were still secret, however, and a subsequent film also obfuscated the facts. Yet the Germans had recovered an unexploded bomb immediately and knew its technical features.

7. See Sweetman, *Dambusters Raid,* 189.

8. See Jones, *Most Secret War,* chaps. 38, 44–46.

9. See Morpurgo, *Barnes Wallis,* 283.

10. Memorandum, Owen to author, 26 August 1993.

11. On torpex, see *U.S. Army Training Manual,* 77–79.

12. Memorandum, Owen to author, 26 August 1993.

13. Britain sent Guy Gibson, VC, on a tour to North America in August 1943 to enlist public support. Too valuable to use on regular operations, he was posted to the Air Ministry, then to 5 Group where he arranged "semiofficial" operations. He was serving as master bomber over München-Gladbach/Rheydt on 19–20 September 1944 when other crews lost radio contact with him. His Mosquito had crashed near Steenbergen, The Netherlands. Civilians buried him and navigator Jim Warwick there.

On Lancasters as tactical bombers, see Tubbs, *Lancaster Bomber,* 128–37; on 617 Squadron's leafleting of Italian cities, see Middlebrook and Everitt, *Bomber Command War Diaries,* 415.

14. See Bennett, *617 Squadron, 9*; see also Middlebrook and Everitt, *Bomber Command War Diaries,* 430–31.

15. For an intimate look at 617 Squadron's leading personalities, see Bennett, *617 Squadron, 8*–15.

16. Letter, Bennett to author, 23 February 1993.

17. Ibid.

18. On the SABS, see Bennett, *617 Squadron,* 10–11.

19. Ibid.

20. Letter, Bennett to author, 23 February 1993.

21. Ibid.

22. Ibid.

23. See Bennett, *617 Squadron,* 11.

24. See Hastings, *Bomber Command,* 256–58. Cheshire's extraordinary personality made him a legendary leader throughout Bomber Command even as Mick Martin won renown as a superior pilot.

25. Bennett, *617 Squadron,* 50.

26. Ibid.

27. Letter, Bennett to author, 23 February 1993. Crews who placed in the "one-bomb category" were always elated by that honor; see Bennett, *617 Squadron,* 72.

28. See Frankland, *Bomber Offensive,* 118.

29. Middlebrook and Everitt, *Bomber Command War Diaries,* 459–60.

30. Ibid., 462.

31. See Bennett, *617 Squadron,* 13.

32. Ibid.

33. Middlebrook and Everitt, *Bomber Command War Diaries,* 471.

34. Ibid., 490–92; see also, letter and memorandum, Bennett to author, 1 September 1993.

35. Middlebrook and Everitt, *Bomber Command War Diaries,* 499.

36. The author thanks Flying Officer Tom Bennett for information on Operation Taxable; letter and memorandum, Bennett to author, 1 September 1993.

37. Ibid. See also Middlebrook and Everitt, *Bomber Command War Diaries,* 525.

Chapter 7 Operation Neptune: Opening Moves

1. "The Use of Special Intelligence in Connection with Operation Neptune, January 1944–September 1944," p. 98, Public Record Office, ADM 223/287; hereinafter cited as OIC Neptune Report.

2. Quoted in Morison, *Invasion of France and Germany,* 83.

3. OIC Neptune Report, p. 100.

4. See Schofield, *Operation Neptune.*

5. See Tarrant, *The Last Year of the Kriegsmarine,* 56–60; see also Kühn, *Torpedoboote und Zerstörer im Einsatz,* 290–92.

6. Interviews, author with Rabe, 29 April 1993, and Schirren, 3 May 1993. FdS Petersen noted that the two flotillas had spotted no enemy vessels, whereas 4th Flotilla boats from Boulogne saw Allied destroyers. See "German E-Boat Operations and Policy, 1939–1945," Section II, B, vi, entries for 6.6. and 7.6.44, p. 87, Public Record Office, ADM 223/28.

7. OIC Neptune Report, p. 101.

8. See Tarrant, *Last Year of the Kriegsmarine,* 60–65; see also Schofield, *Operation Neptune,* 107–8.

9. OIC Neptune Report, pp. 102–8.

10. Tarrant, *Last Year of the Kriegsmarine,* 71–80; see also Hinsley, *British Intelligence in the Second World War,* 3:160.

11. See Weigley, *Eisenhower's Lieutenants,* 94.

12. See Collins, *Lightning Joe,* chap. 10, for preparations for Overlord, and chap. 11 on VII Corps' operations from D-day to the capture of Cherbourg.

13. See Harrison, *Cross-Channel Attack,* 181–83.

14. Ibid., 300–304.

15. Roosevelt received the Congressional Medal of Honor for cool leadership under fire on Utah Beach. See Breuer, *Hitler's Fortress Cherbourg,* 91–93.

16. On Collins's aggressive style of command, see Weigley, *Eisenhower's Lieutenants,* 98–101.

17. The opening of the causeways saved hundreds of lives; see Weigley, *Eisenhower's Lieutenants,* 91–93. See also Keegan, *Six Armies in Normandy,* 108–14.

18. See Weigley, *Eisenhower's Lieutenants,* 96–97.

19. See Gavin, *On to Berlin,* 115–31; for actions by individual airborne regiments see Keegan, *Six Armies in Normandy,* 93–107.

20. 101st Airborne Division veterans recounted their small unit actions in Ambrose, *Band of Brothers,* 76–85; see also Drez, *Voices of D-Day,* 189–97.

21. See Harrison, *Cross-Channel Attack,* 300–304, 386–401. See also Keegan, *Six Armies in Normandy,* esp. 108–10.

22. See Keegan, *Six Armies in Normandy,* 94. After cutting the cable, Lieutenant Colonel Krause's unit established a stout defense around Ste. Märe Eglise just in time to beat off counterattacks. See Harrison, *Cross-Channel Attack,* 289–90.

23. Harrison, *Cross-Channel Attack,* 386–449.

24. On events at the city hall on 27 June, see Breuer, *Hitler's Fortress Cherbourg,* 239–41.

Chapter 8 The Sea Battle, 6–13 June 1944

1. "The Use of Special Intelligence in Connection with Operation Neptune, January 1944–September 1944," pp. 115–16, Public Record Office, ADM 223/287; hereinafter cited as OIC Neptune Report.

2. Ibid., p. 116. See also Rohwer and Hümmelchen, *Chronology of the War at Sea,* 282. Their information is based on war diaries of the Seekriegsleitung and Marine Gruppe West, which vary in some details from the OIC Neptune Report.

3. Quoted in Lund and Ludlum, *War of the Landing Craft,* 170–71. Crews spoke of a new threat: "Out at sea the E-boats were a continual menace. During one night attack on a small convoy of LCIs and LCTs, five out of eight craft were sunk" (Lund and Ludlum, *War of the Landing Craft,* 178).

4. See Hinsley, *British Intelligence in the Second World War,* 3:163–64.

5. See Beesly, *Very Special Intelligence,* 125, 239. Beesly's study details U-boat movements in June 1944 but mostly omits coverage of E-boat activity.

6. See OIC Neptune Report, p. 119.

7. Interview, author with Schirren, 3 May 1993.

8. Interview, author with Rabe, 29 April 1993.

9. The Ultra decrypt as amended in a signal of 1952 hours on 8 June 1944 directed the E-boats to lay mines in an area "which is used by battleships by day for shelling the coast." Minelays had to take place in water less than seventy-five feet deep. Thus Allied naval forces received useful estimates of which sectors to search. See Ultra decrypt, 081952B/June, dated 8 June 1944, Public Record Office, ADM 223/195.

10. OIC Neptune Report, p. 123; see also Rohwer and Hümmelchen, *Chronology of the War at Sea,* 282, which dates the LST sinkings on the previous night.

11. Interview, author with Rabe, 29 April 1993.

12. OIC Neptune Report, pp. 123–24.

13. Ibid., p. 124.

14. Ibid., p. 125.

15. Ibid., p. 126; see also, Schofield, *Operation Neptune,* 108–10, and Rohwer and Hümmelchen, *Chronology of the War at Sea,* 282. Rohwer and Hümmelchen claim three vessels were sunk on the night of 10–11 June.

16. OIC Neptune Report, p. 127.

17. Ibid., p. 128.

18. Ibid., pp. 128–29.

19. See Rohwer and Hümmelchen, *Chronology of the War at Sea,* 282; see also Morison, *Invasion of France and Germany,* 175.

20. Interview, author with Gould, 27 September 1993. See also Lewis, *Exercise Tiger,* 179. Lewis cited a crewman as stating that a torpedo sank LST 496, but Gould and other crewmen knew it was a mine. The sinking occurred close to shore in daylight.

21. The OIC also tracked mines in June; OIC Neptune Report, "Shallow Water Mining and Underwater Obstacles," pp. 49–73, and "Post D-Day Minelaying," pp. 208–20.

22. OIC Neptune Report, p. 131.

23. Ibid., p. 132.

24. Interview, author with Rabe, 29 April 1993; see also OIC Neptune Report, pp. 131–32.

25. Interviews, author with Benda, 8 December 1994, and Zymalkowski, 10 December 1994.

26. Letter, Roeder to author, 5 January 1994. Rabe agrees but notes that the best detectors were passive radar, the FuMB. Once alerted, crews could take evasive action although they could not "turn on the spot"; letter, Rabe to author, 21 February 1994.

27. Hinsley, *British Intelligence in the Second World War,* 3:164.

28. OIC Neptune Report, p. 134.

29. Ibid., p. 135.

30. Ultra decrypt, 121852B/June, dated 12 June 1944, Public Record Office, ADM 223/196.

31. OIC Neptune Report, p. 135.

32. Ibid., p. 136.

33. Ibid., p. 137.

34. Ibid., p. 138.

35. See Ultra decrypt, 150052B/June, dated 15 June 1944, Public Record Office, ADM 223/196.

36. OIC Neptune Report, pp. 138–39.

37. Ibid., p. 139.

38. "Note on Operation Neptune—First Week," p. 2, S.I. 978a, Public Record Office, ADM 223/172.

Chapter 9 Bomber Command Target: E-Boat Pens

1. "War Diary of FdS," 13 June 1944, p. 97, Bundesarchiv-Militärarchiv, RM 55/9. Allied decipherers quickly grasped its import. See Hinsley, *British Intelligence in the Second World War,* 3:164.

2. "The Use of Special Intelligence in Connection with Operation Neptune, January 1944–September 1944," p. 137, Public Record Office, ADM 223/287; hereinafter cited as OIC Neptune Report. At first, Operations Officer Kapitän-leutnant Bernd Rebensburg refused to believe the Allies were reading the Schnellbootwaffe cipher Offizier M (M for "Marine"), which the British called "Dolphin." When the author supplied Rebensburg with the OIC Neptune Report and OIC Ultra decrypts, he informed surviving E-boat veterans in a circular letter, "War es so? . . ." 10 November 1993.

3. See Brookes, *Photo Reconnaissance.*

4. 542 Squadron Operations Record Book, Records for June 1944, p. 5, 14.6.44, Public Record Office, AIR 27/2017.

5. See Brookes, *Photo Reconnaissance,* p. 63, on time interval and technical details on aerial photography.

6. See Babington-Smith, *Evidence in Camera,* 233. She described how fellow PI, Flt. Lt. André Kenny discovered a V-2 rocket at Peenemünde, 203–5. For PRU images of V-weapons, see Jones, *Most Secret War,* photographs 19–21 following p. 300, and nos. 26 and 27a following p. 396. Jones had known of Peenemünde after reading the "Oslo Report." Babington-Smith and Kenny confirmed his suspicions.

The author thanks Gen. James Brown, Maj. James Fitts, and Staff Sgt. D. Taylor Robinson of the 106th Tactical Reconnaissance Squadron, 117th Tactical Reconnaissance Wing, Alabama Air National Guard, for advice on photoreconnaissance and interpretation.

7. 542 Squadron Operations Record Book, Summary for June 1944, p. 6, Public Record Office, AIR 27/2017.

8. Interview, author with Sturrock, 24 October 1992. Sturrock flew with 542 PRU Squadron from 13 June 1944 to war's end, with sorties over Le Havre.

9. On antiaircraft weapons, see Hogg, *The Guns,* 82–109.

10. Godefroy, *Le Havre sous l'Occupation,* 144.

11. See Stanley, *World War II Photo Intelligence,* 165–71.

12. See Brookes, *Photo Reconnaissance,* 197.

13. Babington-Smith, *Evidence in Camera,* 233. Another Medmenham PI gave a similar account but dated her photographic runs and PI examination sequences differently; Powys-Lybbe, *The Eye of Intelligence,* 202.

14. Copy of "Report by the Allied Naval Commander-in-Chief, Expeditionary Force on Operation 'Neptune,'" vol. 1, p. 15, 506.451–490A, U.S. Air Force Historical Research Agency, Report of ANCXF Admiral Ramsay; hereinafter cited as Report of ANCXF Ramsay. Although an Admiralty unit, the OIC served both the Royal Navy and the Royal Air Force; see Beesly, *Very Special Intelligence,* xv–xvi.

15. See chap. 4. See also Report of ANCXF Ramsay, p. 5, as well as his mem-

orandum to General Eisenhower of 10 May 1944, "Appreciation of E-Boat Threat to Overlord" in National Archives, R.G. 331, decimal file 045.93.

16. Letter, Bennett to author, 3 September 1992. The author thanks Bennett for detailed information on the wartime activities of 617 Squadron.

17. "Daylight Operations," Headquarters, Bomber Command Operations Record Book, pp. 8–9, Public Record Office, AIR 24/206.

18. "Narrative of Operations," Headquarters, Bomber Command Operations Record Book, p. 1,802, 14 June 1944, Public Record Office, AIR 24/206.

19. The author thanks Robert M. Owen, Official Historian, 617 Squadron Association, for memoranda of 4 August and 26 August 1993, and 11 April 1995, on assembling Tallboys.

20. "Description of Royal Air Force Bombing," p. 9, and Exhibit 7 (Gaggle Formation), U.S. Strategic Bombing Survey Reports, 137.306-4, U.S. Air Force Historical Research Agency.

21. Some 617 Squadron personnel entered a fourteen-thousand-pound bomb in their logs. Others entered the correct weight of twelve thousand pounds; memorandum, Owen to author, 26 August 1993.

22. For squadron summaries, see "Narrative of Operations," Headquarters, Bomber Command Operations Record Book, night of 14–15 June 1944, p. 1,802, Public Record Office, AIR 24/206. On marking techniques, see Bomber Command Report on Night Operations, 14–15 June 1944, p. 44, Public Record Office, AIR 14/3412.

Chapter 10   The Witches' Cauldron

1. See Middlebrook and Everitt, *Bomber Command War Diaries,* 528–29.

2. 100 Squadron Operations Record Book (ORB), 14 June 1944, p. 11, Public Record Office, AIR 27/797.

3. The author thanks Tom Bennett for details on SABS; memorandum, Bennett to author, 1 September 1993.

4. Memorandum, Owen to author, 4 August 1993.

5. "Description of Royal Air Force Bombing," p. 8, Document 137.306-4, U.S. Strategic Bombing Survey Reports, U.S. Air Force Historical Research Agency.

6. Ibid.

7. Bennett, manuscript, "617 Squadron . . . Le Havre, 14th June 1944," used by permission; hereinafter cited as Bennett manuscript.

8. Letter, Bennett to author, 3 September 1992.

9. For the altitude gap between light and heavy guns, see Hogg, *The Guns,* 104.

10. Bennett manuscript, 1.

11. Ibid.

12. Ibid., 2. For his many acts of bravery, Cheshire received the Victoria Cross. No single event earned him the award, but the citation details one ac-

tion: "In June 1944, when marking a target on the harbour of Le Havre in broad daylight and with no cloud cover, he dived well below the range of the light batteries before releasing his marker bombs, and he came very near to being destroyed by the strong barrage which concentrated on him"; courtesy of Squadron Leader Tom Bennett.

13. Letter and attached log entry for 14 June 1944, McCarthy to author, 17 November 1992.

14. Memoranda, Owen to author, 4 August, 26 August 1993, 11 April 1995.

15. "Ground Survey of E-Boat Pens at Le Havre," 20 November 1944, p. 1, Report No. 5, Public Record Office, AIR 40/1670. A fused delay of 0.5 seconds was unusual for a deep penetration bomb; however, Le Havre was the first maritime target for Tallboys.

16. Letter, McCarthy to author, 17 November 1992. McCarthy was convinced that three Tallboys hit the pens. Photographs showed two hits and a near miss.

17. Bennett manuscript, 2. Owen noted that the huge bunker posed aiming problems: "It was soon discovered that the vast size of the pens made it difficult to aim at a specific point on the roof, and an offset technique was devised whereby the bomb aimer set his sight on a corner, the information fed to the sight being doctored so as to cause the bomb to fall in the centre of the pen." Since Le Havre was the first pens target, experience gained there led to the above technique; letter, Owen to author, 22 October 1993.

18. Bennett manuscript, 2.

19. Ibid.

20. 617 Squadron ORB, 14 June 1944, pp. 6–9, Public Record Office, AIR 27/2128.

21. Ibid.

22. Ibid.

23. Ibid.

24. Ibid.

25. 12 Squadron ORB, 14 June 1944, Public Record Office, AIR 27/168.

26. 166 Squadron ORB, 14 June 1944, Public Record Office, AIR 27/1089.

27. Ibid.

28. 100 Squadron ORB, 14 June 1944, Public Record Office, AIR 27/797.

29. Ibid.; 103 Squadron ORB, 14 June 1944, Public Record Office, AIR 27/816.

30. "Auslaufen entfällt wegen Wetterlage" (Mission canceled because of weather), 14 June 1944, 2232, p. 100, Bundesarchiv-Militärarchiv, RM 55/9.

31. Prisoner of War Reports, box 2, interview no. 39, Grand Adm. Karl Dönitz, 28 June 1945, p. 9, National Archives, R.G. 38, Office of Naval Intelligence, Special Activities Branch, British NID (Naval Intelligence Division), NID/1; hereinafter cited as Dönitz interview, 28 June 1945.

32. In a letter to the author 11 May 1993, Hans Schirren stated that he was unaware of the Tallboys that evening and had not observed tidal waves. "I heard the first time about the use of these 'earthquake' bombs when I saw one coming toward me outside the E-boat bunker in Rotterdam in the autumn of 1944," he wrote. "It is doubtful to me that these bombs should have been used on the 14th of June 1944 in Le Havre when I saw only small bombs, effective enough against E-boats, Torpedo boats and other small craft."

33. Letter, Schirren to author, 19 September 1992, p. 2.

34. Peter Scott and Coastal Forces took a keen interest in E-boat officers. After the war they reconstructed events; see Scott, *Battle of the Narrow Seas,* 196–97. E-boat veterans conveyed the same information to the author; interviews, author with Rebensburg, 1–2 May 1993, and Schirren, 3 May 1993.

35. Interview, author with Rebensburg, 1–2 May 1993.

36. Guillemard, *L'Enfer du Havre,* 190.

37. Godefroy, *Le Havre sous l'Occupation,* 145. Wishful thinking and an optical illusion made Godefroy see Cheshire strafing German positions. His sole mission was to lay markers accurately.

38. Letter and memorandum, Schirren to author, 11 May 1993; memo, p. 2. Schirren's observations contrasted with Krancke's after-action telegram, claiming the boats were tied up individually for quick egress. See Telegram, 0220 hours, 17 June 1944, to Seekriegsleitung, pp. 150–51, Bundesarchiv-Militärarchiv, RM 7/142.

39. "Ground Survey of E-Boat Pens at Le Havre," report by Dr. Solly Zuckerman of 20 November 1944, pp. 4–5, Public Record Office, AIR 40/1670; cited hereinafter as B.A.U. Report with date; see also Summary of Tallboy Incidents, Le Havre (Port Area), pp. 5–6, AIR 20/4805.

40. B.A.U. Report of 20 November 1944, p. 6. When asked after the war what was the most vulnerable port installation, Dönitz replied: "The worst thing, naturally, [is] if you hit the electrical power plant. Then the whole docks are at a standstill"; Dönitz interview, 28 June 1945.

41. Summary of Tallboy Incidents, Le Havre (Port Area), p. 5, Public Record Office, AIR 20/4805.

42. Ibid, p. 6.

43. Telegram, Marinenachrichtendienst (Naval Information Service) to Seekriegsleitung, 15 June 1944, pp. 28–29, 32, 64, 67, Bundesarchiv-Militärarchiv, RM 7/142.

Chapter 11   E-Boats' End

1. Bomber Command Report on Night Operations, 14–15 June 1944, p. 44, Public Record Office, AIR 14/3412.

2. Ibid.

3. 7 Squadron Operations Record Book (ORB), 15 June 1944, p. 430, Public Record Office, AIR 27/101.

4. 514 Squadron ORB, 14–15 June 1944, pp. 286–87, Public Record Office, AIR 27/1977; 622 Squadron ORB, 14–15 June 1944, p. 252, Public Record Office, AIR 27/2137.

5. 514 Squadron ORB, 14–15 June 1944, pp. 288, 289, Public Record Office, AIR 27/1977.

6. 7 Squadron ORB, 14–15 June 1944, p. 430, Public Record Office, AIR 27/101.

7. 635 Squadron ORB, 14–15 June 1944, p. 14, Public Record Office, AIR 27/2155; 7 Squadron ORB, 14–15 June 1944, p. 429, Public Record Office, AIR 27/101.

8. Quotation from Guillemard, *L'Enfer du Havre,* 190. The newspaper *Le Petit Havre* wrote on 16 and 17 June 1944 of heavy damage to public and private buildings and commented on the valor of volunteer units. Military censorship forbade comment on destruction in the port; City Archives, Le Havre. See also Middlebrook and Everitt, *Bomber Command War Diaries,* 528.

9. Letter, Schirren to author, 19 September 1992, p. 2.

10. Interview, author with Schirren, 3 May 1993; letter, Roeder to author, 5 January 1994.

11. Operational Log Book of Lt. H. Nick Knilans, entry no. 36, Le Havre, 14 June 1944. Copy in possession of author. The author thanks Nick Knilans for useful information about 617 Squadron activities.

12. Interview, author with Schirren, 3 May 1993. German records confirmed Schirren's achievement that night. See KTB, entry for 15 June 1944, p. 103, Bundesarchiv-Militärarchiv, RM 55/9.

13. Interview, author with Rebensburg, 1–2 May 1993.

14. Teletype message, "Air Raid on Le Havre, night of 14–15 June, 0501 hours," 16 June 1944, p. 84, Bundesarchiv-Militärarchiv, RM 7/142.

15. Ibid., p. 85.

16. Ibid.

17. "The Use of Special Intelligence in Connection with Operation Neptune, January 1944–September 1944," p. 140, Public Record Office, ADM 223/287; hereinafter cited as OIC Neptune Report.

18. "Note on Air Attacks on Le Havre and Boulogne," 14–16 June 1944, S.I. 975a, p. 1, Public Record Office, ADM 223/172.

19. See Ultra decrypt, 151002B/June, dated 15 June 1944, Public Record Office, ADM 223/196. This first decrypt of 15 June gave lower figures and omitted E-boat losses that were unclear. Later decrypts showed that the Germans had lost nine E-boats; see "Supplementary Summary of German Naval Situation Based on Information Received 1200B/15th–1200B/16th June 1944 Bombing

Attack on Le Havre," Public Record Office, ADM 223/311. The OIC appreciation appears in note 24 below.

20. For a skeptical estimate about wave action, see OIC Special Intelligence Summary, S.I. 975a, pp. 2–3, Public Record Office, ADM 223/172. However, Rebensburg confirmed the destruction in the hangars due to wave action; interview, author with Rebensburg, 1–2 May 1993. See also Bomb Damage Assessment photograph of 15 June 1944, Print 4035, attached to Report K.2491 Le Havre, dated 16 June 1944, box 92, G-2 Target Damage Files, National Archives, R.G. 243. For an account of how heavy explosions on water caused a destructive pressure wave in Halifax, Nova Scotia, in 1917, see MacLennan, *Barometer Rising,* 152–54.

21. "Temporary Report Concerning Bombing Raid on Le Havre of 14–15 June," telex, dated 16.6.44, 0405, to Marine Gruppe West, Bundesarchiv-Militärarchiv, RM 7/142.

22. OIC Neptune Report, p. 141.

23. Signal AOC-in-C Bomber Command to AOsC HQ, 1, 3, 5, and 8 Groups, 16 June 1944, 1730 hours, originators no. A312 16/6; transcription courtesy of Robert M. Owen.

24. OIC Special Intelligence Summary, S.I. 975a, pp. 1–3, Public Record Office, ADM 223/172.

25. 617 Squadron ORB, 15 June 1944, pp. 8–10, Public Record Office, AIR 27/2128. Ultra revealed that R-boat losses at Boulogne on 15 June were high: eight R-boats and three depot ships plus many craft were damaged. See Ultra decrypt, 1036 hours, 17 June 1944, Public Record Office, ADM 223/311. Bomb damage assessment photos showed steady disintegration of Boulogne's pens. See European War, G-2, Target Damage Files, Boulogne, reports, 18 and 24 June, 26 September 1944, National Archives, R.G. 243. See also Middlebrook and Everitt, *Bomber Command War Diaries,* 529.

26. RAF Museum, Hendon, Department of Aviation Records, Harris Archive, File 49H, signal from AOC-in-C, H.Q. Bomber Command, to AOsC H.Q. 1, 3, 5, 6, and 8 (PFF) Groups, 19 June 1944, 1545 hours, originator's no. A313 19/6; transcription courtesy of Robert M. Owen.

27. Marine Gruppe West, Monthly Report for June 1944, dated 6 July 1944, p. 65, Bundesarchiv-Militärarchiv, RM 7/89; hereinafter cited as Monthly Report for June 1944.

28. "German E-Boat Operations and Policy, 1939–1945." Section II, B, vi, "Summary of Invasion Operations up to 16.6.44 by FdS," pp. 91–92, Public Record Office, ADM 223/28.

29. Ibid., p. 92.

30. Monthly Report for June 1944, p. 65.

31. The OIC monitored the Germans' Kleinkampfverbände, or Small Combat Units, and warned of their impending attacks. See OIC Neptune Report, pp.

184–207. German sources described Small Combat Unit Operations including sketches of zigzag patterns for *Dackel* torpedoes in the invasion area. *Linsen,* the small, explosive-laden motor boats, attacked later. Once they rode on E-boats from Dutch harbors toward the English Coast; letter, Rabe to author, 13 October 1993. See also FdS KTB, 1 August–15 August 1944, pp. 8–51, Bundesarchiv-Militärarchiv, RM 55/10; Sieche, "German Human Torpedoes and Midget Submarines," 74–85.

32. Quoted in Tubbs, *Lancaster Bomber,* 135.

Chapter 12   Retreat and Pursuit

1. "The Use of Special Intelligence in Connection with Operation Neptune, January 1944–September 1944," p. 145, Public Record Office, ADM 223/287; hereinafter cited as OIC Neptune Report.

2. OIC Neptune Report, pp. 146–47; "German E-Boat Operations and Policy, 1939–1945," Section II, B, vi, p. 7, entry for 31 [*sic*] June 1944, Public Record Office, ADM 223/28.

3. Conclusive evidence on the explosion is lacking. Early accounts referred to a gasoline fire started by a careless German. Naval authorities, fearing sabotage, increased security. See memo, Seekommandant, Seine-Somme to Marine Gruppe West, 6 July 1944, Bundesarchiv-Militärarchiv, RM 7/145. See also entries for 6 July 1944, pp. 36–37, and 10 July 1944, p. 64, Bundesarchiv-Militärarchiv, RM 35 II/64. French electrician Maurice Leboucher had worked long and well for the Kriegsmarine in Germany and later in Le Havre; the French Resistance, later the French government, rejected his claims to have detonated the torpedoes. Some Havrists believed Leboucher; letter, Sylvie Barot, City Archives, Le Havre, to author, 22 September 1993. See also FC, K3, 34.3, "Rapport concernant M. Leboucher, Maurice," accepting his claims, and FC, K3,34.3, letter, Secretariat d'Etat aux Forces Armées to M. Pierre Courant, Deputy, National Assembly, 23 January 1950, refusing honors to Leboucher, both in City Archives.

4. OIC Neptune Report, p. 151.

5. Ibid., p. 171.

6. See Tarrant, *The Last Year of the Kriegsmarine,* 100–106.

7. Middlebrook and Everitt, *Bomber Command War Diaries,* 577–79. On Le Havre, see Williams, *The Long Left Flank,* 56–60. See also, Tacitus, *Agricola,* 30.

8. The City of Le Havre issued a commemorative history on the fortieth anniversary of its liberation. See Legoy, *Le Havre,* 35–49. Five thousand citizens died during the years of occupation.

9. City Archives, Le Havre, FC, H4, 15.5, copy of undated U.S. Navy Report, "History of the U.S. Navy in Le Havre, France," p. 1. The author thanks Marvin Greene, formerly of the 358th Harbor Craft Company at Le Havre, for this report.

10. Millar, *Isabel and the Sea,* 36.

11. On E-boat operations, September to December 1944, see Tarrant, *Last Year of the Kriegsmarine,* 172–76.

12. Folder, "Aggressive Measures against German E-Boats and Destroyers," memorandum, C-in-C Nore to Admiralty for Air Ministry . . . SHAEF Main, 25 December 1944, National Archives, R.G. 331, decimal file 045.93.

13. See Middlebrook and Everitt, *Bomber Command War Diaries,* 631, 639, 659, 661. Letter, Schirren to author, 30 January 1994. Schirren saw a Tallboy from his crew quarters and dashed for an exit but was trapped in a stairwell. Friends inside were less lucky.

14. "German E-Boat Operations . . ." Section II, B, vii, "Operation from Dutch ports to the end of the war," p. 109, Public Record Office, ADM 223/28.

15. "German E-Boat Operations . . ." Section II, B, vii, entries for 6 February and 8 February 1945, p. 112, Public Record Office, ADM 223/28. Petersen may have considered Tallboys' impacts on pens to be so accurate that he was willing to take the chance that none would fall in the water, causing pressure waves against dispersed boats.

16. See Ruppenthal, *Logistical Support for the Armies,* 53; see also chap. 3, "The Port Discharge and Shipping Problems," on supply difficulties from D-day to D+90.

Chapter 13   How Serious Was the E-Boat Threat?

1. European War, Aiming Point Report, G-2 Target Intelligence, Daimler-Benz: Stuttgart/Untertürkheim (19115), dated 1 December 1943, National Archives, R.G. 243.

2. See Middlebrook and Everitt, *Bomber Command War Diaries,* 455, 474, 477, 481.

3. Report, "Daimler Benz A.G., Untertürkheim, Germany (0011336 4), Survey of 8 May–18 May 1945," p. 12, U.S. Strategic Bombing Survey Reports, 137.308-1, U.S. Air Force Historical Research Agency; interview, author with Rebensburg, 1–2 May 1993.

4. Letter, Rebensburg to author, 18 February 1993. For a life sketch of Petersen, see "Urteil . . . gegen Petersen und Andere" (Judgment . . . Concerning Petersen et al.), pp. 4–8, Bundesarchiv-Militärarchiv, Siebert Papers, N623/v.65; hereinafter cited as Petersen Case. The author thanks Douglas Peiffer for providing this document.

5. Rust, *Naval Officers under Hitler,* 57–58.

6. Interview, author with Rebensburg, 1–2 May 1993.

7. See Petersen Case, pp. 4–8. See also interview, author with Rebensburg, 1–2 May 1993. Rebensburg prepared a manuscript, "Ausarbeitung der KTB [Kriegstagebuch]" (Elaboration of the War Diary), examining Petersen's war no-

tations. Rebensburg detailed Petersen's family background, his difficulties with superiors and with the Nazis; see pp. 44–49. Copy in author's possession.

8. Ruge, *Rommel in Normandy,* 189, 204.

9. Dönitz, *Memoirs,* 312–13.

10. "The Use of Special Intelligence in Connection with Operation Neptune, January 1944–September 1944," pp. 101–2, Public Record Office, ADM 223/287; hereinafter cited as OIC Neptune Report.

11. Ibid., 102.

12. Letters, Rabe to author, 21 February and 2 March 1994.

13. OIC Neptune Report, pp. 143–45.

14. Interview, author with Rebensburg, 1–2 May 1993.

15. "Questions Concerning the Deployment and the Leadership of E-Boats," memorandum from Oberbefehlshaber der Seekriegsleitung der Kriegsmarine [Dönitz] to F.d. Schnellboote [Petersen], 31 January 1945, in private archives of Bernd Rebensburg in Kiel. Copy in author's possession.

16. Ibid. Dönitz ordered the E-boat force to abandon its mind-set of caution in favor of destruction of the enemy: "Great victories only come when supreme efforts are made." He demanded that they change their tactics.

17. Interview, author with Rebensburg, 1–2 May 1993.

18. See Thomas, *The German Navy in the Nazi Era,* 226–52.

19. Interviews, author with Rabe, 29 April 1993; Rebensburg, 1–2 May 1993; and Schirren, 3 May 1993. They emphasized that speed was the supreme advantage in the last year of the war. Angered by insinuations of cowardice by senior SKL officers, Operations Officer Rebensburg has offered detailed rebuttals to Dönitz's criticisms; letter, Bernd Rebensburg to Korvettenkapitän Henning Hoops, 20 August 1986, copy in possession of author.

20. See Tarrant, *The Last Year of the Kriegsmarine,* 212–24.

21. Scott, *Battle of the Narrow Seas,* 222.

22. Letter, Rebensburg to author, 4 February 1994.

23. Smith, *Churchill's German Army,* 53–63.

24. See Petersen Case, pp. 17–69. The case became an object of East German propaganda too. Articles hostile to Petersen appeared in the weekly *Junge Welt,* 13 January to 24 February 1967. See also letter, Rebensburg to author, 4 February 1994; interview, Rebensburg with author, 1–2 May 1993.

25. Quoted in letter, Rebensburg to author, 14 July 1995. On the later trials, see Petersen Case, pp. 70–121.

26. Details on the GBU 28 and high-performance bombs and missiles used in the Gulf War are still classified, but readers can obtain some information from Hallion, *Storm over Iraq;* see 242–43, 306.

Glossary

AEAF Allied Expeditionary Air Force.

ANCXF Allied Naval Commander, Expeditionary Force (Admiral Sir Bertram Home Ramsay).

A/P Aiming point; the exact point designated for bomb impact during a strike.

AVM Air Vice Marshal (RAF).

B-Dienst *Beobachtungsdienst* (German signals interception service).

Benson RAF photoreconnaissance base near Wallingford.

Bletchley Short for Bletchley Park, site of Britain's Government Code and Cypher School where Allies decrypted German signals.

Bofors Swedish-designed quick-firing cannon, usually 40 mm in size; often called "pom-pom" in the Royal Navy.

C-in-C Commander in Chief.

D-day Designated day, often followed by numbers plus or minus referring to days following or preceding commencement of operation (e.g., D+8, D–2); term generally used for invasion dates until 6 June 1944, then retired in honor of the anniversary of the Normandy Landings.

Dolphin Allied term for a German naval code used by Germany's E-boat Force; also known as *Offizier M* (M for "Marine").

E-boat Royal Navy term meaning "enemy boat" or "enemy torpedo boat" (origin obscure).

FdS *Führer der Schnellboote;* senior officer or flag officer of E-boats of the Kriegsmarine (Rudolf Petersen).

FuMB *Funkmessbeobachtungsgerät* (radio signals measuring device); a passive radar detector used by the Kriegsmarine including E-boats.

Gee First British radar navigation system using tracking stations with intersecting radar beams or pulses to guide bombers to target.

H-hour The hour an operation is said to commence, often followed by numbers plus or minus referring to minutes following or preceding commencement of operation (e.g. H+1, H–5).

High Wycombe Headquarters for RAF Bomber Command.

HMCS His/Her Majesty's Canadian Ship.

HMS His/Her Majesty's Ship (British).

I.P. Identification point or initiation point; the orientation point on a bombing mission representing the start of the bombing run.

Kriegsmarine German Navy during World War I and World War II.

Lancaster RAF heavy bomber produced by A. V. Roe Company.

Lauertaktik E-boat tactic of loitering in suspected enemy convoy lanes (in contrast to *Stichtaktik,* or sting tactics).

LCT Landing craft, tank (flat-bottomed craft, displacing approximately 1,500 tons).

LCVP Landing craft, vehicle and personnel (light assault boat with ramp).

Liberty Ship Mass-produced transport; British designed, mostly American built.

LST Landing ship, tank (flat-bottomed ship with heavy decks and clam-shell doors for fast unloading on defended beaches, displacing approximately 5,000 tons).

Luftflotte German aerial armada; equivalent to a U.S. Air Force such as the 8th Air Force.

Marder Wood marten, German Navy human torpedo weapon; successor to *Neger.*

MB Mercedes Benz, usually refers to diesel engine series used to power E-boats (produced by parent company Daimler Benz [DB]).

M-class Ship German minelayer, usually displacing about 800 tons.

Medmenham RAF photointerpretation unit located on the Thames west of London.

Merlin Standard high-performance Rolls Royce aeroengine; an in-line, liquid-cooled engine used on many Allied aircraft and on British MTBs.

Mosquito RAF's fast, twin-engined wooden construction bomber and reconnaissance aircraft built by the DeHavilland Company.

Mossie Colloquial term for Mosquito.

MTB Motor torpedo boat; Royal Navy's fast boats used by its coastal forces, especially against E-boats.

Mulberries Artificial harbors built in Britain and floated to Normandy; intended to increase port facilities for the invasion fleet.

Naxos German 10-cm radar, copied from downed Allied H2S radar and used by the Kriegsmarine.

Neger German manned torpedo, predecessor to *Marder*.

NID Naval Intelligence Division (Royal Navy).

Oboe British radar navigational aid.

Oerlikon Swiss-designed cannon, usually 20 mm in size; used by both Axis and Allied forces in World War II.

OIC Operational Intelligence Centre of the British Admiralty.

ORB Operational Record Book; crew's collective log book for RAF Bomber Command.

OT Organisation Todt; German labor and construction organization heavily involved in building bunkers.

Perspex British term for plexiglass.

PFF Pathfinder Force; Bomber Command's 8 Group crews responsible for finding and marking enemy targets.

PI Photointerpreter, usually based at Medmenham.

PIU Photographic Interpretation Unit based at Medmenham.

Pom-pom Royal Navy colloquial term for 40-mm Bofors cannon.

PRU Photo Reconnaissance Unit, mostly based at Benson.

PT boat Patrol torpedo boat; American equivalent of British MTB.

RAF Royal Air Force (Great Britain).

R-boat *Räumboot* (German coastal vessel) usually displacing 120 to 150 tons;

used for close-in minesweeping but also for minelaying, often mistaken by Allies for E-boats.

RDX High explosive used usually in combination with TNT to produce torpex.

Recce Short for reconnaissance.

Reichswehr Term for German Armed Forces from 1918 until the Nazis seized power in 1933.

RN Royal Navy (Great Britain).

RNVR Royal Navy Volunteer Reserve.

SABS Stabilized automatic bomb sight used by Bomber Command.

Schnellbootwaffe German Navy's E-boat Force in World War II.

Schnorchel Snorkel tube used on late–World War II German U-boats for (mostly) submerged breathing.

SHAEF Supreme Headquarters, Allied Expeditionary Force.

SKL Seekriegsleitung; German Navy's Supreme Command.

S-130 Typical designation for a German E-boat. The S stood for *Schnellboot,* literally "fast boat," followed by the vessel's individual number.

Spout Central sea lane across the Channel from Britain to Normandy Coast, designed to protect Allied convoys.

Stichtaktik Sting tactics; aggressive, fast-penetration E-boat tactics used during torpedo attacks on Allied convoys (in contrast to *Lauertaktik,* or loitering tactics).

Tallboy Deep-penetration earthquake bomb designed by Barnes Wallis.

Task Force O Task force of British and American warships to protect invasion forces at Omaha Beach.

Task Force U Task force of British and American warships to protect invasion forces at Utah Beach.

T-boat German 900- to 1,200-ton torpedo boat such as T-24, with deck guns and torpedo tubes, similar to *Torpedoboote* of the "predator" classes such as *Falke* and *Jaguar;* often called an Elbing.

TI Timed interval; amount of time between takes for an aerial reconnaissance camera.

TIs Target indicators; RAF marker flares for bombers.

TRE Telecommunications Research Establishment located in Malvern in England.

U-boat *Untersee* (underwater) boat; German submarine of World War I and World War II.

Ultra Secret Elaborate system of Allied decryption of German signals; widely regarded as greatest secret of World War II.

USAAF U.S. Army Air Force.

USN U.S. Navy.

USS United States Ship.

Vic V-shaped flying formation; commonly used by Bomber Command on the way to a target.

VP-boat *Vorposten* boat; German picket boat (sometimes just V-boat).

Woodhall Spa RAF base in Lincolnshire frequently used by 617 Squadron.

W/T Wireless traffic or wireless telephone; RAF term commonly referred to by Americans as radio traffic, radio telephone, or simply radio.

Z-32 A specific *Zerstörer* (destroyer) of the German Navy that, like R-, S-, and U-boats, were unnamed, using the letter—in this case Z—followed by the individual vessel number.

Selected Bibliography

Primary Sources
Archives

Bundesarchiv-Militärarchiv, Freiburg im Breisgau. RM 7, Marine Gruppe West, Kriegstagebuch. Vols. 89, 142, 145, 192.

———. RM 35 II, Marine Gruppe West, Kriegstagebuch. Vol. 64.

———. RM 55, Führer der Schnellboote, Kriegstagebuch. Vols. 8–11.

———. Siebert Papers. N623/v.65. "Urteil . . . gegen Petersen und Andere" (Judgment . . . Concerning Petersen et al.). Hamburg, 1953.

City Archives, Le Havre.

———. *Le Petit Havre.* Issues for 16 and 17 June 1944.

Marine Offizier Vereinigung, Bonn. Journal Collection. *Marine Forum.*

———. Naval History Publications (in the German language).

———. Schultz, Herbert Max. "Die deutsche Schnellbootwaffe im 2. Weltkrieg," Erlangen, 1987.

National Archives, Washington, D.C. Cartographic Division. Aerial Photograph Collection, World War II.

———. Still Pictures Branch. Signal Corps Collection, World War II.

———. Military Records Branch. R.G. 38, Records of the Chief of Naval Operations, World War II.

———. Military Records Branch. R.G. 243, Records of the U.S. Strategic Bombing Survey.

———. Military Records Branch. R.G. 331, Allied Operational and Occupational HQ, World War II.

Public Record Office, Kew, London. ADM 223/28, German E-Boat Operations and Policy, 1939–1945.

———. ADM 223/172, Operational Intelligence Centre (OIC), Special Intelligence Summaries.

———. ADM 223/195, Ultra Decrypt Translations.

———. ADM 223/196, Ultra Decrypt Translations.

———. ADM 223/287, Operational Intelligence Centre (OIC), Operation Neptune Report.

———. AIR 14/3412, Bomber Command Report, Night Operations.

———. AIR 20/4805, Report, Tallboy Incidents.

———.AIR 24/206, Operations Record Book, Headquarters, Bomber Command.

———. AIR 27, Squadron Operations Record Books.

———. AIR 40/1670, Bombing Analysis Unit.

Rebensburg, Bernd (Kiel, Germany). Archive Pertaining to E-Boat Force. Includes maps, copies of diaries and reports, manuscripts, and circular letters to E-boat veterans.

U.S. Air Force, Historical Research Agency, Montgomery, Alabama. U.S. Strategic Bombing Survey Reports.

———. Report of ANCXF Admiral Ramsay.

U.S. Navy, Naval Historical Center, Washington Navy Yard, Archives. Special Collection, British Admiralty, Naval Intelligence Division, Prisoner of War Interrogation Reports.

Interviews and Correspondence

Benda, Ernst (Funker [Radioman])
Bennett, Tom (Flying Officer)
Eckstam, Eugene E. (Medical Officer)
Foot, Michael R. D. (Captain, Intelligence Expert)
Gould, William F. (Petty Officer, 3d Class)
Knilans, H. "Nick" (Lieutenant)
McCarthy, Joseph "Big Joe" (Wing Commander)
Owen, Robert M. (617 Squadron Association Historian)
Rabe, Günther (Kapitänleutnant)
Rebensburg, Bernd (Kapitänleutnant and Operations Officer)
Roeder, Ullrich (Kapitänleutnant)
Schirren, Hans (Kapitänleutnant)
Sheppard, Owen (Motor Machinist Mate, 2d Class)
Sturrock, Ian (Flight Lieutenant)

Walker, William C. (Pharmacist's Mate, 2d Class)
Wyman, David B. (Naval Architect)
Zymalkowski, Felix (Korvettenkapitän, Flotilla Commander)

Secondary Sources

Ambrose, Stephen E. *Band of Brothers: E Company, 506th Regiment, 101st Airborne, from Normandy to Hitler's Eagle's Nest.* New York: Simon and Schuster, 1992.

Babington-Smith, Constance. *Evidence in Camera: The Story of Photographic Intelligence in World War II.* Newton Abbot: David and Charles, 1976.

Beesly, Patrick. *Very Special Intelligence: The Story of the Admiralty's Operational Intelligence Centre, 1939–1945.* London: Hamilton, 1977.

Bennett, Donald C. T. *Pathfinder.* London: Goodall, 1958.

Bennett, Tom. *617 Squadron: The Dambusters at War.* Wellingborough: Patrick Stephens, 1986.

Bradley, Omar N., and Clay Blair. *A General's Life.* New York: Simon and Schuster, 1983.

Breuer, William B. *Hitler's Fortress Cherbourg: The Conquest of a Bastion.* New York: Stein and Day, 1984.

Breyer, Siegfried. *Die Deutsche Kriegsmarine, 1939–1945.* 2 vols. Friedberg, Hesse: Podzun-Pallas, 1985.

Brickhill, Paul. *The Dam Busters.* London: Ballantine, 1951.

Brookes, Andrew J. *Photo Reconnaissance.* London: Ian Allan, 1983.

Buffetaut, Yves. *D-Day Ships: The Allied Invasion Fleet, June 1944.* Annapolis, Md.: Naval Institute Press, 1994.

Chalmers, William S. *Full Cycle: The Biography of Admiral Sir Bertram Home Ramsay.* London: Hodder and Stoughton, 1959.

Chandler, Alfred D., Jr., ed., *The Papers of Dwight David Eisenhower: The War Years.* Vol. 3. Baltimore: Johns Hopkins University Press, 1970.

Collins, J. Lawton. *Lightning Joe: An Autobiography.* Baton Rouge: Louisiana State University Press, 1979.

Cooper, Bryan. *The E-Boat Threat.* London: Macdonald and Jane's, 1976.

Dönitz, Karl. *Memoirs: Ten Years and Twenty Days.* New York: World Publishing, 1959.

Drez, Ronald J. *Voices of D-Day: The Story of the Allied Invasion Told by Those Men Who Were There.* Baton Rouge: Louisiana State University Press, 1979.

Fock, Harald. *Fast Fighting Boats, 1870–1945: Their Design, Construction, and Use.* Annapolis, Md.: Naval Institute Press, 1976.

Frankland, Noble. *Bomber Offensive: The Devastation of Europe.* New York: Ballantine, 1970.

Gavin, James M. *On to Berlin: Battles of an Airborne Commander, 1943–1946.* New York: Bantam Books, 1978.

Godefroy, Georges. *Le Havre sous l'Occupation, 1940–1944*. Le Havre: Munici-palité du Havre, 1965.

Gray, Edwyn. *The Devil's Device: The Story of the Invention of the Torpedo*. Lon-don: Seeley, Service, 1975.

Greene, Ralph C. "What Happened Off Devon?" *American Heritage* 35, no. 2 (February–March 1985): 26–35.

Guillemard, Julien. *L'Enfer du Havre, 1940–1944*. Paris: Editions Médicis, 1948.

Hallion, Richard P. *Storm over Iraq: Air Power and the Gulf War*. Washington: Smithsonian Institution Press, 1992.

Harrison, Gordon A. *Cross-Channel Attack*. Washington, D.C.: Government Printing Office, 1951.

Hastings, Max. *Bomber Command*. New York: Dial Press, 1979.

Hervieux, Pierre. "German Torpedo Boats at War: The Möwe and Wolf Classes." Part 1, *Warship*, no. 25 (January 1983): 60–65, and part 2, no. 26 (April 1983): 74–78.

———. "S-Boats at War, 1939–1940." *Warship*, no. 32 (October 1984): 270–76.

Hinsley, F. H. *British Intelligence in the Second World War*. 3 vols. London: Her Majesty's Stationery Office, 1984–88.

Hogg, Ian V. *The Guns, 1939–1945*. London: Ballantine Books, 1970.

Hoyt, Edwin P. *The Invasion before the Invasion: The Secret Battle of Slapton Sands*. London: Robert Hale, 1985.

Hümmelchen, Gerhard. "German Schnellboote (E-Boats)," *Profile Warship*, no. 31 (1979): 153–76.

Johnson, Brian. *The Secret War*. London: Methuen, 1978.

Jones, Reginald Vincent. *Most Secret War: British Scientific Intelligence, 1939–1945*. London: Hamish Hamilton, 1978.

Keegan, John. *Six Armies in Normandy: From D-Day to the Liberation of Paris*. Harmondsworth, Middlesex: Penguin Books, 1982.

Kemnade, Friedrich. *Die Afrika-Flottille: Der Einsatz der 3. Schnellbootflottille im Zweiten Weltkrieg*. Chronik und Bilanz: Stuttgart, 1976.

Kühn, Volkmar. *Torpedoboote und Zerstörer im Einsatz, 1939–1945*. Frankfurt am Main: Motorbuch Verlag, 1983.

Lambert, John, and Al Ross. *Vosper MTBs and U.S. Elcos*. Vol. 2 of *Allied Coastal Forces of World War II*. Annapolis, Md.: Naval Institute Press, 1993.

Legoy, Jean. *Le Havre, 1940–1944*. Le Havre: Municipalité du Havre, 1984.

Lewis, Nigel. *Exercise Tiger: The Dramatic, True Story of a Hidden Tragedy of World War II*. New York: Prentice Hall, 1990.

Leyland, John. "The Spirit of the German Navy Law." In *The Naval Annual*, ed. Viscount Hythe. 1913. Reprint, New York: Arco Publishing, 1970.

Lund, Paul, and Harry Ludlum. *The War of the Landing Craft*. London: W. Foul-sham, 1976.

MacDonald, Charles B. "Slapton Sands: The 'Cover-Up' That Never Was." *Army* (June 1988): 64–67.

MacLennan, Hugh. *Barometer Rising.* 1941. Reprint, Toronto: McClelland and Stewart, 1969.

Massie, Robert K. *Dreadnought: Britain, Germany, and the Coming of the Great War.* New York: Random House, 1991.

Middlebrook, Martin. *Battle of Hamburg: Allied Bomber Forces against a German City in 1943.* London: Allen Lane, 1980.

Middlebrook, Martin, and Chris Everitt. *The Bomber Command War Diaries: An Operational Reference Book, 1939–1945.* London: Viking, 1985.

Millar, George. *Isabel and the Sea.* London: William Heinemann, 1948.

Morison, Samuel Eliot. *The Invasion of France and Germany, 1944–1945.* Vol. 6 of *History of United States Naval Operations in World War II.* Boston: Little, Brown, 1962.

Morpurgo, J. E. *Barnes Wallis: A Biography.* New York: St. Martin's Press, 1972.

Phillips-Birt, Douglas H. C. *Famous Speedboats of the World.* New York: St. Martin's, 1959.

Powys-Lybbe, Ursula. *The Eye of Intelligence.* London: W. Kimber, 1983.

Rohwer, Jürgen, and Gerhard Hümmelchen. *Chronology of the War at Sea, 1939–1945: The Naval History of World War II.* 2d ed. Annapolis, Md.: Naval Institute Press, 1992.

Ruge, Friedrich. *Rommel in Normandy: Reminiscences by Friedrich Ruge.* San Rafael, Calif.: Presidio Press, 1979.

Ruppenthal, Roland G. *Logistical Support for the Armies.* Vol. 2. Washington, D.C.: U.S. Government Printing Office, 1959.

Rust, Eric C. *Naval Officers under Hitler: The Story of Crew 34.* New York: Praeger, 1991.

Saward, Dudley. *Victory Denied: The Rise of Air Power and the Defeat of Germany, 1920–1945.* New York: Franklin Watts, 1987.

Schmalenbach, Paul. "S-Boats: The Genealogy of the Schnellboot." *Warship International* 6, no. 4 (Winter 1969): 10–25.

Schofield, Brian B. *Operation Neptune.* Annapolis, Md.: Naval Institute Press, 1974.

Scott, Sir Peter Markham. *Battle of the Narrow Seas: A History of Light Coastal Forces in the Channel and North Sea, 1939–1945.* New York: Scribner's Sons, 1946.

Sieche, Erwin F. "German Human Torpedoes and Midget Submarines." *Warship,* no. 14 (April 1980): 74–85.

Smith, Arthur L., Jr. *Churchill's German Army: Wartime Strategy and Cold War Politics, 1943–1947.* Beverly Hills: Sage Publications, 1977.

Stanley, Roy M., II. *World War II Photo Intelligence.* New York: Scribner, 1981.

Sweetman, John. *The Dambusters Raid*. London: Motorbooks International, 1990.

Tarrant, V. E. *The Last Year of the Kriegsmarine, May 1944–May 1945*. Annapolis, Md.: Naval Institute Press, 1994.

Taylor, J. C. *German Warships of World War I*. Garden City, N.Y.: Doubleday, 1970.

Teale, John. *Fast Boats: A Guide to Speed under Sail and Power*. New York: St. Martin's Press, 1961.

Thomas, Charles S. *The German Navy in the Nazi Era*. Annapolis, Md.: Naval Institute Press, 1990.

Tirpitz, Alfred von. *My Memoirs*. 2 vols. New York: Dodd, Mead, 1919.

Tubbs, D. B. *Lancaster Bomber*. London: Ballantine Books, 1972.

U.S. Army Training Manual TM 9-1300-214, Military Explosives. Washington, D.C.: Department of the Army, 1979.

Weigley, Russell F. *Eisenhower's Lieutenants: The Campaign of France and Germany, 1944–1945*. Bloomington: Indiana University Press, 1981.

Whitley, M. J. *German Coastal Forces of World War Two*. London: Arms and Armour, 1992.

Williams, Jeffery. *The Long Left Flank: The Hard-Fought Way to the Reich*. London: Leo Cooper, 1988.

Wright, Gordon. *The Ordeal of Total War, 1939–1945*. New York: Harper and Row, 1968.

Index

Merifield, John, 154
Messerschmidt 110 (Me. 110), 186
Millar, George, 211
minelayers, 29, 46, 49, 53, 131, 137, 155–56, 192, 195
mines and mine warfare, 6, 25, 28, 29, 37, 40–42, 47–50, 61, 65, 69, 71, 73, 111, 116, 127, 131–34, 136–37, 144, 155, 182, 196–98, 201, 202, 209–10, 218, 228–29, 232, 233, 239–40. *See also* E-boat Force, minelaying by
minesweepers and minesweeping, 53, 109–10, 135, 143, 155, 195, 197, 230, 239–40; Allied, 110, 197; German, 53, 109, 155, 195, 230; during Operation Neptune, 110
Mirbach, Freiherr Götz von, 32, 52, 54, 56–58, 60–61, 112–13, 130, 136, 138–39, 177, 196
Montgomery, Sir Bernard Law, 214, 230
Moon, Don P., 12, 13, 69, 117
Mulberry (artificial port), 136, 139–40, 166, 203
Munich, Germany, 104, 158
Munro, Les (Smiler), 161, 169, 172, 215
Murdock, James, 15

Naval Intelligence Division (NID), RN: interrogation of E-boat crewmen by, 60–61; use of Ultra intelligence by, 58–59
Naxos. *See Funkmessbeobachtungsgerät*
Niemöller, Martin, 221
Nore, England, 57, 110, 212
Normandy, France, 4, 11–13, 116–18, 137, 164–66, 177, 208, 235; airborne operations in, 116, 118–27; air war over, 116, 151, 153, 158, 164, 192, 203; defense of, 109, 122–27; E-boat operations around, 58, 109; German reinforcement of, 105–7; invasion of, 12–13, 21, 58, 64, 68, 74, 105–7, 109–11, 117–18, 222; ports in, 11, 109, 112–17, 120, 122, 125–28, 213–14; transportation and communications network in, 126–27. *See also* airborne infantry; Cherbourg; Operation Neptune; Operation Overlord
Normandy Battle Zone, 1, 4, 58, 68, 74,

131, 158, 186, 190, 192, 197, 200, 203
Normandy Invasion Fleet, 109–12, 143–45, 192, 206; assembly of, 11, 109–10, 165, 166, 177; attacks on, 1–3, 111, 129, 132, 143; defense of, 110–11, 128, 132, 203; E-boat threat to, 1–5, 24, 58, 65, 68–69, 72–73, 143, 145, 156, 177, 186, 197, 200, 203, 216; losses to, 143–44, 197–98, 200–201; and transit of English Channel, 109–10. *See also* Eastern Naval Task Force; E-boat Force, operations of, in response to Neptune/Overlord; Mulberry; Operation Neptune; Western Naval Task Force
Normandy Invasion Fleet landing craft, 9–22, 136–37, 143; LCT 381, 22; LCT 921, 130; LST 289, 19–20; LST 314, 134; LST 376, 134; LST 391, 237; LST 496, 18, 137, 237; LST 507, 9–10, 14–17, 19–21, 137, 237; LST 511, 18; LST 515, 13–14, 18–21; LST 538, 136; LST 715, 130. *See also* Allied landing craft; Mulberry
North Sea, 5, 23–24, 29, 30, 34, 37, 46–47, 50–51, 68, 142, 208–9, 211–12, 228–29
Norway, 46, 49, 215, 236, 239

Omaha Beach. *See* Operation Overlord
Opdenhoff, Hermann, 32, 58, 178–79, 189–91, 228
Operational Intelligence Centre (OIC), 3, 58–59, 204; analysis of E-boat threat by, 70–74, 113, 145, 208–9, 224–25; analysis of U-boat threat by, 115; and battle damage assessment of Le Havre and Boulogne raids, 194–97, 199–201, 208–9; detects E-boat concentration at Le Havre, 134, 136–37, 141–42; monitors E-boat Force during Neptune/Overlord, 131–37, 141–43, 145–47, 206–9; in planning for Le Havre raids, 156–57. *See also* Special Intelligence
Operational Research Section. *See* Bomber Command
Operation Chastise. *See* Dambusters
Operation Market-Garden, 214
Operation Neptune, 2–5, 67–68, 108–12, 115–17, 121, 127, 225; Allied losses during, 144–45, 197–98; Allied planning

radars (German) (*continued*)
53–55, 61, 132, 139; shortwave centi-
metric radar (Hohentwiel), 55, 132,
139
Raeder, Erich, 220–21, 223
Ramsay, Sir Bertram Home, 63–68, 70, 74,
109, 132, 145, 156–58
R-boat (minelayer), 53, 137, 155–56, 181,
191, 196, 207
Rebensburg, Bernd (Clever Bernd), 53,
57–58, 178, 189, 191, 195, 222, 226,
227, 229, 240
Reichsmarine. *See* German Navy
Reichswehr. *See* German Army
Research Department Explosive (RDX). *See*
Cyclonite
Roeder, Ullrich, 139, 188–89
Rolls Royce Merlin engines, 38, 175
Rommel, Erwin, 118, 122, 223–24
Roosevelt, Brig. Gen. Theodore, 119–20
Rotterdam, the Netherlands, 55–56; E-
boat operations from, 47, 51, 53, 108,
212–13, 229; Waalhaven, 212–13
Royal Air Force, 1, 3, 71–72, 74–79, 84,
93–94, 100–101, 106, 129, 138, 148,
149–50, 155, 158–60, 166, 169, 183,
190, 194, 204, 210, 212, 214–15,
236–37; Air Ministry, 76–77, 79–80,
85–86, 91–93, 214; Air Staff, 76–80,
86, 90–93; Air-Targets Subcommittee,
77; and strategic air war, 75–79, 90;
Western Air Plans, 5, 77, 90. *See also*
Bomber Command; Coastal Com-
mand; Dambusters; Fighter Command; Photographic Interpretation
Unit (PIU); Photographic Reconnaissance Unit (PRU)
Royal Air Force airfields and bases: Benson (PIU headquarters), 84, 148, 150,
153–54, 204; Bentley Priory (Fighter
Command), 79; Conningsby, 97–98;
High Wycombe (Bomber Command),
79–80, 92–93, 102–3, 156–58, 164,
183; Medmenham (PIU), 84, 148, 150,
153, 155–57, 204, 219; Wallingford
(PRU), 148; Woodhall Spa, 96, 104,
106, 157, 161, 167, 190
Royal Air Force bombers: Halifax, 80, 164,
210, 219; Lancaster (Victory bomber),

1, 55, 75, 80–81, 89–90, 92, 96–99,
102–6, 157–63, 164–69, 171–72, 174,
179, 184–87, 192–94, 199–200, 210,
212, 215, 219; Mosquito (Mossie),
80–83, 97, 102, 104, 106, 159, 162, 164,
166–69, 171, 179, 184; Stirling, 80;
Wellesley, 88; Wellington (Wimpey), 84,
88, 90, 130. *See also* Bomber Command
units
Royal Air Force fighters and fighter/
bombers: Albacore, 50, 138–39; Beau-
fighter, 114; Spitfire, 159, 162, 175;
Swordfish, 50. *See also* Coastal Command; Fighter Command
Royal Air Force reconnaissance aircraft:
P-51 Mustang, 214; Spitfire XI, 148,
150–52, 193. *See also* Photographic Reconnaissance Unit (PRU)
Royal Navy, 12, 14, 19, 24–26, 30, 48, 52,
54, 56–59, 65, 70–71, 93, 130, 131, 206,
212, 229, 230, 240; 10th Destroyer
Flotilla, 114–15; consideration of torpedoes by, 25–26; and coordination with
U.S. Navy, 63, 66–68. *See also* British
ships; Coastal Forces; Normandy Invasion Fleet; Operation Neptune
Ruge, Friedrich, 31–32, 222–24
Ruhr dams: Eder Dam, 92; Möhne Dam,
91–92; raid on (Operation Chastise),
92–93, 96, 98, 106, 169; Sorpe Dam, 92.
See also Dambusters; Wallis, Barnes
Ruhr District, Germany, 78–79, 81–84, 87,
91–93, 105. *See also* Bomber Command;
strategic air war

Ste. Marie du Mont, France, 123–24
Ste. Mère Eglise, France, 126
St. Malo, France, 135, 142, 206, 224–25
Saumur, France, and Saumur Tunnel, 106,
158
Schelde River and Estuary, 209, 211–12,
214, 228
Scheveningen, the Netherlands (E-boat
Force headquarters), 47, 57, 59, 61, 108,
112, 175, 178, 189
Schirren, Hans (Seelöwe), 52, 56–57,
112–13, 132, 139, 175–77, 180, 188–90,
212, 241
Schlieben, Karl von, 127

About the Author

James Foster Tent graduated with honors in history from Dartmouth College in 1966, where he studied military history under Louis Morton and participated in Dartmouth's ROTC Winter Warfare program. He earned a Ph.D. in modern German history at the University of Wisconsin in 1973 and has written several studies on the American occupation of Germany after World War II. Tent is currently a University Scholar with the University of Alabama at Birmingham, where he and his wife, Bunnie, live with their son, John, daughter, Virginia, and three cats.

The **Naval Institute Press** is the book-publishing arm of the U.S. Naval Institute, a private, nonprofit society for sea service professionals and others who share an interest in naval and maritime affairs. Established in 1873 at the U.S. Naval Academy in Annapolis, Maryland, where its offices remain today, the Naval Institute has almost 85,000 members worldwide.

Members of the Naval Institute receive the influential monthly magazine *Proceedings* and discounts on fine nautical prints and on ship and aircraft photos. They also have access to the transcripts of the Institute's Oral History Program and get discounted admission to any of the Institute-sponsored seminars offered around the country.

The Naval Institute also publishes *Naval History* magazine. This colorful bimonthly is filled with entertaining and thought-provoking articles, first-person reminiscences, and dramatic art and photography. Members receive a discount on *Naval History* subscriptions.

The Naval Institute's book-publishing program, begun in 1898 with basic guides to naval practices, has broadened its scope in recent years to include books of more general interest. Now the Naval Institute Press publishes about 100 titles each year, ranging from how-to books on boating and navigation to battle histories, biographies, ship and aircraft guides, and novels. Institute members receive discounts of 20 to 50 percent on the Press's nearly 600 books in print.

For a free catalog describing Naval Institute Press books currently available, and for further information about subscribing to *Naval History* magazine or about joining the U.S. Naval Institute, please write to:

Membership & Communications Dept.
U.S. Naval Institute
118 Maryland Avenue
Annapolis, Maryland 21402-5035
Telephone: (800) 233-8764
Fax: (410) 269-7940